SUCH
MEN
AS THESE

Also by David Sears

The Last Epic Naval Battle:
Voices from Keyte Gulf

At War with the Wind: The Epic Struggle
with Japan's World War II Suicide Bombers

SUCH MEN AS THESE

THE STORY OF THE NAVY PILOTS
WHO FLEW THE
DEADLY SKIES OVER KOREA

David Sears

DA CAPO PRESS
A Member of the Perseus Books Group

Designed by Pauline Brown
Set in 11.5 point Berkeley Book by the Perseus Books Group

Library of Congress Cataloging-in-Publication Data

Sears, David, 1947–
  Such men as these : the story of the Navy pilots who flew the deadly skies over Korea / David Sears.
     p. cm.
  Includes bibliographical references and index.
  ISBN 978-0-306-81851-6 (hardcover : alk. paper)
    1. Korean War, 1950–1953—Aerial operations, American. 2. Korean War, 1950–1953—Naval operations, American. 3. United States. Navy—History—Korean War, 1950–1953. 4. United States. Navy—Aviation—History—20th century. 5. Air pilots, Military—United States—Biography. 6. Air pilots, Military—United States—History—20th century. 7. Air pilots, Military—Korea—History—20th century. 8. Aircraft carriers—United States—History—20th century. 9. Aircraft carriers—Korea—History—20th century. I. Title.
  DS920.2.U6S43 2010
  951.904'245—dc22

                                                                    2010000588

PB ISBN: 978-0-306-82010-6
E-book ISBN: 978-0-306-81904-9

Published by Da Capo Press
A Member of the Perseus Books Group
www.dacapopress.com

Da Capo Press books are available at special discounts for bulk purchases in the U.S. by corporations, institutions, and other organizations. For more information, please contact the Special Markets Department at the Perseus Books Group, 2300 Chestnut Street, Suite 200, Philadelphia, PA 19103, or call (800) 810-4145, ext. 5000, or e-mail special .markets@perseusbooks.com.

10 9 8 7 6 5 4 3 2 1

For Virgil A. Stiger
USN and USMC veteran, best man,
and dearly missed friend

CONTENTS

Illustrations follow page 210

FOREWORD

Adm. James L. Holloway III, USN (Ret.)

Although Korea was a war America neither expected nor planned to fight, it had little choice. At dawn on June 25, 1950, when the North Korean Army without warning or provocation stormed across the South Korean border, their purpose was clear—to annex the Republic of Korea, a free and sovereign nation, to the Communist North.

How would America and its free-world allies respond to this transparent Communist aggression? The choices seemed painfully diametric. Counter with diplomatic protests and ambiguous threats, thus risking its influence in the postwar world? Or unleash its arsenal of tactical atomic weapons, possibly triggering a full-scale nuclear war with the Soviet Union?

Instead, as the world watched apprehensively, America took the only option consistent with its national character: Draw a line in the sand, and, despite the extreme sacrifices that lay ahead, go to war with conventional arms.

America was totally unprepared for even a limited war. By early 1950 its massive armies, air forces, and seagoing fleets, so essential to allied victory in World War II, had been dismantled. For their part, Americans had little appetite for war, especially on a piece of the globe so remote and forbidding. As then Secretary of State Dean Acheson put it, "If the best minds in the world had set out to find us the worst possible location to fight a war, the unanimous choice would have been Korea."

Rebounding from a disastrous start during which American and allied forces, acting under United Nations mandate, were nearly driven off the Korean peninsula, Americans mobilized and fought back with characteristic determination. After routing the North Korean Army, they ultimately drove Chinese armies out of South Korea, restored the original borders, and concluded an acceptable truce. The Korean War ended just as it began, along the 38th Parallel.

But the three-year conflict, which embroiled twenty-two belligerent nations and took the lives of over four million men, women, and children, left painful scars, both physical and emotional. For years it was a little considered footnote in history—the "forgotten war." Today, however, fully six decades from its bloody beginning, the Korean War can be seen in a broader perspective: At a pivotal point in history, America and its free and like-minded allies stood firm and turned back totalitarian aggression. The contrasting circumstances of democratic South Korea and totalitarian North Korea speak volumes. Korea may well be the "forgotten win."

While air power alone could not have won the Korean War, it nevertheless played a crucial role in shaping the final outcome. By the Chinese Army's own admission, UN air power was the equalizer to its vast numerical superiority in ground forces.

To fight its part in the air war over Korea, the U.S. Navy had to move quickly to reactivate its mothballed fleets of World War II warships and aircraft. The Navy's active fleet carrier force grew to nineteen; propeller-powered F4U Corsairs, which had once dueled Japanese Zeroes over the Pacific, again flew from Navy carriers. A total of twenty-one carriers of all types ultimately served in the conflict, and carrier-based aircraft flew more than 30 percent of all UN combat sorties.

The Korean War ultimately restored the preeminence of the aircraft carrier task group in the U.S. fleet. But this resurgence would not have been possible had the Navy been unable to adapt these ships to handle jet aircraft. When jet squadrons were first deployed aboard the fleet carriers after World War II, the results were discouraging and often costly in losses of planes and pilots. But Naval Aviation pursued these programs aggressively and determinedly, finally overcoming seemingly insurmountable technical and operational obstacles. (It was during this time that, as a young naval aviator, I made my own professional transition from "props" to jets.) By the time *Essex* class carriers were deployed regularly to combat operations in Korea in the fall of 1950, all pilots and aircraft were mission-capable.

In 1953, during the closing days of the Korean conflict, Pulitzer Prize–winning author James Michener published *The Bridges at Toko-Ri. Bridges* is perhaps the best novelistic depiction of aerial combat and the skills, emotions, and personal trials of carrier-based combat pilots. During two Korean War deployments I personally experienced both the trepidation and exhilaration of twice-daily launches from carrier decks (often over tossing and frigid seas) and going "feet dry" to take out Communist targets ashore. Ironically, after the war, I was also privileged to fly as a stunt pilot in filming the movie version of *The Bridges at Toko-Ri.*

In the pages that follow, David Sears has looked behind the scenes to tell, compellingly and convincingly, the true stories of the U.S. Navy carrier pilots who braved the deadly wartime skies over Korea.

Manchuria

Hoeryong●
Chongjin●

Yalu River

Hyesan●
Kaspan● ●Hapsu

**NORTH
KOREA**

Kilchu●

Songjin●

●Pyoktong

Tanchon●

Yudam-ni● *Chosin
Reservoir*

Koto-ri● Hagaru-ri●

●Antung

Yonpo● ●Hungnam
Yonghung

Samdong-ni● Kowon●
Songchon● Munchon●
Yangdok● Majon-ri● ●Wonsan

★Pyongyang

*Sea of
Japan*

*Cho Do
Island*●

Iron Triangle *Truce Demarcation Line*
Pyonggang●
Chorwon● ●Kumhwa
Kaesong● *38th Parallel*
Panmunjom●

*Yellow
Sea*

**South
Korea**

USSR

Map not to scale.

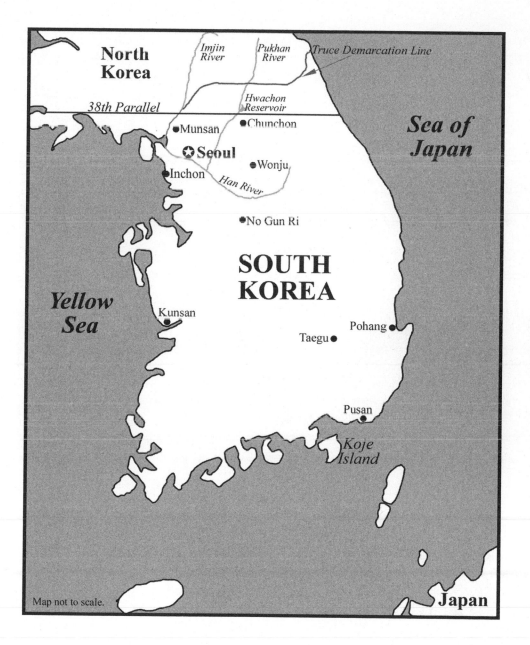

PROLOGUE: MARINERS

February 8, 1952, in the Sea of Japan East of North Korea
If a ship's lineage best conveyed America's dilemma in this war, this place, and this bitter season, it was USS *Valley Forge* (CV-45).* Named for the bivouac site of America's Continental army during the bleak Pennsylvania winter of 1777–1778, the 33,000-ton aircraft carrier had been built in Philadelphia during the closing days of World War II, her construction financed in part by the state's citizens through a special war bond drive.

Valley Forge was launched in November 1945 but not finally commissioned until the following year—a proud, if somewhat belated, symbol of U.S. sea power's global supremacy. Soon, however, with the war over and the decade waning, *Valley Forge*, her dozens of *Essex*-class predecessors, and the handful of even larger *Midway*-class carriers that followed were widely criticized as huge, costly exemplars of the U.S. Navy's obsolescence. The era of seagoing supremacy that large fleet carriers defined—when "flattops" projected global power and airplanes, not ships, won blue-water battles and controlled vital sea-lanes—seemed to be passing before it had much begun.

The atom bomb—the device that had simultaneously closed the war with Japan and threatened unprecedented global apocalypse—pointed to a new mind-set in military preparedness. If mastery of its secrets proliferated and deterrence failed, then war would be quick,

---

* See the Glossary for U.S. Navy ship designations.

decisive—and nuclear. Nuclear war's "delivery system" would not be flattop-based aircraft. Rather, it would be flights of land-based long-range, nuclear-armed strategic bombers, the specialty of the nation's newest military branch, the United States Air Force (USAF).

Such thinking came close to dispensing with the U.S. carrier fleet's future—and with it much of the Navy's as well. In mid-1945 the Navy had nearly a hundred aircraft carriers (of all sizes) in commission; a year later there were just twenty-three and by 1950 just fifteen (including *Valley Forge*), with plans to reduce that number to five. It didn't stop there; fewer flattops also meant 50 percent fewer aircraft and 80 percent fewer pilots.

And it wasn't just the Navy. Wholesale cutbacks in manpower and equipment had left a standing army of just 591,000 men, most of them signing up (as one frustrated U.S. Army company commander put it) "for every reason known to man except to fight."[1] The bulk of U.S. Army troops—especially those stationed in the Far East—were trained for occupation, not combat. They were young, inexperienced, and equipped with obsolete weapons they scarcely knew how to use.

Clearly, the U.S. military was vulnerable when, on June 25, 1950, the North Korean People's Army (NKPA or, in Korean, In Min Gun), seven divisions strong (one-third of its ranks battle-tested veterans of the Chinese Communist People's Liberation Army) and equipped with 150 powerful Russian-made T-34 tanks, peremptorily invaded the Republic of Korea (ROK). The NKPA hordes quickly overwhelmed both the fledgling ROK army and the undermanned U.S. advisory force backing it. The invasion touched off a new breed of conflict, the first of a succession of localized, "limited" wars—"hot" conflicts in the framework of a global Cold War—that would come to define armed conflict for the rest of the century.

This limited war would be dubbed (for reasons of global policy, U.S. politics, and want of a better term) a "police action." However, the conflict's true nature eventually eclipsed most realistic notions of limits or policing: Its fighting would drag on for three full years, involve more than twenty nations, claim more than 1 million military casualties (including 170,000 U.S. servicemen killed, wounded, captured, or missing), and result in a staggering 3 million civilian deaths. Perhaps the conflict's only limit was that actual combat was confined to the Korean peninsula, a piece of geography shaped roughly like the state of Florida and only 25 percent larger.

During the abysmal opening weeks of the Korean conflict, *Valley Forge* was the only U.S. Navy fleet aircraft carrier in the western Pacific. Throughout that summer and fall, with U.S. airfields on the Korean peninsula overrun and the nearest U.S. Air Force resources in distant Japan, *Valley Forge* pilots and airplanes had played an outsized role in destroying the North Korean Air Force and preventing U.S. GIs from being tossed into the Sea of Japan. Now, just months shy of the conflict's second anniversary, with the sides stalemated, *Valley Forge* and her crew and air squadrons were on their second wartime deployment, plying a frigid sea on the outskirts of a fierce but now largely forgotten war in the service of a nation that scarcely knew or appreciated the dangers and hardships they faced.

While it was midmorning in the Sea of Japan, it was midevening of the previous day in the States. Other international headlines often displaced Korea on the front pages of the nation's newspapers. The headlines on Thursday, February 7, 1952, were dominated by the death of Britain's King George VI and the planned coronation of his daughter as Queen Elizabeth II. In the next day's edition of the *New York Times*, news from Korea would be sequestered on page 2. "Carrier-based aircraft launched strikes at Yangdok, Munchon, Wonsan, Hungnam and Songchon," began one paragraph of the three-column digest of UN press releases, "cutting rail tracks and destroying a bridge." Pilots, the article noted, "flew in the teeth of freezing weather and snow squalls" to reach their targets.

***

Virtually every U.S. Navy ship, including *Valley Forge*, bore an informal name—a moniker devised through a sometimes transparent, sometimes mysterious collective thought process by her crew. The name, reinforced by constant usage on decks, docks, and liberty calls, defined the mood, the mind-set, and ultimately the reputation of the ship. On great ships the names were inspiring, on good ships affectionate, on bad ships disparaging, and on hard-luck ships ominous. The war in the Pacific had generated legendary carrier names: USS *Lexington* (CV-16) was "Blue Ghost" (so-called because of a deep-blue paint job that enabled her to "sink beneath the deep blue seas each evening, all hands aboard, only to re-appear each morning"); USS *Enterprise* (CV-6), the most decorated carrier in the war, was "Big E"; and USS *Bunker Hill* (CV-17), famed for her devastating year-ending air strikes against Japan in 1944, became "Holiday Express."

Valley Forge had been coined "Happy Valley" by her first executive officer (XO) Cdr. Frank G. Raysbrook, a leader whose passion for scheduling all-hands cleaning details earned him the crew-bestowed nickname "Field Day Frankie." Happy Valley might have fit the postwar times (or Field Day Frankie's assumptions about crew morale), but names devised by senior officers seldom stuck, and events could change names—as they eventually did for *Valley Forge*'s. By February 1952, six years and many prolonged and far-flung deployments later, Happy Valley had become "Rusty Bucket"—a term of endearment (at least to some of the thousands of ship's company sailors who kept her afloat) but also recognition that the Valley's upkeep and overhaul schedule had fallen victim to the postwar budget squeeze.

However, there was still another name circulating, one hinting at the curse on Coleridge's Ancient Mariner who, at another time in a different cold sea where ice "cracked and growled, and roared and howled," shot the albatross. To the squadron aviators and to the "airdales" working the flight deck (men whose powerful jet- and propeller-driven birds were being shot up or destroyed), *Valley Forge* was increasingly known as "Death Valley."

Since *Valley Forge*'s arrival in the Sea of Japan to join Task Force (TF) 77 the first week in December 1951, Air Task Group (ATG) 1's four squadrons and three specialized air detachments had lost five aviators to flight accidents and enemy gunfire—four of them in December alone. The total, including flyers missing in action, had actually swollen to eight, but this morning offered a wink of hope that the number might dip to seven. A pilot presumed lost in a night crash had reportedly been found alive but badly injured by Korean anti-Communist guerrillas and, after being smuggled to the North Korean coast near Wonsan, was awaiting rescue. At daybreak a rescue combat air patrol, or ResCAP, of *Valley Forge* aircraft had taken off to rendezvous with the helicopter from cruiser *Rochester* (CA-124) and escort it to a remote pickup site.

Lt. Ray Edinger, the XO of fighter squadron VF-653, had been expecting the day off after flying strikes on two consecutive days. But at 10 A.M. he was alerted by the squadron duty officer (SDO) to get ready for a 10:30 briefing, an 11:00 "man planes," and an 11:30 launch. When Edinger asked what was up, he was told only that the mission near Wonsan was in trouble. He was to pull together a division—four planes and four pilots, including himself.

Even as the second-most-senior squadron officer, Edinger was, at age thirty-four, comparatively speaking, an "old man" in a young man's game. "Older" pilots, however, were not uncommon in VF-653; most were reservist "weekend warriors": well into their twenties, World War II veterans, senior lieutenants with wives, families, and budding civilian careers left behind when they were called up.

Edinger was painfully aware that VF-653 had already lost four of its pilots. It was Edinger's job to draft condolence letters to the dead pilots' families for signing by squadron commanding officer (CO) Cook Cleland—himself under pressure about mounting casualties. Already down four pilots and even more airplanes, finding three more aviators and four airplanes ready for them to fly on such short notice was no simple matter.

***

Valley Forge was the flagship of Task Force 77. By World War II standards—when task groups routinely numbered hundreds of warships—TF 77 was a relatively modest formation of a cruiser and a handful of screening destroyers centered on three of the four *Essex* carriers normally deployed to the Far East for stretches of six months or more. However, TF 77's scale did not diminish the pace of activity or sense of urgency in *Valley Forge's* flag plot, the low-ceilinged, red-lit compartment used as command center for carrier division commander Rear Adm. John "Black Jack" Perry.

One flag plot observer was a civilian, sitting unobtrusively amid the noise and bustle, with little to do but plenty to see and record. James A. Michener was a writer of still modest (but fast-growing) acclaim on assignment for two of America's most popular magazines: the *Saturday Evening Post* and *Reader's Digest*.

Michener, forty-five, was of average height and weight, though narrow shouldered and a bit paunchy at the waist. He'd been a Navy officer in the South Pacific during World War II, even rising to the rank of lieutenant commander, but he lacked an officer's bearing even then and displayed less of it now. His thinning hairline, blunt nose, receding chin, and wire-rimmed "porthole" glasses made him easily mistaken (in other settings at least) for the college teacher (at what was then Colorado's Greeley Teachers College, fifty miles north of Denver) and textbook editor he had once been.

Michener's first book, *Tales of the South Pacific*, an interconnected series of anecdotes, impressions, and profiles that chronicled wartime life in the South Pacific, had won him moderate success and then, somewhat unexpectedly, a Pulitzer Prize for fiction. It was a rare World War II novel, one that gave a perspective on life in the backwaters of the Pacific and focused on local island characters as much as it did on American servicemen. "I wish I could tell you about the South Pacific," *Tales* begins disarmingly. "But whenever I start to talk about the South Pacific, people intervene."

The "intervention" of people made the book unique and charmed its audience—both men and women. Although it is about the war, it also resonates with the war's larger substance: not just the brief intensity of combat but also the much longer stretches of separation, isolation, and "timeless, repetitive waiting." It tells of ordinary people coping with suspended lives equidistant from the front lines and home. Uniquely and somewhat boldly for the time, *Tales* also dips into the precarious waters of race. Several of its white protagonists find themselves enveloped in a polymorphous world of races, languages, and cultures in which, for once, their own prejudices and senses of superiority are out of step. Two of its stories—"Our Heroine" and "Fo' Dolla"—had by now been transformed into the hit Broadway musical *South Pacific*. "You Have to Be Carefully Taught," one song from the show, even underscores the damage wrought by prejudice.

Michener had already parlayed *Tales*'s postprize sales into a thriving—and independent—writing career. He'd become, almost by default, an expert on Asian travel and culture, but he also felt committed to write about contemporary events. This combination of circumstances drew him to Korea, often to its front lines where he interviewed hundreds of GIs and wrote passionately of their heroism, isolation, and deprivation. He made five separate Korean reporting trips and each time came away troubled that the fight generated little sympathy among the American public. "We forget," he told an audience of *Saturday Evening Post* readers. "Even those of us who know better forget that today, in the barren wastes of Korea, American men are dying with a heroism never surpassed in our history. Because they are so few, we forget that they contribute so much."

This time he'd come to learn about perhaps the least-known aspect of this forgotten war: its warships and sailors. The trip would last the better part of four months, much of that time aboard either *Valley Forge* or *Essex* (CV-9) with occasional side trips to other carriers and even surface escort ships. Before abruptly leaving the United States in September, Michener had written his lecture booking agent, instructing him to cancel speaking engagements set for October and November. "The bright spot in all this," Michener wrote, apologizing for the late notice, "is that when I do return I shall carry with me fresh news, fresh incidents for discussion, and a generally better collection of information to share with your audiences."[2]

The news, incidents, and information Michener was in the midst of gathering were both stirring and sobering. By his account he flew as observer on several combat missions. For a night mission launched from *Essex*, he had crawled out of bed at three o'clock for the ritual "ready room" briefing and review of reconnaissance photos and then climbed into the rear compartment of a Navy attack plane for takeoff.

Before launch the enlisted man responsible for the preparation—and cleanup—of his aircraft handed him a box of tissues: "Kleenex, Mr. Michener. Them as throws up, cleans up." Michener put both the advice and the Kleenex to good use. "I never knew which was worse," he later wrote, "the sudden leap forward to get us aloft, or the instantaneous stop when we came back down."[3] To his continued awe and amazement, after completing their hazardous combat missions, the naval aviators were routinely able to land their huge prop- or jet-powered planes on the "hellishly small" bobbing deck of an aircraft carrier at sea.

During the mission, in a series of "sickening dives, which left me hawking," the pilot and his wingman attacked a long Communist supply train trying to reach the safety of a tunnel before sunrise. Between them, they cut the tracks ahead of the train and derailed a few cars at its rear, effectively trapping the entire train. The two pilots then combed the full length of the stalled train, dropping bombs and strafing its cars, turning the rail line valley into a "ghostly inferno with four separate big fires."[4]

The pilots' ages—one was thirty-six, the other thirty-five—surprised, even unnerved, Michener. "I used to knock around carriers, a good deal," he wrote later in one news service dispatch. "I was only 37 then, but I felt like a grandpappy. . . . That isn't true now. I'm 45 and an alarming number of our major pilots are in their mid or late 30s. I took three flights over North Korea and each time my combat pilot was over 35. They weren't squadron leaders, either. Nor were they professional Annapolis men making naval aviation their career. These were ordinary run-of-the-mine combat pilots. And I say they were too old."[5]

Their skills made these Navy carrier pilots (young or "too old") unique, but to Michener there was also something singular about their character. "I hold their heroism to be greater than what I witnessed in 1941–45," he wrote. "The soldier on Guadalcanal could feel that his entire nation was behind him. . . . But today the fighter in Korea cannot feel this sense of identification with his own nation." Instead, Michener believed, "we have told a few men, 'You do it, bub. You be the hero.'" They went out on their missions (he was "ashamed to say") alone.[6]

***

On even the most routine days, the intense atmosphere of *Valley Forge*'s flag plot took its cues from the demeanor and reputation of Black Jack Perry. Michener would later describe Perry to his readers as the "epitome of the historic, crusty, taciturn Navy man. . . . He is lanky, dour and relentless—a holy terror to inefficiency, and one of our greatest living air admirals."

Perry's résumé, rank, and demeanor combined for singularly intimidating effect. A 1920 U.S. Naval Academy graduate, he'd served on destroyers, cruisers, and battleships before taking flight training during the 1920s. Stationed as a squadron XO at Pearl Harbor when the

Japanese attacked, he'd stepped in to reorganize its devastated remnants. Perry had advanced to skipper small jeep escort carriers early in the war and then a fleet carrier at Iwo Jima and Okinawa.

In person Perry was quiet to the point of surliness, and he rarely smiled or laughed. Clad in black shoes and khaki slacks and shirt, sometimes bareheaded but usually wearing a nondescript baseball cap (and usually drinking coffee), Perry, then in his fifties, paced the flag plot relentlessly. When he talked he leaned forward from the hips, often using the coffee cup and saucer to make a point. When Perry listened, he might sit and even lean back, but he always seemed to be critically surveying the speaker.

With good reason, staff officers and aviators often quaked in Perry's stern presence. Despite this, most men also understood Perry possessed the qualities essential to running air operations in the unforgiving wintry expanse of the Sea of Japan. Stoked with caffeine, Perry had the stamina for eighteen-hour flag plot days and the brainpower to coordinate hundreds of operational details, dozens of ships, and the efforts of thousands of airmen and sailors. Perry also had an uncanny skill in judging water and weather: He had an expert sense of timing with sea swells that could cripple flight operations and the clairvoyance to sidestep snowstorms that otherwise shut operations down.*

Perry was as gruffly exacting as he was inspirational. Regardless of day-to-day outcomes, the admiral was determined that his ships, aircraft, and aviators would do their jobs relentlessly—as if the accumulation of risk, destruction, and loss might at long last tip the scales of the enemy's own stubborn determination. It was not that specific results didn't matter—in this Perry was also relentless: "No use claiming work that you haven't done." To be credited with destroying a Communist target, Perry's pilots had to supply irrefutable proof—gun-camera footage or multiple confirmations. "When that old buzzard reports a locomotive destroyed, it's destroyed," Michener was assured by one pilot. "Because he makes us bring back a signed chit from the engineer: 'My engine was knocked to hell. . . . Signed, Fung Il.'"[7]

---

* In the sort of irony that would characterize much of the Cold War's convoluted dealings, Task Force 77 ships routinely relied on weather conditions and forecasts broadcast from Moscow and Peking. They were available because none of the three nations was, officially at least, a combatant.

Perry was also a fanatic in the smallest of details, demanding, for example, that radio circuits be kept free of trivial chatter. The lives of men and ships depended on immediate access to radio circuits. "If some damn fool pilot is gossiping about a ball game," Michener had once heard Perry complain, "you could lose an entire squadron."

Perry had reason to be upset about the volume of traffic this morning, even though none of it was gossip. Instead (despite being transmitted with the same spare, almost nonchalant, "business-as-usual" monotone), it was the chatter of things going wrong and of people fighting to master their distress, rein in their emotions, and somehow set things right.

***

The enemy bridges to be hit by today's late-morning mission carried rail lines and roads across a valley chasm fifty miles west of Kowon near a valley town called Samdong-ni. The Korean rail grid was shaped roughly like a capital letter *H*: One north-south leg followed the curves and typography of the east coast, another leg hugged the west coast; a connecting line (with its eastern terminus at Kowon and western terminus at Yangdok) stretched across the peninsula's mountainous waist well north of the 38th Parallel—North Korean territory. Michener had seen the bridges from a distance during the morning bombing run on the freight train.

Today's bridge-strike "package" consisted of six aircraft: four from squadron VF-194 joined by two more from VF-653, all led by VF-194's CO, Lt. Cdr. Robert Schreiber, a pilot with a reputation for hard living ashore and, aloft, for getting in close to enemy ground targets (in part to get the camera-footage evidence that Perry required) and getting riddled with flak. Schreiber's flight was already on its way by the time Ray Edinger reached VF-653's ready room.

***

As expected, Ray Edinger had to scramble and improvise to pull together the four-plane division. Most of VF-653's fourteen remaining Corsair fighter aircraft were already committed to missions—as combat air patrol (CAP) protecting task group ships, or the day's strikes and reconnaissance missions—while nearly all the rest were down for repair or scheduled maintenance. Edinger was finally able to track down three VF-653 planes and two other squadron pilots, Ens. Richard G. Jensen and Ens. Roland G. Busch, to fly them. But the fourth aircraft and its pilot, Ens. Joe Akagi, had to be borrowed from VF-194. Edinger knew little about Akagi—only that he was part Japanese, the first ever to fly for the U.S. Navy. But to World War II Navy veterans such as Edinger, Akagi's last name had a certain ironic resonance: The Japanese aircraft carrier *Akagi* had played a prime role in the Japanese 1941 attack on Pearl Harbor and had later been sunk by U.S. Navy aircraft from the aircraft carriers "Big E" and *Yorktown* (CV-5) in the Battle of Midway. At least symbolically, the U.S. Navy seemed to have come a long way in seven years.

By the time the four pilots sat down for the 10:30 briefing, Edinger already knew the bare bones of the problem. The rescue whirlybird was down; its crew had apparently survived, but there was no information about their current status—or the status of the injured ATG-1 pilot they were supposed to extract. One of *Valley Forge's* ResCAP aircraft had already gone missing, and others were low on fuel and ordnance. Edinger, Busch, Akagi, and Jensen were being sent as ResCAP replacements.

***

The Korean climate is one of extremes as distinct as its topography, as brutal as its history, and as withering as its ground warfare was proving to be. Summer high temperatures are frequently 110 degrees with 90 percent humidity in the South, while winter temperatures are consistently subzero in the rugged North. In February the same winds that howled down from the Arctic to dump snow on Korea's barren mountains swept unchecked across the Sea of Japan. The winds froze the salt spray that lashed *Valley Forge's* towering prow. Sometimes, during heavy storms, the spray spilled over the carrier's flight deck; even on the gentlest days it routinely iced over the weather decks, bulkheads, topside gear, and exposed watch standers of the smaller ships in her company.

To the sailors on *Valley Forge* and her escort ships, Korea was a place they'd likely never set foot on, much less see. Ships mostly stayed well outside the hundred-fathom curve, away from the dangers of coastal mines and shoals. The carrier task force ships needed to be only as close to Korea as the operational range of their aircraft required. For flight operations their fictive home address was Point Oboe, a geographical reference point, about 125 miles east of the North Korean coastal town of Wonsan. From Point Oboe, Task Force 77 aircraft were within striking range of most Northeast Korean targets from Wonsan north to Chongjin. At the same time, Task Force 77 ships rode far enough out to sea not to be visible to enemy aircraft flying high above the Korean and Chinese landmass.

Even the pilots like Ray Edinger who saw Korea up close got little sense of it. They flew as high above its terrain as mission objectives allowed, and when they flew low it was never for sightseeing. Approaching the "coast-in point," there was inevitably a buildup of tension and anxiety. Just as inevitably, these emotions colored the landscape—made North Korea's cliffs more jagged and bleak, cast its valleys in deeper shadow.

In truth, Korea always looked better outbound. Only then did the mountains claim some majesty or did the drifting snow soften the escarpments' edges and crevices. Once a pilot was "feet wet" over the Sea of Japan he was apt to feel home free. In some ways he really was—out of range of the antiaircraft (AA) guns trying to shoot him down, away from the risks of crash landing on rocky slopes, free especially from the reach of North Korean or Chinese soldiers anxious to capture or kill him.

Just as danger built on the way into Korea, so it seemed to ease on the way out. With a good reserve of fuel and with plane and self intact, a pilot had every reason to believe he had reached the fair circle of home. Somewhere in the vast sea there was the task force, a flight deck, and a landing signal officer (LSO) waiting to bring him home. But if fuel was low, the plane was crippled, or he was injured, the pilot still had to contend with the sea. In those circumstances, because of its vastness and sheer indifference, the sea was perhaps the most frightening and treacherous adversary of all.

***

In February the Sea of Japan was an ice bath. A man immersed in its waters without protective gear could expect his face and hands to freeze within five minutes. Seven more minutes would incapacitate his arms and legs. Eight minutes later he would most likely be dead. Wearing protective gear was essential if he hoped to survive the time it would take a rescue helicopter or ship to reach him.

While these were risks faced to one degree or another by everyone aboard these ships, they were especially real to the carrier pilots. When Edinger, Busch, Jensen, and Akagi rode the flight deck elevator to Death Valley's flight deck, they were doubly protected—and doubly constrained—by garments designed to help them survive the frigid atmosphere aloft and the frigid sea below. They not so much strode as awkwardly waddled to their aircraft: Edinger, the tallest of them at six-foot-three, like a walrus; Akagi, at barely five-seven and 140 pounds, more like a penguin. Their visible gear—flight suit, C-1 land survival vest, a Mae West life jacket, knife, .38-caliber pistol, gloves, crash helmet, flight goggles, oxygen connection, harness strap, dye marker, shark repellent, flashlight, and whistle—was just the top shell of five or six garment layers weighing more than forty pounds in all.

For all jet pilots and many prop pilots (including Edinger), the base layer was a G-suit, an interconnected series of air bladders positioned at the pilot's calves, thighs, and abdomen. The valve-controlled bladders were set to inflate, constrict blood flow, and thus increase blood pressure whenever flight acceleration impeded the heart's pumping power. First issued to combat pilots in 1944, G-suits were initially shunned until wartime studies revealed that G-suit-wearing pilots were more successful in air-to-air combat. Atop the G-suit and skivvies, most pilots donned long woolen underwear followed by a wool shirt and flannel-lined trousers. Next came a quilted pajama-like blue coverall, the inner liner for a rubberized Mark III exposure suit—the "poopy suit." The poopy suit was at once the pilots' most vital and most loathed piece of gear. A neck-to-toe, one-size-fits-all galvanized-rubber affair, the suit—just as often called a poofy suit or poopy bag—had the smell, inflexibility, and texture of an inner tube or pair of galoshes. The poopy suit's discomfort—a blend of sweat, odor, and claustrophobia—was only made worse by the reality that gave the suit its name. As Edinger ruefully recalled years later, "Either you couldn't do anything that your body may want to do for four and a half hours—or you did it in the suit."

Just climbing into the poopy suit (via a long slash running from the left shoulder of the suit across the chest and down to the right hip) was hell. After pushing his legs and feet into the suit's extremities (leg tubes ending in boot galoshes) and his head and hands through cinch-tightened apertures, the pilot rolled the flaps that flared from either side of the slash into a bulky seal that resembled a huge diagonal scar. With the tightening of the neck aperture (early models used a choker belt whose brass buckle pressed annoyingly into neck and chin) and sleeves, the poopy suit was supposedly watertight. If the seals held, the poopy suit could be the salvation of a pilot ditched and adrift in the Sea of Japan; any leakage, however, could quickly make it a death trap.

***

During flight operations *Valley Forge's* nine hundred-foot-long timbered flight deck (because of its ability to withstand high loads, Douglas fir was the flooring of choice for aircraft carriers) was constantly in motion and, because it was both a parking lot and a one-way drag strip, constantly in the process of being reconfigured. One-way, it was also one-lane; the current crop of U.S. fleet carriers had yet to be built or reconfigured with a British innovation: a flared and angled appendage at middeck that provided extra space and allowed for simultaneous launches and landings. Although there was a massive hangar deck below for longer storage and for maintenance and repairs of ATG-1's eighty or so aircraft (with three huge elevator platforms to lift and lower), there was inevitably the need to park a "stack" of aircraft topside. As airplanes joined or left the stack, the stack itself was in motion—shuttled aft during launches, forward during recoveries.

The agents of the flight deck's activities—arming, fueling, moving (called "respotting," as if it were chess instead of multiton moving and storage), launching, and recovering—were the flight deck crews. In locales and conditions much balmier than the Sea of Japan in February, the flight deck was a riot of bold colors: the red shirts of ordnance handlers, the purple of fuel handlers, the green of mechanics, the yellow of plane directors, the blue of "plane pushers," the white of medical personnel, and the brown of mechanics and plane captains. Today, with these "blue-collar airdales" bundled against the winter sea's extremes (with skull caps or small swatches of colored cloth stitched to their cold-weather gear, denoting their functions), the less colorful work was inestimably harder because both deck and stacked airplanes accumulated sheens combined of ice, oil, hydraulic fluid, and gasoline that made footing treacherous and launches even more so. In fact, nothing on the deck—from big things like aircraft engines and catapults down to small gaskets and air valves—worked particularly well in cold weather.

***

The four ResCAP airplanes were out of the stack and waiting at middeck—the three VF-653 Corsairs with their long nose cowlings, distinctive gull wings, and four-blade propellers and one huge straight-wing VF-194 Skyraider. The unpredictable placement of aircraft within the stack, and the fact that there were more squadron aviators than squadron aircraft, meant that no one pilot was normally assigned a particular aircraft. Each, as in a corral full of horses, might have its idiosyncrasies, but, for the most part, you got what you got.

Teardrop tanks—the reserve of fuel that would allow the propeller-driven airplanes to stay over target for extended periods—hung from fuselage bellies. Their wings were unfolded (the plane pushers' job), each slung with four high-velocity aerial rockets (HVARs, pronounced "hi-vars"). The Skyraider's distinctive heft made Joe Akagi look particularly small and high-perched as he settled into its cockpit.

Plane captains (mechanics, but also squires to unhorsed knights) helped the four pilots into their cockpits, handed them sheaves of maps, got them strapped into their parachute harnesses and seat shoulder straps, and helped plug in radio jacks and oxygen and G-suit hoses.

Military pilots now wore crash helmets made of hard plastic, remarkably similar to college and professional football helmets of the day. They were a relatively recent innovation: made necessary by the bubble canopies in most postwar aircraft—especially the jets—which could easily collapse and crush unprotected skulls. When VF-653 was activated, its pilots became part of "Cook Cleland's Flying Circus," and their new helmets had accordingly been tricked out in circus colors—white polka dots on a background of metallic red. A garish red-lipped clown's smile was painted on the right, or inboard,

side of each squadron aviator's helmet. Because Edinger, as XO, was
VF-653's "bad cop" when it came to disciplinary matters (allowing
squadron CO Cleland to play benevolent "good cop"), the smile logo
on his helmet was inverted—a clown's frown instead of a clown's
smile. Although Edinger considered it a sort of badge of honor, it was
also now a reminder of the squadron's heartrending losses.

Although *Valley Forge* was equipped with two flush deck aircraft
catapults—topside "shuttle" tracks linked to immense hydraulic pistons
belowdecks—the "cats" were seldom used to launch the propeller-
powered Corsairs and Skyraiders. (Their use was mostly confined to
launching jets—the newest and hottest but also, relatively speaking,
the heaviest and lowest endurance of ATG-1's mixed aircraft inven-
tory.) Instead, the Corsairs and Skyraiders usually took off from middeck, giving them roughly 450 feet to get airborne.

It was always crucial to have the right amount of relative wind
(the offsetting combination of wind and ship's speed) streaming over
the flight deck during launches. Thirty-five knots (a little less than
forty miles per hour) was the ideal combination, but with the wind
conditions ever changing in the Sea of Japan, it was a judgment call.
If there was insufficient relative wind, the consequences were immediate and could be disastrous—a plane heavily loaded with explosive
ordnance and volatile fuel stalling at the absolute worst possible instant. It was something pilots couldn't control and thus, at least at the
moment of takeoff, tended not to worry about.

Engine ignition systems for the Skyraider and the newer Corsair
production models flown by VF-653 used heavy-duty solenoids. During World War II, Navy aircraft including the Corsair used a cruder
and simpler device: essentially a shotgun charge fired internally. In
winter use the solenoid systems, although ultimately more reliable,
occasionally displayed the same sluggishness as ignition systems in
cars left out in subfreezing weather. At such times the pilots had to
grind and grind them like any frustrated motorist before they engaged.

Another frightening moment for pilots making a deck run—and
another that they couldn't control—was when the carrier turned into
the wind. If his airplane was spotted amidships as the ship's prow
lifted and the flight deck "banked," a pilot often had the weird sensa-
tion that he was about to topple backward into the sea or skid into

the stack. On winter days like this, with the cockpit canopy open—a requisite for takeoffs and landings to enable visibility and easier escape from the cockpit in an emergency—the turn also brought the icy wind painfully across the pilot's exposed cheek.[8]

Into a socket just outside the stern-facing, glass-fronted primary air-control station, sixty feet above the flight deck on the inboard side of the carrier's superstructure "island," the air boss had stuck a green flag. Simultaneously, a sailor perched high on *Valley Forge's* signal bridge hoisted the "Fox" flag—a signal flag representing the letter *F* and indicating to nearby ships that *Valley Forge* was beginning flight operations. A bullhorn then blared, "Clear deck. Commence launching aircraft."

Once engine, prop, and pilot were set, a plane handler using hand signals guided each plane as it taxied to "fly one," the actual takeoff point. As the aircraft moved, the plane captain walked alongside, keeping a watchful eye on the bird's wheels and control surfaces, meanwhile listening intently (despite the vortex of wind and the proximate roar of other planes), like a doctor with a stethoscope, to the beat of the patient's multipiston heart. Because of the Corsair's particularly long nose cowling—one of its many nicknames was "Hose Nose"—its pilot had to crane his neck to see what was directly ahead of him. This was a small annoyance during takeoffs, but it could be treacherous when it came to carrier landings; it was like parking without being able to see the curb or the car in front of you, but vertically, headfirst, and at much higher speed.

When Ray Edinger's Corsair was positioned for takeoff, control passed from the plane handler to the launch signal officer—usually a nonflying officer in the air group—responsible for controlling launch. With brakes engaged, Edinger watched the launch signal officer, whose arm pointed skyward, two fingers showing and spun in a tight, conical, and ever-accelerating circle. This was the signal to bring the plane's engine to full throttle. The plane captain stared and listened more intently now. When the flight deck officer thought the aircraft was ready to go, he gave a final "now-or-never" glance toward the plane captain and then, catching the pilot's eye and receiving his salute, deftly lunged like a duelist, his twirling arm locked and extended straight forward, his two fingers pointing at the bow like a foil tip to an opponent's heart. When Ray Edinger released his brakes, the Corsair not so much lunged as lurched forward, simultaneously yanking its pilot's clown helmet head and walrus torso back as though he were nothing more than a string puppet.

***

During flight ops (operations), the carrier deck's well-organized takeoff routines (usually ninety-minute cycles alternating between prop and jet launches) always held the risk of suddenly turning into chaos. If an airplane, because of mechanical malfunction or poor wind, stalled and tumbled off the deck and into the water (perhaps squarely in the path of the onrushing 33,000-ton flattop), the race was on, especially in winter, for the ship's helicopter—its "pinwheel"—or the "plane guard" destroyer to get to the scene. It was a game of chance whose odds and disastrous possibilities lured sardonic kibitzers (mostly off-duty pilots) to the rail of "Vulture's Row," a narrow observation porch just aft of primary air control.

Leaving flag plot to watch from Vulture's Row as the ResCAP launched, James Michener had the perspective of his own backseat takeoffs in one of the lumbering Skyraider beasts: "the fantastic leap forward, up to ninety miles an hour within the short length of the carrier, the takeoff and the perilous drop, more terrifying to witness from the bridge than to experience in the plane itself, because as the heavy bomber leaves the end of the runway it automatically drops down, down, down toward the clutching waves until it seems to crash into them and sink, except that at the last minute the engines [*sic*] whine, the nose lifts up, and the plane miraculously gains altitude."[9]

Michener had it right about the pilot's perception of the "perilous drop." Drop or dip, perilous or insignificant, Ray Edinger paid it scant attention as he "cleaned up" his plane: retracted his landing gear, slid his canopy closed, pulled back on the control stick, eased up slightly on the throttle, checked his gauges, and adjusted his wing flaps. With Edinger as division leader, the other three airplanes launching would be forming up on him. To accomplish this, Edinger continued climbing slowly with the carrier deck still astern. When he reached fifteen hundred feet he leveled off and banked left until his Corsair headed downwind parallel to *Valley Forge*'s flight deck. By the time he was abreast of the ship's stern each of the other planes—first Jensen's (Edinger's wingman), then Akagi's (his Skyraider the outsized odd bird of Edinger's flock), and finally Busch's—would be coming into line at Edinger's starboard wing.

With all four planes assembled, the division headed west. Soon the coastal mountains would come into view—not beckoning, instead (like big-shouldered sentries) warning. Edinger would check in with cruiser *Rochester* (code name "Above Board"), the ship coordinating the troubled rescue mission, before crossing the coast-in point and going "feet dry" over North Korea.

PART 1

WE INTERRUPT THIS COLD WAR

1

THE HOLLOWAY

As a child, Jesse LeRoy Brown's dreams of flying seemed to hinge on speed and endurance—his ability to outrun and outdistance a tobacco-spitting redneck named Corley Yates. Yates was the mechanic and caretaker of an airfield—really little more than a five hundred–foot dirt runway and a corrugated tin hangar—on the outskirts of Palmer's Crossing, a small town in northeastern Mississippi. For Brown, a black sharecropper's son whose ancestry sprinkled Choctaw and Chickasaw blood, the spark had been his first glimpse of a red biplane operating from the field's dusty strip. Brown was irresistibly drawn to the field where, sometimes hidden in the tall grass bordering the runway and other times behind the ramshackle hangar, he could watch the red plane or any other aircraft that chanced to pass through. All the while, though, Brown had to keep a watchful eye for Yates, who invariably chased after the wiry, barefoot ten year old whenever he spotted him. "I'll get you someday, nigger!" Yates always screamed, but he never did—and never much deterred his prey from returning. Brown, who was born on October 13, 1926, had by then already experienced a full share of the curses, indignities, and exclusions that defined a black childhood in rural Mississippi. The names and murderous threats intended to keep Brown in his place could not kill his insatiable fascination with aviation and his dream—however objectively outlandish—of becoming a pilot.

***

In what were then still the nascent days of aviation, Jesse Brown's dream was shared by perhaps hundreds of thousands of American boys. (It doubtless figured in girls' dreams as well, but those dreams, with a handful of exceptions, were about as far-fetched as Jesse Brown's.) For some, the spark was a brief glimpse of an aircraft soaring overhead, still a rare phenomenon in the 1920s and 1930s. For others it was a barnstorming aircraft dropping in at a local field to offer demonstrations and rides.

For still others, it was aviation's depiction in movies, magazines, and newspaper comics. In 1930, for example, a still young tycoon named Howard Hughes had produced and directed a thrilling aerial epic called *Hell's Angels*. The movie filled the screen with graphic air combat scenes shot by daredevil cameramen strapped into (and sometimes onto) a fleet of resurrected World War I biplanes. Monthly magazines such as *Model Airplane News*, *Flight*, and *Air Trails* also fueled the fascination; in daily newspapers it was the likes of "Tailspin Tommy," a strip whose characters were inspired by Charles Lindbergh's solo crossing of the Atlantic.

For most, the aviation spark, though momentarily intense, was also fleeting. For a core, however, the dream came early and never faded. Royce Williams, for example, a Wilmot, South Dakota, grocer's son born in 1925, felt the spark surge through him at age four when he, his brother Lynn (then six), and their grandmother went for a ride in a Ford Tri-Motor "Tin Goose" barnstorming out of a local piece of pastureland. Soon, the two brothers reached a pact—both would become aviators. Royce agreed to call his brother Lindy (after "Lucky Lindy" Charles Lindbergh) if Lynn in turn would call him Roscoe, a tribute to (Kentucky) Colonel Roscoe Turner, a barnstormer turned stunt pilot turned racing pilot.

In 1940 a fifty-cents-a-head hop in another (by then ancient) Tin Goose, a field trip arranged by a Texas educator, lit the spark for eleven-year-old Joe Akagi. Mr. Naill, Akagi's grade school principal in Henderson, Texas (and himself an aviation enthusiast), encouraged Joe and Joe's older brother Henry by getting them involved in model airplane construction. The flight—a field trip to Houston for the principal and the two boys—was an electrifying event.

Small, smart, and nimble, Akagi was the second oldest of five children raised on a truck farm in the small town of Sheldon, outside Houston. The Akagis worked year-round six-and-a-half-day weeks growing okra and watermelons during the hot, muggy coastal Texas summers and turnip and mustard greens in the fall and winter. His modest farming background seemed no deterrent to Akagi's new unbounded dream. Neither did his ancestry, at least at the time. Akagi's father, Torata, was second-generation Japanese; his mother, Beatrice, a Texan, traced her roots to Mexico.

Like Joe Akagi, Ohio-born Neil Armstrong also caught the spark in grade school—actually in a series of schools, as his parents moved through a string of Ohio towns: Warren, Jefferson, Moulton, St. Mary's, and Upper Sandusky before finally landing in Wapakoneta. Armstrong, a serious and cerebral boy a year younger than Akagi, was inspired by the aviation magazines of the time and determined to be an aircraft designer. To Neil Armstrong, becoming a pilot was a logical and necessary first step. A good designer ought to know the operational aspects of an airplane.

***

When Japan attacked Pearl Harbor on December 7, 1941, Royce Williams, then sixteen, and his brother Lynn, then just shy of eighteen, sat glued to the radio console at their home in Clinton, a western Minnesota town where their father had purchased a grocery store. Both were anxious to do something, anything, and right then to get involved in the war effort. The first step for both was to join the Minnesota Guard, the state militia that soon had to reconstitute itself with younger volunteers like Royce and Lynn once the prewar unit was mobilized, nationalized, and sent off to war.

After that the two boys' paths diverged. Royce, still just a high school sophomore, would not be graduating until 1943. Lynn, meanwhile, was at the prime age, both for military service (just months later the draft age was reduced to eighteen) and for military aviation. He soon joined the V5 Navy College Training Program, one of an alphabet soup of "Victory" programs designed to meld education with military training, in this instance to prepare Navy and Marine officer aviators.

Well to the east, in Newport, Rhode Island, George Schnitzer and his older brother Robert also listened to the Sunday broadcast bulletins. George at age twelve was already into flying "in a big way." He had first flown in an airplane at age four (the same age as Royce Williams but a few years later), sitting on his father's lap in the open cockpit of his Uncle Charlie's World War I–era Jenny. The flight made a big impression. For as long as he could remember he'd been building and flying balsa-framed model airplanes powered by rubber bands. In the months after Pearl Harbor he would redirect his hobby to the war effort, building solid-wood scale model aircraft used by the military for aircraft recognition purposes, and even standing civilian aircraft spotting watches in the tower on the Middletown, Rhode Island, campus of St. George's Boys School. The Schnitzer brothers shared a bedroom, and its ceiling was strung with wires from which dangled a growing fleet of model aircraft. At night with the lights out, the boys used flashlights to practice spotting and identifying individual aircraft.

Some 1,200 miles due south of Clinton, Minnesota, and 1,800 miles southwest of Newport, Rhode Island, Joe Akagi's family had spent the morning of that same fateful Sunday working their winter crops in Sheldon, Texas. The family had a small battery-operated radio (their home's electricity was supplied by a gasoline-powered generator), and, when they returned from the fields for lunch, someone turned it on. The static-filled reception made listening difficult, but the news and its implications were clear enough. A pall of dread soon filled the house.

Joe Akagi's father was not a first-generation Japanese immigrant, but his grandfather Fukutoro—who lived with his son's family—was. Within days of the Pearl Harbor attack, FBI agents were at their door. After rummaging through the Akagi home, the agents confiscated several firearms used for hunting. Soon, the elderly Fukutoro Akagi was also involuntarily whisked away, bound for incarceration in a Houston detention center.

***

It turned out that, in addition to motivation, aptitude, and even pedigree, realizing the dream of flying was also a matter of timing. In particular, it mattered when these boys came of age and how closely that coming of age dovetailed with the manpower needs of a nation at war. Almost without exception, the path for the dream's realization was military aviation. In a war whose first blow, at least in the Pacific, was struck from the air, there was a burning (though highly selective) need for a steady supply of flyers: young men with the education, acuity, and aptitude to pilot single-engine fighter and dive-bombing planes as well as multiengine "horizontal" bombers and cargo aircraft.

In the case of the Navy the need extended to the controlled recklessness it took to launch and land on short, heaving aircraft carrier flight decks in the middle of the ocean. For carrier pilots—more precisely naval aviators—these takeoffs and "recoveries" were just the stage entrances and curtain calls to every operational or combat mission. The carrier-borne aviators defied death even before they got to fire a shot, launch a torpedo, or drop a bomb.

Military flight training had to begin young, ideally while candidates were still in their teens. Combat pilots had to be put in action before the erosion of reflexes and the softening effects of maturity—and awareness of mortality—took hold. (A Royal Air Force study of the time concluded that the very best age for a combat pilot was sixteen.) Though often truncated in the war's first years, thorough preparation took nearly two years, a long time in the pressing calendar of war and an eternity for young men trying to get past the hurdles.

Groundwork began as early as 1939, when thousands of college undergrads enrolled in the U.S. government–sponsored Civilian Pilot Training Program (CPTP), which financed ground schooling and rudimentary flight training at eleven colleges across the country. Eventually, even more structured and extensive programs like V5—two years of college, Officer Candidate School, and then flight training—were falling into place. For the U.S. Navy, the combination of recruiting, screening, education, and flight training would produce, by war's end, a superb corps of Navy and Marine aviators numbering upward of 60,000.

***

In the thick of the war, for adolescent pilot aspirants like Neil Armstrong, George Schnitzer, and Royce Williams, it was a matter of reaching graduation. Advancing through their high school years, they saw waves of graduating senior boys ahead of them go off to military service, many of the most talented of them into the respective aviation branches.

Adolescent blacks, like Mississippi's Jesse Brown, saw the same thing, but in a humbling and blatantly discriminatory form. During the war more than 125,000 black Americans served overseas in both the European and the Pacific theaters, but virtually all were in segregated units. A few served in illustrious units, including the 332nd Fighter Group (Tuskegee Airmen). Most, though, were assigned to auxiliary and noncombat organizations for backbreaking tasks such as construction, cargo handling, and transport.

Examples for boys such as Joe Akagi were even more limited. The Akagi family's faith in country was somewhat buoyed when a petition campaign by their Texas neighbors spurred federal officials to release Joe's grandfather from detention and allow him to return home. For his part, Joe Akagi moved on to high school in Houston, where he was well received, popular, and even took a leadership role in school Reserve Officers' Training Corps activities. Despite this, for the balance of the war, his family's travel was restricted to the confines of their county.

It was just as well that Joe Akagi, because of his youth, was not eligible for military service during the war—it would have almost surely squelched his aviation dreams. While the U.S. Navy enlisted blacks, Hispanics, and Asians, it used them mostly as cooks, cleaners, and food servers in Officers' Clubs and ship wardrooms. Indeed, the only combat example was the Army's 442d Regimental Combat Team, an Asian American infantry unit composed of mostly Japanese Americans (many of whose parents were subject to internment) that fought with distinction (and enough casualties to be nicknamed "the Purple Heart Battalion") in Italy, southern France, and Germany. The 442d paid a particularly heavy price in proving their loyalty and worth to their distrusting country.

***

When the war ended triumphantly in 1945, most U.S. veterans were as weary and exhausted as they were joyous. Few equated the triumph with glorious—or even fond—memories of their service during the war. Frontline combat was almost invariably a dirty, distasteful, and humbling experience; rear-echelon duty, though immeasurably safer, was tedious, mind-numbing, isolating, and depressing. Though the harsh edges of their experience would often be softened and embellished by time, what most took away from the experience was the depth and quality of the relationships forged on ships, in squadrons, and in foxholes. They hated the war (and, for good measure, the military branch in which they toiled) but cherished the deep, often life-long bonds with comrades in arms.

As it was in the trenches, so it was at home. Once the ticker tape was swept away, the end of the Second World War fed a nationwide fever for demobilization—"demobe," as it was sometimes called. At war's end, America had 12 million men and women in uniform, including 3.3 million in the U.S. Navy. Within two years, the overall number was down to 1.5 million, and what wasn't discharged was mothballed. A military budget that had reached a wartime peak of $90.9 billion had dwindled to $10.3 billion in 1947.

The service ranks depleted as most war veterans—superbly trained and battle tested—stampeded for the exits. Replacing them (though by no means in the same numbers) was an influx of raw recruits. Though they may have been as eager and potentially capable as the departing veterans (many entered based on recruiters' promises that they'd learn a trade), there were fewer old hands to train them and show them the ropes. The military professionals who remained found themselves saddled with deteriorating facilities and equipment, fewer choice billets, and slower promotions—as well as a citizenry that no longer participated in war bond drives, honored them in glowing newspapers accounts, or even bought them drinks.

For the U.S. Navy, the revolving door of manpower had an undeniably adverse impact on the teamwork, cohesion, and overall readiness of ships and air squadrons. Although still riding its global reputation, the Navy quickly began fraying at the edges: understrength, poorly trained, and ill-equipped.

Meanwhile, although it couldn't be said that victorious peace quashed or evaporated the flying aspirations of teenagers like Neil Armstrong, George Schnitzer, and Royce Williams, it certainly did change the mood, immediacy, and certainty of their plans. In the fall of 1945, for example, Schnitzer and Armstrong were both about to enter their junior years in high school, Schnitzer in Newport, Rhode Island, Armstrong in Wapakoneta, Ohio. Armstrong had earned his pilot's license at age sixteen, but gone now was the motivation to "get out and enlist" that had driven the lives of boys graduating during the war years.

Royce Williams, meanwhile, was well along in the U.S. Navy's flight pipeline. During his high school summers in Clinton, Williams had fed his hunger for flying in the backseat of a Travel Air biplane owned by a local garage owner and "speed merchant." In 1943, his graduation year, Williams was high school valedictorian and had even written his esoteric senior thesis on military aviation—specifically, the need for each service's infantry branch (e.g., the U.S. Army and U.S. Marine Corps) to have its own integrated aviation corps to provide aerial ground-fighting support.

Following the March commencement ceremonies, Williams went immediately into the V5 program. His first stop was not college; instead, it was boot camp at the U.S. Navy's aviation facilities in Corpus Christi, Texas. With war raging and the Allies' ultimate victory, though perhaps no longer in dispute, still nowhere in sight, Williams seemed to be on the fast track. Then, inexplicably, things began to slow down. First it was the increased "washout" rates from boot camp: A beginning class of more than two hundred was whittled down to fewer than twenty. Exhaustive physical training was one tool to winnow the swollen herds.

The cadets it couldn't wear out the Navy tried to wait out. Williams, an Eagle Scout in addition to being a Minnesota Guardsman, survived this grinder to be sent on to something called "Flight Prep" at Murray, Kentucky. This program lasted three to four months, only to be followed by another program called "War Training School" in Conway, Arkansas. At one point during his time assigned to Conway, Williams was even detached for a brief seagoing stint on a U.S. Navy destroyer.

Beyond Conway, Williams finally seemed to get back on track—first with Pre-Flight Training at the University of Georgia, Primary Flight Training in Memphis, and single-engine training in Pensacola. The war in Europe ended while he was in Memphis. There remained the expectation that the conquest of Japan would require a long haul. In August, however, the dropping of the atomic bombs—electrifying news—was quickly followed by Japan's capitulation. The war that had been the background benchmark of Royce Williams's progress toward becoming a naval aviator was over. When he at last received his Wings of Gold, it was November 1945.

***

Jesse Brown's aspirations to become a pilot, though far-fetched because of race, didn't lack for a foundation. Despite impoverished circumstances, Brown came from a tightly knit family and excelled in both academics and athletics (especially in track as a runner and long jumper). When he graduated second in the 1944 class at Eureka, Hattiesburg's segregated high school, teachers, family, and friends fully anticipated Brown would go on to college. But they expected it would be a Negro college—a school such as Alcorn, Hampton, Howard, Wilberforce, or perhaps even Tuskegee, the wellspring for the already illustrious Tuskegee Airmen.

Instead, Brown applied to Ohio State University (OSU), the university that had produced Jesse Owens, the equally illustrious gold medal–winning track-and-field phenomenon of the 1936 Berlin Olympics. At the time, Ohio State's black student population was well below 1 percent, but Brown was determined to test himself in the white world—both on the field and in the classroom. It was a momentous occasion, both for Brown and for Hattiesburg's black community, when he learned OSU had accepted him and even offered a track scholarship.

Early that September, carrying the contents of two cardboard suitcases, Jesse Brown took the night train north from Hattiesburg to Columbus, Ohio. He brought with him a new copy of *Popular Aviation*, an issue devoted to carrier warfare. As the train clacked along, Brown read about the planes and pilots who flew them in air battles against the Japanese in the Pacific. By two o'clock, when he fell asleep, Brown had made up his mind about the particular pilot he planned to be: a Navy pilot flying from flattops.

In Columbus Brown took up off-campus residence in a boarding-house in the heart of "colored town." In three of his four classes in OSU's College of Engineering, there were no black students, but, aside from being ignored, Brown didn't sense any particular animosity. In downtown Columbus, however, things weren't that much different from Hattiesburg. Blacks couldn't eat at any of the city's restaurants, and seating in its movie theaters was restricted to a few back rows in the balcony.

After a little more than a month of school, Brown realized he'd need more than athletic scholarship money to survive. So he dropped out of track and began working after class, eventually in a night-shift job unloading boxcars for the Pennsylvania Railroad. Brown also gave some thought that first year to joining OSU's Naval Reserve Officers' Training Corps (NROTC).

Gaining admission to the Navy's college training program was no straightforward matter for a black man, even at OSU. Indeed—still three years ahead of Executive Order 9981 that would mandate (and eventually, although slowly, effect) integration of the military services— it was unprecedented. While wartime needs had chipped away at some of the most rigid racial restrictions, the U.S. Army and Navy remained essentially segregated institutions.

This was especially so for the Navy. At the outset of the Second World War, aside from its mess stewards, the U.S. Navy had only six black enlisted sailors. Two years later, while the ranks of black enlisted men had swollen to eighty-two thousand, there were still no black officers. It was only in 1944—the same year as Brown's enrollment at OSU—that the Navy grudgingly began training its first black naval officer candidates: a small crop of seventeen men, thirteen of whom would eventually receive commissions. The future of such efforts, however, didn't look bright. But then, in his sophomore year, Brown caught wind of a new program called the Holloway Plan.

***

The Holloway Plan was named after Navy admiral James L. Holloway Jr., a "black-shoe" (nonaviator) sailor with (according to a *Time* cover story) "square, salt-cured features," who, at war's end, had commanded battleship *Iowa* (BB-61) under William "Bull" Halsey in the Pacific. Born the son of a Fort Smith, Arkansas, osteopath, Holloway grew up in Dallas with ambitions of attending West Point. Failing to win an appointment there, Holloway instead settled for the Naval Academy.

After graduating in 1918, just before the end of the Great War, Holloway reported to his first assignment, tiny destroyer *Monaghan* (DD-32), operating out of Brest, France, with enough baggage to fill the wardroom. ("I was a very unpopular young officer for that," he later admitted.) Following World War II, as a flag officer stationed in Washington and known for his taste in fine wines, his neo-British accent, and his penchant for writing erudite letters (one of his favorite words was *vouchsafe*), Holloway became "Lord Jim" to the D.C. press corps. "Lord Plushbottom" was his behind-the-back Navy nickname.

"If he will ever be known for any command," said one former staff officer, "it will be for his command of the English language." Still, Holloway made the most of his opportunities, especially ashore. Serving as assistant chief of naval personnel, it was his unenviable responsibility to quickly and evenhandedly demobilize much of the Navy's manpower. Holloway did it (as described in the same cover story) with "chin-out style," deflecting special pleadings from congressmen to get favored constituents home ahead of their time by intoning, in his best "Plushbottom" voice that congressmen came to understand and even admire, "I look to you, senator, to help me maintain my probity."

Before leaving Washington to become Annapolis superintendent, Holloway laid the foundation for rebuilding the Navy he'd just downsized. At Navy secretary James Forrestal's urging, Holloway empaneled a prestigious group of Navy officers and civilian educators to create a trailblazing plan using the nation's colleges not only to produce NROTC reservists but also to train regular Navy and Marine Corps officers. The Holloway Plan, which was approved by Congress in August 1946, was initially criticized as a waste of taxpayers' money—a path for young men to get a free college education only to quit the Navy after completing a three-year military service requirement. But, in the years to follow, the plan revolutionized both the makeup and the operational flexibility of the U.S. Navy's officer corps.

The actual terms of the Holloway Plan varied depending on the type of service. It was structured over a seven-year period: two years of university study, three years of commissioned active duty, and, finally, completion of the last two years of college. For pilot candidates, under a variant called the "Flying Midshipman" or "Aviation Midshipman" Program, the structure was somewhat different: two years of college as a seaman recruit, two years of active duty as a midshipman (first as a flight midshipman in training and then, after earning wings, the balance of the time in a fleet squadron), then two more years as either a full-time naval aviator or an active naval reservist completing college.

Despite the criticism, the Holloway Plan took shape at fifty colleges nationwide, including Ohio State. The plan's ubiquity, in fact, spurred a new quip in Navy commissioned-officer circles: "Did you get your commission the hard way [meaning Annapolis] or the Holloway?"

***

One young man who took the "hard way" (albeit before there was a "Holloway") was the admiral's own son James. James Holloway III had entered the U.S. Naval Academy in 1939, as part of the class of '43. With "salt water in his veins," the younger Holloway was certain he'd make the U.S. Navy a career and equally certain that he would eventually become a carrier pilot. The war, it turned out, both accelerated and delayed these plans.

First, the class of '43's graduation date was advanced to 1942. Next, Holloway was assigned to the "Tin-Can Navy" aboard USS *Bennion* (DD-662), a swift and lethal destroyer, one of the acknowledged "greyhounds" of the fleet. Advancing to become *Bennion's* gunnery officer, Holloway eventually saw action in the October 1944 Battle of Surigao Strait in the Philippines, in retrospect the last major engagement of U.S. Navy surface ships unaided by supporting aircraft.

Surigao Strait was a heady victory and pulse-throbbing experience. During a two-day period, Holloway later reflected, *Bennion* and her crew had "silenced two shore batteries, shot down three Zeros, battled a Japanese cruiser, sunk a destroyer by gunfire and torpedoed a Japanese battleship." It was enough to tempt Holloway to continue his career in destroyers had it not been for a letter he'd received from his father earlier that summer.

As *Iowa* CO, then as captain, James Holloway Jr. had just participated in the Battle of the Philippine Sea during which it was clear (as it had been since nearly the beginning of the war) that the carriers and their aircraft were the principal actors in modern sea warfare. While *Iowa* and her consorts shielded fleet flattops, naval aviators, during what would be termed the "Marianas Turkey Shoot," shot down nearly 350 Japanese aircraft, dealing a fatal blow to the Imperial Navy. Writing later from his stateroom, the elder Holloway counseled his son: "The future of the U.S. Navy lies in naval aviation." James Holloway III's application to naval flight school "went off in the next mail bag headed east."[1]

***

When Jesse Brown talked to the OSU Holloway Plan coordinator, a burly Navy lieutenant (and naval aviator) named Earl Dawkins, he got only discouragement. Dawkins pulled no punches about Jesse Brown's biggest obstacle. The Navy now had four decades of carrier-based aviation tradition—a tradition that separated being "just a pilot" from becoming a naval aviator. It was a proud tradition, Dawkins told Brown, "a lot of white tradition." No black man had ever been admitted to a Navy flight program.

Earl Dawkins was the cleaned-up, dressed-up embodiment of Palmer's Crossing's Corley Yates. But, in the way that he had shrugged off Yates's rants, Brown now shrugged off Dawkins's warnings of insurmountable odds. Determined as ever to fly, he completed the Holloway Plan application paperwork and pressed on, traveling next to Cincinnati for a daylong series of tests and screening interviews followed by a second day of physical tests. Brown qualified for the program—although his overall rating was a cautionary "desirable" instead of "outstanding" or "superior"—and enlisted as an apprentice seaman, United States Naval Reserve (USNR), on inactive duty. With the enlistment came tuition plus a $50 monthly stipend, the end for now to Brown's financial problems.

***

As expected, Brown became the first and only black cadet among the six hundred in his Selective Flight Training class at the Naval Air Training School at Glenview, Illinois—the first hurdle in the long process of qualifying as a naval aviator. At Selective, each candidate was watched from the moment he climbed into a cockpit until he left his instructor at the end of the day. Any hint of fear or lack of flight aptitude, and the cadet was gone.

Hands-on flight training started right away, and right away Brown caught a break in the form of his flight instructor, Lieutenant Junior Grade (LTJG) Roland Christensen, USNR. Chris, as he was known to other Glenview instructors, was a Nebraska native of Danish descent and had his own farming roots. A six-year Navy veteran who had hoped to be a combat pilot, Christensen nursed the bittersweet feeling of "having missed the war" and saw the assignment to cadet training as a letdown.

Christensen was strict on flight procedures but otherwise easygoing. Best of all, Christensen came across as indifferent to Brown's race. Growing up in Nebraska, he'd not encountered many blacks; he was even naively surprised at not having seen a black flight cadet before now.

It was sitting behind Roland Christensen in the backseat of a bright-yellow Stearman N2S-5 biplane that Jesse Leroy Brown finally got a chance to fly. The Stearman N2S-5 (or another of its many variations) had been the primary flight trainer for virtually every Army pilot and Navy aviator during World War II. Its color and its function explained its nickname: the Yellow Peril.

The Yellow Peril was rugged, highly maneuverable, and, except in crosswinds, easy to control, even for beginners. It was on that first day of Selective Flight Training, March 18, 1947, and within minutes of first meeting Roland Christensen that Jesse Brown took his first flight. He would always remember the experience: It was late morning, the sun strong and the sky deep blue, with all of Glenview and its surrounding farmland and the distant shore of Lake Michigan spread below him. It was a new world, almost a private one, far from the complications of earth. Jesse Brown felt like a bird, like a kite, like he was living an impossible dream.

***

His first taste of flying helped steel Brown for the earthbound racial indignities that, though usually not as flagrant as they'd been in Mississippi, continued. On at least one occasion, Brown overheard Chris's fellow instructors tease him about having developed an "oil leak." Slights even came at the hands of the black stewards who served student pilots. They seemed to take immediate offense at Brown (as if his presence were somehow intended to humiliate them), treating him rudely, giving him only half portions at meals, and almost conspicuously ignoring his requests for service.

But perhaps the worst indignity was the military's inability to curb its own segregationist culture. After playing in a pickup game in Glenview's base gym, Brown was recruited to play for the base basketball team. Five days after his heady first flying experience in the Stearman, Brown traveled with the Glenview team by air for a "road game" against the Pensacola Naval Air Station (NAS) team. There, once again, presumption caught up with Jesse Brown. Already dressed and ready for the game, Brown suddenly learned he couldn't play. Florida was segregated, a norm carried to events on the base; Brown had already violated the rules by stepping into Pensacola NAS's all-white locker room.

Still, Brown forged ahead, almost as if the aspects of Selective Flight Training best calibrated to wash him out were actually the least challenging of the hurdles he faced because of race. After surviving eight weeks at Glenview and soloing in the Yellow Peril, Brown went next to Pre-Flight Training at Ottumwa, Iowa.

At Ottumwa, Jesse Brown was sworn in as an aviation midshipman (although only after the base commander stepped aside and left his executive officer to administer the oath). Aviation midshipman was the new rank created for the Holloway Plan that required two years of service before commissioning. The status was a blow to pay, prestige, and even family life: A midshipman could not marry until he was commissioned.

After the war, Ottumwa Naval Air Station's fleet of Stearmans and support aircraft had, like so many migratory birds, flown south to Corpus Christi, emptying the sky over the base's drab sprawl of sixty-four buildings near the muddy banks of the Des Moines River. To aviation midshipmen, Ottumwa was little more than books, lectures, marching, regulations, discipline, and inspections. Brown was usually up well before reveille—a sharecropper's habit—and, as at Glenview, had little trouble with either the classes or the military regimen. His only real obstacle at Ottumwa was swimming—passing an increasingly difficult series of qualifying tests capped by a mile-long swim and escape from the "Dilbert Dunker," a cockpitlike device inverted and submerged in the pool to simulate escape from an aircraft forced down over water.

For a time, it looked to be Brown's undoing: Though an athlete, he was barely able to swim a stroke. Still, it was a hurdle he never questioned. As a naval aviator he had to be able to survive a water landing; if he was unable to overcome this obstacle, the failure would be his alone. It took him long days of remedial swimming lessons—followed by nights when he crawled into bed shivering and aching all over—before Brown was able to complete all the water tests. When he surfaced after escaping the Dilbert Dunker (the final test), Brown, who all along had likened his aviation goal to climbing Mount Everest, felt as though he had put another ten feet of sheer cliff below him.

***

Jesse Brown returned to Pensacola Naval Air Station in August 1947, just five months after the humiliating basketball debacle. Pensacola's graduates, including illustrious carrier admirals like Bull Halsey, Mark "Pete" Mitscher, and John "Slew" McCain (though Halsey and McCain had earned their wings at midcareer), and its ambiance—the sandy beaches of Pensacola Bay, its buildings' moss-stained walls, its rustling palm trees, and its ancient oaks dripping Spanish moss—bespoke history and proud tradition. But for Jesse Brown it also bespoke his return to the Deep South: still a dangerous place for a black man trespassing on white men's dreams.

As it was, Brown's entire Pre-Flight contingent arrived at Pensacola through an administrative back door. Ottumwa NAS had been closed, the victim of continuing cuts in military spending. With eight weeks of Pre-Flight still to go, both the class and a contingent of ground-school instructors were transported by air to Pensacola.

Other than the searing heat and exhausting humidity, not much seemed to change in the outward routine of Pre-Flight in Pensacola. Brown, though, found himself deeper in an even whiter world, fully anticipating that Old Dixie sooner or later would step forward to speak its venomous mind. It happened within a matter of weeks when an instructor overtook him in a classroom building corridor and, as he passed and walked on, said directly and clearly: "Go home, nigger boy." Stunned, Brown froze in his tracks, losing the opportunity to identify the culprit.

Another threat came three days later, this time scrawled in red letters on a white card placed on Brown's barracks bunk pillow: NIGGER GO HOME. He was both enraged and conflicted about what to do. He had been called nigger more times than he could count, but this was different. It came at a time, place, and circumstance where he'd come to believe he had achieved a new stature that would shield him. Still, he risked fingering the wrong man. And who would he be taking his case to? The same base command that just months before had banned him from a basketball game?

Brown also realized he had a long way to go before qualifying as an aviator. Becoming one depended on the goodwill of the instructor staff, a group that as likely as not would line up against him if he challenged one of their own. It was best, at least at this stage, to shut up and move on while being more on guard than ever.

***

In August 1947, after completing Pre-Flight—one of thirty-six graduates from a class that started with sixty-six trainees—Aviation Midshipman Jesse Brown advanced to Basic Flight Training. Basic would prove to be more grueling than Pre-Flight in ways that surprised and frustrated Jesse Brown, because it challenged (almost for the first time) qualities in him that had little to do with race.

At the same time, Basic's burdens would be both eased and intensified by a decision Jesse Brown made during its first weeks. He had learned that Jack Keefer, another aviation midshipmen and his barracks roommate, had, despite the prohibition and the possible consequences, gotten married and even secretly arranged for his wife to join him in Pensacola. By now nearly swamped by his sense of isolation, Brown made up his mind. On a weekend pass, Brown made a quick visit to Hattiesburg, arranged for a marriage license and church ceremony, and married his fiancée, Daisy Pearl Nix. He returned to Pensacola that Sunday and began making secret arrangements for Daisy to join him there.

Hands-on flight training, this time in an SNJ, an all-metal two-seater monoplane with retractable landing gear, continued in earnest when Brown returned from his wedding. From the very beginning, it did not go well. Day upon day, week after week, reports by Brown's instructors read like a frustrating litany of stupid mistakes and mental errors: "Does not keep plane trimmed up . . . Over controls badly on takeoffs . . . Has trouble holding nose straight . . . In spin entry became confused . . . Coordination in climbing and gliding turns poor . . . Doesn't look around enough in the air . . . Did not observe wind direction."

The culmination came in early December when Brown's instructor for the day, a lieutenant named Ross Tipton, turned out to be the racist tormentor who had overtaken him in the classroom corridor back in October. Although Tipton's presence in the airplane's backseat clearly unnerved him, Brown also realized that by any objective measure his flight performance that day was poor enough to give Tipton the opportunity he sought. "Nigger," Tipton told him while they were still aloft, "you're the sloppiest student I've ever flown with." On the ground, going by the book, Tipton exercised his instructor prerogative: Two emphatic "downs" for the day's flying sent Brown before what was called a Summary Flight Board—a panel of officers who would decide whether Brown would get another chance or be washed out.

***

Before facing the panel, Jesse Brown was presented with another agonizing choice. One item on a questionnaire that he was required to fill out before the panel took up his case asked: "Have you any complaint or criticism to make concerning your treatment or training?" It was, if there would ever be one, a prime opportunity for Brown to spill out his grievances: the anonymous card on his bunk, Tipton's racist remarks, the indignity of being banned from the basketball game, and even the Ottumwa NAS CO's refusal to swear him in at the start of Pre-Flight.

The righteousness of his complaints seemed to burn through Brown as he prepared to respond. But tempering his indignation was the realization that the racial humiliations would not explain or correct the gaps in his flying skills. He knew his skills weren't up to par—not yet. Race was undoubtedly a contributing factor, but another reality overshadowed it. Brown was all alone in trailblazing this path. If he fell back on race now, he'd still be burdened with his poor flying and make things only more difficult for those who followed in his footsteps. Race would become the flag that Jesse Brown flew; waving it would somehow be surrendering the individual passion and determination with which he had begun his personal assault on Mount Everest.

Brown looked again at the question and simply answered: "No." A different question followed: Would he like to be retained? Here he had no hesitation: "I desire very much to be retained."

The next hour, as he stood before the panel and answered their questions, something remarkable happened. One of Brown's earlier instructors, a Navy lieutenant named Bill Zastri, was on hand and asked to address the panel before they made their decision. "Brown is a much better pilot than indicated," Zastri began. "I think all of us went though a bad period sometime. I know I did. I remember that after I got into trouble and went before a board like this one, my flying ability quickly increased."

It was a moment of unsolicited and unexpected support from Zastri. In a way it was a counterweight to all the forces that were conniving to exclude Jesse Brown from his dream. It was a sign that perhaps the best people in this still exclusive club of naval aviation identified less with society's unyielding prejudices and more with the aspirations of men like Jesse Brown enduring the very trials they had endured. Having seen Brown get this far, they were as inclined to reel him in as they had been inclined before to keep him out.

"You're retained," Zastri said gruffly as he emerged later from the boardroom and walked by the anxiously waiting midshipman. "Don't let me down."

***

In October 1948 Jesse LeRoy Brown became the first black American naval aviator. Following Zastri's intervention and the reprieve of Summary Flight Board, Brown's flight ability did indeed improve quickly— just as Zastri had predicted—and he was able to set aside the distractions and regain focus. There were more good hops than bad hops and more good days than bad days.

In June Brown had passed the single biggest hurdle: landings on and takeoffs from the pitching deck of an aircraft carrier, the USS *Wright* (CVL-49) in the Gulf of Mexico. It was anticlimactic, certainly when compared to what had gone before. He easily made a series of "touch-and-goes" and his first arrested landing on the first try. Five more landings and six takeoffs on the same afternoon made him eligible for flight pay, increased his rank slightly to aviation midshipman first class, and, most important, punched his ticket to go on to Advanced Flight Training at Jacksonville Naval Air Station. Meanwhile, Brown's marriage remained secret but with a new complication: Daisy was pregnant and beginning to show, so she returned to Hattiesburg to await the baby's arrival.

At Jacksonville he qualified to fly the Grumman F6F Hellcat, naval aviation's Pacific war dream machine and primary fighter-bomber. Jesse Brown's pinning-on ceremony took place on October 21, a brief ceremony, but one marked by significant differences from Ottumwa. Jacksonville's commanding officer did the pinning, this time with a Navy photographer snapping photos that would accompany a Navy public information release: FIRST NEGRO NAVAL AVIATOR. The release in turn prompted an Associated Press wire story, and Brown's photo appeared in *Life*.

In December, still a midshipman, Brown received orders to report to his first squadron, VF-32, stationed in Quonset Point, Rhode Island. The orders coincided with the birth of the Browns' daughter, Pamela. It was April 1949, another six months, before Brown finally became a Navy ensign. It was more or less automatic; its true significance was that Jesse and Daisy Nix Brown could now be officially and openly acknowledged as married.

***

By spring 1949 the Holloway Plan was proving to be the fertile seedbed of a whole new crop of naval aviators. Joe Akagi, Neil Armstrong, and George Schnitzer were each Holloway Plan products as well—Akagi at Texas A&M, Armstrong at Purdue, and Schnitzer at Brown.

Although it might have not meant much then to a struggling Jesse Brown, the path he pioneered was already, directly or indirectly, becoming smoother for members of racial minorities. Joe Akagi, reflecting many years later on his own experience becoming the first Japanese American to earn Wings of Gold, described it as remarkably free of race-based resistance or prejudice. The United States, in ways both real and symbolic, had moved rather quickly away from its bitter distrust of all things Japanese.

Akagi and Armstrong both began Pre-Flight Training as part of the same flight training class. Classes began each month, and "Class 5-49" indicated the fifth (May) class of 1949. Another 5-49 class member was Kenneth A. Schechter. Schechter, nineteen, born in New York City but raised in Southern California, was a gregarious and optimistic nineteen year old with an easy grin beneath a commanding nose and a shock of dark hair The three were marked contrasts: the diminutive southeast Texas farm boy, Akagi; the studious midwesterner, Armstrong (who already possessed a private pilot's license earned in high school); and the jovial, laid-back Southern Californian, Ken Schechter. Different, but each—teamed with many more—taking the "Holloway" toward a distant, fateful, but little-anticipated war then brewing on the Asian mainland.

2

DISTURBING THE PEACE

KOREA, THE PAW-SHAPED peninsula stretching from the northeast shoulder of Asia's mainland south toward Japan, had never lived up to the imagery of its ancient name: *Chosun*, Land of the Morning Calm. Instead, as a strategic crossroads to the territorial ambitions of China, Japan, and Russia, Korea has always possessed a troubled history, much of it subsumed by the rising and ebbing influences of its neighbors.

For most of a millennium, China exerted the greatest pull, establishing a Confucian "father-son" relationship with Korea. The ties—more mystical than legal or diplomatic—supplied Korea's kings with the rationale for rebuffing imperialistic and commercial intruders.

Then, in 1905, on the strengths of its success in the Russo-Japanese War (the first victory of an Asian army in a clash with Europe), Japan claimed Korea as a "protectorate." U.S. president Theodore Roosevelt, who'd mediated the treaty ending the war, saw Japanese hegemony as a way of achieving regional peace in Asia. Five years later (with another approving nod from the United States) Japan fully annexed Korea, effectively wiping it from the political map and embarking on a harsh, systematic process of turning the peninsula into a semi-industrialized Japanese colony. Koreans suffered more than thirty years through repressive policies aimed not only at exploiting their country's resources but also at dismantling its traditions, language, and culture. After Pearl Harbor Japan converted Korea into a major military base.

Japan's demise in 1945 only set the stage for more disruption. After the surrender, U.S. president Harry Truman and Soviet dictator Joseph

Stalin—the Red Czar—reached a bilateral accommodation whereby Japan's forces in Korea's North would surrender to the Soviets while forces in the South would surrender to the Americans. The agreed-upon line of demarcation—the 38th Parallel—was one of convenience and self-interest. For the Koreans, though, the boundary was puzzlingly artificial: It aligned with no recognizable geographical, cultural, or political frontier.

If anything, the topographic frontiers of the peninsula's landmass (roughly 600 miles long and, except for a pinched neck, roughly 150 miles wide from coast to coast) run north to south instead of east to west: a perimeter of jagged coastal cliffs on the east; high, spiny mountain ranges traversing its center; and, in the west, gentler plains sloping toward the Yellow Sea. The line in effect separated the food-producing fields in the South from fertilizer minerals available only in the North, and it disconnected Korea's cities and population from lifeblood sources of coal and hydroelectric power.

The line also embittered Korea's people, stalled Korean nationalist dreams of unified independence, and, under the pervasive influence of Cold War animosities, effectively turned a homogenous population into two armed and fiercely hostile camps. The uneasy relationships across the 38th Parallel were shaped by the barometer of hardening postwar diplomacy. Early low-level proposals to permit movement between the two zones disappeared into the failed workings of an American-Soviet "Korean Joint Committee" ostensibly convened to prepare the way for a unified democratic government. When this committee "adjourned," divisions only deepened.

For America, support of Korea was costly, troublesome, and, at least according to an assessment by the new Joint Chiefs of Staff, not strategically viable. Looking for disengagement, the United States placed the question of Korean independence on the agenda of the UN General Assembly. The nascent United Nations' response was a nine-country "Temporary Commission on Korea" to sponsor elections, assist in the formation of a government, and arrange American and Soviet troop withdrawals. Though the USSR withheld cooperation and refused access to the North, commission members journeyed to South Korea, where they set up the structure for a national assembly in which a third of the seats would be reserved for a North Korean delegation. Elections were held, though in the face of Communist-inspired riots and the eventual cutoff of power lines coming from the North.

A race to set up competing governments followed, with each government, in varying degrees, controlled or sponsored by the United States or Soviet Union. The face of the U.S.-sponsored government in South Korea was Syngman Rhee, a fierce but aging Korean nationalist educated in the United States; for North Korea it was Kim Il Sung, a guerrilla fighter against the Japanese and an equally passionate Korean nationalist, but also a man rigidly molded by his sponsors into a Soviet-style Communist.

While the Korean situation finally boiled over in June 1950 with North Korea as the first-move aggressor, both camps had played a role in triggering the face-off. There were reports of frequent guerrilla-scale cross-border intrusions by North and South. Perhaps more telling was a January 1950 policy speech by U.S. secretary of state Dean Acheson suggesting that Korea might lie outside America's Asian-defense perimeter.

The speech signaled a window of opportunity to Kim Il Sung and his Soviet sponsors. Both Rhee and Kim harbored fantasies of storming the North (Rhee's dream) or the South (Kim's) to unify Korea, each believing that crusade would be swift and triumphant. Aside from the cross-border forays, the United States kept a tight leash on Rhee, as did the Soviets on Kim. But now, using Acheson's ill-considered words, Kim pressed his case with Joseph Stalin, arguing for a preemptive strike and assuring Stalin that he would be welcomed with open arms by South Koreans. Stalin was persuaded to let Kim off his leash but only if it did not involve a direct Soviet-American confrontation. Stalin promised background support but pointed Kim to China's Mao Zedong and Mao's newly triumphant Chinese Communist regime for primary sponsorship—and, in the event of a military reversal, for backup.

***

Meanwhile, below the 38th Parallel, following the withdrawal of fighting forces (at the request of the South Koreans), America had left behind a 50,000-man Korean Military Advisory Group (KMAG). KMAG had been instrumental in building up the strength and capability of the Republic of Korea's army and navy.

Although appearing, on paper at least, to be a credible military infrastructure and effective deterrent shield, neither the ROK Army nor its KMAG advisers were a match for the seven NKPA divisions and the Soviet tank–equipped armored brigade that, after weeks of assembly and staging, finally poured across the 38th Parallel at four o'clock on the morning of June 25, 1950.

None of the first bulletins trickling from the chaotic and ever-changing front lines played well—if at all—back in the States. Unlike Vietnam (and wars ever since), the news did not come back to America either instantly or in color. Even radio reports and newspaper accounts were skimpy or confused, lost in a babble of unpronounceable place-names. The names were usually reeled off from north to south as U.S. Army troops and their hapless South Korean counterparts retreated pell-mell down the length of Korea's peninsula. They seemed incapable of withstanding the North Korean onslaught.

If the ability of U.S. and South Korean forces to hold back the threat was in question, so (though admittedly to a somewhat lesser degree) was the readiness of the supposedly powerful U.S. Navy to supply or support friendly ground forces. When hostilities broke out, the U.S. Navy had only a third of its active-duty strength in the Pacific and only a fifth in the Far East. Closest to the scene were twenty ships (only five of them combat types and none armed with anything larger than a five-inch naval cannon) stationed in Japan—all effectively sublet to Douglas MacArthur's Far East command. In the Philippines, meanwhile, 1,700 miles south, were the ships of the Seventh Fleet, the embodiment (in name at least) of U.S. Navy muscle in the Pacific. But the Seventh Fleet, commanded by Vice Adm. Arthur D. Struble, wasn't very impressive, either: three task groups totaling nineteen ships, including one aircraft carrier (*Valley Forge* with eighty-six aircraft), one cruiser, and eight destroyers.

Such as they were, Seventh Fleet ships quickly formed the core of an Anglo-American naval squadron—eventually dubbed Task Force 77. TF 77 assembled and set sail for the Yellow Sea on July 1. Once on station, TF 77 attack squadrons directed "do something/anything" strikes on the North Korean capital of Pyongyang and its airfields, rail yards, and bridges. Fitfully at first, TF 77's war work had begun. Already, back in the United States, elements of the Navy's admittedly thin carrier, air-squadron, and support-ship reserves were being hastily assembled for deployment.

***

On Independence Day, the pilots and aircraft of Carrier Air Group 11 (CVG-11) boarded *Philippine Sea* (CV-47), one of two *Essex*-class carriers docked in San Diego. The other was *Boxer* (CV-21), which, until *Valley Forge* relieved her that same spring, had been the western Pacific "duty carrier." While *Boxer* waited to enter a navy yard for much needed repairs, *Philippine Sea* had just arrived from Atlantic Fleet duty and was, until the Korean crisis intervened, in the early stages of preparing for an October departure to the Far East to relieve *Valley Forge*. Departure was now just hours instead of months away.

Leading CVG-11's five squadrons was Cdr. Raymond William (Sully) Vogel Jr., a Naval Academy graduate and World War II veteran a month shy of his thirty-sixth birthday. On the eve of deployment, Vogel's air group was chronically handicapped by a shortage of both aircraft and pilots. Ironically, many of his younger pilots had recently received orders separating them from the Navy effective June 30— a loss reversed only by an emergency appeal to BuPers (the Navy's Bureau of Personnel). VF-111 and VF-112, two of CVG-11's fighter squadrons, were among the first Navy air units to make the transition from Grumman Bearcats to Grumman F9F-2 Panthers—the U.S. Navy's first combat jet aircraft. But the price of the pioneering transition had been felt in ongoing struggles to secure enough operational aircraft (and the personnel to maintain them) and accomplishing the training needed to bring the squadron up to fighting trim.

***

The Grumman F9F Panthers were the first operational output of the Navy's toddling steps into the jet age four years before. In July 1946 test pilot Lt. Cdr. James Davidson from the Naval Test Center (NTC) in Patuxent, Maryland (affectionately known as "the River"), flying a twin-engine, straight-wing prototype, made a successful series of takeoffs and landings from the aircraft carrier *Franklin D. Roosevelt*

(CV-42) off the coast of Virginia. Already late to the jet-aviation party, the Navy pressed ahead to develop jet-familiarization aircraft as well as three fighter-aircraft projects, one of which led to the production of the Panther.

The F9F, which (through various models) would be the Navy's mainstay carrier jet in the months ahead, had a number of drawbacks. First and foremost were flight characteristics—high landing-approach speed, tendency to stall without warning, and slow takeoff acceleration—that made all first-generation jet aircraft difficult to adapt to carrier operations.

Although classified as a fighter, the F9F was used primarily as a ground-attack aircraft. This meant the addition of bomb racks to its wings, a modification that shaved thirty knots off maximum airspeed. With external ordnance attached—a maximum of 500 pounds later upped to 1,200 pounds in subsequent models—the Panther's stall problems increased, and it was no longer an air-to-air combat threat.* What it became instead was a heavy, fuel-hungry, "short-legged" (low-endurance) fighter-bomber. Because of limited cockpit instrumentation, the F9F had reduced all-weather capability, and because of its added operational weight, it was difficult to launch from the "short-stroke" H4B hydraulic-powered catapults in use on the *Essex*-class carriers. In other words, flying the Panther (especially in combat) required pilots with exceptional confidence and extraordinary reflexes and skills.

Still, all these limitations never seemed to diminish naval aviators' affection for the Panther and, perhaps even more, for the company that produced it. To new and veteran pilots alike, the Grumman name meant a lot. Leroy Grumman (the firm's founder and himself a naval aviator during World War I) and his vice president of engineering, Bill Schwendler, prided themselves in producing aircraft designs that enabled "a 21-year-old pilot coming back from a tough mission" to land safely aboard a carrier. "We don't want the fastest, or the most maneuverable aircraft," Grumman constantly reminded his design teams, "if it compromises the chance of that kid getting back to his carrier."[1]

---

* It wasn't until April 1951 that two bomb-laden Panthers were carrier launched for their first operational air strike against a ground-infrastructure target—a small bridge that they succeeded in taking down.

Grumman possessed a rich heritage of stubby radial-engine fighter aircraft, beginning with its first biplanes: the FF, the F2F, and F3F. The F4F Wildcat, the company's first production monoplane, was the precursor to the legendary F6F Hellcat, followed, after the war, by the twin-engine F7F Tigercat and the F8F Bearcat—a much loved "pilot's plane" that took the single-radial-engine fighter to its ultimate performance frontier.

Grumman's reputation went far beyond design. To no less an authority than Vice Adm. John "Slew" McCain, the commander of Task Force 58 under Halsey during World War II (and the grandfather of Sen. John McCain), "the name Grumman on a plane or a part is like sterling on silver." To the naval aviators flying Wildcats, Avengers, and especially Hellcats (which produced some three hundred aerial combat aces, more than any other American fighter during the war), Leroy Grumman's company was known affectionately as the "Grumman Iron Works."[2]

Still, Grumman-brand loyalty went only so far. In mock combat trials staged at the River, the new jet-propelled Lockheed F-80 Shooting Star (itself a lightly armed, low-endurance interceptor) dominated even the hot-rod Bearcat. The F8F was simply unable to position itself for an attack on the F-80, an undeniable augur that, at least as a fighter-aircraft power plant, the radial engine's days were done.

However, the bad news for Grumman didn't end with the demise of the Bearcat. It would soon become apparent that, although jet powered, the straight-wing Panther was no match for its most likely adversary, the swept-wing MiG being produced by the Communists. Early on, straight wings had been a conscious design choice by the U.S. Navy and Marine Corps: The tricky low-speed performance of early swept-wing models was thought altogether unsuitable for carrier aircraft. Now, years later, combat performance far outweighed operational safety considerations. As one Marine jet squadron commander ruefully put it: "Having the second-best fighter is like having the second-best hand at poker."[3]

***

Beyond the catapult problem, there were, it soon turned out, a host of difficulties with operating the new jet aircraft at sea. In the most basic terms, World War II–era *Essex*-class carriers such as *Philippine Sea*, *Valley Forge*, and *Boxer* were simply not configured to handle them.

Take fuel, for example. The jets were essentially "flying gasoline barrels" whose added speed and performance came at the expense of voracious fuel consumption. It was estimated that each jet sortie cost its carrier a full minute in replenishment time alongside a tanker. When air group complements included two jet squadrons, full-scale operations could siphon off a carrier's aviation gasoline stores in less than two days.

And it wasn't just the amount of fuel that posed a logistics problem; it was also the type. The F9F used a rugged J-42 turbine jet engine. However, its Turbo Jet Control (TJC) unit's many small working parts required the use of lubricant-enriched JP-type aviation jet fuel. The fuel storage tanks and pumping units on *Essex*-class carriers were equipped to handle only "dry" aviation gas. The carrier operational "fix" for this problem was to add lubrication oil to the Panthers' after-main fuel tanks. This was a stopgap measure at best; pilots and crews would learn soon enough that, because of inadequate lubrication, TJC small parts sometimes froze, causing the TJC to fail and the engine to flame out.

And the fuel problem didn't end there. The Panthers' auxiliary fuel tanks were mounted on the airplanes' wing tips, and standard procedure at sea was to refuel aircraft with wings folded. This meant that deck crewmen had to use ladders just to reach the tanks, dragging with them a heavy fuel hose. Atop the ladder—and often perilously close to the lip of the flight deck—the sailors still had to unscrew the tip tank's cap and insert the hose nozzle. It was small wonder that carrier pilots (despite the many challenges they faced aloft) stood in awe of the dexterity, skill, draconian work hours, and death-defying choreography of flight deck crews.

***

Aviation pilot (AP) Duane Thorin and six other personnel, a detachment from the Navy's fledgling Helicopter Utility Squadron, might well have been lost in the shuffle created by CVG-11's arrival and the stowing of its aircraft had it not been for the curiosity generated by its single aircraft—a deep-blue Navy Sikorsky HO3S helicopter. Most

"Phil Sea" sailors had never seen a "pinwheel" before, and they marveled at its oddity.

It was an understandable reaction. Nearly two years before, when he first saw an S-51 (an early prototype for the HO3S) sitting on the tarmac in a remote corner of Connally Air Force Base outside Waco, Texas, Duane Thorin was struck most by its odd and suggestive shape. A long tail boom, drooping main rotor blades, and the sunlit reflection from the curved Plexiglas of its latticed cabin "greenhouse" combined to make the S-51 look like a huge dragonfly.

The S-51 was designed and manufactured by Sikorsky, a U.S. aircraft firm founded a quarter century before by Kiev-born Russian American aircraft engineer Igor Sikorsky. Although Sikorsky did not invent the helicopter concept, just before the war his company (part of United Aircraft, later United Technologies) developed the S-47, the first stable single-rotor, fully controllable helicopter to enter full-scale production.

The S-51, the first commercially available helicopter and also the first model put in use by U.S. armed forces, came three generations of refinements later. While the S-51 had bigger rotors and greater load capacity, endurance, speed, and altitude limits than its predecessor models, it was still a long way from deserving the workhorse reputation of later-generation rotorcraft.

Indeed, the U.S. Air Force flight instructor who gave Thorin his first orientation flight at Connally had taken great pains to reveal its frailties as well as extol its virtues—as if the Sikorsky was his oddball, much maligned, but still dearly beloved friend. The S-51's main features were indeed its shortcomings: Flimsy main rotor blades, he told Thorin, relied for strength on the power of high-speed centrifugal force, yet too much of that force was apt to shred and strip off their fabric covering. The S-51's primitive piston-powered engine supplied barely enough horsepower to lift the helicopter and a couple of people (even though it had seats for three). Its ability to "hover" was also extremely limited; the S-51 could suspend itself just a few feet off the ground, riding on a "ground cushion" of denser air generated by the downwash of the spinning rotors. Successful flight, meanwhile, depended on a sort of "flying saucer" effect. Only by moving forward with the rotors at the correct angle and spinning at the right speed could the Sikorsky create enough additional "translational lift" to stay aloft and keep moving. The S-51, in other words, didn't "fly itself."

After demonstrating the basics that *day*, the instructor gave Thorin the controls. Almost at once, Thorin could feel the Sikorsky's vibrations flowing directly into his hands. The craft seemed to respond to the gentlest of pressures on stick, pedals, and throttle, almost as though he were part of the machinery. Thorin also got the sense he was experiencing something of what the earliest aviation pioneers must have felt as they first flew their fledgling aircraft. If anything, Thorin thought, those earlier pioneers should be envying him the pioneering opportunity to pilot this "flying eggbeater."

***

If any World War II veterans faced the prospect of war's end with mixed and bittersweet emotions, it was the corps of U.S. Navy aviators. There had been nothing quite like the opportunity they'd had: the combination of youth, the opportunity to fly, the singular rush of testing skills in aerial combat and in landings and takeoffs from aircraft carriers. Nor were there many precedents for the indispensable role they and their aircraft had played in systematically dismantling Japan's formidable surface fleet along with the world's then most advanced air force. The June 1944 Battle of the Philippine Sea, the engagement that sealed Japan's aerial doom, had given carrier *Philippine Sea* its name.

The risks and casualties of war may have had their impact and age might yet catch up, but like Duane Thorin, then just shy of age thirty, few veteran flyers could resist the adrenaline surge of beholding a new and unfamiliar aircraft or contemplating the never-old challenge of unfettered flight. If anything, Thorin's fragile AP status linked him inextricably to the supreme era of naval aviation, an era to be savored even as it seemed to be passing.

Thorin was the youngest of seven sons of Swedish immigrants turned Nebraska farmers. Thorin,[*] whose matinee-handsome face was

---

[*] The last name is pronounced "Toreen" (emphasis on the second syllable), although, to people who knew him in the service, the pronunciation was most often "Thorin" (emphasis on the first syllable).

topped by an orderly thatch of fine straw-colored hair, enlisted in the U.S. Navy in 1939 and steadily advanced to chief petty officer rank as an aviation mechanic (the formal job rating was aircraft machinist mate). Selected for flight training, Thorin had then qualified as an enlisted aviation pilot—one of roughly 5,000 U.S. sailors and marines who piloted aircraft during the still formative stages of naval aviation. Thorin had wartime assignments as an SBD (Dauntless) dive-bomber pilot and later as a carrier test pilot. By war's end, Thorin figured he had flown virtually every type of carrier-launched aircraft.

While aviation pilots (a title used to differentiate enlisted pilots from commissioned-officer "naval aviators") got little separate recognition, to most APs, including Thorin, the opportunity to fly was enough reward for men who'd entered the Navy's elitist world on its lowest rung. However, as naval aviation matured and the AP designation was being phased out, holdovers like Thorin struggled with the disparity between his enlisted rank and his well-honed aviation skills.

The postwar status gap was most evident when Thorin ended up copiloting multiengine transport aircraft in China, often paired with commissioned naval aviators. Naval aviators, he quickly learned, could always "pull rank" in the cockpit, even when doing so risked lives—including Thorin's. Disillusion with such indignities almost drove Thorin to quit the Navy and fly instead with China Air Transport, an Asian commercial airline founded by Claire Chennault of Flying Tiger fame. Counseled by cohorts to bear with these peacetime circumstances, Thorin finally reenlisted in 1947 only to find himself (in company with many other Navy veterans) a pawn in bitter postwar military turf and budget battles.

***

Accompanying the steamroller of postwar demobilization was a rethinking of the traditional balance between the country's War and Navy Departments. In December 1945 President Harry Truman signaled his desire for a unified military establishment. The Navy and Marine Corps both stood out as potential losers in Truman's proposed shift. One Army Air Force brigadier general labeled the Marine Corps as a "small bitched-up Army" and proposed to "put those Marines in the Regular Army and make efficient soldiers of them." For his part,

Truman made no secret of his criticism of the Navy: He had once accused his predecessor Franklin Roosevelt (a former assistant secretary
of the Navy) of running a "damned wardroom."

The upshot of all this unification turmoil was the National Security
Act (NSA) of 1947, which created both the Department of Defense
and the U.S. Air Force as a separate service branch. The National Security Act's passage further polarized postwar debate about the roles
and missions of the various armed services.

At the highest level, the disputes devolved to a fight over two hardware platforms symbolizing the strategic visions of each branch. For
the U.S. Air Force (and, by extension, the U.S. Army) the hardware
was the B-36, a massive six-engine propeller-driven strategic bomber.
For the Navy it was the 65,000-ton supercarrier *United States* (CVB-
58). The competing claims for the B-36 and CVB-58 were actually
based on virtually identical premises. Top Air Force, Army, and Navy
brass—ever sensitive to accusations of planning for the *last* war—were
collectively certain they'd drawn a bead on the *next* war. It would un-
questionably pit the United States directly against the Soviet Union,
and victory would hinge on the ability to rapidly deploy—and even
use—thermonuclear weaponry.

Battles over such astronomically priced pieces of military hardware
meant deeper cuts in postwar military budgets. Defense Secretary Louis
Johnson (no fan of the Navy, unlike his effective but erratic predecessor James Forrestal) proposed the abolition of land-based naval aviation and the eventual replacement of aircraft carrier–based naval
aviation squadrons with U.S. Air Force squadrons. The squeeze was
put on Navy aviation research and development, slowing the Navy's
emergence into the jet age.

Many individuals, of course, got caught in the crosshairs of this
high-stakes budget and procurement squeeze. One was Duane Thorin.
Another was Harry E. Ettinger, a Milford, Massachusetts, native, who
at the time of the NSA's passage was a twenty-year-old fledgling naval
aviator. A product of the V5 program (following graduation from
high school in 1944) via Williams College, Ettinger had, in July 1947,
just earned his wings and been assigned to VA-55, a San Diego–based
"attack" squadron transitioning from Avenger torpedo bombers to
Skyraiders.

The Skyraider was both a throwback and a step forward for naval aviation. It was propeller powered, a product of Douglas Aircraft (with Grumman, one of the two aircraft firms with particularly strong ties to the U.S. Navy), which had manufactured generations of slow but effective SBD Dauntless dive-bombers—stalwarts at the Battle of Midway. At the same time the "AD" (while the initials technically stood for "Attack/Douglas," they soon stood, in pilot usage at least, for "Able Dog") also carried the appearance and performance heritage of its Avenger predecessor: big, beefy, and built to take punishment as well as deliver it. U.S. Navy (and U.S. Marine) squadrons equipped with these powerful, sturdy aircraft became attack squadrons (VA in U.S. Navy vernacular, VMA in Marine), shedding outmoded World War II designations as scout, torpedo, or bombing squadrons.

The "Able Dog" was powered by a powerful Wright "Cyclone" engine, a power plant first used on the Boeing B-29 during World War II. The Cyclone enabled the single-engine AD to carry up to four tons of ordnance, exceeding the bomb-carrying capability of the four-engine Boeing B-17 Flying Fortress.

Another of the Able Dog's primary virtues was its adaptability. Before being phased out of military combat use (not until 1968, well into the Vietnam War era), the AD had been manufactured in seven major models configured in twenty-eight distinct variations. It was in effect an earlier generation's version of a "transformer" or "go-bot," an aerial weapons "platform" upon which a number of capabilities could be built. Its wing racks, normally used for mounting rocket and bomb ordnance, could also carry packages of sophisticated radar, photographic, and electronic gear. Accommodating extra crewmen (either by lengthening the pilot cockpit to add a backseat for one man or by using interior fuselage space behind and below the pilot to add two), the AD could stand in as an aircraft capable of night, all-weather, antisubmarine, photo reconnaissance, or electronic countermeasure (ECM) missions.

At the time, as he trained and flew this versatile addition to the Navy's postwar air arsenal, Ettinger assumed he was starting out on a promising military aviation career. Over the next two years he married and even started a family. Then, abruptly, in March 1950, he was released from the Navy, along with thousands of other USNR (reserve) officers. Although Ettinger had to scramble for work, he soon cobbled together two jobs. One was as a flight instructor for a local private aviation school; the other, ironically, was as a production-line assembler for the Air Force's B-36 strategic bomber.

***

One incidental cost-cutting counterstroke devised by Navy brass to combat these pressures was to use aviation pilots as flight instructors. Duane Thorin was one of eighteen APs assigned to the Navy's Pensacola naval aviation training facility to test the concept—and thereby keep his job.

At Pensacola—the Rome, Jerusalem, and Mecca of U.S. Navy aviation—the APs met widespread resistance to the notion of enlisted flight instructors. Objections were many, among them the potential awkwardness of having enlisted instructors evaluating trainees newly graduated (and newly commissioned) from the U.S. Naval Academy.* In the class-conscious Navy, the two instructor categories also meant separate privileges and accommodations. For example, when Thorin and six other AP instructors (fresh from instructor training) first reported to Pensacola's Basic Training Unit Two in 1947, they learned the "Instructors Ready Room" had become the "Officers Ready Room," and choice parking spaces reserved for flight instructors could not be used by AP instructors.

Although this pattern of slights annoyed and soured the APs, sticking out this training tour nonetheless gave Thorin the opportunity to fly an entirely new category of military aircraft: the helicopter. While the B-36 and CVB-58 were table-stake bets of gigantic proportion, the helicopter was initially a technical breakthrough without a specific use. The Navy had quickly embraced its potential, and there was already a waiting list for the Navy's first-ever helicopter training facility at Lakehurst, New Jersey. USAF brass, meanwhile, were as yet unimpressed. After stamping the USAF logo on a fully equipped helicopter

---

* The Navy had by now begun to relax its policy to permit some Naval Academy cadets to enter flight training directly after graduation.

training facility inherited from the Army, the operation was virtually ignored. Refusing to sit on their hands, the ex–Army Air Force helicopter instructors at Connally connived to invite Navy trainees.

So it was that Duane Thorin got his first introduction to the helicopter at Connally, where he excelled during training and soon came to share every bit of his instructors' passion for the awkward S-51. Near the end of the program, one dispirited Air Force helo jockey pulled him aside to confide his own jealousy at the opportunities open to Thorin as a Navy pilot. "You've got people in Washington who see the potential of this machine. The wild blue yonder boys in this outfit aren't interested in anything but big bombers and flying blow torches."

From the start, the helicopter seemed an ideal fit for enlisted pilots, and, indeed, a high proportion of the Navy's first helicopter pilots were either APs or "mustangs"—former enlisted men who'd received officer commissions. Rotor-wing aviation's small scale and the uncertain future made it a risky choice for career- and promotion-minded naval aviators. By contrast, these same factors made helicopters appealing to many APs. Plus, because the earliest military helicopters had only one "driver's seat," an experienced AP could avoid flying copilot with inexperienced "junior birdmen" naval aviators.

***

When he reported to the Navy's Helicopter Utility Squadron One (HU-1) at Miramar Naval Air Station, Duane Thorin became Navy helicopter pilot number 216. This meant two things. First, there were enough pilots qualifying before Thorin to provide a cadre of "old-timers" to learn from and emulate. At the same time, few if any of the veteran pilots (many of them APs or mustangs) were disposed to be "know-it-alls." There were still many unknowns about the machine and its foibles, and still plenty of room for "newcomers" to collaborate and contribute ideas.

One of these old-timers was "Cap" Kembro, the fifth Navy pilot to qualify on helicopters and the first AP. Just having the opportunity to listen to Kembro talk about helicopters was a thrill for Thorin. Thorin had plenty of opportunity when he accompanied Kembro on a Bering Sea exercise aboard the Navy icebreaker *Burton Island* (AG-88) in January 1950. As it turned out there was little opportunity for Kembro to fly (and none for Thorin) during the time aboard *Burton Island*. Still, it was an opportunity to learn that important modifications would be required before helicopters could operate reliably and safely in such harsh weather conditions.

One of the modifications had to do with the helicopter pilot's own equipment. As Kembro prepared for one of his few flights, a Navy diving chief noticed the flimsy antiexposure suit he was wearing: "Chief—I wouldn't be caught dead in that thing you're wearing! And you sure as hell will be if you go into these waters!" The diver fitted Kembro into one of his own cold-water suits, stressing the absolute necessity of covering the head and neck when immersed in frigid water. It was a piece of advice Thorin never forgot.

***

Within days of *Philippine Sea*'s departure for the Far East, carrier *Boxer* followed in Phil Sea's wake. While *Boxer* awaited Navy-yard overhaul, a desperate need developed for a transport carrier to ferry Air Force and Navy planes to the front lines. Lacking other ready alternatives, *Boxer* was designated for the task. Following emergency repairs at San Diego, *Boxer* sailed for Alameda, where, after loading 170 aircraft (including 145 World War II F-51 Mustangs scraped together from Air National Guard squadrons), she steamed out the Golden Gate and headed west. One of the pilots from an NAS Alameda detachment embarked to assist with the ferrying of these aircraft was twenty-two-year-old ensign Dick Kaufman. Kaufman, a native of the North Bay town of Richmond, California, was yet another product of the Holloway Program, in his instance via San Jose State College. Kaufman would be getting an advance—albeit distant—glimpse of a war that would later shape all their lives.

Boxer's imminent presence in a conflict disputing control of a country bordering China struck a strangely symbolic note—and, for those in China with reasonably deep memories, likely an angering and discordant one as well. In November 1899, little more than fifty years before, members of the Chinese Society of Right and Harmonious Fists (called Boxers because of their penchant for martial arts and organized calisthenics) staged an uprising in protest against foreign influence in trade, politics, religion, and technology.

The uprising began as an antiforeign, anti-imperialist peasant-based movement in northern China with attacks on foreigners building railroads (and thereby violating feng shui) and Christians, but spread in June 1900 when the Boxers invaded Peking (now Beijing) and killed hundreds of international diplomats and foreigners. Foreigners retreated to the city's legation quarter, holding out for fifty-five days until a multinational coalition of 20,000 troops came to their rescue. Japanese soldiers and ships formed the coalition's core, but the United States lent U.S. Army and Marine troops backed by warships based in the Philippines. The force, called the China Relief Expedition, broke the siege, and a resulting peace protocol exacted the execution of rebellion leaders and the payment of reparations.

The Chinese imperial government's failure to hold off the foreign intervention was just one link, but nonetheless a seminal one, in a chain of events that fed revolutionary nationalism in China. Five decades later the chain would end in the triumph of the Chinese Communists. Now *Boxer*, emblematic of that imperialist intervention—and the humiliating reparations that followed—was going back to the region.

In a real sense *Boxer* would be limping into the fray, returning after stopgap repairs and subject in the months ahead to a plague of problems that could, in a more tranquil time, have been avoided by a much needed overhaul. In that sense, the ship was also a symbol of the U.S. situation in the festering conflict. If the United States was to have an impact in Korea, there would need to be a quick "remobilization" of its dormant military strength.

3

THE PITTSBURGH CORSAIRS, THE LONG ISLAND PANTHERS

SEVERAL YEARS AFTER the Korean War, Ray Edinger came close to dying, taking with him the lives of dozens of others. Edinger was then serving with the Military Air Transport System, captaining a propeller-driven four-engine Lockheed Constellation (an airliner whose distinctive triple-tail design and graceful dolphin-shaped fuselage was widely rumored to be the brainchild of maverick aviator, film producer, and Trans World Airlines owner Howard Hughes). Less than one hundred feet off the runway during a night landing at Kwajalein, a South Pacific atoll northeast of what was then New Guinea, Edinger's "Super Connie," carrying seventy-eight passengers and a crew of nine, suddenly ran into an unexpected patch of moisture, stalled, and almost crashed.

Edinger was by then a deeply experienced pilot with years of duty as a flight instructor and in single-seat fighter aircraft as well as multi-engine transports. But, even for veteran pilots qualified as plane captains on the biggest passenger aircraft of the day, all it need ever take was one mishap, one slip, or one moment of inattention to lose it all. That moment always lay in waiting whenever, wherever, and whatever they flew.

***

Ray Edinger grew up in Pittsburgh and, like many boys who would later become wartime aviators, built model airplanes and was devoted to the adventures of "Tailspin Tommy." After graduating from high school in 1934, Edinger attended Pittsburgh's Todd School of Aeronautics and later earned his private pilot's license via CPTP. Edinger was eager to join the Navy as a pilot. Edinger's timing was right, but his circumstances were wrong: He had gotten married the year before, and neither the Navy nor Army then accepted flight-duty applications from married men.

The entry door cracked open a bit in late 1942, when Edinger, then working for Curtiss-Wright Corporation, became an AV(T), or "aviation volunteer temporary," a commissioned Navy officer limited to Stateside flight instruction. In 1943, newly promoted to LTJG and still eager to become a full-fledged naval aviator, Edinger finally got his opportunity. Although he'd trained hundreds of pilots and flown thousands of hours, Edinger arrived in Pensacola as just another fledgling trainee. At one juncture, he even had the awkward experience of having his progress "checked out" by a former student.

After Edinger earned his Wings of Gold, he qualified on multi-engine aircraft, including seaplanes. In 1946 Edinger transferred to the River for test-pilot duty. It was exciting and sometimes dangerous duty (including, among other things, testing the propeller-driven successor to the Hellcat, the Grumman F8 Bearcat), but by 1947 the Navy was undergoing huge cutbacks in all areas, including research and development. Edinger's string finally ran out: He was separated from the Navy in December, and he and his wife, Margery, returned to Pittsburgh where he found work, first as an automobile insurance adjuster and eventually as a General Motors service representative.

***

In memory at least, the U.S. postwar years—during which Ray Edinger and millions of others left the military and settled into civilian jobs—seem slow, orderly, and affluent times captured in black-and-white pictures of slicked-back, buttoned-down, upbeat, and uptight people. This was a generation that exercised its freedom not in social or political dissent (that would be for the generation of the 1960s and 1970s) but in economic terms. Veterans out of the service (courtesy of demobilization), many of them just out of college (courtesy of the GI Bill) as the decade closed, pursued the sorts of material ambitions that were beyond the reach of many Depression-era households: a good, career-long, white-collar job; a house in the suburbs; a manageable number of children (many of whom grew up to reject their parents' achievements); and the accoutrements (from schools and club memberships to household appliances and automobiles) to go with them.

These consumer needs made America in the years immediately following World War II one of the all-time great sellers' markets. At first there were shortages: Americans, for example, had to pay something under the table to car dealers just to get on the waiting list for the relatively few new cars finally rolling off retooled war assembly lines. With marriages and birthrates soaring, there was also a housing shortage—actually a crisis, with people in some regions using military Quonset huts and even old trolleys as single-family homes. In March 1949, when Bill Levitt, the soon-to-be housing tycoon, first advertised mass-produced homes to be built (at first for veterans only) in Long Island's Levittown, 1,400 sales contracts were drawn up the first day.[1]

The lifestyle frenzy seemed to preoccupy all Americans, with the revolution extending to entertainment and communication (by 1952 there would be 19 million television sets in the United States beaming programming underwritten by aggressive consumer advertising), transportation and energy (automobile ownership depended on cheap oil and access to refineries, as well as the financing, insurance, and dealer service sectors where Ray Edinger took up his postwar career), food (California's McDonald brothers first prototyped their fast food restaurant concept in 1948), and even sex (in 1947 University of Indiana professor Alfred Kinsey published a blockbuster with the clinical yet scandalous title *Sexual Behavior in the Human Male*). But in the midst of this remarkable behavioral revolution, the last years of the 1940s were also mean times, times ripe for suspicion and witch hunts. An unwanted European and Pacific war had not brought a true peace. Triumphant, unscarred, and wealthy as the United States was, the rest of the world, much of it strange and hostile, was pressing unsettlingly closer.

One wartime ally, the Soviet Union, had shown its true expansionist colors by reaching its tentacles into Eastern Europe, and seemed to have aspirations for controlling the peoples and politics of the entire globe. China—another ally and, during World War II, more nearly a supplicant—had shorn its Western ties after going Communist and staking out all of mainland Asia as its hegemony. The specter of Soviet Communism and the unconscionable "loss" of China fueled suspicions of a rampant Communist global conspiracy with deep, secret tendrils in America. "The traitors," intoned Joseph McCarthy, Wisconsin's then obscure Republican junior senator, "must no longer lead the betrayed." Traitors, at least to "Tail-Gunner Joe's" way of thinking,* meant the elite and effete eastern establishment represented by the likes of Truman's secretary of state, Dean Acheson. Opportunistic politicians like McCarthy and power-hungry bureaucrats like FBI director J. Edgar Hoover appointed themselves avenging champions and set out to track down clandestine Communist cells in such hotbeds of subversion as the media and government—regardless of the innocent victims they bullied and skewered along the way.

In the midst of all this chilling, not altogether baseless, but often unsubstantiated fury about the internal threat of Communism, there was little maneuvering room—for the president or either political party—when faced by external and overt Communist aggression. Despite (or perhaps because of) Acheson's verbal gaff about Korea just months before, Truman had little choice but to take a military stand. And an otherwise restive and hostile U.S. Congress had little choice but to let him—even though Truman never approached them for a formal declaration of war. Korea was to be a "sour little war" no one wanted fought in "the worst possible location," but it was also, because of this chain of circumstances, unavoidable and inevitable.

***

One further measure of the depthless fear and loathing of Communism came in an initially unheralded article written by journalist Edward Hunter and published in the September 24, 1950, edition of the *Miami Daily News*. Hunter, who, while based in Hong Kong, had interviewed former Chinese Communist prisoners, was convinced that the Chinese Communists were using a process called *xi-nao* (mind

---

* As a Marine Corps captain in the wartime Pacific, McCarthy was attached to an air squadron as an intelligence briefing officer. In that capacity he flew a dozen or so missions as a gunner/observer in the backseat of a Dauntless dive-bomber.

cleanse) to reform errant Communists. To capture the attention of its readers, *Miami Daily News* copy editors gave Hunter's article a provocative title: "'Brain-Washing' Tactics Force Chinese into the Ranks of Communist Party." *Brainwashing* quickly found its way into the Cold War lexicon.

Brainwashing, wrote Hunter in this newspaper article and a subsequent book, involved the calculated use of mistreatment followed by measured rewards and punishments to "change a mind radically so that its owner becomes a living puppet—a human robot—without the atrocity being visible from the outside." Later, before the House Un-American Activities Committee (the congressional forum for all things that smacked of Communism), Hunter went even further. "The United States is the main battlefield," he testified, "the people and the soil and the resources of the United States."

Although Hunter had pioneered a term that riveted the attention and fears of the general public, he was not alone in investigating such practices, nor was speculation about their use confined to the Chinese Communists. Indeed, Hunter along with other researchers, such as psychiatrist Lawrence Hinkle and neurologist Harold Wolf (two CIA-sponsored experts), were convinced that brainwashing-style practices had actually originated in the Soviet Union before spreading inevitably and systematically (though with some variation) to its satellite and client states. Soon after the Russian Revolution, their research found, Bolshevik leader Vladimir Lenin had invited Russian physician and experimental psychologist Ivan Pavlov to the Kremlin and pressed him to extend his work on behavioral conditioning of dogs to humans. Pavlov purportedly produced a manuscript convincing Lenin that Pavlov's methods could be used for the mass conversion of Soviet citizens (and the citizens of other countries as well) to the ways of Communism. The power and practicality of these techniques, researchers believed, were displayed on a grand stage for the Moscow Show Trials of the late 1930s during which dozens of "conspirators"—many with impeccable Communist Party credentials—literally demanded to be executed for committing heinous crimes against the Soviet state.

Soviet interrogation techniques used heavy doses of solitary confinement to persuade victims they were alone, unloved, and abandoned, with fear as their only companion. Soviet objectives—extracting complete confessions to blatantly fabricated charges—differed from the Chinese focus on "reeducating" subjects so that they might be "usefully" returned to society. But success for both uses apparently hinged on Pavlov's three stages of conditioning and reeducation: a straightforward stage where subjects responded directly to a stimulus (e.g., the ringing of a bell or the constant repetition of a philosophy), a confused stage where both stimulus and behavior became unpredictable, and a traumatic final stage where expected behavior was inverted—the mind stopped functioning and went haywire. Here, theory went, honest individuals turned to liars, spiritual individuals to apostates, and loyal individuals to traitors. As the Moscow Show Trials' chief prosecutor put it following an inspection tour of the vast Soviet gulag: "These prisoners have deteriorated to the point of any resemblance to human beings."[2]

These queasy fears about Communist "mind control" were just taking hold when the first amped-up reports emerged about the fates of South Koreans and neutral civilians in the hands of the North Koreans. As the invaders moved in, they blanketed newly occupied territory with propaganda pamphlets extolling their humanity. "Quite contrary to the propaganda of Syngman Rhee," read one such pamphlet, "the People's Army is a kind, modest and merciful lot of young people."[3] Yet despite a patina of reform, including a promise of landownership to South Korean tenant farmers, the victors were quick to display their ruthlessness, summarily liquidating local South Korean leaders and conscripting thousands of students into a "volunteer force."

Things often got worse when North Korean frontline unit commanders and their troops were left to their own devices. Homes were occupied and ravaged by invaders. Some civilians were summarily selected to be "migrated" north. Inhabitants of religious missions (many Koreans but also private citizens of America, Australia, Belgium, France, Germany, Ireland, and Turkey) were rounded up, hauled before peremptory "People's Courts," and then sent north by train for internment in Pyongyang.

Even worse treatment for American GIs was widely anticipated from the outbreak of hostilities. As routinely demonstrated in the war with

Japan, captivity in the Far East was, for many American prisoners of war (POWs), effectively a death sentence. Living conditions in remote island jungles, peasant villages, and even continental cities were often horrid, with the captors themselves living hand to mouth on the edge of survival, with scant food and virtually no access to medical treatment. Layered atop these factors were febrile (and robustly two-way) racism and, at least in the case of the Japanese, a brutal disdain for any so-called warrior who would deign to surrender short of death. The resulting attitudes on both sides, especially in ground combat, led to a simple dictum: no quarter expected and none given. Could anything better be expected of the rampaging—and likely brainwashed—North Koreans once they were in widespread mortal combat with Americans?

***

To deal with the immediate military crisis of the Korean conflict, Congress loosened hitherto taut purse strings on military spending to rush through an $11 billion supplemental appropriation bill for Truman's signature. The infusion was of little short-term help to a military sector that had been starved of funds for weapons development—at least for capabilities short of nuclear annihilation—and whose infrastructure had been allowed to molder.

The impact for the ex-veteran man on the street, however, was immediate and earthshaking. On June 30 Congress authorized mobilization. Within weeks, the president called up 25,000 individual and inactive reservists (those not drilling or assigned to units), with another 135,000 to follow by year's end. Pentagon brass, fearful Korea might be just the first step toward a global conflict, chose not to strip active reservists (those attending drills) from established units, instead keeping these units intact and in the States for training and refit prior to deployment. Thus, inactive reservists—those with the slimmest of residual ties to the military—were actually the first to go to Korea and into the front lines.

For many if not most of these veterans, the call to duty was a shock. Orders came so swiftly that few got time to dig out their enlistment contracts (if they'd even bothered to save them) to check the fine print. Many infantry and armor reservists were dispatched to Korea so quickly that they found themselves, without additional training, in frontline positions within one day of their arrival in Korea.*

The call-up also gave a jolt to the otherwise stagnating progress of racially integrating the active-duty military. Despite Truman's Executive Order 9981, most black GIs were still assigned to all-black units. Now, pressed by the exigencies of armed combat, that began to change. One U.S. Army 9th Regiment battalion commander whose Korea-based infantry unit was at less than half strength received a call from a division personnel officer alerting him that almost 200 from black labor units in Pusan were eager to transfer to the infantry. The commander, who had previously led a unit of black troops during the Second World War, readily agreed and considered himself fortunate to have them.

Though there was a difference in scale, the need to ramp up Air Force and Navy strength also precipitated call-ups (some would even say "press-ganging") of reserves. In the case of the U.S. Marine Corps—a force whose active-duty manpower had dwindled from a Pacific-war high-water mark of nearly a half-million leathernecks down to fewer than 80,000—it involved, within three months, the full mobilization of the Corps' Organized Ground Reserve: nearly 35,000 officers and enlisted men. For the Navy, a Pacific Fleet manned by about 11,000 sailors in June 1950 would balloon to more than 60,000 sailors over the next six months; nearly all the added manpower would come from the ranks of the naval reserve.

***

After Ray Edinger left the regular Navy, he remained in the reserves. The Navy had established a system of reserve naval air stations spaced regionally across the country as a means of maintaining bonds with former naval aviators and enlisted aviation specialists. Equipped with one squadron's worth of surplus aircraft, each station supported four reserve squadrons—"weekend warriors"—whose personnel would report for paid duty one weekend a month and for an additional extended and intensive period of two weeks each year.

---

* Inexperienced American soldiers weren't the only ones being rushed to the front lines. Thousands of bewildered South Korean youth (sharing the fate of other young South Koreans in areas controlled by the invaders) were taken off the streets, given ten days' training, and assigned to U.S. units.

Edinger would have welcomed the opportunity to join one of these squadrons, but there was no station or organized squadron in the Pittsburgh area. Because of his unabated joy in flying, Edinger instead kept involved by cadging occasional assignments at NAS Willow Grove, near Philadelphia, where he would serve, for a couple weeks at a time, as the station's on-call pilot.

Finally, in 1949, a squadron opportunity opened up when he was part of a group of Pittsburgh-area pilots invited to join VF-653, a reserve Corsair squadron flying out of NAS Akron, Ohio. VF-653 was headed by a hotshot Navy aviator named Cook Cleland. In World War II, Cleland flew Douglas SBD Dauntless dive-bombers from the deck of carrier *Wasp* (CV-7), first in the Atlantic and Mediterranean and then in the Pacific until, in September 1942, *Wasp* was sunk by a spread of torpedoes from a Japanese submarine. Rescued along with other survivors after four hours in the water, Cleland was later based on *Lexington* (the famous "Blue Ghost"). During his time in the Pacific, Cleland amassed two Japanese aerial kills and, among other decorations, won a Navy Cross (for scoring a bomb hit on a Japanese battleship) and a Purple Heart.

After the war and a stint as a tactical test pilot, Cleland took up pylon air racing—aviation's latest envelope-pushing incarnation—a vocation that he supplemented with other aerial-business sidelines: flying boat charters for North Woods anglers, a flight training school, and a flight-banner advertising business. Flying production models of the Navy's bent-winged Corsair fighter-bomber manufactured by Goodyear Aircraft, Cleland entered the Cleveland Air Races (a prestigious prewar event revived after a wartime hiatus) only to finish a dismal sixth behind surplus Army Air Force Mustangs and Airacobras. When Cleland discovered that a better-performing version of the Goodyear Corsair existed, he approached no less than famed admiral William "Bull" Halsey (who had known Cleland during the war and was eager for Navy aircraft to whip the surplus Army aircraft being entered in the races) to have three of the planes quietly declared surplus and just as quietly purchased before potential rivals found out.

The muscular Goodyear-manufactured Super Corsair (designated F2G) sported a huge twenty-eight-cylinder Pratt & Whitney R4360 engine (called a "corncob" engine because of its four seven-cylinder stacks) rated at more than 3,000 horsepower. The result for Cleland's race team was a record-setting 396 mph victory in the 1947 Thompson Trophy Race. Beaten by an Army aircraft (by a razor-thin 1-mph margin) the next year, Cleland bounced back to sweep first, second, and third places in the 1949 race.

The Corsair was a 1940 design inspired by the Navy's need for a carrier aircraft that could match the performance of land-based fighter planes. In early tests the Corsair became the first U.S. single-engine production aircraft capable of level flight speeds of 400 mph. The first production Corsairs, however, proved to be controversial aircraft, loved by Marine aviators but thought by many Navy aviators to be unsuitable for carrier duty.

The Corsair's particularly long nose (among its nicknames were "Hose Nose" and "Hog") made it difficult for its pilot to see straight ahead when taxiing on the ground. This was true to some degree of most World War II fighter aircraft, in large part because their three-point stances (undercarriages combining two wing or fuselage wheels with a tail wheel or strut) thrust the plane's nose into the pilot's field of vision. But the "Hose Nose" added a new degree of difficulty. If taxied for any great distance, a Corsair was often accompanied by a man on the ground to prevent the Corsair pilot from hitting and chopping up unseen obstacles. A more pressing problem for carrier operations was that the Corsair's long nose also made it difficult for the pilot to see the LSO and follow his signals for carrier landings.

Other problems compounded this particular drawback. During slow-speed carrier approaches, the "U-bird's" port wing tended to stall before the starboard wing (the sort of stall problem that also plagued early-generation Navy jets). As it touched down, the Corsair's propeller blades (despite the gull-wing design that in effect raised the fuselage) came uncomfortably close to scraping the flight deck. Later Corsair versions came with fixes: the substitution of a four-blade propeller (with somewhat shorter individual blades) and the installation of a short metal "spoiler" on the starboard wing to balance out the stall.

Despite these quirks, the Corsair's speed and ruggedness earned it a reputation as a formidable and versatile carrier-based weapon. The F4U boasted a ten-to-one "kill ratio" in combat with Japanese aircraft. That was years before, of course, and there was little argument the

Corsair's best days were behind it. The quirky, advanced fighter of 1943 and 1944 was by now pretty much outmoded—fit for reserve duty, perhaps, but seemingly out of place in frontline use, unless perhaps the aviation gods were bent on making amends for their earlier misgivings about its capabilities.

***

VF-653 (an active reserve unit) was an ideal setup for Edinger and other Navy reserve pilots (all of them lieutenants except for a lone ensign and Cleland, who was a lieutenant commander) living in Ohio or western Pennsylvania. When the Korean War started, however, it was no longer such a good deal—at least for pilots with families and community roots who, despite their active reserve status, never anticipated being called up. It didn't help these men that their skipper—his racing career on hold because the Cleveland Air Races were once again suspended—was rumored to be lobbying Washington brass to target VF-653 for early activation.

By no means were all VF-653 pilots reluctant reservists. Ray Edinger, now thirty-two and married but with no children, was as eager as ever for operational, even combat, flying. Another ready-to-go pilot was Bobby Balser. Texas-born Balser, twenty-six, was a veteran who, despite flying Hellcats in the Pacific, had never seen combat. He'd gone to Pittsburgh to attend the Pittsburgh Institute of Art on the GI Bill and afterward landed a job as a staff illustrator for the *Pittsburgh Post Gazette*. He soon found that he loathed the routine of his job; a bachelor unencumbered by family obligations, Balser now saw reactivation as the escape hatch from his deskbound life in Pittsburgh.

Edinger, Balser, and other like-minded VF-653 reservists got their wishes. In January 1950 VF-653 pilots and ground crews were ordered to report for active duty, first for training out of Alameda, California, and then combat deployment.

"Thousand of Reserves Ready Here for Quick Plunge into Battle" trumpeted the Monday, July 24, 1950, edition of the *Pittsburgh Press*: "Many of Pittsburgh's 'week end guardians of peace' will soon become fighting warriors on the Korean front. . . . These veterans are ready for the already ordered mobilization and prompt movement to the battle lines because they have been working and drilling while the rest of

the population dozed in the complacency of peace." Emphasizing
that the manpower of Guard and reserve outfits in the Pittsburgh District numbered in the many thousands—nearly 4,000 of them Navy
reservists—the *Press* article turned its attention to VF-653, "Cleland's
Clippers," a "top notch fighter squadron" of "24 young Corsair pilots,
five ground officers, six chiefs (petty officers) and 80 enlisted men."

Each of the VF-653 pilots, *Press* staff writer Waldo L. Russell reported, had more than 1,000 hours' flight time ("Lt. Ray Edinger of
206 West Prospect Ave. . . . has 3000 hours and holds all Navy flight
ratings"), "with many a Jap to their credit." The *Press* reporter pronounced them eager to go as a squadron: "About the first thing I heard
was from their peppery leading chief, W. J. Zielinski of 710 Woods
Ave. Addressing Lt. Edinger, he said: 'Sir, when can we get going? Let's
take the whole squadron and lick the h— out of those Commies.'"

Stressing that VF-653's pilots were "as at home in the cockpits of
their 2400-horsepower Corsairs as . . . in their week day jobs as business and professional men," the article concluded with a listing that
demonstrated the variety in their backgrounds and walks of life. It
was a résumé true both to Pittsburgh and to the times. There was
heavy representation from the Allegheny region's coal, steel, and mate-
rials base: Lt. William R. Clarke ("oil company researcher"), Lt. O. G.
Cramer ("with oil company"), Lt. Ralph Evans ("researcher for steel
company"), Lt. Frank W. M. Frankovich ("chemical engineer"), Lt.
John F. Gibbons ("engineer with testing laboratory"), Lt. Joseph D.
Sanko ("with coal company"), Lt. Robert L. Sobey ("engineer with
steel company"), and Lt. Hull L. Wright ("with steel company laboratory"). But it also reflected other burgeoning sectors. For example,
construction: Lt. G. Dunn ("bricklayer"), Lt. William Geffel ("con-
struction electrician"), Lt. Richard A. Graciano ("building contractor"),
Lt. Robert E. Kempmiller ("building contractor"), and Lt. James T.
Porterfield ("masonry contractor"). And the "GI Bill industry": Lt.
Thomas Davis ("on staff of business college"), Lt. Robert Hermann
("Pitt graduate student"), Lt. D. E. London ("law student at Dicken-
son"), Ens. David W. Robertson ("student at Pitt"), and Lt. Henry R.
Sulkowski ("with Mellon Institute"). And, not least, the 1950s-style
revolutions in communications and finance: Lt. B. G. Balser ("news-
paper artist"), Lt. William L. Hartman Jr. ("partner in television busi-

ness"), Lt. J. R. Rohleder ("in telephone company offices"), and Lt. G. N. Wilson ("insurance broker").

***

VF-653's personnel had the advantage of knowing their aircraft—if not fully envisioning how the old Corsair would be employed over Korea. They were rusty in skills and qualifications. Most had not flown off or onto a carrier deck in years—a handful, including XO Ray Edinger, had never done so. Still, they knew the airplane's strengths, quirks, and limitations. They could brush up on, or quickly learn, the rest. However, this wasn't the case for other activated squadrons who had the advantage—and for some the inestimable challenge—of going to war flying the Navy's first jet aircraft.

In early May 1951, George Schnitzer reported to Squadron VF-831, part of Air Group 15 (CVG-15) based at NAS Alameda, across the bay from San Francisco. Schnitzer had begun Pre-Flight in July 1949 (two months after Joe Akagi, Neil Armstrong, and Ken Schechter began theirs). A tall, slight New Englander, Schnitzer was not accustomed to the Florida Gulf's midsummer swelter, conditions made only worse by the intense physical activity and the fact that many of Pensacola's work and living spaces were not air-conditioned.

Although Schnitzer, who'd been a math major at Brown, had an easy time with the classroom training, he was a bit taken aback by how outdated some of it seemed. Aerial navigation, for example, used manual plotting boards and emphasized slow-moving search patterns. Wind velocity was to be judged visually by looking at wave motion and height instead of cockpit instrumentation. And his meteorology class taught the students virtually nothing about weather conditions at high altitude.

Schnitzer graduated from Pre-Flight on November 19, 1949—an occasion marred only by his being called to the front of the formation to receive his diploma as "Midshipman Schitzer." Two months later, on January 18, 1950, Schnitzer made his first solo flight (a milestone that called for the snipping of his black uniform tie four inches from the top) and a year later earned his wings.

Still ranked a "flying midshipman," Schnitzer was one of eight young aviators (six LTJGs and one ensign, with Schnitzer the lone lowly "middie") assigned several months later to fill out the ranks of what turned out to be a reserve unit activated in February 1951 from NAS Bennett Field on Long Island, New York. As the unit's lowest-ranking aviator (VF-831's grizzled veterans didn't know what to make of someone who was neither officer nor enlisted man), Schnitzer was assigned the role of squadron first lieutenant, responsible (he soon found out by asking the squadron's equally grizzled chief petty officer) for managing the movement of squadron personnel and equipment when VF-831 finally deployed.

VF-831, which had been flying World War II–era Hellcats (the same aircraft Schnitzer qualified on during Advanced Flight Training) on Long Island, would instead be flying F9F-2 Panther jets in Korea. It was an awkward transition, both in receiving aircraft (the last of sixteen airplanes did not arrive until July) and in learning to fly them tactically as a squadron. It was a particularly uneasy transition for young pilots like Schnitzer who, after earning their wings, had spent the intervening months training and soloing in jets. Because of their lowly status, they knew they had to keep quiet as they "learned" from the more senior pilots who were themselves just confronting the intricacies of jet aircraft in general—and the challenging and quirky F9Fs in particular.

The young pilots were "taught," for example, to start their climbs as soon as they raised landing gear and flaps—even though they knew that in a jet it was best to build up airspeed before climbing. In similar fashion, VF-831's veterans fell back on the "Thach Weave" as an aerial defense tactic despite the fact that the weave was impractical for high-altitude jet aircraft that, because of speed, fuel consumption (tight formations required too much fuel-guzzling "throttle jockeying"), and turning radius, flew better and longer if widely spaced. They never learned tactics that seemed crucial to them: how best to defend against speedier jet aircraft with faster climb rates like the much feared Communist MiG-15. The weave had been developed early in World War II based on the concept of "dissimilar air combat tactics"—in other words, "thinking outside the box." Such dissimilar thinking had not yet seemed to emerge for air combat in Korea; if it had, they hadn't heard about it.[4]

The list of things not practiced—but later to be found essential during deployment—only seemed to grow in the weeks and months that followed. They included: instrument flying, especially in descents; diving and strafing attacks in divisions or sections instead of one aircraft at a time; visual reconnaissance, especially spotting camouflaged ground targets; close air support (CAS) bombing and strafing against small targets the size of trucks or tanks; shallow dives or steep pullouts from bomb runs in rugged terrain; and, always, air defensive tactics that went beyond what had already been picked up in Advanced Flight Training.

As a group, the young pilots (and perhaps some of the older reservists as well) felt that they were getting ready for war without learning particularly much. Admittedly, some of it was competitive fun. (The "warheads" of aerial rockets they fired at a mountainous desert range in Southern California's Imperial Valley contained white powder to mark the point of impact. Schnitzer's bachelor officers' quarters roommate and flight training buddy, Larry Quiel, proved to be the squadron sharpshooter, once putting all six of his rockets into a six-foot bull's-eye, while Schnitzer "couldn't come close to his score.") Still, to George Schnitzer's mind, the preparation "didn't fill the bill." Instead, it was insular training, an earnest but misleading look back at World War II rather than at what lay ahead. They had reason to sense that Korea would be altogether different, if for no other reason than that they were flying jets now, not props. It was, in a way, like readying for World War II by learning from World War I aces who were just learning to fly monoplanes (and whose war stories were about fighting the "Huns," not the Japanese).

What galled all the pilots later was that much of this fresh insight, information, and tactical savvy was already being built up through hard wreckage- and casualty-strewn practice. Each day Navy and Air Force pilots were flying Korean combat missions, and each day their experience was being captured in debriefings, gun-camera footage, and after-action reports. The problem was that, for no discernible reason, not much of this vital information was yet finding its way back to where it could be of most benefit—to rookies like Schnitzer and ill-prepared veterans like the reservists from Bennett Field.

4

ONIONSKIN ANGEL

ON AUGUST 1, *Philippine Sea* finally reached Buckner Bay, a vast harbor stretching along the eastern (Pacific) shoreline of the island of Okinawa. Five years before, the Hagushi beaches fronting the East China Sea on the opposite shore had been the landing site for what proved to be the last—and biggest—Pacific-war assault by U.S. Marines and GIs.

Originally called Nagagusuku Wan, Buckner Bay had taken its new name (at least for the duration of the American occupation) to honor U.S. Army general Simon Bolivar Buckner Jr., the invasion commander (and son of a Civil War Confederate general) killed during its last days by a ricocheting coral chunk dislodged by a Japanese artillery round. The island's rugged cave-pocked ridges and escarpments had been the killing grounds of perhaps the fiercest and bloodiest ground combat of any battle—Pacific or European—during the entire war.

The three months it eventually took to subdue Japanese defenders had resulted in upward of 75,000 combined U.S. casualties, including 12,500 killed or missing; more than a third of these were U.S. Navy sailors killed by aerial kamikaze attacks. Japanese casualties, the product of a never-surrender mind-set and (in the case of many civilians) wild propaganda about the bloodlust of the American invaders, tolled infinitely worse: the deaths of 110,000 Japanese troops and 75,000 civilian men, women, and children.

Conquered Okinawa was to have been the arsenal for Operation Downfall, the massive two-stage invasion of Japan's home islands just three hundred miles to the north, a campaign anticipated to result in a million more U.S. casualties—and who knew how many millions of Japanese. In large part to avoid Downfall's ground-combat abattoir, the United States had forced war's end by dropping atomic bombs, first on Hiroshima and then Nagasaki. Now Okinawa's bays, beaches, bases, airstrips, and depots were the U.S. Seventh Fleet's staging point for a new conflict, this time on Asia's mainland, where diplomats, politicians, and military planners alike had hoped never to fight.

***

Upon arrival, Duane Thorin and Lt. Harry Sundberg, Helicopter Utility Squadron One's detachment officer-in-charge (OinC or O-I-C), were kept busy flying their "pinwheel" to shuttle personnel between Task Force 77 ships and to military facilities ashore for rounds of staff meetings. For radio communication purposes the helicopters (objects to marvel at wherever they first appeared) were called "Angels," and their call sign combined *angel* with their ship's call sign. *Philippine Sea's* call sign was "Onionskin," so its helicopter was "Onionskin Angel."

The three-week, 12,000-mile Pacific crossing was hectic for everyone aboard but especially for pilots in Air Group 11, many of whom had deployed with just a few days' notice. Although the helicopter was often used for courier duty, shuttling of personnel, and other errands, its priority, once the fleet returned to sea, was to be a guardian angel during flight operations. It was left to Sundberg, Thorin, and aviation machinist Chester Todd, Thorin's usual crewman, to familiarize air group pilots with the procedures to follow if they bailed out, "punched out" (the new bailout vernacular for jet aircraft equipped with powered ejection seats), or ditched.

The most important thing in the case of ditching, they stressed to pilots, was getting away from the wreckage. For parachute landings in the water it was even more important to get rid of the chute. In so many words, the underpowered HO3S "couldn't lift a sick whore off a couch"; the combined weight of a downed pilot and his wet parachute could pull them all into the drink. As it was, during plane guard duty, the pinwheel took off with its fuel tanks just half full. Still, if a pilot went into the drink during launch or recovery, Thorin and

Sundberg promised, he should be picked up in a minute or two, maybe even less.

***

Phil Sea joined *Valley Forge* on August 5 with first-day sweeps (on station in the Yellow Sea) by Air Group 11 aircraft over South Korean airfields lost during the North Korean invasion. That first day the group also experienced its first fatality, when VF-113 Corsair pilot Ens. John Frederick Kail, twenty-five, from Upper Sandusky, Ohio, crashed and burned fifteen miles south of Kunsan. Kail's loss, although officially a combat casualty, resulted not through enemy gunfire but from a midair collision with another strike aircraft (whose pilot survived and was rescued). That same day "Bunny" McCallum, a VF-113 Corsair pilot seconded to *Valley Forge* (to make up for Air Group 5's pilot losses), crashed his plane in Inchon Harbor after plowing through high-tension wires while on a strafing run. McCallum survived (he was rescued by British destroyer *Cockade* after a night spent clinging to a rock outcropping), but both incidents underlined the kinds of risks pilots faced in the first weeks of combat flying. In essence they were working out the kinks—the nautical equivalent was "shakedown"—in the midst of combat.

Such risks were by no means confined to the Korean skies. Rusty or inexperienced pilots also grappled with the hazards of flying postwar combat aircraft (like the jet-powered Panthers) off the narrow, cramped flight decks of *Essex*-class carriers. During this stage of the war, flight deck mishaps often outpaced North Korean ground fire as the cause for plane damage and pilot casualties. During July and August, for example, launch and takeoff accidents (twenty-five) for one *Valley Forge* jet squadron contrasted, starkly and somewhat embarrassingly, with squadron battle damage for the same period (one confirmed enemy bullet hole).

In August VF-111 pilot Lt. Carl E. Dace earned the dubious distinction of being the first Navy jet pilot to punch out in combat. Hit while strafing a North Korean ground target, Dace climbed from 2,000 feet up to 6,000 feet—ejection-seat use had been cleared only for altitudes above 5,000 feet—and turned out to sea. When Dace tried to jettison his Plexiglas canopy, it stuck on its tracks, forcing him to wrestle with the balky bubble's frame until the wind finally carried it away. Then, as his wingman looked on apprehensively, Dace pulled his face curtain and punched out. To both men's immense relief, the ejection mechanism—a solid-propellant charge inside a telescoping tube that shot seat and strapped-in pilot like a bullet from a gun—worked as advertised. After separating from the seat, Dace deployed his chute and drifted down to the Yellow Sea, where he floated the next seven hours in his life raft before being picked up by a destroyer.

Meanwhile, across the peninsula, *Valley Forge's* propeller squadrons (VF-53, VF-54, and VA-55) got more productive results when a July 18 morning reconnaissance flight spotted a dream target on North Korea's east coast. It was the Wonsan Oil Refining Factory, originally built by the Japanese, but now jointly operated by North Koreans and Russians and daily producing hundreds of tons of petroleum products, including automotive gasoline. It would prove to be a rare find in Korea— a bona fide twentieth-century industrial target. VF-53 Corsairs armed with rockets and VA-55 Skyraiders carrying bombs, twenty-one aircraft in all, took off for Wonsan that very afternoon.

Swarming over the factory complex, first with rockets and then bombs, the aircraft left the refinery an inferno of flames and plumes of black smoke visible to *Valley Forge's* flight deck crews some sixty miles away in the Sea of Japan. The refinery continued to burn for the next four days until it was finally reduced to little more than islands of rubble surrounded by vast shallow lagoons of black crude.

There followed an intense interservice squabble as to who could rightly claim the Wonsan Oil Refining Factory's destruction. Air Force high-altitude B-29 strikes had targeted the facility during the first and second weeks of July, and another B-29 raid followed on the nineteenth. While later evidence sustained the Navy's case, it only begged the bigger question: With such "strategic targets" in the crosshairs, was this really just a "police action"?

*   *   *

Better (or at least more visible) results not surprisingly brought higher casualties, including one at the top. Late in the afternoon on August 19, Phil Sea launched eight VF-114 Corsairs lead by Air Group Cdr. (CAG) Sully Vogel to strike a bridge crossing the Han River, near

Seoul. While the four-plane CAP rode top cover unmolested, the four-strike Corsairs hit a bridge span with a five hundred–pound bomb during a first pass. When Vogel came around again for a second pass, however, enemy antiaircraft fire set his Corsair afire.

Vogel bailed out of his burning Corsair; other pilots saw his chute stream but fail to deploy, leaving him to plummet like a stone to his death. Vogel, an "old man" still in a "young man's" game, left behind a widow and five children in Ann Arbor, Michigan. Although the target bridge was destroyed, it brought little satisfaction and no solace to Air Group 11 personnel. The somber mood only deepened when, the very next day, another group pilot, VF-112's Ens. Curtis L. Smith, was lost to antiaircraft fire during a rail strike near Pyongyang. Smith died a week to the day after his twenty-fifth birthday.

* * *

Meanwhile, in late June, on the other side of the world, aircraft carrier *Leyte* (CV-32) was nearing the end of the second month of her Mediterranean deployment. Near midnight on the twenty-fifth, the day of the North Korean invasion, while *Leyte* was anchored off Leghorn, Italy, an operational command put all pilots on standby alert. There were as yet, it turned out, not enough carriers in America's depleted naval arsenal to simultaneously support NATO in the Mediterranean while stepping up to the unanticipated hot spot in Korea. The shortfall was to be made up by borrowing from the Atlantic Fleet while simultaneously lengthening deployments and curtailing carrier maintenance and training. Within days, *Leyte* was ordered back to Norfolk where, after a breakneck ten-day overhaul period, ship, crew, and Air Group 3 would be sailing for Korea.

The beginning of 1950 had brought VF-32, one of CVG-3's two propeller fighter squadrons, a new CO. Lt. Cdr. Dugald (Doug) T. Neill, USN, was a twelve-year naval aviator, now in his midthirties and a confirmed bachelor, who'd distinguished himself as a Hellcat fighter pilot in the Pacific war. Neill was dark-haired, dapper, and physically fit, with a precisely trimmed mustache and a jut-jawed profile that reminded some pilots of comic-strip character Dick Tracy. Though not particularly inspiring, Neill was organized and competent. He was also a stickler for military bearing, spit, and polish—a rude awakening for some squadron aviators accustomed to the more lax style of his predecessor.

To the dismay of many VF-32s pilots, there was also a change in aircraft from Bearcats to Corsairs—for many a step back. Despite its cramped cockpit (a tight fit for anyone above average height), the Bearcat bore the Grumman brand and was as fast and muscular as its name implied—a true pilot's airplane.

One man who wasn't disappointed was Tom Hudner, a VF-32 aviator who doubled as assistant maintenance officer for the squadron. Hudner had flown the F4U Corsair during advanced training. To his mind the U-Bird had some special virtues, especially as a ground attack and support plane. Its engine was more robust than the Bearcat's and its fuel-tank capacity nearly 50 percent greater. The Corsair was also a good gun platform, rock steady even when firing rockets.

***

Thomas J. Hudner Jr., then nearing twenty-six, was born in Fall River, Massachusetts, the oldest of five children (four boys and one girl) of a successful Irish businessman and proprietor of Hudner's Markets, a grocery store chain originally founded by his Irish immigrant grandfather Michael. The Hudners had a summer home in Westport Harbor, Massachusetts, and Tom Jr. early on developed a passion for sailing and naval lore. He and his three brothers each attended Phillips Academy in Andover, Massachusetts, where Tom Jr.'s athletics (football, lacrosse, and especially track) invariably outshone his academics. Still, his grades and family connections were good enough to earn him a congressional appointment (via Republican congressman Joe Martin) to the U.S. Naval Academy.

Tom Hudner was part of a 1947 class that would distinguish itself with a future president (Jimmy Carter) and fourteen admirals. It was the last of a string of classes whose curriculum was shortened to meet wartime needs (Jim Holloway's had been the first); the class of '47 actually graduated in June 1946. Because of their abbreviated stay at Annapolis, the class of '47 (like its wartime predecessors) had missed out on some of the academics, but they were by no means short-changed on the Naval Academy's core experience: a harsh campaign of bullying, brutality, and psychological manipulation administered by upperclassmen. The implicit idea behind this circumscribed warrior regimen was to subject new students to the kinds of intense stress experienced in wartime. Experience and tradition held that those who didn't crack in the cauldron emerged equipped with unflinching instincts toward duty, obedience, and honor.

Steeled by the experience, Hudner graduated fully intending to make the Navy his career, but, like all his classmates, he was joining a service suddenly without a war to fight and, some argued, without that much of a role in postwar defense. Class of '47 graduates who aspired to be naval aviators (a cadre that, at the time, did not include Hudner) could not be assigned immediately to flight training. Their first billets were to the blue-water fleet. Hudner's own first duty preference was for large conventional ships (battleships or cruisers), a once prestigious Navy fleet segment that in future years would be relegated to the scrap heap.

Hudner's first seagoing assignment—seven months as a signal officer aboard the cruiser *Helena* (CA-75)—was followed by staff duty in Pearl Harbor. Hudner was still stationed at Pearl when, in early 1948, BuPers distributed an announcement encouraging commissioned officers in the fleet to apply for naval aviation training—a sure sign it was facing a pilot deficit. Hudner, newly intrigued by the prospect, decided to apply. It took some wrangling—the Navy was losing as many signal and communication specialists as aviators—but, in April 1948, Hudner received his orders to Pensacola.

Academy toughened, Tom Hudner breezed through Pre-Flight and, though his Basic began inauspiciously (he threw up in the cockpit during his first SNJ flight), went on to earn his wings in August 1949. That November, still a fledgling aviator but with enough service to be promoted to lieutenant junior grade, Hudner joined VF-32 aboard *Leyte* in time for its 1950 Mediterranean deployment.

***

Before departing Norfolk, Air Group 3 marked the arrival of eight "flying midshipmen" and ensign aviators and, owing to their arrival, a reshuffling of berthing assignments. Because of his senior ensign status, VF-32's Jesse Brown moved into one of the three-man berthing compartments normally reserved for lieutenants and LTJGs. One of his two new roommates was twenty-four-year-old LTJG Bill Koenig from Des Moines, Iowa, whose path into naval aviation had been through the wartime V5 program. After schooling at the University of Oklahoma and commissioning, Koenig served tours as an engineering officer onboard a Pacific Fleet destroyer (USS *Rogers* [DD-876]) and a patrol craft (where he'd briefly crossed paths with Tom Hudner) before reporting to flight school in the fall of 1948.

Stored in *Leyte's* hold for the Pacific crossing were six Marine helicopters; the ten Marine Corps pilots who would be flying them were along as passengers. Although the marines were transients, most hung around in the officers' mess to chat and drink coffee. One was 1st Lt. Charlie Ward, a compact, gray-haired Alabaman in his early thirties. Ward, who possessed a deep southern drawl, had a laid-back, mild-mannered way about him that disarmed even Jesse Brown's predisposed wariness. "Ah don't know the meaning of the word 'fear,'" Ward would sometimes say. "Not because Ah'm brave. Ah jus' don't understand big words."

Despite his self-deprecations, Ward was indeed reputed to be fearless. He'd started his Marine Corps career as enlisted grunt and advanced to boot camp drill instructor before becoming a dive-bomber pilot during the war and a chopper pilot after. He was said to be the tenth marine to qualify on helicopters. The Navy Sikorskys added a new dimension to the rescue of downed airmen, but the Marine craft and pilots would have a different primary role when they reached Korea: as spotting aircraft for Marine infantry and artillery.

Like the Navy's helicopter pilots, Ward and the other Marine flyers openly bemoaned their choppers' limitations. Poor instrumentation, for example, made the Sikorsky virtually useless for night flying, and it was incapable of hovering at altitudes of 5,000 feet or more. "Yuh guys gonna crash," Ward kidded the Navy pilots, "do it at sea level."

***

Just occasionally, the string of flight deck mishaps and growing battle casualties plaguing the first carrier air groups to reach Korea was redeemed by feats of operational brilliance and near-miraculous survival under the direst circumstances. One such feat occurred on

September 17, when VF-112 ensign Edward D. Jackson Jr. was injured during a mission near Seoul.

Jackson, twenty-five and married (his wife, Grace, back in Georgia, was expecting the couple's first child in November), was a Holloway product via the University of South Carolina. A strapping six feet tall and 195 pounds, he had played two-way tight end for the Gamecocks and later, during Pre-Flight in Chapel Hill, North Carolina, fielded the same position for an undefeated Navy football squad coached by then lieutenant commander Paul "Bear" Bryant. After receiving advanced training in Corsairs, Jackson had transitioned to Bearcats when he joined VF-112 and finally, just months before deployment, to F9F-2s.

This day Jackson was leading a section dispatched to strafe an airfield near North Korea's capital, Pyongyang, and, afterward, to backtrack south along the railroad toward Seoul, looking for targets of opportunity. Flying on Ed Jackson's wing was Ens. Dayl E. Crow, just turned twenty-two. Born and raised in Stillwater, Oklahoma, Crow was also a Holloway product, via the Universities of New Mexico and Oklahoma. Newly graduated from advanced training in jets, Crow had joined VF-112 in January 1950; less than six months later, he was on his way to war. Crow was the squadron rookie, the "Tail End Charlie": inexperienced, quick to learn, but learning, it turned out, under very high-stakes conditions.

* * *

The Pyongyang airfield Jackson and Crow were assigned to hit proved to be little more than a grassy strip littered with the burned and shattered carcasses of Russian-type aircraft. Along the rail line winding south through a mountain pass into Seoul, the hunting for Jackson and Crow was little better: a single locomotive that their strafing set afire. But then, as the two Panthers swung north around the outskirts of Seoul and started on a leg down the Han River leading to the Yellow Sea, Jackson spotted something more promising.

It was a string of small boats—perhaps seventy-five in all—crossing the Han in lines, south to north. Realizing they might be refugees, Jackson dipped to two hundred feet to have a look. Almost at once he heard the distant but distinct pops of small-arms volleys; many passengers were aiming rifles while others dove into the Han.

***

Enemy soldiers caught in plain sight were at once the easiest and most difficult targets confronting American pilots. There was foremost the often difficult matter of ensuring they were in fact enemies, not friendly troops or innocent civilians—always a concern given the crowded and chaotic flux of wartime's human traffic seen from the air, especially near a big city like Seoul. Sorting this out was hard enough on the ground, where it was often suspected that crowds of Korean civilian refugees fleeing south concealed North Korean enemy infiltrators.[*]

The difficulty for most pilots, however, didn't end there. During their first combat strafing runs, pilots were often startled by the sounds of their airplane's .50-caliber machine guns or 20mm cannons—and by the smell of cordite wafting through their cockpit ventilation systems. This despite having made dozens of practice gunnery runs during predeployment training—as if the guns had a different combat volume and meter and the cordite a different combat aroma. And even after many combat missions, most found it vastly easier to shoot at things (roads, bridges, railroad tracks, vehicles, and buildings) than at people standing, running, or riding out in the open, often far from the front lines.

Fighter pilots were trained (and mentally steeled) for aerial combat, not ground slaughter, which, stripped of its rational details and without much opposing antiaircraft fire, this essentially was. It was perhaps one reason many pilots—despite admonitions not to—pressed their attacks by flying as low as possible and why some took sardonic pleasure in having their wings and fuselages peppered with bullet holes. Even with such "handicapping," the need to pit aerial technology against "human wave" tactics was to be among the war's

---

[*] U.S. ground troops and strafing jets would eventually be accused of several atrocities during this period, including the machine gunning in late July of allegedly hundreds of helpless civilians by American GIs near No Gun Ri in central South Korea.

most disturbing and continuing aspects. It was a crude means of "leveling" the playing field to which pilots grew accustomed only grudgingly—if at all. Almost aside from the pilots' contempt for an enemy whose leaders seemed indifferent to exposing and sacrificing their troops this way was the nagging sense that seeking them out and destroying them was, imperceptibly but no less inevitably, eroding their humanity.

***

Crow followed Jackson as they strafed the lines of boats.* Their 20mm cannon rounds—each with the explosive impact of a hand grenade—splintered the boats and turned the otherwise muddy brown waters of the Han to a cloudy vermilion. There was only small-arms fire and no flak to contest them. But while the North Koreans lacked antiaircraft defenses, they didn't lack ingenuity.

As he reached the last line of boats, flying now barely fifty feet above the water, Jackson glanced at the south bank and caught sight of a man kneeling and aiming his rifle. Jackson decided to ignore him and, as he looked forward, caught "just a whisker" of something dead ahead. There was a roar, a flash, and then oblivion.

It was an "aerial booby trap"—steel cables strung across the Han to "clothesline" low-diving planes. VF-113's Bunny McCallum had experienced something similar a month before; the difference (aside from the purposeful positioning of the cables) was that Jackson's jet lacked a propeller to run interference.

The nose of Jackson's F9F's snapped the cables like twine, but, in the process, it was split open halfway back to the cockpit. Meanwhile, one or more of the whipsawing cable ends caught the starboard wing, partially dislodged it at the root, shredded the wing's tip tank, and finally snapped across the bubble canopy. The final lash might easily have swept away the entire canopy and decapitated Jackson. Instead, it shattered the windscreen and punched out its side panels while leaving the canopy bubble intact. The impact dislodged Jackson's gog-

---

* Crow's recollection is that the troops were wading rather than riding in boats.

gles (he was not wearing his oxygen mask at such low altitude), and shards of glass cut deep into his face.

Jackson's nose was split open from its bridge to the end. Both his eyebrows were laid open, and his left cheek was torn to the bone, almost to the ear. Of more consequence, Jackson had been knocked unconscious.

***

Still flying astern of Jackson, the first thing Dayl Crow noticed was that he was gaining on his section leader. That shouldn't be. Their strafing run complete, Jackson should be (they both should be!) "balls to the walls," gaining speed and altitude. Then he noticed that Jackson's plane was streaming gas—never good but worse now because they were a full one hundred miles away from Phil Sea's flight deck.

When Crow drew even with Jackson he could see the problem, if not the cause: a ripped starboard wing tip tank now apparently drained of gas and a partially shattered canopy, its inner surface splashed with a mist of blood. Crow screamed into his radio: "Power, Jack! Power! Jesus Christ!" Crow's brain intercom was also insistently booming. "Tail End Charlie or no Tail End Charlie, you've got to get us out of here!"

***

For nearly twenty seconds Jackson sat slumped and unconscious as his plane faltered. Fortunately, before going into the strafing run, he'd put plenty of back-trim tab on his elevators so that, as he lost control and his nose dipped too steeply, the plane automatically climbed. It was the sudden jolt from one of these recovery climbs that brought Jackson back to consciousness, but he was still disoriented and, worse, blinded by gushes of blood from his forehead, eyes, nose, and cheek. Mustering muscle memory to locate his controls, Jackson managed to cut his speed down enough to ease the wind rushing at him. He also began responding to Crow's frantic radio calls.

Meanwhile, Crow realized he had to rally his own composure and dampen the tenor of those radio transmissions. He had been shouting at his section leader, detailing all the grisly damage to his airplane, and even urging Jackson to line up on his wing until Jackson finally screamed back, "For God's sake, Dayl, I'm blind!"

Panic wouldn't help either of them. "I'll fly wing on you," a chastened Crow told Jackson.

First he coaxed Jackson to climb with him to about 2,000 feet. Next he got Jackson to orient his aircraft toward *Philippine Sea*. "OK, Ed," Crow told him reassuringly, "I'm taking you home. Ease to your right."

As Crow and Jackson reached the Yellow Sea, their radio cross talk was picked up by Jack Butts, VF-112's CO. His voice came faint but familiar: "Magnetic heading to ship is two-three-zero."

Crow coached Jackson to the correct heading. Meanwhile, though, Jackson was beginning to slip. The wind no longer seemed so harsh, and he felt himself floating in a kind of warm fog. Each time he began to drift off, Crow's voice knifed in: "Add power, Ed. Pull up! Pull up!" It made Jackson angry—just what was needed then to keep going.

In a clearer moment, Jackson had dismissed the idea of punching out. During a catapult launch (Jackson's first in a jet) off Hawaii, his ejection seat had malfunctioned and nearly killed him. The locking mechanism that secured the seat to the cockpit deck had failed just as Jackson left the deck; with the plane climbing, the ejection seat slid up its vertical rails, yanking Jackson's hands from the controls. Luckily, the canopy was open, but, still strapped to seat, Jackson now hung momentarily half in and half out of a plane that was about to crash. Fortunately, rather than escaping the rails, the seat slid back into the cockpit, allowing a shaken Jackson to grab the controls and stabilize the plane's flight. Although still in shock, he somehow managed to fly the F9F back to an island landing. Now, even if the seat were to perform flawlessly, Jackson lacked even the strength to try ejecting, never mind the endurance to survive a water landing.

***

As Jackson and Crow finally neared Phil Sea's flight pattern, another voice came on the circuit. "Keep talking to him, Dayl." It was Doug Hagwood, their division leader.

Crow calmly talked the fading Jackson through their descent. "Put your wheels and tailhook down. You're doing fine." For a moment,

Crow thought he had Jackson positioned for an approach, only to have him turn downwind instead of up. Below them Phil Sea's flight deck was as clear as possible, with the stack of aircraft moved well forward and the barriers in position.

"Flaps down now," Crow radioed when he finally talked Jackson—flying purely on reflexes now—back into the groove. Then, to his great relief, Crow heard yet another voice: "Ed, this is Les. Ed, I got you."

* * *

Les was LTJG L. K. "Les" Bruestle— one of Phil Sea's landing signal officers. Perched atop a tiny platform jutting over the flight deck's port quarter, Bruestle wielded two paddles framed in reflective fabric: semaphore flags to visually guide pilots through approach and touchdown.

The LSO's ultimate call was whether to give the "cut-power signal" (telling the pilot to cut off engine power and land) or the "wave off." To make the call he had to know the conditions of each oncoming plane and its pilot. Priority care went to aircraft returning low on fuel, wounded pilots, and damaged aircraft. In each case, a bad approach and a wave off might condemn plane and pilot to the drink. Alternatively, a botched landing (missing the deck entirely or hitting it so hard that the plane's tailhook leaped over each of the arresting cables) might kill the pilot, destroy his aircraft, and foul the flight deck in a jumble of wreckage, explosions, fire, and casualties. Smack center in the vortex of these possible nightmares were the pilot and the LSO; the LSO had to know his stuff, and the pilot had to trust the LSO unquestioningly to bring him home safely no matter what.

The LSO notwithstanding, of course, the pilot still had the controls. During the routine recovery of a flight of aircraft, each pilot was responsible for keeping the proper interval between him and the plane landing directly ahead. Thirty seconds was the standard interval. Poor intervals—too long, but especially too short—screwed up everything. Too long an interval prolonged recovery and made things harder for the planes behind; too short (not giving the plane ahead enough time to clear the landing area) was often the seed of a problem snowball: a wave off to another approach, consumption of precious fuel, a ratcheting of pilot tension, more work for the deck crew, and compression of the interval needed for respotting, refueling, rearming, and relaunching.

During the last ten seconds in the groove—routine or emergency—the pilot of a jet was all but committed to touch down or go around. Corrections in altitude, speed, or flight deck alignment were nearly impossible without the sort of panicky emergency maneuvers that all but ensured a bad landing or crash. Easing power to slow down, for example, could easily send pilot and plane into the aft edge of the flight deck (the rounddown), causing the jet to break in half at the cockpit, with flaming pieces caroming along the flight deck at more than a hundred miles per hour.

Prop planes, while slower and more forgiving, were hardly immune from such calamities. Duane Thorin's vantage from his plane guard station off *Philippine Sea*'s port quarter gave him a clear view of the sometimes calamitous ways things went wrong. Although the Sikorsky cockpit's wraparound greenhouse gave him a good panorama of ship and returning aircraft, Thorin learned to play closest attention to the plane making its final approach.

Once, with *Philippine Sea*'s stern down, Thorin saw the LSO signal an AD pilot to continue his approach, apparently expecting the stern to lift and hold steady just as it had through a series of small swells. But this time a much deeper trough approached; the ship's bow suddenly plunged, and the stern just as suddenly rose. When, as a result, the AD slammed early onto the deck, its tailhook grabbed a wire, but the impact literally snapped its engine loose. The engine, its propeller still turning, tumbled forward, trailing a stream of fuel that burned like a fuse straight back to the AD's tailhooked wreckage. In an instant, "hot papas," flight deck crewman wearing oversized fireproof asbestos suits, rushed into the flames while others advanced with fire hoses, removed explosive ordnance, or moved nearby planes clear of the fire. The AD pilot managed to escape only by leaping from the cockpit and outrunning the flames.

Another time an LSO "wave off" came too late for an F9F on a low approach. The jet's fuselage snapped in two, and its racing engine carried the forward fuselage up the deck, through the barrier, and into a flaming crash with a dozen planes parked forward. The F9F's pilot survived even this crash, although, in the midst of the turmoil, he was initially reported missing. Eventually he was found, sitting alone, shivering, and in shock in his squadron's ready room.

***

"Ed, this is the LSO," Bruestle radioed. "Don't answer. Just listen. Take it easy."

Les Bruestle's challenge in landing Ed Jackson was to translate paddle semaphore into voice commands. More than ever it required Jackson's implicit trust as well as the muscle memory to operate his cockpit controls.

Crow circled and watched, praying that the landing would succeed—for Jackson's sake, of course, but also for his own. He had less than six hundred pounds of fuel left, about enough to make one landing approach before he had to ditch.

"Too fast," Jackson heard Bruestle say, and he cut his speed. It felt as though Bruestle's voice was running like a current through his muscles.

"You're angling in too steep. Roll it out a bit." Jackson tried.

"You're in the slot now," Bruestle said calmly, but then with startling urgency: "High and to the right!" Obeying, Jackson adjusted.

There was silence—probably just a microsecond of it but enough to make Jackson think he'd overshot the deck—and then: "Cut it."

Without a thought, Ed Jackson dipped his nose and then pulled back on his stick to flare. He felt the arresting hook grab a wire. His plane lurched and stopped. He was down.

***

Ed Jackson had come in a little high and off centerline with only one flap down—the other had been taken out by the whipsawing cable. His tailhook had grabbed the number-nine wire. Emergency personnel (this time including the ship's flight surgeon) raced to the plane and carefully lifted him from the cockpit. "I can walk," Jackson insisted, only to fall before he took a step. Strapped to a stretcher, Jackson got his first clear view of the flight deck before he was hurried below to sick bay.

Jackson's landing was soon followed by the more routine recovery of Dayl Crow's airplane. Tail End Charlie to the last, Crow caught the third wire, his Panther returning with barely enough fuel to taxi forward.

Jackson, meanwhile, after taking thirty-six stitches and an emergency transfusion, spent the next several days in sick bay. Although the loss of blood had been nearly fatal and his wounds were ugly—his left cheek would remain a scarred mass of dead skin—there was miraculously no damage to either eye.

Jackson was back on his feet in days along with his plane. Although initial thought had been given to pushing the damaged F9F over the side, the shortage of serviceable jets gave it new life. Instead of being sent to the bottom of the Yellow Sea, the Panther went instead to the hangar deck for repair. Within a week it was ready to go back on the flight line, and so was Jackson—to take it up for a check flight before both were cleared to resume combat.

***

Jackson's, Crow's, and Bruestle's coolheaded performances added one more notch in the lore of both carrier aviators and the corps of LSOs who brought them home. Meanwhile, the Onionskin Angel that stood by during Jackson's and Crow's landings was a loaner—from battleship *Missouri* (BB-63)—and was flown by Sundberg instead of Thorin. Six days before, during a mail-delivery run to a fleet oiler entering the harbor at Sasebo (a port city on the western shore of Kyushu, Japan's southernmost main island), Duane Thorin had crashed *Philippine Sea's* only helicopter.

It was a freak accident, but one that nonetheless underlined the pinwheel's fragility. Just as the mail drop was nearing completion, Sasebo Harbor's air currents combined with the oiler's stack gases to abruptly disrupt the air cushion into which the rotor blades could "bite." The helicopter began to drop like a stone. To avoid crashing, Thorin simultaneously "redlined" the engine, flattened the rotor blades using pitch control, and allowed the craft to "torque" with the blades. After two complete turns of the fuselage—the helicopter's wheels now brushing the wave tops—rotor speed finally recovered enough for Thorin to reduce engine power. But it was too late—the redlined engine blew.

As the machine toppled and settled into the water, Thorin had the alertness and just enough stick control to lay it to starboard—where the cabin door was closed. The rotor blades spun several times through the water, tossing up sheets of spray as their fabric covering shredded and was stripped away. When the blades finally stopped churning, one spiked up and forward from the surface like a long skeletal arm.

Two passengers were aboard, both pilots from *Valley Forge*, and both quickly escaped through the open door of the passenger section. Thorin, meanwhile, picked up the remaining mail packet from beside his seat and followed. A small Japanese fishing boat hauled in the three men. Within minutes they were transferred to one of the harbor's pilot boats and from there to a U.S. Navy destroyer accompanying the oiler into Sasebo.

Thorin, still wet and still carrying the mail pouch he'd rescued, was immediately escorted to the destroyer CO's cabin.

"Jehovah's on the line," the CO said, with a nod toward a speaker on his desk. "He wants to talk to you."

"Jehovah" was the call sign for carrier division commander Rear Adm. Edward C. Ewen, one of Thorin's frequent passengers. "Chief Thorin, are you okay?"

Thorin assured Jehovah he was fine, just wet and embarrassed.

"Good," said Jehovah and then, "What happened to the packets you were carrying?"

"One was delivered, sir. I have the other one here in my hand."

There was a pause on the command net, long and pregnant enough, it seemed to Thorin, for a flag-level sigh of relief. Then, very deliberately, Jehovah was back on the line: "Chief Thorin, I authorize you now to give that packet to the man you are with."

The destroyer CO took the still dripping pouch, placed it deliberately in his cabin safe, and immediately closed and locked the safe's door.

"We're glad that you're okay, chief," Jehovah said. "We'll have you back with us very shortly. Jehovah out!"

***

Thorin soon learned that the contents of the mail pouch he rescued from the sinking helicopter were operational plans for the amphibious invasion of Inchon. The invasion, which kicked off September 15 (this was two days before Ed Jackson's "blind" landing and accounted for the fact that the North Koreans were crossing the Han River from south to north), marked a startling reversal for the North Korean invaders and a new direction in an "accordion war" of rolling advances and retreats up and down the peninsula's length. After a hot, disheartening, and beleaguered summer on the defensive, American troops under the banner of the United Nations and the overall command of Douglas MacArthur at last turned the tide on the NKPA's seemingly unstoppable juggernaut. The tide turner had been a bold strategic gamble devised and championed by MacArthur: an amphibious assault far behind enemy lines at Inchon, the west coast port closest to Seoul, South Korea's capital.

From the beginning, nobody thought much of MacArthur's plan, least of all the U.S. Navy. Inchon had no natural beach, one sunken ship could block the narrow channel into its harbor, and the currents through that channel fed daily tide swings of as much as thirty-two feet. Incoming landing craft could easily become stranded on mud. The site looked so unpromising that, late in August, U.S. Navy chief of staff Adm. Forrest Sherman was dispatched to Tokyo in an effort to dissuade MacArthur. But the Supreme Commander Allied Forces in Japan (SCAP) was determined. "We shall land at Inchon," he intoned, "and I shall crush them."

Though Sherman still had his doubts—"I wish I had that man's optimism," Sherman was heard to say after the meeting—MacArthur got both Navy cooperation and the go-ahead to proceed. The result, an assault by 13,000 U.S. marines against marginal resistance (and with light casualties), caught the North Koreans completely by surprise. The stroke—without doubt MacArthur's finest hour—enabled the U.S. Eighth Army, trapped inside an ever-shrinking perimeter fronting the port city of Pusan at Korea's southeast tip, to break out and steamroll north, with the overextended NKPA collapsing in disarray before it.

The Marine 1st Division (the muscle of X Corps that also included U.S. Army units), after successfully spearheading this assault, had been withdrawn and transported to the opposite coast for a landing at Wonsan, North Korea's principal east coast port. But they arrived offshore behind the northward thrust of Eighth Army, and even the arrival of Bob Hope's frontline USO troop. ("It was the first time," Hope quipped, "that I ever had to wait for the marines.")

***

That same September, still operating from the Yellow Sea, *Philippine Sea*'s pilots flew strikes on the Yalu River bridges that linked North Korea with Chinese Communist Manchuria. For most pilots, it was another reminder of just how difficult it was to destroy a bridge from the air, even when the structure was poorly defended. Bridge floorings, though easily hit, were also easily replaced, while their vulnerable points—trusses, supports, and abutments—were hard to pinpoint with bombs.[1] It required extremely low flying and multiple bomb runs to have an impact.

In this case it also required added finesse: being careful to avoid entering Chinese airspace while keeping a weather eye for Chinese MiGs pouncing from the havens of Manchurian bases. On September 30 a VF-113 pilot spotted a Russian-built MiG-15 jet fighter in the skies some thirty miles northwest of Seoul: a talisman of what might be lurking to challenge U.S. air supremacy as its strikes flirted with Chinese airspace. Barely a month later, VF-111 squadron skipper Lt. W. T. Amen shot down a MiG-15, scoring the first Navy kill in jet aerial combat.

5

OTHER EVERESTS

AFTER A MIDOCEAN stop at Pearl Harbor, where CVG-3 aviators squeezed in three days of operational flying (their last chance before the real thing), the *Leyte* task group headed for the western Pacific. Its first destination was a port call in Yokosuka, a city south of Tokyo and Yokohama on Honshu, the biggest of Japan's home islands.

Yokosuka was one of two Japanese ports used by Task Force 77 ships. The other was Sasebo, where, lore held, the private dining room at Sasebo Naval Base's Officers' Club—planning site for the December 1941 Pearl Harbor attack—was now an Allied officers' mess. If so, it was another humbling image of a ruined imperial empire, though hardly the most astonishing aspect of Japan's remarkable fall—or its equally remarkable transformation. Indeed, for the Pacific-war veterans aboard *Leyte* (and other ships new to Task Force 77), who had never set foot in Japan, the sights, sounds, and atmosphere of Yokosuka, Sasebo, and other Japanese cities were causes for equal measures of pity and wonder.

When it came to Japan, America (now undisputed ruler of the Land of the Rising Sun) was in the midst of its own transformation—at least in attitude. Just a few years before, military servicemen (indeed, all of America) had been steeped in propaganda lore about the subhuman "monkey men" of Japan. America's incarceration of more than a hundred thousand Japanese American citizens and resident aliens was an indication of the single-monochrome brush with which the Japanese race was painted. The attitude was bolstered by the never-surrender savagery that Japanese soldiers had displayed during scores of island invasions—and, in the very last days of the war, the inexplicable determination of Japan's aerial kamikazes.

While the minds of the newest and youngest Navy recruits were more amenable to postwar reeducation about the Japanese, for many Navy war veterans (including those called back from the reserves) the reindoctrination effort was, to say the least, a hard sell: that, for example, Japanese brutality and fanaticism were products of the "heat of wartime emotions," or that wartime atrocities were the regrettable outbursts by men subjected to a life of repression.

In fact, according to one postwar civil affairs guide, when it came to "other traits of character [like] reliability, ingenuity, industriousness, thrift, bravery, aggressiveness, honesty . . . the average Japanese displays these characteristics in about the same manner and measure as other people in other lands."[1] It was time, they were being told, to redirect animus once reserved for the Japanese onto Communists in general and North Koreans in particular.

***

For their parts, in this sixth year of U.S. occupation, Japan, its government, and its people had built a survival culture aimed at servicing their conquerors while adopting new patterns of authority and norms of behavior. Under the administration of Douglas MacArthur, Supreme Commander Allied Forces, Japan had been radically and fundamentally transformed to "SCAPan."

During the war, the notion of "one hundred million Japanese hearts beating as one" had fed stereotypes of a robotic and fanatic population. Much of Japan's ultranationalism and regimentation had since fallen away, opening the way for its population to think, say, and do things in ways that had been impossible under the militarists. American servicemen in the occupation forces had already witnessed this, although the average GI, airman, and sailor saw just the surface layers of this evolving culture and its catering to occupiers, tourists, and shore-leave hedonists.

The first and crudest stages of this evolution had followed fast on the heels of defeat. Rumors that the American conquerors, once ashore on the sacred home islands, would systematically rape all of Japan's women spread like wildfire—in no small part because of awareness of the rapacity demonstrated by its own troops against populations in China and Korea. In hopes of staving off this imagined cataclysm (and with the government's explicit endorsement and discrete financing), procurer "entrepreneurs" established a series of "comfort facilities," among the first of them in the Tokyo-Yokohama area. The facilities were not unprecedented; similar "pleasure quarters" to accommodate the "water trade" had been set up a century before when U.S. Navy commodore Matthew Perry had forced Japan out of its seclusion.

The first Recreation and Amusement Association (RAA) facilities opened at the end of August 1945 in Tokyo's Ōmori district, just in time for the arrival of the occupation force's lead elements. RAA facilities quickly spread to twenty Japanese cities (with access to separate facilities designated for officers, white enlisted men, and black enlisted men) before just as quickly being ordered to close—ostensibly because "public prostitution" was undemocratic and demeaning, but just as likely because of soaring rates of "state-sponsored" venereal disease.

In their place, at least for officers, SCAP brass substituted access to the exquisite suites and gardens of elite—but isolated—Japanese resort hotels. Near Tokyo it was the Fuji-san, perched high on a mountain with commanding views of Mount Fuji. For many U.S. officers, such R&R (rest and recreation) hotels were perfect lures: plush accommodations, fine food and drinks, and access to superb summer and winter recreation facilities, all at below-bargain prices. Although a challenge to reach (often by a combination of taxi, overnight train, and, during winter, a tracked "snow weasel" up steep icy roads to the hotel's lobby entrance) because of their remote locations and limited R&R time, the hotels' ambiance satisfied both lodgers (as a chance to fully unwind from combat stresses) and SCAP authorities (as a means of luring Americans away from their sometimes combustible encounters with port cities' facilities and citizens).

For enlisted sailors and officers with earthier appetites, government-sponsored RAAs gave way to more traditional "red-line" districts (so-called because of their demarcations on city maps used by police) in which, over time, an estimated 55,000 to 70,000 full- and part-time prostitutes—called *panpans*—plied their trade.[2] Remembered for their bright lipstick, nail polish, flashy possessions, and sharp clothes, these women epitomized Japan's postwar urban nightscapes in much the way that bar girls symbolized urban Saigon during the Vietnam War a generation later.

The women (who even devised their own polyglot vernacular called "panglish" or "SCAPanese") had different specialties and different names to go with them: A prostitute who flitted from customer to customer was called a *batafurai* (butterfly), while a woman loyal to one American was called an *onrii wan* (only one).[3] Although condemned by much of society—and even by many of their patrons—the women of these districts (sometimes called *shimas*, literally "islands" in Japanese) also seemed attractively bold and subversive, as if they alone, through their sensuality, had transcended race barriers, at least in the furtive after-hours lives of the occupiers. As one American historian put it, "Their self-indulgent carnality was as sharp a repudiation as could be imagined of the stultifying austerity and discipline the [Japanese] militarists had demanded."[4]

The impact of the occupation, not so subtly displayed in the red-line *shimas*, was just as evident in a rampant gangster-infused black-market economy. Sometimes euphemistically called the "free," "open-sky," or even "blue-sky" market, for many Japanese the black market was the only market. Initially, a lot of the trade was in the selling of household treasures for money and food but eventually expanded to include food supplies from the countryside, fish from seaside villages, and even military stockpiles, both Japanese and American. In August, when carrier *Philippine Sea* had first pulled into Sasebo, Duane Thorin had flown over the harbor, noticing bomb craters and burned-out neighborhoods, but also marveling at the antlike speed and efficiency of Japanese removing packing crates and other discards from the Navy's docks.

Japan's big changes were also mirrored in smaller but just as fundamental ways, such as play activity in children. Though few children in any nation had commercial toys in the late 1940s, one produced by a Kyoto toy maker right after the war caught on quickly in Japan. It was a ten-centimeter replica of an American jeep. Jeeps were easily associated with the chewing gum and chocolate handed out by GIs and sailors, among the few treats that most postwar Japanese children ever received. Children picked up common catchwords and phrases besides *jeep* and used them like mantras: *hello*, *good-bye*, and *give me chocolate*. For good or ill, they also learned to emulate servicemen's public style and behavior. Harmless enough, boys learned to fold newspapers into GI-style caps instead of traditional samurai helmets; however, another popular activity for boys and girls was *panpan asobi*—prostitute play during which little boys, often wearing GI-style paper hats, walked arm in arm with little primping girls.[5]

***

In early October, when *Leyte* finally joined Task Force 77 in the Sea of Japan, it marked the first time four large *Essex*-class carriers had operated together since the war in the Pacific. VF-32 flew its first air strike over Wonsan on October 10. Most strikes, including this first one, consisted of at least a division: four aircraft composed of two two-plane sections. The first strike mission for Jesse Brown, Tom Hudner, and Bill Koenig came the next day: two VF-32 divisions (eight aircraft) joined by divisions of Skyraiders and "top-cover" Panthers targeting North Korean shore gun installations in Wonsan Harbor— the run-up to the planned Marine amphibious landing soon outpaced by the North Korean's pell-mell retreat after the mid-September Inchon invasion.

During the dawn briefing, VF-32's Doug Neill admonished his aviators: "If a plane goes down, that's one down. We don't need any Hollywood stuff." No grandstanding heroics, in other words. "If we lose one, that's one. We can't afford to lose two."

Most knew what the Hollywood reference meant. During one scene in *Fighter Pilot*, a 1948 film about the air war in Europe, an Army Air Force pilot lands behind enemy lines, rescues a downed squadron mate, and then takes off with guns blazing. It was a ridiculous and most unlikely stunt.

***

October was the harvest season in Korea, but already cold. There was a frigid sting to the wind that whipped across *Leyte*'s flight deck, and the airdales wore buttoned-up jackets and heavy gloves. Strike pilots likewise dressed for the elements.

Climbing to the flight deck from VF-32's ready room, Brown was sweating profusely by the time he had corseted himself in the Corsair's cockpit. Helped by his plane captain, Brown adjusted his harness straps and lashed his flight board to his right knee.

When the flight deck bullhorn blared, "Start your engines!" the Fox flag was hoisted. The deck was almost instantly filled with the throbbing of Corsair engines and the mad whir of propellers encased in halos of vapor. Brown completed his cockpit check and, when he reached fly one, locked his brakes and applied full power.

Brown's F4U was last in the mission's first division, making him the fourth airplane off the deck. When the launch officer finally dropped his checkered flag, Brown's Corsair lurched forward, rumbling along four hundred feet of deck (a race for power as much as for speed) before gaining the sky. Behind him the next four Corsairs (including Hudner's) were already lining up. The bigger, slower, and more heavily armed ADs were next, followed, finally, by the catapult launch of the jets.

After assembling at higher altitude, the four Corsairs nosed west. Approaching the coast-in point they spread out, armed bombs and rockets, and tested machine guns. Once they were over Wonsan, the division leader, VF-32's XO Dick Cevoli, established communication with the flight controller, himself flying in a twin-engine R4D—the Navy version of the Douglas DC-3. After Cevoli relayed the division's "package" to the controller ("four Corsairs, each carrying one 500-pound bomb, eight 5-inch rockets and a full load of ammo"), the planes circled until he gave them target coordinates on a hilltop gun emplacement.

And so, just two days shy of his twenty-fourth birthday, Jesse Brown's war began. He'd felt a claw of anxiety ever since waking up that morning with the uncertainty of what he would do when the moment came. Now there was surprisingly little room for panic. In a very real way, the mission's routine, its elements practiced so many times before, took over. He had taken off when his turn came, formed up with his division, stayed in formation en route, and now, regardless of anxiety or fear, would simply make a run when his turn came.

While the Corsairs were better suited for ground-support missions than the "short-legged" jets, they had their own Achilles' heels. They were old aircraft by now: Many had already gone through their fourth overhaul cycle, one more cycle than prescribed in the original aircraft design specs. And, of course, that original design was for a fighter aircraft, not a dive-bomber. The Corsairs weren't equipped with air brakes to slow airspeed during steep dives. On occasion pilots lowered their wheels to create impromptu dive brakes only to learn that steep approaches also risked dropping the bomb load directly into the propeller. Most pilots accordingly used shallow thirty-degree dives. Even then the Corsairs could develop too much airspeed, forcing pilots to pull out early, often with the target passing out of sight before bomb release. Although the Corsair's cockpit was shielded by armor and its fuel tanks were self-sealing (a key advantage over Japanese aircraft in the Pacific war), its engine's vital oiler coolers were installed in the wings, making the aircraft especially vulnerable to ground fire (even small-arms rounds) and shrapnel from below.

***

Following the division's lead planes, Brown pushed his nose over and swept down to drop his five hundred–pound bomb. Diving lower, the pilots spotted the first ground flashes from antiaircraft fire and the black aerial puffs as rounds exploded on either side. Brown released—"pickled"—the bomb (by pressing a button atop the pistol grip of his control stick) and pulled back on the stick. He climbed back to safer altitude and got ready for the next run—HVARs first and then strafing.

Brown's wingman, Bill Koenig, meanwhile, had spotted a camouflaged truck and swept down, intending to take it out with a wing rocket. Koenig came in low and flat—what squadron CO Doug Neill was forever admonishing his pilots never to do. He fired a single HVAR and quickly pulled up through the cloud from the explosion—a thick, dark brew of smoke, shrapnel, and splattering mud.

The division then worked over additional ground targets around Wonsan before rendezvousing off the coast with other "feet-wet" strike units and returning to *Leyte*. It was a good inaugural mission—everyone launched also returned. Because his Corsair was so splattered (a splotch of mud had even blacked out his wing gun camera), Bill Koenig was "invited" by CAG to land last. As soon as he touched down, a fire crew raced out to hose down Koenig's U-bird as well as the flight deck across which, like a messy toddler, he'd tracked mud.

***

On through the next weeks, *Leyte's* Corsairs, Panthers, and Skyraiders flew missions on target locations with names like Chongjin, Hapsu, Hyesan, and Kilchu. All the while, the UN troops rolled north toward the Yalu River, the dividing line between North Korea and Manchuria.

The pattern of carrier operations, CVG-3's veteran pilots came to find out, was much different from the near-legendary days of Task Forces 38 and 58 under Bull Halsey and Raymond Spruance. World War II carrier tasks groups had specialized in making surprise high-speed runs to the vicinity of Japanese target objectives. For air squadrons this translated to two-month cycles of training, refitting, and planning culminating in four or five days of intense air combat—battling Japanese aircraft, attacking Japanese ships, and striking ground targets—before moving into another cycle and on to another objective.

Task Force 77's flight operations were to be more like factory shifts—not nearly as exciting but, in their own way, equally or more dangerous because of day-in and day-out exposure. For now at least, with the front lines fluid, the missions varied: sometimes troop CAS, sometimes preplanned strikes, and sometimes "armed reconnaissance"—high-speed, low-level trolling for targets of opportunity.

The operations actually involved three "shift" cycles, the longest of which were the seven-month Task Force 77 deployments—what *Leyte* was just beginning—though in truncated form.* Deployments were seemingly endless stretches for young men in a seaborne world with relatively few off-hour diversions and limited communications (mostly letters) with lives, loves, and families back home.

For some sailors, even this expected term of separation and tedium was being doubled through a fiendish process called "cross-decking." When a carrier finished its deployment and sailed Stateside, some key officers and enlisted specialists—especially ship's engineers and flight

---

* Having been diverted two months into its Sixth Fleet deployment in the Mediterranean, *Leyte's* Korean War deployment would last five, not seven, months.

deck crews—stayed behind where, after a short leave period, they would cross-deck to another carrier just beginning its deployment. Although crippling to morale, there were scant manpower alternatives to these back-to-back tours until mobilization and training caught up with operational needs.

Within the seven-month deployment shift, carriers and air groups worked thirty-day-at-sea cycles broken further into four-day stretches. Within these stretches, three consecutive days of flight operations would be followed by a fourth day of replenishment—the restocking of supplies, ammunition, and especially fuel—with an underway replenishment group (URG) ship waiting fifty miles east of the carrier group.

Although there were no flight operations on this fourth day, there was little respite for most ship or flight operations personnel. While ship's company loaded ammunition, transferred stores, and pumped fuel, air group mechanics worked furiously to repair damaged aircraft and flight deck crews used their "downtime" to perform essential maintenance on catapults and other crucial flight deck equipment. The only individuals who got any meaningful rest were the squadron pilots. At five o'clock on the eve of replenishment day, flight surgeons made the rounds of the squadron ready rooms, delivering to each two bottles of "medicinal spirits" (alcohol consumption aboard ship was otherwise prohibited, at least officially), one containing bourbon and the other scotch. When not sleeping—another replenishment-day favorite—pilots could lounge in the ready rooms, screening movie reels on a 16mm projector, munching popcorn, and quietly getting stewed.

***

At the end of October, *Leyte*, in company with *Valley Forge* and *Philippine Sea*, detached from Task Force 77 and sailed for Japan. It marked the end of thirty days at sea and the beginning of a roughly weeklong period of rest and recreation. As *Leyte* and *Valley Forge* rode at anchor off Sasebo (*Philippine Sea* went onto Yokosuka to off-load munitions in preparation for a return to the States), the conflict seemed both far away and, more important, nearing its end. The NKPA, by all accounts, was beating a chaotic retreat toward (and probably across) the Yalu. General MacArthur predicted it would all be over by year's end with many troops home by Christmas.

Then, as was becoming sort of a pattern when it came to Korea, assumptions and expectations abruptly jumped the rails. During the evening of November 4, shore leave was abruptly canceled, and all Task Force 77 personnel ashore in Sasebo and Yokosuka were recalled—whether from sightseeing, shopping, red-line carousing, or *panpan* embraces—and ordered back to their ships. The very next morning, *Leyte*, *Valley Forge*, and their escorts lifted anchors and steamed back into the Sea of Japan. *Philippine Sea*, her journey home postponed, followed the next day. Sensing that a serious Chinese Communist intervention was under way, General MacArthur, without consulting leaders in Washington, had ordered intensified bombing of the Yalu bridges.

***

Liberty and leaves were simultaneously being canceled for nearly all West Coast Navy aviators and ground crews, including those at NAS Alameda across the bay from San Francisco. Personnel were placed on standby and told to get ready for immediate deployment to Korea.

A recent transfer to Alameda and Air Group 2 was Aviation Midshipman Joe Akagi. Akagi had completed Advanced Flight Training in Pensacola, received his Wings of Gold in October, and then gone on to advanced training as a ground-attack specialist flying the Corsair. Initially assigned to the Fleet Air Service Squadron at North Island near San Diego, Akagi had wangled an assignment to Alameda in hopes of attaching to a CVG-2 Corsair squadron. He had succeeded, only to learn that while the group would be readying for Korean deployment, no aviation midshipmen would be going along.

Instead, Akagi got orders to VF-194, another Corsair squadron. VF-194, nicknamed the Yellow Devils, although nominally part of Air Group 19, was being orphaned as the group prepared for Korean deployment on *Princeton* (CV-37). Heretofore, U.S. Navy air groups deployed with five squadrons and usually on the same carrier, but the resource pinch and the nature of air-combat operations in Korea were forcing changes. One trend was the use of specialized air detachments—small units drawn from squadrons "configured" (in Navy parlance) to perform such roles as antisubmarine warfare, night operations, and high-altitude photo reconnaissance. Adding planes from these detachments to the limited flight deck and hangar space on *Essex*-class carriers in effect crowded out a fifth squadron. VF-194, one of CVG-19's two Corsair squadrons, was, for now at least, the "odd squadron out."

But substituting air detachments for a squadron was robbing Peter to pay Paul—hardly a solution to overall manpower shortages. Aircraft carriers were being rushed out of mothballs. Air groups were needed to fill out their flight decks.

***

Back on station in the Sea of Japan, VF-32's strike missions took on new intensity and urgency over a landscape that the pilots considered almost unearthly. Navigation and target spotting were tricky even for the best-planned missions. The maps of North Korea the pilots used were sometimes based on old or sketchy information dating to Japan's occupation of Korea. More often they depended on reconnaissance photos, but even with using those it was guesswork. North Korea consisted for the most part of primitive preindustrial terrain where there were few navigational aids or reliable reference landmarks. Instead, pilots had to dead reckon across a landscape of barren mountains, narrow rivers, nameless villages, and dirt roads.

The riskiest missions, of course, were along the Yalu, where, tapping their limitless supplies of manpower, the Communists continued to repair and resurrect bridge crossings. Pilots scrupulously avoided straying into Chinese airspace by making bombing runs along the axis of the river, which made precision bombing nearly impossible and made the aircraft fatter targets for enemy gunners on the ground.

Flying up north also increased the chance that the props might stumble into duels with China's fast and maneuverable MiG jets. Although Panther jets flew top cover for the Corsairs and Skyraiders, MiGs could strike with impunity from bases just beyond the Yalu. As they lined up Yalu targets, VF-32 pilots often saw the silver glints of MiG fuselages rising from Manchurian air bases to confront them. MiG pilots knew that the Panthers' time over target would be limited; if things got tight, the Chinese (and, many suspected, Russian) pilots could bug out, knowing the Americans could not pursue them across the border.

In their recco (reconnaissance) missions CVG-3 pilots saw something in its way even more ominous than the Yalu MiGs: ever-larger groups of Chinese soldiers on the North Korean side of the river infiltrating south just as the American and South Korean troops continued their headlong rush north. It gave all of them a sense of an impending collision. Day after day they included Chinese troop sightings in their after-action reports and debriefings, but it seemed, amid the still heady optimism and still highly anticipated conclusion of the war, that no one was willing to take notice.

***

Jesse Brown's wingman for most missions was his roommate, LTJG Bill Koenig. Although Koenig nominally outranked his section leader, Brown had earned his wings earlier and had more flight experience.

It was one more sign that Jesse Brown had found his way into the fabric of VF-32. He remained the U.S. Navy's only black pilot, and Navy public relations types never lost the opportunity for photo opportunities: Ens. Jesse Brown on the flight deck, checking out the ordnance package on his Corsair, playing acey-deucey in the wardroom. Always his black face framed by white faces. There also seemed no end to the press releases: Jesse Brown, the first black fighter pilot, the first in Korea, the first this, the first that. It was an approach almost calculated to impede his becoming just another naval aviator.

Brown did benefit from a crucial but—on the face of it—unlikely ally. *Leyte's* skipper was Capt. Thomas U. Sisson Jr., like Jesse Brown a native of Mississippi, but (very unlike Brown) also the scion of a family with deep patrician roots. Sisson's father, who died in 1923, had been a product of the post-Reconstruction South, a lawyer, and a six-term Democratic—and staunch segregationist—congressman. The younger Sisson, a Naval Academy graduate with an aviation background, had the manners, speech, and bearing of a courtly southerner—but his firm, unwavering insistence on Brown's rightful place in the structure and community of *Leyte* broke the apparent mold. Sisson made it clear that Brown would suffer no outward indignities in the actions or words of *Leyte's* officers and petty officers.

And, at the same time, just as firmly, something else worked in Brown's favor. As he piled up flight hours, launches, recoveries, and sorties, the same Navy traditions that had so fiercely excluded him now worked relentlessly in his favor to include him. The Navy, but more important VF-32, measured Jesse Brown in the only way they knew how. If he flew well, then he moved up in the pecking order. When new pilots joined, Brown moved a notch higher: a squadron veteran and then a section leader, with Bill Koenig flying on his wing instead of Brown on Koenig's.

This support also spilled ashore, where squadron personnel were fiercely protective of Brown when it came to accommodations in shopping, restaurants, and other facilities—or to the disapproving stares or callous actions of civilians or other military personnel. VF-32 was not without its internal cliques and social distinctions. Tom Hudner, for example, was both a lieutenant junior grade and a product of the bonding rigors of Annapolis; thus, he was more apt to be close with other JGs and with fellow Trade School graduates. By all appearances life in the midst of war seemed, for once in Jesse Brown's arduous and convoluted race-determined life, relatively straightforward. He was respected and (even beyond the circle of his marriage, family, and childhood friends) embraced as a comrade.

***

Still, Jesse Brown had trouble sleeping. Late on December 3, when he'd crawled exhausted into his rack on the eve of a scheduled afternoon mission, his mind's eye kept looping a scene from the day's mission: a Chinese soldier caught on the fringes of a napalm blast, running for his life, his back wrapped in flame. It was the type of unsettling vision that could gnaw at the delicate balance between confident certainty and deep remorse.

To it was added the equally unsettling possibility of never returning home. Although CVG-3 had been relatively lucky as to casualties, there had been one loss that sent a chill up the spine of nearly every aviator. On November 11, Lt. (jg) Roland Batson, a pilot attached to *Leyte*'s VC-35 detachment of night flight–equipped Skyraiders, was lost during a bridge strike near Chongjin. Batson had crash-landed about one mile north-northeast of Kwick-tong; he was spotted walk-ing away from his aircraft, but he was never seen again.

There was an unspoken pact among combat pilots: If you are down, we will come get you. And, with it, the corollary: You will do the same for me. But how could that pact hold in the face of such appalling conditions on the ground and at sea?

It was the cumulative weight of these factors that convinced Brown he would be leaving the Navy and returning to Ohio State when his active-duty commitment was up the following year. He'd been married for three years and in all that time had seen very little of Daisy—and even less of his new daughter, Pamela.

Brown had already reached the summit of one Everest: his Navy wings. But it was a young man's Everest, more precisely a young black man's Everest. He had climbed an unprecedented, almost unimagin-able, pinnacle. And it was not so much the climbing that made it that way. It was the resistance—the time taken by others (involved, of course, in their own climbs) to frustrate him, slow him down, even stop him.

Now, he realized, there were only more pinnacles ahead. Navy avia-tion had given ground: first, because he'd displayed the unreasonable audacity to presume it would, and then because he'd demonstrated the skills that were, it turned out, the keys, the passwords, the secret signs, and handshakes to the brotherhood of naval aviation. For some who witnessed these skills (as Bill Zastri had two years before when he chimed in for Brown before Summary Flight Board in Pensacola), it was almost as if, despite all that they might have been "carefully taught" about the inferiority of other races and cultures, they saw something of themselves. It was almost as if they couldn't resist bring-ing Jesse Brown across the threshold.

But he now had doubts if this minor miracle would ever be re-peated if he made the Navy his career. It was, at best, even for the anointed, a cutthroat business climbing through the officer ranks. It was made somewhat easier now because of the war, but that was a whole other factor. Knowing aviators—comrades and friends—who'd crashed and died made Jesse Brown a realist. In a way, he was playing a high-stakes poker game. He'd bet his chips. If the hands continued to play out during the next months, that would be the time to fold and go on to other "Everests"—but ones climbed with friends and, most important, with Daisy and Pamela.

In a long postmidnight letter to Daisy, Jesse Brown poured out some of his thoughts:

> The last few days we've been doing quite a bit of flying, trying to help slow down the Chinese Communists and to give support to some Marines who were surrounded when the Chinese launched their big drive. Knowing that he's helping those poor guys on the ground, I think every pilot would fly until he dropped in his tracks. This morning we were flying in weather so bad we could hardly see each other at times—snowing—yet the air was full of planes. Navy planes for close support of the troops. Air Force transports dropping supplies by parachute, etc. We know a few Marine officers down on the ground because they were with us in the Med. But my biggest hope still is that somehow, thru the mercy of God, this war can come to a close without us getting into an all-out war with China.
>
> Darling, heaven alone can know how much I need you and how badly I want to see you.
>
> Often when I climb into my rack at night all the loneliness of the day seems to descend upon me and I'm haunted by seemingly a thousand sweet memories of you. Then all the tears that I've been holding back all day long refuse to be held any longer, and I just lay there in loneliness and misery and cry my heart out.
>
> Don't be discouraged, Angel, believe in God and believe in Him with all your might and I know that things will work out all right. We need Him now like never before. Have faith with me, darling, and He'll see us thru and we'll be together again before long too.
>
> Darling, I'm going to close now and climb in the rack. I honestly dread going to bed, but I usually dream of you, so I'll manage to make it until we'll share our bed together again—darling, pray that it'll be soon. I have to fly tomorrow. But so far as that goes my heart hasn't been down to earth since the first time you kissed me, and when you love me you "send" it clear out-of-this-world.
>
> I'll write again as soon as I can. I'll love you forever.
> Your devoted husband
> lovingly and completely yours
> forever
> Jesse

6

IROQUOIS FLIGHT

HELP X CORPS—the 5th and 7th Marines and 31st Army GIs—break out from Chosin. In the first days of December 1950 that was the sole mission for Task Force 77's pilots and planes, as it was for Marine and Air Force squadrons. Round-the-clock air strikes on six Chinese Communist divisions, perhaps as many as 60,000 enemy soldiers: This was the gauntlet through which the 15,000 frostbitten 1st Division Marines and 7th Division GIs were fighting en route from the rim of Chosin Reservoir seventy-five miles south to the port of Hungnam.

The divisions were half of a self-styled "People's Volunteer Army" led by fifty-two-year-old Peng The-huai. Peng, born into an impoverished peasant family, had become a soldier at eighteen, first in the Hunan Provincial Army, then in Chiang Kai-shek's Nationalist Army. Though promoted to regimental commander, Peng became increasingly disillusioned with Chiang. He joined the Communist Party in 1928 and six years later aligned himself with Mao.

Peng, like Mao, was convinced that the United States, once at the Yalu, would inevitably find an excuse to invade China. "Sooner or later the tiger devours the man; the timing only depends on the tiger's hunger."[1] To combat the tiger and thereby "help the future construction of the fatherland," Peng employed the same tactics he'd devised for the already legendary "Battle of a Hundred Regiments," a massive offensive that had stunned the Japanese in central China a decade before: this time using stealth to move into positions across the Yalu, engaging the enemy in dual efforts to gain fighting experience and thin the opponent's ranks, and then withdrawing to lure the tiger forward before finally springing the trap.

It was a trap whose jaws had been widening through all of November, and, as it sprung, Americans for once cast their uninterrupted gaze toward a war they would rather have ignored. In late November reports in Stateside newspapers like the *New York Herald Tribune* were announcing a potential disaster. "U.N. forces are now paying the price for the unsound decision to launch an offensive north of the peninsula's narrow neck," wrote *Herald Tribune* correspondent Homer Bigart. "The overall picture is grim."[2] Several days later the worst fears were realized.

***

The marines, operating as part of X Corps, had been ordered by Army general Edward "Ned" Almond, X Corps commander and a MacArthur protégé (who doubled as SCAP chief of staff), to kick off a drive northwest, beginning November 27, to link up with Eighth Army troops eighty miles away on the western flank of the peninsula. Suspecting a trap, Maj. Gen. Oliver Prince Smith, Marine 1st Division commander, followed orders but also made it his job "not to go too far out on a limb."

Smith, a ramrod-straight Texan, thirty-three years a marine and sometimes called "professor" because he'd attended L'École Supérieure de Guerre while assigned to the U.S. Embassy in France, had loathed his commander since the day Almond (a four-star general) called Smith (a three-star general) "Son" despite Smith's being just ten months younger. Before Inchon, Almond had also been dismissive of the skill and planning required for amphibious assaults, but neither insults nor loathing fueled Smith's caution. What did were his memories of the murderous 1944 assault on the Japanese-held island of Peleliu. As the 1st's assistant division commander for a scheduled three-day operation that stretched for a month and cost the lives of more than a thousand marines, Smith had learned never to underestimate (as the marines had then) his Asian enemy's fighting capacity, intelligence, or skills in deception.

The Chinese had in truth set a formidable trap. There were as many as 150,000 Chinese troops on the eastern front, but through all of November they remained concealed and illusive, striking at American lead elements and then melting away. Peng was certain that persistent baiting would inevitably lure the Americans and South Koreans into "pre-selected killing zones."

When the Chinese finally struck, the marines, despite their caution, were out on a limb that stretched, depending how you measured it, anywhere from sixty-five to seventy-five miles. The limb in fact was actually a thin, perilous branch—a single mountain road surrounded by Chinese-held high ground and locked in subzero temperatures. The marines themselves looked, in the words of journalist-historian David Halberstam, "like Ancient Mariners who had sailed too close to the North Pole, all of them bearded; their beards, filled with ice shavings."[3]

Despite their spectral appearance, they fought like marines, obstinate enough to act as if they were not retreating. In the midst of the fighting, when a journalist asked Smith what he thought of the retreat from Chosin, the general quickly snapped back: "Retreat, hell, we're simply attacking in another direction."

***

An even bigger trap was waiting on the western front where assaults by 250,000 People's Volunteers staggered Eighth Army. The U.S. Army's 2d Infantry Division's forced withdrawal down a single road culminated in a horrendous traffic jam and a deadly enfilade of Chinese Communist rifle, machine gun, mortar, and light artillery fire. The Army's 24th and 25th Divisions—battered but still intact—also fell back.

On November 28 MacArthur cabled the Pentagon from Tokyo: "We face an entirely new war." Convening an expanded session of the National Security Council in the wake of what Joint Chiefs of Staff head Gen. Omar Bradley termed MacArthur's "rather hysterical" cable, President Harry Truman—himself calm—admitted, "This is the worst situation we have had yet." While no specific decisions were made at the session, the strategic posture going forward was clear: Avoid war with the Soviets. "We must consider Korea not in isolation," Secretary of State Dean Acheson warned others at the meeting, "but in the worldwide problem of confronting the Soviet Union as an antagonist."

To prevent World War III, Acheson concluded, the United States had to somehow end its involvement on the Asian mainland. His reasoning was basic, almost elemental: "We can't defeat the Chinese in Korea. They can put more in than we can."[4]

Meanwhile, after alerting the Pentagon, MacArthur had returned his attention to matters in the field. He conferred with his two field commanders—Ned Almond of X Corps and Eighth Army's Gen. Walton Walker—in a face-to-face meeting that stretched into the early morning of November 29. While Almond clung to his optimistic assertion that the offensive thrust toward the Yalu from Chosin could continue, Walker, his more seasoned and battle-tested counterpart, was more pragmatic about their plight. In previous days, despite his own orders to continue advancing north, Walker had sensed the trap, even relaying a message to one infantry commander to pull back immediately if "he smells Chinese chow."[5]

***

Eighth Army commander Walton H. "Johnnie" Walker, then just days short of his sixty-first birthday, had long been the "odd man out" when it came to MacArthur's fighting strategy in Korea. Walker (the nickname "Johnnie" was a nod to the general's favored brand of Scotch) had developed enduring friendships with Dwight Eisenhower (both had skirmished with Pancho Villa along the Mexican border just before the Great War) and George C. Marshall and was a devoted acolyte of Gen. George S. Patton—three allegiances that excluded him from the orbit of MacArthur's "Bataan Gang."

During the First World War Walker had earned two Silver Stars in the Meuse-Argonne. Later, as a Third Army Corps commander in the Second World War, Walker had spearheaded Patton's dash across France in the late summer and fall of 1944 and later pushed forward to relieve embattled GIs at the Battle of the Bulge. Noted—as was his boss—for propelling his jeep with reckless speed, Walker was always positioned close to his leading tank columns. At war's end, Patton had lauded Walker as "my fightingest son-of-a-bitch."

Walker's World War II résumé helped him not a bit when, fleeing a desk job, he took command of Eighth Army, MacArthur's American occupation force in Japan. Walker's simultaneous efforts to satisfy

MacArthur and rehabilitate Eighth Army (little more than a soft, minimally trained, underequipped constabulary when he took command in 1948) both came up short. Eighth Army (consisting of the 7th, 24th, and 25th Infantry Divisions and the dismounted 1st Cavalry Division) was nowhere close to fighting trim when war broke out in Korea and its GIs were thrown into the fray.

In August, little more than a month into the war, the Pentagon's rising star, Lt. Gen. Matthew Bunker Ridgway, then the U.S. Army's deputy chief of staff for administration, had been dispatched to inspect Walton Walker and his Korean command. After visiting embattled field units and interviewing Walton and his deputies, Ridgway had come away appalled. Walker had problems of all sorts, but perhaps the biggest, Ridgway determined, was the poor quality of his subordinate commanders—a situation that Walker himself bemoaned. SCAP got the cream of the crop of U.S. Army officers assigned to the Far East, while Walker settled for the dregs: scores of "ticket punchers" who had been bypassed for field commands during the Second World War and were trying now to leverage their way to final promotions before retirement.

But Ridgway was also unsparing in his judgment of Walker. While he had few equals as a fierce and combative tank commander, Walker's lack of leverage with MacArthur, combined with his weaknesses in organization and high-level strategy, placed him over his head as Korean ground commander. In fact, Walker's being a tank commander systematically undermined the tenor of field combat operations: His troops had become prisoners of their vehicles—and thus victims of Korea's abysmal system of roads. Ridgway felt strongly that Walker should be replaced, but he was also wary about the immediate impact of relieving a commander in the midst of an already perilous situation and of being seen as the usurper of another's command. The decision on Walker was left in MacArthur's lap.

After Ridgway's inspection, Walker's strained relations with both MacArthur and Almond had only worsened. His reputation with them undercut his battlefield assessments, strategic recommendations—he had advised against the Inchon landing—and pleas for resources. It seemed Walker was at his fighting best only when his back was against the wall, as it had been in the Pusan perimeter and looked to be now.

This time, for once, MacArthur sided with Walker. He was convinced that the Chinese were intent on pushing on both fronts as a prelude to a spring 1951 offense aimed at no less than tossing UN troops entirely out of Korea. He dismissed Almond's pleas to continue pushing north, and ordered that X Corps go on the defensive. He ordered the same for Eighth Army, and asked that Walker attempt a defensive stand at Pyongyang.

***

Task Force 77's VF-32 pilots flew ground-support strikes exclusively every day beginning December 1, the first day of the breakout on the eastern front. Jesse Brown had flown sorties on December 2 and December 3—Saturday and Sunday—and was on the schedule for Monday's afternoon launch.

The Marine breakout route from Chosin, a fourteen-mile-long road that coursed from the town of Yudam-ni on the western flank of the reservoir down to Hagaru-ri at its southern tip—called the MSR (major supply route)—turned into a killing ground devoid of restraint or pity by either side.

The marines, burdened by their equipment and the 1,500 wounded they were evacuating, moved slowly, fighting as they went. Overhead, the pilots could easily see the ChiCom (Chinese Communist) troops enveloping the MSR, practically all of them on foot, some wearing white parkas and capes in an effort to blend in with the snow.

Had this perilous drama unfolded a few months before, the Navy's efforts to provide CAS for the marines and GIs would likely have been stalled or altogether confounded by an intricate, top-heavy communications and control protocol. The postwar shuffling of U.S. Air Force, Army, and Navy responsibilities had given the Air Force control of all tactical air support for ground fighting. What had emerged from this mandate was a cumbersome system in which requests for air support fed to a high-level Army/Air Force/Navy Joint Operations Center and then filtered through two more layers—an Air Force–manned Tactical Aviation Control Center (TACC) and frontline Tactical Air Control Party—before targets were finally matched with strike aircraft under the direction of a forward air controller (FAC).

Such a system would have made sense had the infrastructure to support it been in place. But it proved disastrous when ground forces were in headlong retreat (as they'd been in July and August 1950) or fast-moving advance (as they had been since September). As early as August, with the Pusan perimeter shrinking by the hour, Eighth Army's Walker had authorized the Navy to arrange missions and conduct strikes while in direct communications with ground troops.

This day, as a result, there were planes available everywhere, often as many as eight flights at a time: Navy, Marine, and Air Force planes directed by marine and GI ground controllers. The cold affected the airplanes as well as the infantry, sometimes freezing up the wing guns or the ordnance pylons. Still, the "ambush-busters" (as one marine ground controller called them) were numerous enough and well-enough equipped with rockets, bombs, and napalm tanks to cut down, atomize, and incinerate the Chinese.

It was a pitting of strength against strength. The U.S. Marines had the upper hand in airpower and artillery. They also had the disciplined leadership and ferocity so characteristic of Marine units. Still, as the Marines' Smith suspected, the Chinese had discipline and ferocity in equal measure. The indisputable advantage on China's side of the ledger was the seeming inexhaustibility of its manpower: numberless Chinese infantrymen pummeling Marine ground forces with mortar barrages, automatic weapons fire, and grenades from the MSR flanks. They could wield this store of humanity like a commodity—almost as if it were devoid of humanity. In this running battle between the Marines with their close-covering air power and the Chinese, the snow-covered track of the MSR was stained pink for miles as the U.S. troop column edged its way south.

***

Iroquois Flight, Monday's afternoon sortie, was a recce (reconnaissance) mission of six Corsairs led by squadron XO Lt. Cdr. Dick Cevoli. In addition to Cevoli and Brown, Iroquois Flight included Lt. George Hudson (the air group's LSO, but also an experienced pilot anxious to participate in strikes), LTJG Tom Hudner, LTJG Bill Koenig, and Ens. Ralph McQueen, a VF-32 rookie. The addition of Hudson and McQueen to what would otherwise have been a division-size mission required a shuffling of wing assignments. Hudson replaced Hudner on Cevoli's wing, with Hudner instead on Brown's wing and McQueen on Koenig's.

Monday afternoon's weather was about as bad as Sunday's. Intermittent snow squalls tumbled from a dark-gray sky onto the white-caps of an even darker-gray sea. It was just another day in the Sea of Japan—and not nearly bad enough to cancel launches.

After Iroquois Flight's Corsairs (first Cevoli and Hudson and then, in quick succession, Brown, Hudner, Koenig, and finally McQueen) launched, they quickly gained altitude, formed up, and pointed northwest toward Chosin, a distance of about 100 miles, a flight time of forty minutes. Once they'd crossed the rugged coastline north of Hungnam, the aircraft dropped altitude to 500 feet and readied to check in with flight controllers, flying a line of valleys between dull, snow-specked mountains, many of them shrouded in overcast. The widely spaced Korean hamlets that occasionally drifted into sight were little more than collections of dun-colored mud huts.

***

Iroquois Flight soon approached the reservoir, recognizable this time of year as little more than a flat, desolate, windswept expanse of white about 3,500 feet above sea level. When VF-32's pilots had first seen Chosin earlier that fall from 10,000 feet, its three splayed fingers of water were cast in deep blue under bright sun, a contrast to the dusky green of the pine forests that in some places marched right up to its shoreline. The blue waters and green forests were still there, of course, but now bleached out by snow and ice.

Most pilots preferred recce missions because they offered the best chances for visible targets. Next to air-to-air combat—jet-to-prop battles the Corsair pilots hoped to avoid—the recce missions also required the highest level of flying skill, marksmanship, and daring. They supplied an adrenaline rush that went hand in hand with the implicit danger. It was a little like playing a pinball game while on an extended roller-coaster ride—though with life-and-death consequences.

For recce missions over remote locales during this early stage of the war there was usually no systematic antiaircraft fire to worry about, but there were multitudes of Chinese Communist soldiers taught to hit the ground when aircraft approached, point their rifles and machine guns straight skyward, and squeeze off concentrated volleys. Pilots tended to joke about it, calling the tactic the "Golden BB." Counting bullet holes was a standard postflight procedure, one that amused the pilots but drove young plane captains and older maintenance crew chiefs crazy. To the pilots they were little more than a nuisance, almost badges of honor. Still, as the name Golden BB implied, the ChiComs could get lucky, especially against vulnerable Corsairs flying low and slow to drop bombs, fire rockets, or strafe.

***

Everything seemed to be going smoothly until Bill Koenig, crossing to the right astern of Brown's Corsair, noticed a stream of vapor trailing from Brown's cowling. The Corsairs carried drop tanks that used an automatic transfer switch to pump fuel when needed. It looked to Koenig as if the fuel might be pumping but not reaching Brown's engine, instead streaming from the cowling and vaporizing. Koenig jumped on the circuit: "Jess, check your fuel status!" As the aircraft approached a ridge and pulled up in unison to clear it, Brown came on the line, his voice calm, matter-of-fact: "This is Iroquois 1-3, I'm losing power. I have to put it down." Iroquois Flight was now flying behind enemy lines, altitude too low to bail out, in terrain that was simply one wooded mountain after another. Bill Koenig, still astern of Brown, was back on the circuit: "Mayday, Mayday . . ."

As the distress call went out, Brown was occupied: lowering flaps, dropping belly tank and rockets, getting ready for a wheels-up crash landing. Wingman Tom Hudner had pulled alongside and was calling into his mic: "Okay, Jesse, I'll walk you through the check-off list." Doing this would allow Brown to focus his mind on the landing. "Lock your harness," Hudner began—especially important in order to keep Brown's head from spearing into the cockpit gun sight when he hit the ground. "Open your canopy and lock it," a time saver for exiting the cockpit quickly. Opening the canopy required using a hand crank mounted on the right side of the canopy; once it rolled all the way back, a latch mechanism held it in place. "Watch your airspeed." Brown was trading elevation for airspeed so he had to compensate. As he neared the ground his speed should be less than a hundred knots.

There wasn't much landing space to choose from, but Brown had spotted a bowl-shaped clearing about a quarter mile in diameter on a mountain slope. The slope had maybe a twenty-degree gradient—steep, but probably the best to be found. The snow there was likely at least a foot deep, enough to conceal who knew what. Brown began his approach into the wind—his six-ton aircraft heading for a wheels-up dead-stick landing in the tree-fringed clearing. The overall elevation was perhaps 5,500 feet, the temperature bound to be hovering near or below zero. It was now 2:30 P.M.

Iroquois's other pilots watched and winced as Brown's Corsair finally slammed uphill into the clearing, plowing a track through the snow and the frozen ground beneath. The Corsair's four-blade propeller splintered, as did pieces of the long engine cowling. The impact sent up a cloud of powdery snow that momentarily obscured the crash site, but as the white cloud settled and dispersed, the other pilots could see the wreckage. The Corsair's wings were intact, as was its fuselage aft of the cockpit, but its fractured nose was twisted to the right at nearly a thirty-five-degree angle just forward of the cockpit. A tangle of wires and steel frame protruded—much like the ends of a compound bone fracture—from the break. Wafts of smoke surrounded the cowling, meaning something volatile was either on fire or about to be. Worse, the Corsair's canopy was shut, and there was no sign of movement from Brown.

***

When Bill Koenig saw the smoke, he knew for certain they'd need some sort of fire extinguisher. He immediately got on the guard channel: "Any heavy transport in the area," Koenig almost shouted. "Come in! Come in!"

Cevoli meanwhile left the circuit, climbing higher to call for a helicopter. The others—Hudson (for now in charge of the flight), Hudner, Koenig, and McQueen—circled the clearing, looking for signs of enemy movement. Bill Koenig could pick out a few small farm buildings perhaps a quarter of a mile from the crash site but no sign of people or evidence of tracks in the snow. If anyone showed up, they

still had their strike packages—rockets, napalm, and machine guns—
to shield Brown until a rescue helicopter could extract him.

Despite their vigilance, they were all becoming pretty much convinced that Jesse Brown was a goner. His canopy should be open and
he should be getting out of the cockpit before the Corsair erupted in
flame or exploded. Then, when Hudner circled one more time, he noticed this time the canopy was open. Descending to get a closer look,
he saw Brown sitting in the open cockpit waving his arm. But something else must be wrong. Brown didn't seem to be making any effort
to get out of the cockpit.

Hudner went on the circuit to tell the others what he saw. It was
already apparent to Hudner that any help needed right away—stopping
the smoke, getting Brown out of the cockpit and clear of the wreckage,
waiting for the chopper—had to come from Iroquois Flight.

There was some circuit cross talk, but none of it very helpful.
"Jesus, why doesn't he get out of there?" someone said. "That plane's
gonna blow up before the chopper gets here," another said. It was by-
stander talk.

By then Hudner had already made his decision. He wasn't going to
ask Hudson's permission, knowing full well Hudson wouldn't (indeed
couldn't) give permission. The Navy would be losing another plane and
quite possibly another aviator. As VF-32 CO Doug Neill had put it: "If
a plane goes down, that's one down. We don't need Hollywood stuff."

"I'm going in," Hudner radioed—a fact of the matter instead of a
request. Hudson rogered the transmission without comment.

***

Hudner continued to circle, expending rockets and ammunition to
reduce weight and the chance of an explosion when he touched down.
Then he reduced power and lowered his flaps. Hudner's watch showed
2:50 P.M. as his airspeed indicator slipped below one hundred knots.
He planned to come in low, just a few feet off the ground but nose
up, then add power and fly up parallel to the slope before chopping
power and flaring down. Very much like a carrier approach.

He hoped the snow might cushion the impact, but instead he
landed harder than he'd ever experienced. It felt like he was bouncing
along concrete, and his windscreen shattered. The Corsair finally

scraped to a stop about a hundred yards uphill from Brown's wreckage. Hudner was still in one piece, but his back hurt and he found himself thinking: "What in the hell am I doing here?" He cut his control-panel switches, clambered out of the cockpit, and stumbled downhill through the crust of snow toward Brown.

By the time Hudner reached the wreckage the soles of his boots were packed with snow, making it difficult to get a foothold on the wing to climb up to the cockpit. He was finally able to pull himself up by grasping the canopy track. Brown was still conscious, but Hudner could sense by his eyes and face and the strain in his voice that he was in horrible pain. "I'm pinned in here, Tom. We need to figure a way to get me out."

Hudner clung to the canopy railing and inspected the cockpit area. Brown was in bad trouble. It was like the side impact of a car collision at an intersection. The buckling of the fuselage and cockpit area had jammed Brown's right leg between the fuselage and the central instrument column. Just as bad, Brown had already been on the ground for almost a half hour, exposed to subfreezing temperatures at high elevation. In working to escape the wreckage, he had removed his flight helmet, exposing his head to the cold. He had also removed his gloves in order to release the parachute harness; the gloves had dropped out of reach into the wreckage. Brown's hands were already like claws—totally frozen. Hudner was wearing a wool scarf and carried a watch cap in a pocket of his flight suit. He put the cap on Brown's head and wrapped the scarf around his hands. Hudner realized it was more of a gesture than a remedy. With Brown's limbs already frozen, there was no body heat left to retain. It would take more than a wrap to warm them now, but it was all he could do.

"Don't worry, Jesse. We're getting a chopper in."

Hudner tried to help Brown get his leg free, but it was no use. Hudner carried a survival knife, but even if it came to sawing through Brown's leg, he couldn't get the footing or angle to reach the leg. He needed tools, more sets of hands, and better leverage. If a helicopter was en route to rescue them, it wouldn't do Brown any good unless he could somehow get out of there. Brown's cockpit radio was apparently still working, but turning on the battery power to use it risked igniting the fuel that surrounded the wreckage.

Hudner slid off the wing to the ground. "Back in a minute!" he shouted over his shoulder as he ran back to his own Corsair, powered its radio, and went on the circuit, telling Iroquois Flight that the rescue helicopter should bring an ax and a fire extinguisher.

When he returned downhill, Hudner found Brown was still conscious, speaking occasionally but now very slowly. Hudner's back still hurt; he assumed Brown must have internal injuries, but he never heard him cry out or complain. There was no sense of fear or desperation, just stoicism. "Tom," he'd said at one point, "if anything happens to me tell Daisy how much I love her."

Thinking of nothing else he could do as he waited, Hudner scooped up handfuls of snow and pack it on and around the cowling where the smoke was rising. It didn't seem to do much good.

Finally, Hudner heard the throb of the rescue helicopter. "The chopper's here!" he shouted up to Brown before igniting a red smoke flare to help the chopper pilot judge the wind direction. The Sikorsky landed downslope, its engine idling and its rotors still turning slowly in the frigid air. When Charlie Ward, the tough Marine chopper pilot who had ridden *Leyte* on the voyage over, stepped out of the Sikorsky cockpit, Hudner could hardly believe his eyes. He well knew that Ward was taking a big gamble trying to pull off a rescue at this elevation and in these conditions. That Ward had somehow gotten in was no guarantee that any of them would get out.

Ward had received the message about the need for a fire extinguisher and an ax. He had doubled back in order to get them, which had delayed his reaching the scene. Learning he'd have to pick up two men, Ward had also dropped off his crewman. The fire extinguisher he brought was small, but they tried it anyway. Though it reduced the smoke briefly, its contents were soon used up, and the embers on the cowling continued eating their way toward the fuel tank.

Hudner and Ward then took turns with the ax, but it was useless: The blade simply bounced off the aluminum plating. They would need torches to cut the metal, and that would mean a trip back to Hagaru. Not enough time. They could get neither sufficient leverage nor footing to lift Brown by standing on the wing. Even if they had, the effort would likely kill him, as would the last option—severing his right leg. Brown was too far gone for that.

And by now it was getting dark. Concerned about being able to restart the Sikorsky, Ward had kept its engine running all this time. It was running low on fuel and wasn't equipped for night flying. Time, in other words, was running out for all of them. Brown was fading in and out of consciousness, speaking less often and even more slowly. In the fading light, Hudner peered once more into the cockpit.

"Jesse, we have to leave," Hudner told Brown. "But we'll come back with help." Brown was motionless and unconscious. Ward and Hudner walked downhill, climbed in the helicopter, and took off.

The four Iroquois Flight Corsairs also had to leave. Cevoli and Hudson, both night qualified, went "feet wet" back to *Leyte* while Koenig and McQueen (neither of whom were) vectored toward the Marine landing strip at Yonpo.

***

Ward and Hudner touched down first at Hagaru, the bustling shambles of a crossroads through which thousands of freezing marines were making their way south. While Ward left the helicopter to get further instructions, Hudner stayed in the cockpit and watched as twin-engine aircraft roared in and out of a makeshift airstrip. A few from the long line of iced-over, bedraggled marines passing through the crossroads stopped to plead to be flown out. There was little Hudner could say or do.

Keyes Beech, a *Chicago Daily News* reporter, captured the mood of Hagaru in his account of a regimental commander briefing his battalion commanders for the journey ahead of them. Nothing like this, he told his men, had ever happened to the Marines before. "But, gentleman, we are going out of here. And we're going out like Marines. We are sticking together and we are taking our dead and wounded and our equipment."[6]

When Ward returned with his orders, he flew them farther south to Koto-ri where they spent the night under canvas in a transient tent city. Hudner had no sleeping bag, but an enlisted marine offered him his: "Sir, you look like you could use this more than me." Hudner gratefully accepted the offer, but ended up sleeping hardly at all that night—the twin effect of the cold and the realization that Jesse Brown, whether dead or still alive, was spending the subzero night alone and exposed on a barren, snow-covered mountain.

***

Bill Koenig and Ralph McQueen flew out of Yonpo on the morning of the fifth, but with *Leyte* detached for refueling, their first stop was *Philippine Sea*, the TF 77 flagship. A staff officer, knowing Koenig was a VF-32 aviator, reached him after his landing and asked him to check over a press release that was about to go out. The draft turned out to be tragically wrong, indicating that Brown had been saved with the help of Hudner's heroics and Charlie Ward's helicopter. Koenig could just imagine Daisy Brown reading this mistaken press release and later getting official notification of Jesse's death. Koenig was all over the staff officer: Jesse Brown, he told him, was all but certain to be dead.

Tom Hudner and Charlie Ward reached Yonpo on the morning of Koenig's and McQueen's departure. Bad weather grounded flights for two days, so it was December 7 before a *Leyte* Skyraider was able to reach Yonpo to retrieve Hudner. On the return flight Hudner learned *Leyte*'s skipper, Sisson, wanted to see him as soon as he touched down. Communication, to say the least, had been confused and conflicted since the day of the mission: It turned out nobody knew reliably what had finally happened, either to Hudner or to Brown.

After listening to Hudner's account, Sisson said he was ready to send in a helicopter with a flight surgeon to retrieve Brown's body. Hudner advised him not to—it was a good gesture, but it was too dangerous and would only risk the lives of two more men. If he'd been stuck there, Hudner knew he wouldn't want that, and he doubted Brown would either. Enough lives had been risked—and lost—on that mountain.

So Sisson decided on a backup plan—a makeshift warrior's funeral. Within the hour, seven Squadron 32 Corsairs left the carrier bound for the crash site. Six carried napalm, and while they were diving to drop ordnance, the lone seventh plane soared above them—tribute to a fallen comrade.

***

Meanwhile, X Corps' breakout in the east and Eighth Army's staged fallback in the west continued. Leaving Hagaru in stages beginning on December 6, the Marine column battled its way south to Koto-ri.

UPI correspondent Maggie Higgins, who flew to Koto-ri in the backseat of a Navy COD (Carrier Onboard Delivery, a TBM Avenger modified for passengers and cargo), described "an aerial curtain" of Navy and Marine aircraft protecting the column "as it wound over the road." She also described the casualties: faces swollen and bleeding from icy winds, hatless men with blue ears, barefoot men no longer able to shove their frostbitten feet into frozen footwear. When Higgins asked one reluctant casualty to explain how he survived the cold and to describe the hardest thing he ever had to do, he replied with a weak grin: "Get a three-inch prick out of six inches of clothing, lady."[7]

By dusk on December 6, lead elements had covered just two miles of the distance to Koto-ri, but with light casualties. To clear Chinese roadblocks between the way stations, Marine controllers called in air strikes as ground infantry and armor assault teams waited to mop up and press on. When the final marine reached the perimeter at Koto-ri on the night of the seventh, the next and more formidable obstacle lay three and a half miles south—a chasm-spanning bridge at Funchilin Pass that had been blown by the Chinese. It took a daring Air Force cargo drop—six 2,500-pound bridge sections flown from Japan successfully parachuted into the Marine perimeter on December 8—and an even more intrepid feat by Marine engineers, transporting and installing the bridges on the ninth as Marine companies (commanded by iconic 1st Marine commander Col. Lewis "Chesty" Puller) seized and held the high ground, to get the column of troops, casualties, and vehicles continuing south.

On that day, David Douglas Duncan, a *Life* photographer traveling with the column, snapped a marine trying to eat from a frozen C-ration can.

"If I were God and it was Christmas," said Duncan, "what would you ask for?"

The marine, after struggling to form words, finally raised his eyes and said, "Give me tomorrow."[8]

Most who crossed Funchilin Pass that day and the next would get their tomorrows, though the breakout would ultimately cost the Marines dearly: 561 battle deaths, 182 missing, 2,894 wounded, and 3,600 nonbattle injuries (most victims of frostbite). The small number of missing was a particular testament to the Marines' discipline and single-minded obsession with leaving no one behind.

The casualties on the Chinese side of the ledger would remain objectively inestimable. All told, perhaps as many as twelve Chinese divisions (120,000 men) had been involved in the fighting; speculation held that perhaps as many as four of these divisions had been put out of action with 30,000 fatalities.

On December 10 the southbound Marines linked up with reinforcements from the South; the next day the combined column entered the port city of Hungnam with its wounded, its weapons, most of its equipment, and its morale and reputation for valor intact. As Marine and Navy aircraft flew a protective umbrella, dockworkers set to the task of systematically loading 105,000 military personnel, 91,000 refugees, 350,000 tons of cargo, and 17,500 vehicles aboard waiting ships for the voyage south to Pusan.

***

After returning from his meeting in Japan with MacArthur in late November, Walker had turned his focus to saving Eighth Army; after surveying his front lines by air, Walker concluded he could not hold Pyongyang as MacArthur had hoped. Instead, heeding George Patton's battlefield adages ("Once you've decided, don't delay. . . . A good plan violently executed *now* is better than a perfect plan later"),[9] Walker decided to pull back, regardless of distance, to his best defensible position. He would fight delaying actions along the way; destroy roads, rail lines, and bridges behind him; and, above all, avoid envelopment by the People's Volunteer Army.

Walker's retreat brought him to a defensive perimeter at the Imjin River thirty miles north of Seoul where he faced an opposing force estimated at 115,000 men. Although just as hard fought as X Corps' withdrawal in the east, Walker's retreat went largely unheralded, even though it bought precious time for X Corps' perilous evacuation at Hungnam. Walker's forces would get no miraculous exit.

Despite threats of a full frontal assault across the Imjin, Walker was more concerned about strikes on his flanks, positions held by often-panicky ROK troops. To counter this, Walker bolstered the ROKs with elements of the U.S. Army's 2d Division. On the morning of December 23, Walker set out by jeep to inspect this fragile portion of the line.

A lap robe tucked tightly around his legs against the bitter cold, seated next to Master Sgt. George Belton (his driver since World War II) and with his senior aide and a bodyguard seated in back, Walker sped north along a clogged southbound column of ROK trucks and vehicles. Suddenly, an ROK weapons carrier pulled out of line, ramming Walker's jeep and causing it to skid broadside across the ice and roll into a snowbank. The driver, aide, and machine gunner were thrown clear, but Walker, pinned to his seat by the lap robe, was killed instantly when the jeep's windshield smashed his skull.

Walton Walker's death was eerily reminiscent of the death of his idol both in circumstance and timing. George S. Patton had been killed in a traffic accident on December 9, 1945, when his staff car was hit by a U.S. Army two-and-a-half-ton truck on a country road near Mannheim, Germany. Paralyzed from the neck down, Patton survived until December 21, when an embolism finally claimed him.

Both Patton and Walker died during perhaps the lowest reach of the pendulum swings of their respective careers. Patton's fatal accident occurred just one day before he was to return to the United States. Refused a command in the Pacific war and shoehorned into a poor (and controversial) fit as military governor of postwar Bavaria, Patton was depressed at the prospect of not having another war to fight. Just before his own death, Walker had good reason to believe that MacArthur was about to relieve him. He agonized that, as a consequence, his final legacy would be the retreat from the Yalu instead of his valiant stand in the Pusan perimeter or his exploits with Patton's Third Army.

***

Within minutes of being informed of Walker's frontline death, Douglas MacArthur was on the phone to the U.S. Army chief of staff, Gen. J. Lawton "Joe" Collins, in Washington. Both had agreed that if anything happened to Walker, his replacement would be Matthew Ridgway, then still assigned to the Pentagon. Ridgway was finally located at a party with friends next door to his own quarters at Fort Meyer; it was near midnight when Collins (a West Point classmate) reached him by phone, instructing Ridgway to "get your things together and get out there as soon as you can."[10]

Months before, Ridgway had hesitated and MacArthur had procrastinated on Walker's fate. Now, however, the need and timing for change had eclipsed all three men. Meanwhile, if mirrored epitaphs would somehow be written for Patton's and Walker's deaths, there were still sharp contrasts in the global events that overshadowed their untimely ends. Patton undoubtedly would have preferred Walker's death—speeding in a jeep to the front lines instead of being chauffeured to a day of pheasant hunting (as was Patton). Of more consequence, Patton left behind a world ostensibly at peace—a condition for which he was ill-suited. Walton H. Walker, meanwhile, as he lay stretched out in the makeshift morgue of the 8055th Mobile Army Surgical Hospital, bequeathed a conflict now closing just its first—and by no means its longest or costliest—chapter.

PART 2

THIS AWFUL WAR
YOU'LL TERMINATE

7

THE RIDGWAY

At FIRST LIGHT one late-February morning in 1951, as they wrapped up a night heckling mission over North Korea, pilots from VC-35, carrier *Princeton's* detachment of night-flying Skyraiders, spotted several long trains making a dash for the mouth of a mountain tunnel. The flight leader was Lt. Frank Metzner, the detachment's OinC, a World War II veteran and reservist who, before being activated for Korea, had been a writer and radio announcer in civilian life. Metzner's flight circled overhead and waited, but the trains never emerged from the other side. This told them one thing: The tunnel—and others like it—was being used as a daytime hideout for Communist supply trains.

Several days later on March 2, returning to *Princeton* from a morning strike against North Korean bridges near Kilchu, VF-193 Corsair squadron CO Lt. Cdr. Clement Craig spotted a different target opportunity: a high four-span railroad bridge, parts of it still under construction, connecting three rail lines with two tunnels across a deep canyon near Songjin, inland from the coastal plain and the Sea of Japan.

Pinpointing the bridge from the air, apparently for the first time, was a real coup. Like most choice North Korea target sites—the exceptions were those hugging the narrow coastal plain—the Songjin bridges were built into a landscape of canyons, mountain ridges, and narrow valleys often obscured by clouds or morning mist. The excitement of spotting the target, Craig realized only too well, would soon enough be tempered by the risks and costs of going after it.

The rugged terrain, augmented in some cases by mobile radar-equipped antiaircraft weaponry, was more and more working to the Communists' advantage. There was often only one flight path in and one out. For the attacking pilots there was little margin for error and little wiggle room for evasion. It took lots of nerve to go in and even more luck to emerge unscathed. Already, since the start of its deployment in November aboard *Princeton*, Task Force 77's flagship, Air Group 19 had lost four prop pilots in combat, all flying Corsairs. Three of the four—each an ensign and each just twenty-two years old—were from Craig's VF-193. Ron Paris, the first, went down on a CAS mission over Yonpo on December 15. The next, on Christmas Eve, was Hugo Scarsheim—a crash northwest of Hungnam. The most recent, February 10, was Harold Trolle, whose F4U inexplicably stalled, crashed, and exploded northwest of Inchon. Craig had already sent condolence letters to Paris's, Scarsheim's, and Trolle's families. As was nearly always so, there was grieving to be done but a singular lack of tangible remains—other than the pictures, clothes, and personal effects stored in lockers or scattered across stateroom bunks.

Not surprisingly, Craig's sighting generated an immediate stir as soon as his Corsair touched down on *Princeton*. In a hastily prepped strike, CVG-19 pilots set out that same afternoon to hit the bridges. Challenged as much by a race against the early-setting late-winter sun as by enemy ground fire, strike results were modest—some damage to the approaches but little or none to the bridge spans themselves. They would have to return another day and however many days it took to bring them down—and keep them down. Meanwhile, the matter of the tunnels and the hidden trains lingered. The tunnel entrances were inviting target propositions, but until someone came up with a reasonable tactical plan, they were not worth the risk.

***

In the wake of the UN forces' headlong December fallbacks from their equally heedless advances toward the Yalu in the fall, the Korean War's front had, in January and February, stopped its accordion-like swings and settled into more or less fixed and fortified lines north of Seoul but south of the 38th Parallel. For Navy, Marine, and Air Force pilots, the shift from a war of movement to a static front (almost like the

World War I trenches in France) meant shifts in missions and targets. With troops neither advancing nor retreating much, CAS gave way to what was collectively called interdiction: strikes on transportation targets such as bridges, tunnels, dams, rail lines, and roads. The logic—to cut or strangle exposed Communist supply lines and thereby starve their trenches of everything from food and medicine to ammunition and uniforms—seemed to make perfect sense. Armies, whether Napoleon's, Kim's, or Mao's, moved on their stomachs.

In mid-December 1950, anticipating this shift, the U.S. Air Force (which had primary responsibility for interdiction) segmented North Korea into eleven zones, and within those zones targeted 172 bridges, tunnels, and supply centers for destruction. Far East Air Force (FEAF) commander Lt. Gen. George Stratemeyer envisioned including Navy and Marine air units in this effort. Stratemeyer was rebuffed at first but persisted until, in late January, the Navy reluctantly agreed. Task Force 77's first interdiction strikes—against bridges along North Korea's east coast—were launched before the end of the month.

This first step led inexorably to an ever-deepening commitment. In mid-February Task Force 77 took on "temporary" responsibility for interdiction strikes on Korea's northeastern transportation routes. Within weeks this responsibility escalated, becoming formal, intensive, and almost exclusive. The targets were nearly always in Communist-held territory. The fact that they were widely dispersed required pilots to concentrate as much on navigation as formation flying and aerial assault tactics. The aviators of VA-195, *Princeton's* AD squadron, for example, spent off-duty hours painstakingly cutting large charts (most of them Japanese) into small sections and then covering them with clear plastic. The use of these homemade pocket laminates was better than having blanket-size navigational charts draped across the cockpit while trying to stay in formation or line up for a strike. Still, as squadron pilot K. W. "Tex" Atkinson recalled years later, "you never knew when you would suddenly find yourself on your own, flying over snow-covered mountains that all looked the same."

***

North Korea's narrow eastern coastal plain was particularly target rich. The coastal sites were more concentrated, the navigation surer, and the relative safety of the sea closer at hand. But their allure was also deceptive. Despite appearances, the road and rail lines were not necessarily easy to disrupt—at least with lasting effect. The roads were not much to begin with—the best-placed bomb often just rearranged the gravel or added another crater-sized pothole to what had already seemed impassable. Rail-cut missions ("working on the railroads," as some pilots took to calling them) had their own challenges; put simply, the narrow-gauge rails were hard to hit from the air at high speed or any altitude. Early Air Force efforts using jet planes had yielded abysmal results. The slower-flying Navy Corsairs and Skyraiders did better but, predictably, with higher casualties. Even when rails were cut, the North Koreans quickly got them back in service—often overnight—using an inexhaustible supply of manpower. Destroying bridges took more effort: A scorekeeper here estimated twelve to sixteen Skyraider sorties dropping a combined thirty-six to forty-eight tons of bombs were needed to take down just one.[1] And even when a bridge fell, the North Koreans were masters at combining manpower with engineering ingenuity—riverbeds, for example, frozen rock hard in winter, could serve as impromptu temporary rail beds.

From that vantage, taking out tunnels held a special allure: Done right, ideally with supply-laden rolling stock trapped inside, no amount of manpower could easily or quickly reverse the damage. But doing it right also required the most ingenuity and involved the highest—most thought prohibitive—risk. Once, Frank Metzner and several other pilots intent on solving the conundrum sat down in a ready room to watch films of F6F Hellcats (configured as remote-controlled pilotless drones) attempting to replicate the job. When the lights came on after a particularly graphic cliff-face crash, everyone in the room was in a cold sweat.

***

In the two months since the death of Eighth Army general Walton H. Walker, the UN forces' ground war in Korea had shifted firmly into the hands of Matthew Bunker Ridgway who, detached on Christmas Eve from his Pentagon post, reached Tokyo just before midnight on Christmas Day, 1950. Though he arrived barely forty-eight hours after first being alerted to his new assignment, the task of packing and moving was, like nearly everything else in Ridgway's life, just one more opportunity to apply organization and precision. The general, it turned out, had already cataloged every article stored in the twenty suitcases and trunks that made up his baggage train.

The next morning, after breakfasting alone in his embassy quarters, Ridgway met with Douglas MacArthur. The two had known each other since the time MacArthur was superintendent at West Point and Ridgway (a hockey player and football team manager as a cadet) its director of athletics. Ridgway remained impressed by the force of the old general's personality even under such trying circumstances.

After receiving MacArthur's gloomy and cautionary assessment of the situation, Walker's successor had just one question for the man who, despite all his tribulations, was still supreme commander of UN forces in the war. "General, if I get over there and the situation warrants it, do I have your permission to attack?" Grinning wearily, MacArthur spoke like a beleaguered patriarch relieved to be passing on a practically bankrupt family firm to his first son. "Do what you think best, Matt," MacArthur told him. "The Eighth Army is yours."[2]

***

If MacArthur's response (with its apparent willingness to cede authority) was uncharacteristic, Ridgway's question (which revealed his laserlike instincts for taking the offensive) was not. The son of a Regular Army artilleryman who had served in China during the Boxer Rebellion, Matthew Ridgway, fifty-five, three times married, twice divorced (now the father of a toddler, Matt Jr.), marched (careerwise) a half pace behind the West Point generation that had produced Dwight Eisenhower, Omar Bradley, and George Patton (along with MacArthur, the undisputed American lions of World War II). As a two-star general in the European theater, Ridgway had successfully assembled, trained, and led the famed 82nd Airborne Division through Italy and France— despite the handicap of taking command as a "leg" (not qualified in parachute jumping) and only belatedly earning his jumper wings.

Putting aside early career advice from no less a mentor than George Marshall (who later became wartime chairman of the Joint Chiefs of Staff) to "cultivate the art of playing and loafing," Ridgway was an unsparingly focused and domineering bulldozer, whether in a staff meeting, on the front lines, or off duty.[3] There was, his subordinates took to saying, "a right way, a wrong way and a Ridgway." At war's end, fully recovered from a shrapnel hit (the wound, recalled one of his staff officers, seemed to spill more rage than blood) received during the spring 1945 invasion of Germany, Ridgway had been posted to the Pacific to take command of an airborne corps (under MacArthur) for Operation Downfall.

Peacetime scarcely flattened the trajectory of Ridgway's rising stars, at least in the cloistered universe of the Pentagon. After two postwar diplomatic assignments (both in Washington) and a tour as commander of U.S. Caribbean forces, Ridgway set up shop in the Pentagon as the Army's deputy chief of staff for administration. His boss, Omar Bradley, was singularly impressed, lauding him as both an amazingly competent staff officer ("He can plan an action . . .") and an outstanding commander ("and he can execute it").[4] Now, in Korea, under the scrutiny of Truman and the Joint Chiefs of Staff and with the apparent "hands-off" blessing of Douglas MacArthur, Ridgway would have the opportunity to do both.

***

Ridgway reached Korea the same day as his meeting with MacArthur, touching down that afternoon at an airfield in Taegu, northwest of Pusan. Early the next morning, strapped into the bombardier seat in the Plexiglas nose of his staff plane (a B-17 Flying Fortress now christened *Hi Penny!* in honor of his third wife) to get a better perspective on Korea's terrain, he flew north to Eighth Army advance headquarters in embattled Seoul.

Ridgway arrived poorly clad for cold weather that struck to the very bone, but he radiated confidence and determination. He wore the signature battle accessories—a grenade affixed to the right strap of his parachute chest harness, a first aid kit to the left—that earned him sardonic ridicule from the jaded corps of war correspondents and the nickname "Old Iron Tits" from his troops. After paying a courtesy visit to bolster a forlorn Syngman Rhee ("I'm glad to see you, Mr. President, glad to be here, and I mean to stay"), Ridgway embarked on a sobering inspection of demoralized field units that left him convinced his highest priority was to restore morale and fighting spirit. In the meantime he would somehow have to keep Eighth Army intact, fighting delaying actions in a continuing retreat south while inflicting what punishment it could on the steamrolling Chinese.

The New Year began with a withdrawal from Seoul, though this time in a controlled and organized fashion. The Chinese moved in on January 4, triggering a triumphant celebration in Peking, but soon the Communists were experiencing their own problems. Each day Ridgway pulled his mobile units back roughly thirty miles—about as far as the foot-bound Chinese could march in the same amount of time. When they reengaged UN forces it was usually at strong points preplanned by Ridgway where the exhausted Chinese were battered and then counterattacked. Finally in mid-January, with his command chain regrouped to his satisfaction (a chastened Ned Almond now reported directly to Ridgway—as did Marine units who, after Chosin, adamantly refused to be led by Almond) and a modicum of fighting spirit returned, Ridgway began taking the offensive.

The tactics of the new Eighth Army advance northward were far different from the previous fall's rush toward the Yalu. Like a cautious driver going downhill in second gear, wary of losing control and ending up in a collision, Ridgway worked his divisions ahead very slowly, sending armored spearheads in front to keep constant contact with the Communists.

This time there was no bypassing the enemy and no risk of lunging into a trap. Exhorted by Ridgway to "find the enemy and fix him in position," units pushing into new areas consolidated and mopped up before moving on. Despite this slower pace, Ridgway encouraged greater tactical mobility ("Nothing but your love of comfort binds you to the road," he admonished commanders and troops alike) and, in true paratrooper fashion, stripped down his army's cumbersome transportation, communication, and supply systems. Even the names of Ridgway's counterattacks and offensives bespoke their clawing, grinding spirit: Operation Wolfhound, Operation Killer, and Operation Ripper. By the middle of March, Ridgway's leaner, tougher, and newly invigorated army would recapture Seoul.

The battle landscape of this new "Ridgway" increasingly pitted American against Chinese forces on Korean soil and on either side of the 38th Parallel. Native North Korean forces had been all but destroyed during the summer and fall of 1950. The remnants had been withdrawn and were slowly being rebuilt; in the months ahead rehabilitated units would be plugged into the line at select points, usually opposite ROK troops, positioning guaranteed to spur fierce, fratricidal combat.

In all, the fighting locked into a frustrating and attritional deadlock, a stalemate struck in a curious inverse balance between the fortunes of the opponents. Any push north by the Americans ended up only increasing the frontline density of Chinese Communist troops, shortening their supply lines and making interdiction air strikes that much more difficult. Conversely, Chinese pushes south risked outrunning their fragile logistics while simultaneously exposing them to ravages from the air.

***

It was against this developing backdrop that on March 3, a day after the first impromptu strike, VA-195 squadron CO Lt. Cdr. Harold G. "Swede" Carlson returned to the bridges near Songjin, this time leading two divisions of Skyraiders. Carlson, a 1940 Naval Academy graduate, had served two years aboard cruiser *Nashville* (CL-43) before receiving flight training and finishing out World War II as a torpedo bomber pilot and squadron XO with twenty-two Pacific combat missions, an Air Medal, and a Purple Heart. During the postwar doldrums Carlson had skippered an escort carrier—*Lunga Point* (CVE-94)—and even taught NROTC classes at Villanova University, but now he was back heading a squadron and this day leading a flight in combat. Equipped with a better tactical plan, more daylight, and heavier ordnance, Carlson's beefy Skyraiders produced better results: dropping one bridge span and damaging three others. His planes returned on March 7 to drop a second span.

Following these strikes, Rear Adm. Ralph Ofstie, then the TF 77 commander, nicknamed the battleground "Carlson's Canyon." But if the gesture was intended to be commemorative, it was premature. Instead, it marked just the first three rounds of what turned into a monthlong test of wills and wits pitting the aerial destructive power of Task Force 77 aircraft and pilots against the manpower resources, persistence, and ingenuity of the Chinese and North Koreans. After the March 3 and 7 missions, the North Koreans worked diligently to reconstruct the bridges and continued their efforts despite unrelenting day and night harassment strikes.

***

Meanwhile, as Carlson's VA-195 Skyraiders (and his own night-flying ADs) worked over the Songjin bridges, VC-35 OinC Frank Metzner believed he had devised a way to take on the train storage tunnels. He eventually took his plan to Task Force 77's Ofstie, himself no stranger to either daring aerial tactics or risky propositions. Ofstie had been a fighter squadron commander before the Pacific war and CO of a carrier (*Essex*) and a carrier division during the height of it. Promoted to rear admiral and riding escort carrier *Kitkun Bay* (CVE-71), Ofstie had been part of Task Unit 77.4.3, the famed "Taffy III" that, though surprised, outrun, and outgunned, used its carrier aircraft (mostly Grumman Wildcats and Avengers) to turn back a superior Japanese naval force (including battleship behemoth *Yamato*) off the Philippines in October 1944.

For their part, Metzner and his VC-35 pilots already flew CVG-19's loneliest and most perilous missions. Catapulted after dark and recovered before dawn, the Skyraider aircrews (in addition to a pilot, each night-flying AD carried a radar operator and radioman crammed into a small compartment behind and below the cockpit) worked the combat graveyard shift. It was a surreal existence: As other squadrons' personnel relaxed, watched movies, or slept, the night crews prepped for strikes in a nearly deserted, red-lit ready room, felt their way across a blackened flight deck to their aircraft, and, once aloft, flew over North Korea's towering mountains and into its rugged valleys, depending mostly on radar and cockpit instrumentation to navigate and maneuver. The aircraft usually attacked in pairs—one aircraft dropping multimillion candlepower flares to illuminate the target while the other struck with bombs, napalm, and 20mm cannon.

Despite these tactical pairings and the incessant radio chatter among pilots and crews, the night flights had a way of isolating each man aloft in bubbles of solitude. Boring missions gave each the sense of being a night watchman standing a needless vigil. When things got hot—the combination of the Skyraiders' flares and the tracer-lit flak made for a sudden and almost mesmerizing fireworks display—the loneliness was, if anything, only more acute. This despite the fact that the three-man crew almost invariably shared the same fate: Either all survived a mission or none did.

Perhaps the most surreal aspect of a night's work (frequently two missions, a sort of split shift) was its end. Turning out the light and going home was no afterthought; instead, the airplane's crew had to navigate a black sea to find and touch down on a deck whose only beacon was the LSO—a spectral figure in a green- and orange-striped black-lit fluorescent suit waving a matched set of fluorescent paddles.

Metzner's pitch to Ofstie was simple enough (although perhaps skewed by Metzner's bias that any daylight tactic had to be easier than what he routinely did at night): Come in low to drop a one-ton bomb with a delayed fuse onto the tracks at the mouth of a tunnel. If the bomb hit the tracks with a flat-enough trajectory, it would then "skip" into the entrance, and explode deep inside.

Understandably, the admiral was skeptical. The bombing aircraft would have to come in low, slow, and straight—therefore a sitting duck for any guns placed near the tunnel's entrance. The largest of the North Korean tunnels was only seventeen feet wide, making both accuracy and pilot survival problematic.

Metzner's response was a plan that, though hardly foolproof, offered some promise. Four Corsairs could, he argued, lead every run, strafing the hills surrounding the mouth of the tunnel. Only ADs—carrying three one-ton bombs fixed to their inboard wing and centerline racks (only their Wright Cyclone engines possessed enough power to clear the mountain face after the drop)—would be used for the actual bombing. As to accuracy and consistency, Metzner argued that a test of the concept would provide the answer. It was convincing enough for the naval aviator in Ofstie. "Give it a try." As Metzner and his VC-35 pilots set out to test their tunnel-busting concept, the indefatigable North Koreans' rebuilding of the Songjin bridges was far enough along to trigger plans for a another full-scale aerial assault. Group 19 planes set out on March 15, this time equipped not only with bombs but also with napalm pods intended to torch the temporary wooden bridge beams and scaffolding that supported the repair work. A photo reconnaissance flight the next day confirmed impressive results: not only the demolition of the new construction (including the incineration of the scaffolding) but also the destruction of yet another of the original spans. The Air Force followed with what seemed a final valedictory to the pounding of Songjin. B-29s, flying at high altitude, seeded the bridge site and its approaches with delayed-action fused bombs: booby traps to discourage further repair work.

***

Douglas MacArthur (according to biographer William Manchester) saw war "not as an extension of politics, but as the consequence of a complete collapse," and during that collapse, MacArthur reasoned, power should be in the hands of professional soldiers, "whose sole mission would be eventual triumph."[5] Once he was sent into battle, he contended, it should be with an unfettered mandate to win.

MacArthur, an extreme egoist, also saw himself as a symbol of national destiny. Even so, MacArthur, like other U.S. military and civilian leaders (not least Truman), was also bound by an oath of allegiance. And it was over their differing interpretations of their respective oaths (rather than Cold War ideology) that Truman and MacArthur inevitably collided. Truman was convinced that if MacArthur was allowed to disobey civil authority, as president he would be violating his oath to uphold and defend the Constitution. For his part (as he later testified before a Senate committee), MacArthur felt he owed his allegiance directly to the Constitution and not "those who temporarily exercise the authority of the executive branch."

It didn't help in all this that MacArthur's conservative champions in Congress—many of whom supported bombing Chinese supply lines and wielding Chiang Kai-shek's Nationalist troops and even nuclear weapons as strategic options in Korea—encouraged him to believe he was untouchable. His seemingly meek capitulation of field operations to Ridgway back in December was never complete; MacArthur had a habit of visiting Korea whenever there was an opportunity to reap press coverage and plaudits—he was at Ridgway's side on January 20 to bask in the success of Operation Wolfhound and a month later for the kickoff of Operation Killer.

More important, MacArthur never ceded the field when it came to strategy, politics, and efforts by Washington to control him. With his senior staff in Japan serving as ego enablers (assuring him that Washington could be ultimately converted to his views), MacArthur decided, at some point in March 1951, to challenge the president openly.

Truman's White House remained silent through MacArthur's initial provocations—impromptu press conferences and sidebar contacts with reporters in express violations of a gag rule on unauthorized policy statements. Short of outright insubordination, Truman hoped to keep MacArthur in the Far East. That hope essentially came apart on March 24 when, learning from a Joint Chiefs dispatch of UN and U.S. intentions to lay the diplomatic groundwork for a truce overture to the Communists, MacArthur issued what he called a "military appraisal" of the situation in Korea.

In it MacArthur taunted China, asserting that it lacked sufficient industrial capacity and ground firepower "to accomplish by force of arms the conquest of Korea." Further, any UN departure from efforts to contain the war would "doom Red China to the risk of imminent military collapse." MacArthur's manifesto enraged the Chinese Communists, the Soviets, and even some U.S. allies, effectively shelving any prospect of a peace initiative. It also set Truman's course. "By this act," Truman recalled later, "MacArthur left me no choice—I could no longer tolerate his insubordination."[6]

* * *

As spring 1951 approached, Harry Truman was just one of many politicians and leaders facing—or hoping to sidestep—hard choices about this unpopular war and its consequences. While the war had loosened congressional purse strings, it hadn't fortified the average congressman's stomach for the legislative turmoil or raised his pain threshold for accountability.

Each military branch was spending aggressively. For its part, the Navy was using the new flood of dollars to reactivate fleet carriers, aircraft (mainly Corsairs), and reserve squadrons. Its problem, ironically, was the lack of congressional authorization to create new organizational units—in particular carrier air groups—to which planes, pilots, and squadrons could be assigned. Reactivating mothballed ships was relatively easy—they were tangible pieces of property that had previously been "commissioned." Commissioning new air groups, on the other hand, required separate congressional approval. Having already run the war-funding gauntlet, most congressmen (given America's discontent with the war) wanted passionately to avoid the public scrutiny that would follow from expanding the Navy's (or other service arms') organizational pyramid. The problem of finding a creative way around this bureaucratic conundrum soon fell into the lap of James Holloway III when he was reassigned to Naval Air Force headquarters in San Diego.

Holloway arrived in San Diego expecting an assignment to a Korea-bound carrier squadron and hoping to transition to jets—though he knew it was unlikely. In Bombing Squadron 3, Holloway flew the Curtis SB2C Helldiver, a dive-bomber that, in the wartime Pacific, had destroyed more Japanese shipping tonnage than any other carrier-based attack aircraft. However, the SB2C (it was variously called "Son-of-a-Bitch Second Class," the "Beast," or, by its disconsolate mechanics, "the flying hydraulic leak") also had a reputation for poor manufacturing quality control and sloppy flight characteristics. Having mastered the "Beast" all but guaranteed Holloway a ticket to a Skyraider squadron until, ironically, the Navy's organizational dilemma conveniently opened a path to jets.

Holloway's task—a two-week assignment handed him by a Navy captain who knew Holloway from his Bombing 3 days—was to satisfy the Navy's need for a "by-the-book" command chain while providing cover for a nervous group of congressmen. At the assignment's conclusion he came up with a model that ultimately evolved as a reliable template used in a string of limited, "undeclared" conflicts like Korea.

To sidestep the present hurdle, Holloway suggested the creation of air task groups. The ATG, he reasoned, could have the look and feel of air groups, but the CAG, group staff, and individual squadrons would report to a carrier CO, in effect making them part of the ship's company. It was smoke and mirrors, but it was also workable. ATGs could be assembled in two steps: Some existing five-squadron air groups would be pared down to four, and then these "extra" squadrons would be matched with activated reserve squadrons.

The formation of the first of these—ATG-1, scheduled to deploy with *Valley Forge* in the fall—also created a personal opportunity for Holloway. Wangling assignment as ATG-1's operations officer, Holloway also arranged to be attached to VF-111 (a squadron pulled from CVG-11) for flight duties. VF-111, which had returned to San Diego in March from its deployment with Phil Sea, flew F9F-2s, ensuring Holloway a transition to jets. Three more squadrons would eventually round out ATG-1: VF-52 (an F9F squadron just returned from Korea with *Valley Forge*); VF-194, the AD squadron "orphaned" from CVG-19 when it deployed with *Princeton* back in November; and VF-653, Cook Cleland's "Flying Circus" reservists.

VF-653's personnel were by then assembling at NAS Alameda in preparation for their Korean deployment. Their arrival (along with other Navy reserve squadrons) would usher in a new stage for the Navy's Korean air operations, one where the vast majority of combat air strikes would be flown by reservists. During the training at Alameda, VF-653's pilot contingent swelled to twenty-eight with the addition of four young pilots—three ensigns and a JG. The number of aircraft increased from sixteen to eighteen, all of them relatively new F4U-4Bs equipped with four-blade propellers, more horsepower, and four 20mm cannons instead of six .50-caliber machine guns.

A handful of VF-653 pilots, including XO Lt. Ray Edinger, had never qualified on carriers, so they spent their first days at Alameda practicing "field carrier landings" before qualifying for real on carrier *Antietam* (CV-36), whose own air group was also readying for deployment.

***

Tex Atkinson first learned of Frank Metzner's tunnel-busting concept when VA-195's pilots were briefed on the basic idea and ordered to stage test hops. On the first practice runs the pilots dropped too soon and too fast, causing the bombs to bounce instead of skip. They concluded that a flaps-down approach barely above stall speed—almost like a carrier landing—gave them the best chance of skipping the bomb into the tunnel mouth. Atkinson, strongly convinced that the idea would work, was assigned to fly temporarily with VC-35 as a tunnel buster.

Tunnel busting joined Air Group 19's evolving mission repertoire at about the time the work on Carlson's Canyon wound down. Or, perhaps more fittingly for both sides, wore out: The North Koreans remained undeterred even by the mid-March scorched-earth strikes. Their persistence even stirred feelings of begrudging admiration among the pilots. It was as if reconstruction of the Songjin bridges was bred into the minds and muscles of the hordes of men who scrambled through the ruins (booby traps notwithstanding) and immediately set back to work. By month's end repair and reconstruction were essentially complete, lacking only the laying of tracks to finish this work. This triggered Air Group 19's final major air strike on April 2 that left the bridges' concrete pilings as the only visible testimony to their adversaries' tireless efforts.

As far as Rear Admiral Ofstie and CVG-19 were concerned, it was over. With so many competing targets, full-scale concentration on Carlson's Canyon simply could not continue. It was over for the North Koreans as well—but only insofar as the specific bridges were concerned. While ceding the battle for this particular set of bridges to the "blue planes," the Communists embarked on construction of a four-mile bypass consisting of eight shorter, lower, and less conspicuous bridges. More targets, in other words—and more difficult ones to hit.

It was as if the Songjin debris had, instead of settling, been cast to the wind as seed corn for other North Korean projects. For the most part, CVG-19's aviators were single-minded tacticians. And for good reason: Their survival depended on it. But by the same token (and for the same reason), most were also unflinching pragmatists. It dawned on them that what was being tested here was not just building bridges or tearing them down. What was at stake instead was the movement of supplies; the Communists would spare no effort to stoke the stomachs—and the guns—at the front.

***

In mid-March, just before MacArthur's "military appraisal" toughened the psychological resolve of the Chinese Communists, unraveled the prospects of peace talks, and guaranteed an imminent showdown with MacArthur's commander in chief, Matthew Ridgway's Eighth Army was pushing north under the banner of Operation Ripper, one of a chain of ground offensives designed ultimately to return UN forces all the way to the 38th Parallel. At first, MacArthur had equivocated about actually crossing the line, but then, infuriated by the Joint Chiefs' dispatch, he turned his Eighth Army commander loose. Ridgway was awakened early with news that he could cross when the time came.

During the days of diplomatic and political turmoil that followed, Ridgway kicked off yet another offensive conceived to reinvigorate the push north. As a concession to U.S. State Department complaints about the indelicacy of giving operations names such as Ripper and Killer, Ridgway christened it Operation Rugged. Though its title suggested more a scouting expedition than a murderous assault (subsequent operation names included Dauntless, Thunderbolt, and Detonate), Rugged ground ahead successfully. At the operation's completion on April 9, Eighth Army's central front had reached the approaches to the Hwachon Reservoir, just above the 38th Parallel, fifty miles northeast of Seoul.

Built in 1944 by the Japanese for hydroelectric power generation, the reservoir—its three branches arranged like an inverted T—impounds the waters of Pukhan River by means of a "mass concrete gravity" dam located at the reservoir's northwest corner. The steel floodgates of the Hwachon Dam—a structure 900 feet long and 275 high with walls no less than 20 feet thick—controlled the Pukhan's flow into its confluence with the Han River east of Seoul.

Based on hydrologic studies, U.S. Army Corps of Engineers had already advised Ridgway that the dam posed a problem. Opening the gates, the Chinese could flood Route 17 (a critical route in and out of the strategic town of Chunchon) and, beyond it, the Han River itself. Closing the gates would in turn lower the Han, threatening its value as an essential east-west defensive barrier.

The first effort to tackle the problem of the Hwachon Dam came from the air using Air Force B-29 bombers. Aerial bombing of enemy dams had been tried before, but with much more advance planning. In May 1943 British Lancaster bombers had successfully blasted two dams in Germany's Ruhr Valley, the culmination of three years of painstaking research. Blasting a thick masonry dam, research found, was similar to depth charging a submarine; to succeed, explosives had to be detonated midway down the upstream face of a fully filled dam, setting off a "water hammer" effect in which expanding gases displaced water to fracture the structure.

The Ruhr raid used huge cylindrical depth charges ("bouncing bombs," each weighing 9,250 pounds and packing 6,000 pounds of high explosives) whose postimpact backspin skipped them like rocks across the surface and into the dams' inner walls. (It was, in its way and on a grander scale, the real precedent for Frank Metzner's tunnel-busting idea.) British planners anticipated that destroying each dam would require three to five well-placed detonations; in fact, a single bouncing-bomb hit brought down each dam.

While the British successfully applied an almost surgical precision to a brute-force objective, Air Force planners seemed to do just the opposite. High-altitude Superfortresses dropped huge (but conventional) six-ton bombs, all of which drifted wide of the dam. Even if the bombs had fallen squarely atop the dam walls, it was unlikely they would have accomplished anything more than pockmarking a concrete mass estimated to be 240 feet thick at its base. The bombing did, however, spur the North Koreans into action: They blew most of the bridges across the Pukhan River and briefly opened the floodgates. Surging waters soon raised the Han River level by four feet, destroying one bridge and forcing the dismantling of another to avoid damage. Realizing that control of the floodgates (rather than destruction of the entire dam) was the real objective and, accordingly, high-level bombing too crude an instrument, Ridgway ordered the gates disabled from the ground. The U.S. Army's 1st Cavalry Division was ordered to mount a ground assault to be spearheaded by elite troops from 4th Ranger Company.

Within a few weeks, the results of this courageous but ill-fated assault on the Hwachon would have an impact on the aviators of Swede Carlson's VA-195 and Frank Metzner's VC-35. But events in Korea—on the ground, in the air, and at sea—were already being overshadowed by the high drama of an unprecedented showdown between Douglas MacArthur and Harry Truman.

8

ROADS, RAILS, BRIDGES, TUNNELS, DAMS

As FAR AS Harry Truman was concerned, Douglas MacArthur's fate was sealed just before noon on Thursday, April 5, 1951, when Massachusetts congressman Joe Martin stepped to the well of the House of Representatives to read a document into the *Congressional Record*.

Just a few weeks earlier, Martin, who was House Republican minority leader, had baited MacArthur with a copy of a stump speech assailing Truman for blocking the use of Formosa-based Nationalist Chinese troops to open a second front against the Communists. "If we are not in Korea to win," Martin's provocative speech concluded, "then this Truman administration should be indicted for the murder of thousands of American boys." Martin invited MacArthur to comment, either privately or publicly.

MacArthur, predictably, could not resist the public route. Responding on March 20—just days before he would issue his "military appraisal" and authorize Ridgway's Eighth Army to broach the 38th Parallel—MacArthur wrote that Martin's views were in keeping with the wartime necessity of "meeting force with maximum counter-force." Then he added words that for Truman were the real "clincher": "If we lose the war to Communism in Asia the fall of Europe is inevitable; win it and Europe would most probably avoid war and yet preserve freedom. As you point out, we must win. There is no substitute for victory."[1]

When Martin put MacArthur's letter before Congress, the answer to "when" the ax should fall became "now"—and "how" soon followed. After feverish internal debate and maneuvering among Truman, his cabinet, and the Joint Chiefs, a plan was set in motion: The news would be delivered directly and personally to MacArthur by Secretary of the Army Frank Pace, who was on an inspection tour in Korea. But soon after, amid mounting fears that MacArthur would somehow get the word and resign before he could be fired, the plan began to unravel. Lurching off-script, the White House hastily assembled correspondents for a postmidnight press conference on Wednesday, April 11. As Truman slept, news of the dismissal (and the promotion of Matthew Ridgway to replace Douglas MacArthur) beamed around the globe, reaching MacArthur's embassy at 3:00 P.M. on April 11, Tokyo time.

MacArthur was lunching with a small group of guests, including a U.S. senator and an airline executive, when staff intercepted the news in the form of a radio news bulletin. They delivered the news to MacArthur as he prepared for his afternoon siesta.

Despite the awkward mode of its delivery (the official cable subsequently arrived in a brown Army envelope stamped ACTION FOR MACARTHUR in red block letters), MacArthur took the news with stately outward equanimity. While a typhoon of reaction built and swirled around him, he began preparing for his return to the United States. He would finally leave Japan by air on Tuesday, April 16, ending fifteen years of near-imperial exile in Asia.

Meanwhile, as news of the dismissal spread, reaction was swift and impassioned in all corners. America's European allies were generally pleased (MAC IS SACKED, crowed one London newspaper headline) and her Asian allies, especially Japan, dismayed. The response in the United States, according to a later account by presidential historian Arthur M. Schlesinger Jr., swelled to a "violent and spontaneous . . . discharge of political passion" unmatched "since the Civil War."[2] While the editors and working press of large U.S. city news dailies largely supported the decision (though MacArthur's histrionics made great headlines, many were tired of his rogue behavior and theatricality), Republicans and conservative press critics went into full, anguished cry.

So did millions of Americans who, initially at least, landed squarely on MacArthur's side; even U.S. senators publicly supporting Truman reported that "telegrams from home were running ten to one against the President." There was also talk among caucusing Republicans, not surprisingly led by Joe Martin, of a congressional probe into "the whole conduct of foreign and military policy," of getting the "complete views of General MacArthur," and even "impeachments" of Truman, Secretary of State Dean Acheson, and other cabinet officers. The Republicans extended an invitation for MacArthur to speak before a joint session of Congress—a move the Democratic administration thought it best not to oppose.

Well ahead of the crest of this political and emotional tidal wave, arrangements were already in motion for a ceremony to be presided over by Truman himself on the morning of Friday, April 13. In keeping with the somewhat solemn nature of the occasion (and perhaps with an eye on its superstitious timing), the ceremony had originally been planned as a small, subdued affair staged inside the White House. Accordingly, there were strict limits on the number of guests and witnesses.

However, as the day approached, the ceremony inevitably took on larger implications. Although Truman had already made a radio broadcast to the American public explaining his actions with regard to MacArthur, the ceremony, low-key or not, would be his first public appearance since the MacArthur firing. Somehow and at some point it was decided that the press and the politicians (and, by extension, the country's citizens) should bear witness to a moment portraying the president to better, perhaps even unassailable, advantage while reminding the nation of the mingled emotions of sadness, sacrifice, and pride in which everyone could share. The ceremony was moved outside to the White House Rose Garden.

***

Between his early-December crash landing in North Korea and the end of *Leyte*'s Korean deployment, VF-32's Tom Hudner had logged his share of combat missions. Still, he found it difficult to sit in a Corsair cockpit for much more than a half hour without experiencing excruciating back pain. He likely could have stood down for medical reasons, but the last thing he wanted, given all the scuttlebutt about his being in hack for losing a squadron aircraft, was to be pulled from the flight line. So Hudner soldiered on through January 20 when, after a stop in Yokosuka to off-load excess ordnance, *Leyte* departed for the West Coast, its Far East deployment completed. When the ship reached San Francisco at the end of January, CVG-3 personnel were detached, and squadron pilots were flown by transport cross-country to Quonset Point. Returning to the home base in Rhode Island, with squadron aircraft still aboard *Leyte* and weeks from arriving via the Panama Canal (*Leyte* herself would begin overhaul in Norfolk at the end of February), most air group pilots went on leave. So close to Fall River, Tom Hudner took the opportunity to recuperate at home.

There had been some furtive speculation that in the process of trying to help Jesse Brown, Hudner might have damaged his career as well as his back. Hudner had kept his equanimity throughout, taking comfort in the conviction he'd done the right thing. Although he thought himself ready for whatever his fateful decision brought (or didn't bring), Hudner wasn't prepared for news he got by phone from Washington after returning to Quonset Point in March. He had been chosen to receive the Medal of Honor, with the ceremony set for the White House on Friday, April 13.

***

VC-35 Skyraider pilot Atlee Clapp was the first tunnel buster to actually fly a bomb inside the mouth of one of the North Korean tunnels. As Tex Atkinson (the seconded VA-195 pilot who usually flew with Clapp's division) later pictured it, the explosion drove dirt and debris so far out the other tunnel entrance as to resemble a cannon shot from a twenty-foot muzzle. Although visually awesome, this first direct hit (sealing an apparently vacant tunnel) was by no means the tunnel busters' most rewarding execution of Frank Metzner's tactical vision. A vastly more consequential result came days later when, as pilots lined up for runs on one tunnel entrance, an accelerating locomotive exited the opposite side. Breaking off their bomb runs, Clapp's division joined up with their Corsair escorts to chase and strafe the fleeing locomotive. They pressed the assault until one of the flight's pilots—dispatched ahead to reconnoiter—radioed back, urging them to continue the pursuit but aim wide with their fire. The locomotive, it turned out, was cannonballing heedlessly toward a nearby marshaling yard crowded with rolling stock. The pursuit's finale, according to Atkinson, was a spectacular train crash with locomotives and boxcars flying in all directions. After circling the calamity, Clapp's flight moved on to another target.

The tunnel busters' aerial successes (they were, Atkinson later trumpeted, "putting nearly 50 percent of our bombs into our targets") were in stark contrast to the frustrations and casualties suffered by ground troops trying to gain control of the Hwachon Dam. April 9–10—the time window chosen for the initial 4th Ranger Company assault—coincided with the close of Operation Rugged (and the eve of MacArthur's dismissal). Troops from the Army's 1st Cavalry Division who had been spearheading the offensive were scheduled to leave the line for rest and recuperation. Instead, the 1st Cav's 7th and 8th Regiments were ordered to bolster the Ranger operation.

Almost immediately, the planned assault faltered. After advancing through rugged hills along the western rim of the reservoir's northern branch, rangers and 1st Cav GIs were within a half mile of the dam when they collided with a stubborn defense mounted by two well-entrenched companies of Chinese Communist troops. The American advance ground to a halt, leaving them pinned down. They were in desperate need of more firepower, but efforts to bring up supporting tanks and artillery were frustrated by mud and steep terrain.

As GIs pressed the assault the next day (backed now by a single battery of long-range howitzers), rangers simultaneously tried to stage a flanking amphibious assault across the reservoir. Nine assault boats were somehow muscled to the western banks of the Hwachon, but only four turned out to have working engines. Efforts to shuttle the rangers across proceeded, only to be called off as darkness fell.

The plan to disable the dam's floodgates was scrubbed, at least for the time being. Battle-weary rangers and GIs returned to the news of MacArthur's removal, Iron Tits's promotion, and the installation of yet another Eighth Army commander—Gen. James Van Fleet.

***

The Rose Garden, the 7,500 square feet of manicured landscape bordering the White House's Oval Office and West Wing, was resplendent on a clear, sunny, and cool mid-April morning and filled with a crowd of Navy brass, press representatives, and civilians. The garden had been established in 1913 by Woodrow Wilson's first wife, Ellen, and it had since been used by succeeding presidents as a backdrop for events as varied as press briefings, public policy pronouncements, and visits by prominent citizens. The phrase "Rose Garden strategy" would eventually be synonymous with presidential efforts to orchestrate strategy from the confines of the White House. In that sense, a bit of Rose Garden strategy most likely underlay Tom Hudner's Medal of Honor ceremony.

In advance of the event, Hudner had placed calls to the White House military liaison, a temperamental lieutenant commander charged with coordinating the ceremony and managing the attendee list, to make arrangements for his allotment of guests. However, as the day drew near, ever more friends and family members jockeyed to attend. With each Hudner call, the liaison officer grew grumpier, allowing a few new guests (two of Hudner's mother's brothers with their spouses and another uncle on his father's side) but warning there would be no more room.

Then, on April 12, when some of his Washington-area relatives asked to attend and Hudner worked up the nerve to call the liaison, he found him even more exasperated, but this time because of the last-minute change in venue. It was as though the floodgates had opened. Hudner could invite whomever he wished.

***

The Medal of Honor (often misnamed the Congressional Medal of Honor; strictly speaking, it is awarded by the Department of Defense "in the name of Congress") is the highest decoration—and the sole "neck award" (the medal dangles from a collar of blue silk)—bestowed by the U.S. government on its military personnel. Although first conceived by the Civil War Union navy in 1861 (and called the "Navy Medal of Valor") to honor "petty officers, seamen, landsmen and Marines as shall most distinguish themselves by their gallantry and other seamanlike qualities during the present war," use of the Philadelphia Mint–engraved medallion expanded within a year (under the unifying name "Medal of Honor") to encompass all U.S. service branches and armed conflicts.[3]

Despite the lofty intent, the Medal of Honor's luster was almost immediately tarnished by overuse. The medal had first been bestowed almost as an afterthought by Lincoln's secretary of war, Edwin M. Stanton, to honor survivors of a band of Union guerrillas who had staged a daring raid deep in Confederate territory to highjack a locomotive and destroy vital railroad tracks as they fled north. These awards, although impromptu, were at least fitting. Later in the war, however, facing a manpower crisis, Stanton promised the same award to every man in a Maine infantry regiment who agreed to extend his enlistment. Most did—for an extra four days—and the result was the wholesale issue of 864 Medals of Honor.

These 864—along with 41 others judged frivolous—were eventually rescinded by a 1916 military review panel as the United States anticipated a new war; still, it was not until 1942 that both service branches finally settled on a single Medal of Honor, awarded only for extreme bravery "beyond the call of duty" in combat. Not surprisingly, given the criteria, more than half the 440 medals earned during World War II were awarded posthumously, a proportion that would climb to 70 percent for what would eventually be 131 Korean War honorees. There was ample reason, in other words, for the tradition of calling those awarded the Medal of Honor "recipients" rather than "winners."

While the Medal of Honor may sometimes be awarded through a special act of Congress (as it has been to correct earlier, mainly race- and ethnicity-based, injustices), the much more usual path—and the one followed in Tom Hudner's case—is nomination and approval up through the chain of command. Despite this "bottom-up" protocol, the Medal of Honor approval process doesn't usually originate with a Medal of Honor recommendation. In part to restore the Medal of Honor's reputation, the military services had (with congressional approval) configured a constellation of subordinate awards for heroism— the Bronze and Silver Stars and the branch-specific Crosses.

In Tom Hudner's case, the spark evidently came from *Leyte*'s skipper, Thomas Sisson, the same patrician Mississippian who had championed and vouchsafed Jesse Brown's shipboard stature. It was most likely at Sisson's direction that Doug Neill, VF-32's squadron CO, first drafted Hudner's award recommendation. After the recommendation passed speedily from Neill through CAG Wally Madden and then to

Sisson, Sisson forwarded it (and, in the weeks that followed, likely shepherded it) to higher authorities: first to the commanders of Task Force 77 and 7th Fleet; then to the commander in chief, Pacific Fleet; then to the chief of naval operations, and, through him, to the Joint Chiefs of Staff and the secretary of defense. Somewhere in the upper reaches of this firmament, what once may have been a Silver Star or Navy Cross recommendation was raised instead to the pinnacle: the Medal of Honor.

Even awards for combat heroism have political and social purposes; they have lessons to teach. Wars, especially unpopular wars during times of social upheaval, beg for star-power heroes, and, in that sense, Tom Hudner's feat perhaps did double duty: a conspicuously heroic act in which one man risked his own life to save a comrade—and in the process pierced a racial barrier. And while nobody could doubt the award's justification, that didn't remove it from potential controversy.

Bonds within military "bands of brothers," though tight, are also competitive—and nowhere more so than within the brotherhood of naval aviators. Awards for military heroism set men and women apart—and the Medal of Honor does so more than any other. In a real sense the awards do so unfairly, as most hero recipients readily attest. The stars, crosses, ribbons, and accompanying citations acknowledge relatively few instances of witnessed and documented heroism while simultaneously (however unintentionally) ignoring others. They inspire, but they can also test the strongest bonds.

Finally, with the Medal of Honor, there is sometimes an onus that attaches to its recipients. More than one Medal of Honor recommendation has stalled or derailed because someone in the chain of approval has refused to believe the potential recipient could possibly have survived the exploits described. It might well be added that living recipients are also subject to the unspoken and unknowable judgment of posthumous recipients. For all those reasons, on a splendid Friday the thirteenth spring morning in the Rose Garden, Tom Hudner, Medal of Honor recipient, was bestowed both a big honor and an equally big burden. He was being recognized and elevated. But he was also, in a way and at a very young age, receiving a big piece of his inevitable epitaph.

***

The ceremony marked the first presidential presentation of the Medal of Honor since the Second World War, when Truman, elevated to the office after Roosevelt's April 1945 death, was likewise the bestowing official.* Just prior to the ceremony, Hudner and his fifteen family members and friends were cloistered in the White House cabinet room. But as they filed outside to the Rose Garden, Hudner saw Daisy Brown standing among the luminaries, with a black U.S. Navy lieutenant escort at her side.**

Daisy Brown (then residing with her daughter, Pamela, in Daisy's parents' Hattiesburg home) had flown unaccompanied to Washington at Navy expense the previous day. It was Daisy's first visit to the capital, and the whole experience (etched as it was in personal grief as well as unfamiliarity) was made even bigger, noisier, and more chaotic by the uproar surrounding MacArthur's much anticipated return to the States.

A page 4 article (complete with photo) in Saturday's edition of the *New York Times* described the twenty-minute ceremony: "While Ensign Brown's widow sobbed quietly in the background in the rose garden of the White House, Mr. Truman recited the stirring details of Lieutenant Hudner's 'conspicuous gallantry and intrepidity at the risk of his own life above and beyond the call of duty.'" The article noted that Hudner was "the first naval officer to win the highest decoration in Korea"; that he'd been appointed to the Naval Academy by "Representative Joseph W. Martin Jr. of Massachusetts, the Minority Leader" (Martin did not attend the ceremony); that Hudner and his VF-32 squadron mates had "raised a $2,700 scholarship fund for Pamela, 2-year-old daughter of the dead flier"; and that "Lieutenant Hudner's heroism occurred at the peak of the Chinese Communist effort to destroy the Tenth Corps after General of the Army Douglas MacArthur's 'end the war' offensive had failed in late November."

"Congratulations, son," Truman told Hudner as the audience stood and applauded. And then—off the mic but loud enough to be heard

---

* There would be subsequent ceremonies for Korean War Medal of Honor winners, including several for actions that preceded the Jesse Brown rescue effort.
** The officer was Lt. Dennis Nelson, one of the original thirteen young black men to receive U.S. Navy commissions at the close of World War II.

by most of the crowd—Truman (the World War I national guardsman and artillery captain) spoke words that, although used at other Medal of Honor ceremonies, most likely had a particular resonance because of the MacArthur uproar: "At this moment I'd much rather have received this medal than been elected president." Finally, Truman stepped over to a still tearful Daisy Brown. "I am so very sorry for your loss," he said softly, this time unheard by the crowd. Then he reached over to embrace her.

***

In his West Point yearbook, James Van Fleet (who took formal command of Eighth Army from Matthew Ridgway on April 14) was described as "a brusque, outspoken individual and not much of a mixer."[4] Following his 1915 graduation (he was a classmate of Dwight D. Eisenhower and Omar Bradley), Van Fleet had commanded a machine-gun battalion in World War I. Though considered an outstanding officer, Van Fleet's career stalled between the wars and even during the advancement frenzy of early World War II because his service jacket was routinely confused with another Van Fleet reputed to be an incorrigible alcoholic. Once this matter was cleared up, James Van Fleet's advance was meteoric; he ended the war (as had Walton Walker) as a corps-level commander in Patton's Third Army.

"A rugged combat soldier and crack commander" was *Time's* take on the new Eighth Army leader. Van Fleet made "Iron Tits" Ridgway look like a suave and polished statesman, while, in contrast, the rough-hewn and more physically commanding Van Fleet resembled, as one veteran United Press (UP) correspondent put it, "the fellow next door, good-natured, strong but no world-beater at turning a phrase." His workmanlike demeanor was among the qualities that best suited him to the job at hand.

Van Fleet was not to revitalize the ground offensive or take it in a new direction. Instead, firmly tethered by both Ridgway and the Joint Chiefs, Van Fleet was to be the loyal caretaker of Ridgway's "find them, fix them, fight them, finish them" approach. Ridgway was not so much concerned with capturing or holding real estate as he was in wearing down the Communists. And now that same grinding attrition served a larger strategic objective: convincing the Communists that they could not win the war outright, thus inducing them to engage in peace talks aimed at a negotiated settlement.

For the moment, now that spring had arrived, both Ridgway and Van Fleet anticipated a renewed Chinese ground offensive. Even as Van Fleet superintended a new offensive called Operation Dauntless, Ridgway cautioned his replacement to be prepared to fall back, killing as many Communists as possible as he retreated.

Dauntless, as expected, turned out to be the prod that stirred the Communist hornet's nest. As early as April 16, an uneasy quiet (one reminiscent of the doomed race to the Yalu six months before) fell over the advancing UN front. Three days later, with the Chinese apparently disengaging without a fight, a suspicious Van Fleet called a temporary halt, ostensibly to prepare for two new thrusts: one aimed at evicting the Chinese from the Iron Triangle (the important Communist communication and supply area bounded by Chorwon, Kumhwa, and Pyonggang), the other pushing the UN front lines north to enfold the Hwachon Reservoir.

It was just before ten o'clock on the night of April 22—on what had been an otherwise quiet, cool Sunday under a clear Korean sky—that the Chinese, clad in cotton khaki uniforms, their tunics bulging with potato-masher grenades and crisscrossed with ammunition bandoliers, forded the Imjin River en masse, using a classic invasion route that pointed to Seoul, thirty miles south. By the twenty-fourth, UN forces all along the front were in full (but organized) retreat from a Communist attack that ultimately numbered close to 350,000 troops. On the left flank, UN troops fell back to the Lincoln line, a defensive position consisting of well-fortified trenches and bunkers just north of Seoul. The Chinese clearly seemed intent on retaking the South Korean capital. On April 29 the Lincoln-line defenders repelled a Chinese effort to cross the Han River. There would be more such attacks, and, because of the continued failure to secure the Hwachon Reservoir on the right flank, Chinese hands still held the crucial floodgate levers of the Hwachon Dam.

***

The string of train-demolition and tunnel-busting successes for Frank Metzner's night-flying Skyraiders continued through most of that

same April. During one memorable midnight sortie, VC-35 planes
dropped bombs on two trains parked side by side in a railroad yard
north of Hungnam. Reconnaissance photos later suggested that one
train contained ammunition and the other gasoline. The resulting explosion and conflagration displayed all the noise, heat, and light of
an ammunition dump triggering a refinery fire. On another equally
spectacular predawn mission over a valley west of Wonsan, Metzner
and his wingman, John Ness, spotted four long trains—three separate
locomotive-towed trains chugging uphill in one direction while a
shorter string of boxcars connected to a switching engine passed them
going downhill. Metzner immediately dropped flares, and both pilots
followed up with bomb hits that cut the rails ahead and behind all
four trains. Leaving Ness below to continue strafing, Metzner climbed
and radioed for backup. Soon, four Panthers thundered into the area,
the vanguard of a continuous stream of Task Force 77 planes that not
only destroyed the four trapped trains but ended up flushing out and
destroying two additional locomotives towing thirty supply-laden
boxcars.

It seemed nearly every mission had its own great story to tell. As
Eighth Army moved slowly and relentlessly north, the Task Force 77
pilots grew increasingly convinced that, aside from the admirable obstinacy displayed by the Communists at Carlson's Canyon, they were
playing a major role in strangling the enemy's logistic lifelines.

Not that the day and night successes came cost free: Air Group 19's
combined aircrew losses for March and April climbed to a sobering
total of six pilots. In early March VF-191 lost its thirty-two-year-old
skipper, Lt. Cdr. John Magda, when his F9F crashed at sea after being
crippled by antiaircraft fire. Swede Carlson's VA-195 pilots had all survived the canyon campaign (although one pilot, twenty-two-year-old
ensign Evan Charles Harris, had been killed in late January), as had
all of VC-35's tunnel busters. VC-3, however, the detachment of
night-flying Corsairs, lost two of its most experienced pilots: twenty-
eight-year-old LTJG Baxter Cook in March and twenty-six-year-old
Lt. Al Tiffany little more than a month later. Individually and collectively, these losses continued to hurt and, as ever, left not a scrap of
mortal remains. But the losses at least came in the context of missions
that seemed decisive and, on a personal level, gave combat pilots the

best they could hope for: a chance to test their mettle and demonstrate an impact while showcasing their flying skills and tactical ingenuity. That was why, when the assignment finally came to solve the thus far intractable problem of the Hwachon Dam, CVG-19's pilots approached it with a sense of élan and a quiet certainty that they were up to the challenge.

***

The assignment came in the afternoon of April 30: an urgent request from Eighth Army HQ to Task Force 77 commander Ralph Ofstie to take out two or more of the Hwachon Dam floodgates. Late that same day eight VA-195 Skyraiders escorted by five VF-193 Corsairs set out to give it a try. The ADs, led by Swede Carlson himself, were equipped with 2,000-pound bombs and racks of Tiny Tim air-to-ground rockets, each fitted with a 500-pound warhead.

When they reached the valley, Carlson and his wingman went in first to draw antiaircraft fire. As dirty dark puffs of flak erupted in the valley skies, the VF-193 Corsairs swooped in to chase the puffs to their source. In the ensuing runs through the target gantlet, the ADs dropped sticks of bombs that appeared to straddle the dam and at least one rocket that, according to pilot reports, knocked a hole squarely in the middle of its downstream face.

All planes survived the mission, and some pilots touched down on *Princeton* convinced they'd done a good if incomplete job. However, the day's photo reconnaissance revealed otherwise. In fact, the low-flying Skyraiders had achieved no better results than the high-altitude B-29 sorties of a month before. None of the conventional bombs came anywhere near the vital gates; the one direct rocket hit shook loose only a bit of the dam's surface concrete, while the rest, despite their powerful warheads, simply skittered off.

Swede Carlson, for one, had anticipated what the photos showed, and he returned with an idea of what might be tried next. Carlson had begun his naval aviation career as a torpedo-bomber pilot—why not, he wondered, fire torpedoes at the troublesome sluice gates? It was an idea that immediately appealed to the old aviator in Ralph Ofstie.

Aerial torpedo bombing was by now all but a lost combat art; although occasionally practiced, its weapons and tactics had not been

updated—or applied under combat conditions—since the demise of
the Japanese Imperial Fleet in World War II. Within the air group pilot
ranks only Second World War veterans like CAG commander Richard
C. Merrick, VA-195's Carlson, and VC-35's Frank Metzner and his
wingman, Atlee Clapp, were adequately trained to do it, and none, of
course, had any experience targeting a concrete mass planted at the
head of a narrow freshwater dam surrounded by rocky and gun-
bristling cliffs.

Princeton, it turned out, still carried, tucked away in magazines well
belowdecks, a supply of Mark-13 aerial torpedoes. The torpedoes
were successors to an earlier generation of torpedoes that had performed so abysmally against Japanese shipping early in World War II.
The Mark-13s could, if need be, survive drops from altitudes as high
as 2,400 feet at speeds up to 410 knots; their white protective "heads"
would break away after hitting the water, leaving the actual warhead
(packed with 600 pounds of Torpex, a custom explosive concoction
50 percent more powerful than TNT) to do its destructive best.

For the task at hand, however, these extra margins for altitude and
speed would be unnecessary. And, because the "torps" would be
launched at a stationary object, there were none of the complications
of "leading" a fast and maneuverable target. It was hoped only that
the torps would run hot, straight, and free of surprises as they sped
at 34 knots toward the waiting sluice gates. It took considerable work
(by ship's ordnance men with little or no torpedo expertise), but eight
of the one-ton, thirteen-foot-long torpedoes were wrestled topside,
attached to the bellies of eight Skyraiders (four each from VA-195 and
VC-35), and rigged for the next morning's mission.

CAG Merrick (sporting his signature accessories: a long-barreled
German Lugar, a pair of 7x50 binoculars, and a K-20 aerial camera)
led the division of torpedo-laden VC-35 ADs, while Lieutenant Commander Carlson headed the VA-195 contingent. Flanking them was a
two-division escort of Corsairs. As Carlson had learned the day before,
the approach to the dam itself was no simple matter. The aircraft had
to thread their way two by two through the 4,000-foot heights of the
same mountain passes that had stalled the Army ground attacks. This
day, perhaps because of the previous day's flak-suppression work,
there was remarkably little antiaircraft fire to evade, either going in or

over the reservoir itself. The Corsair pilots made quick work of silencing what little there was and then stood back to watch.

The trick for the ADs—once more making their runs in pairs—was to approach in a shallow dive, low and slow to ensure accurate torpedo placement. All eight torpedoes—four pairs of two—dropped clear of the AD bellies, plunged briefly beneath the surface of the pristine waters and then, just as designed, surfaced and began their runs.

The AD pilots climbed out of flak range, waited, and watched as the torps carved wispy straightaway wakes toward the steel gates. One Mark-13 ran astray—tracing an erratic, blind, and futile path across the placid surface. A second proved to be a dud, its passage ending in a dull, unheard clank. But the remaining six ran "hot and true," each exploding in sequence to send towering columns of water, concrete, and steel all the way up to the dam's crest.

As before, all sixteen planes returned to *Princeton*, but this time to evidence of considerably better results. Panther reconnaissance photos showed that two of the fish had combined to completely demolish one sluice gate, while yet another blasted a hole in a second. Longer-distance shots documented the effect: torrents of water tumbling in long, white, high-pressure columns into the downstream bed of the Pukhan River.

***

The waters of the Hwachon Dam now no longer posed a threat to the UN defensive line in front of Seoul. Bleeding—instead of cascading—through the fractured floodgates, the waters were incapable of overwhelming the banks of the Pukhan and then the Han. On the other hand, the Communist gatekeepers could not for now impound the waters as a means of smoothing an invasion path on and beyond the South Korean capital.

The singular tactical success of the Hwachon Dam mission would inspire a nickname change for VA-195, from "Tigers" to "Dambusters"; however, it could not forestall a dramatic shift in Chinese strategy. Having pinned UN forces above Seoul with what turned out to be a massive feint, the Communists now instead massed farther east and, on May 16, unleashed a huge offensive push aimed at Wonju and Pusan instead of Seoul. Hordes of Chinese and North Korean troops were soon (in the words of Ned Almond, corps commander) "flowing like water around my right flanks."

However, despite the initial surprise and near panic, the UN right flank ultimately held and, with the help of intense close air support, blunted the Communist offensive. A UN counterattack kicked off a week later, and, though the push faced the usual rough going through rain, mud, and mountainous terrain, it found the enemy's supply lines overextended and its forces in disarray. Communist troops, most arriving at the front after long, foot-weary overland journeys, found themselves starved for food and ammunition; droves of them took the opportunity to surrender, "coming over" to the side of democracy.

Within days, Chairman Mao, who had been dictating the action from a modest house near China's ancient capital, was forced by increasingly dire conditions to adopt a new strategy. Realizing that his forces could not mount another major ground offensive, Mao instead ordered his troops to turn the war into a test of endurance. The Communists would shorten their supply lines and begin securing their positions in an elaborate system of deep underground tunnels along the 38th Parallel.

Mao vowed that the North Korean and Chinese Communist troops would "crush the Americans a little at a time." He also exhorted China's population to launch an all-encompassing grassroots campaign to support the Korean War effort. "We are totally dedicated to the fighting in Korea," Mao pledged on behalf of his people. "Whatever Korea asks, we shall supply."[5]

***

While Mao's fierce rhetoric seemed to presage a greater escalation of the conflict, in truth it was the precursor of efforts by both sides to begin the quest for a negotiated settlement. At the end of May, the U.S. Joint Chiefs cabled Ridgway a new set of clearer and more restrictive directives. In the event of a Communist breakthrough he was to forgo retaliatory strikes outside Korea's geographic boundaries. He was to "inflict maximum personnel and matériel losses" on the Communists while simultaneously creating "conditions favorable to the settlement of the Korean conflict."

Meanwhile, behind the scenes, a U.S. diplomatic envoy was reaching out to Soviet UN envoy Joseph Malik, who in turn signaled that his government wanted a peaceful solution in Korea. Malik even advised that the Americans get in touch with the North Korean and Chinese Communists directly, suggesting that the Soviets had already exerted leverage on their clients. On June 23 Malik helped this effort even further by stating that the Soviets believed that "discussions should be started between the belligerents for a cease-fire and armistice."

Days of silence by Peking Radio and Pyongyang Radio on the Soviet suggestion ensued, a sign that both were dissatisfied with the meddling by their big Communist neighbor. Finally, on June 29, the Joint Chiefs instructed Ridgway to broadcast a message to the chief of Communist forces in Korea offering the possibility of preliminary talks. Two days later the Communists responded in their own broadcast, agreeing to meet with a designated UN representative. There followed some haggling over location and schedule, but finally on the morning of July 8, a three-man UN liaison team headed by a U.S. Marine colonel flew north by helicopter across the Imjin River to Kaesong, the launching point for the North Korean invasion a year before. Upon landing, they were driven in two battered American jeeps to the meeting site, a one-story building, formerly a teahouse. The three men stepped out of the jeeps to enter the teahouse and a new, even more frustrating phase of a lengthening war.

***

As the Kaesong peace talks began and the ground fighting continued, there were departures and new arrivals at Point Oboe. Already, of the first crop of fleet carriers rushed to Korean waters, *Valley Forge* had left in December, *Leyte* in February, and *Philippine Sea* in March. By now, even their replacements, ships such as *Princeton*, *Boxer*, and *Bon Homme Richard* (CV-31), were either gone or set to go. Slated to arrive were "new faces" such as *Essex* (in late June) and *Antietam* (in September) and (as deployment calendars settled in for the long haul) repeats like *Valley Forge*.

Inevitably toward the end of their deployments, pilots who had shown such daring, faced such peril, and, in the process, lost so many friends had to ask themselves whether their attacks on roads, rails, bridges, tunnels, and dams had amounted to little more than deadly sideshows. Had their accomplishments and sacrifices been decisive or just counterweights (witness the Marines' retreat from Chosin) to the limitless manpower of Communist ground forces? Were they flying to help win a war or merely prevent its precipitous loss?

It was a dilemma whose urgency understandably faded as ships and squadrons sailed east, bound for the United States. For those leaving, the changing of the guard was a way to put the dilemma aside, at least for now. For those arriving, it was a dilemma obscured (at least for now) by inexperience.

The ships still on station but slated to depart had a tradition of welcoming new arrivals with poetic doggerel laced with good-natured jabs, insider jokes, and a cautionary, albeit caustic, touch of experience-bred wisdom. "Welcome Essex," Bonny Dick's greeting to *Essex*—a triumph of strained rhyme and fractured meter later published in the *Essex Daily News*—read:

> *Great joy to all the ships at sea*
> *And fear to all our enemy.*
> *This awful war you'll terminate*
> *The seed of peace you'll germinate.*
>
> *We know 'twas tough to leave the coast*
> *Where many months you were the toast.*
> *But all good things you know must end,*
> *Your place is here not there dear friend.*
>
> *We hope you had a merry stay*
> *While basking out Hawaii's way,*
> *Cause sister now you're gonna sweat*
> *The roughest schedule you've ever met.*
>
> *From dawn to dusk the planes you'll launch*
> *Until the crew has lost that paunch,*
> *And maybe in a month or so*
> *For ten short days to port you'll go.*
>
> *You'll need the rest we'll all avow*
> *For you'll have worked damned hard and how,*

And soon you'll find that actually
Recuperations best at sea.

We're sure that your conditioned air
Will prove a boon and serve you fair.
The "Bonny Dick" has naught so fancy,
Not even one MacDonald Banshee.

We scramble still from deck to deck
By power of sturdy legs by heck,
You see we haven't reached the state
Where we're required to escalate.

We envy not your dandy thrills
Oh! Welcome to Korean hills,
We're sure the commies cringe in fear
For they heard at last you're here.

9

OH! WELCOME TO
KOREAN HILLS

"USE CAUTION WHEN ditching damaged airplanes in Wonsan Harbor," warned an impromptu sign posted in VF-54's ready room aboard *Essex*. "Don't hit CDR Gray."[1]

CDR Gray was Paul Gray, CO of VF-54, one of Air Group 5's four squadrons. Muscular (he worked out daily in the ship's small gymnasium), with a cue-ball pate ("Bald Eagle" was his nickname) shored up by a small mustache and a steely jaw, the thirty-five-year-old Kansan seemed to live for danger, to embody it—forever, it seemed, thinking up new ways to assault the enemy. As one of his admiring Skyraider pilot acolytes put it (in the vernacular of the day), Gray could "fly lower and harder and raise more hell than anything since Donald Duck."

Gray was as cocky and brash as he was fierce—no slave to Navy protocol, even when it came to matters as mundane as radio call signals. For reasons of precision, secrecy, and—not least—Carrier Division Commander Black Jack Perry's obsession with radio-circuit discipline, pilots were to use numerical call signs during radio voice transmissions. Many instead used first names or nicknames, but Gray went a step further. Claiming he was "no good with figures," Gray used the call sign "Snow White" for himself and "Grumpy," "Sleepy," and "Dopey" for the pilots who flew in his division.

Gray's attitude and manner inevitably rubbed off on all the men who flew with him. Ceding Snow White his advantages in experience, savvy, and pure flying skill, none of his "dwarves" admitted a gap when it came to courting risk. As a result, few of VF-54's ADs returned to *Essex*'s flight deck without some flak damage. For his part, Gray all too frequently ruined—or outright lost—aircraft. The first loss came in the early fall of 1951 with a ditching after an interdiction mission; for this baptismal in the Sea of Japan, Gray had the good fortune to be scooped up by a South Korean Navy picket boat. "Snow White is safe," Grumpy, his wingman, assured flight control, but, as Gray admitted afterward: "I ditched at sea once. That's all a man has a right to expect."

Gray ruined his next aircraft just days later when he went after a North Korean locomotive concealed in a cave. To get the "loco" with one of his HVARs, Gray made a flaps-down low-level run straight for the cave mouth. Gray reportedly got the loco, but the blowback from the rocket explosion all but tore his plane from the sky. As it was, Gray knew right away his crippled AD would never make it back to *Essex*. To avoid a second water landing, Gray instead opted to crash-land south of the bomb line. Once more his luck held; Gray found an emergency field and glided in for a wheels-up crash landing. "This plane can't fly again," Air Force ground crews dutifully pronounced after inspecting the frightful damage, then added: "and this pilot oughtn't to." Gray, however, returned to the *Essex* that same day and put himself on the schedule for another mission.

Gray's exploits infuriated VF-54's own crew chief, a bull-chested Brooklyn-born chief petty officer named Andrew Szysmanski who was apt to be more distressed about lost aircraft than lost pilots. Given his way, Szysmanski would probably have none of his beloved Able Dogs exposed to combat. Time and again Gray's risk taking drove the normally affable chief beyond the limits of his composure.

When Gray actually managed a deck recovery after a subsequent mission, he walked back to the ready room as if everything had been routine. The AD he left behind, however, was riddled with fifty-nine separate shrapnel holes—another total loss, making three in a row. "What is he trying to do," the crew chief wailed to anyone who would listen, "break 'em up faster than I can fix 'em?"

***

When *Essex*, fresh from overhaul, joined Task Force 77 in August 1951, CVG-5's squadron personnel had access to several amenities that made them the envy of air groups on the other TF 77 carriers. For example, portions of *Essex's* interior spaces—including the pilot ready rooms—had been retrofitted with air-conditioning. Though climate control was a welcome feature anytime, AC would actually be most welcomed in the fall and winter when aircrews donned poopy suits. Snug (instead of stewed), flight crews could sit comfortably for briefings in a compartment climate best suited to polar bears.

"Conditioned air" was just one of the "dandy frills" called out in the welcoming doggerel penned by Bonny Dick's CVG-102 pilot laureate. Another was an escalator between the ready-room level and the flight deck—installed, most likely, to discourage pilots from routinely hitching rides on the flight deck elevators. The third—and dandiest—was the F2H Banshee, McDonnell Aircraft's answer to Grumman's Panther, getting its full operational introduction with VF-172.

Nicknamed "Banjo," the F2H had, thus far at least, played second fiddle to the Panther—in part because of the F9F's operational head start (even though the first Navy jet test prototype was a McDonnell design), in part because of a Navy decision to deploy the new aircraft first on Atlantic-based carriers. The Banshee was a larger, more rugged, and, it turned out, more flak-resistant aircraft than the Panther. It was to prove ideal for the low-level air war of interdiction and attrition that awaited its arrival in the Far East. The Banshee could reach a ground target with a more potent ordnance package than the Panther, dive more steeply, and (with its twin engines) climb faster. The Banjo's bombing accuracy was also better than the Panther's—even when pilots adhered to official task force doctrine that jets (to avoid explosion damage to sensitive turbine rotors) descend no lower than 3,000 feet during bomb runs. Perhaps most important, the F2H could stay over target up to a half hour longer than the F9F.

But the airplane's superior endurance also came with at least two practical flaws. When F2Hs were equipped with wing-tip fuel tanks, flight deck crews were hard put to fold the forty-five-foot wingspan. If a tip tank–equipped Banshee was scrubbed during launch, it was equally hard to "respot" the aircraft on a crowded deck. In simple terms, a disabled Banjo quickly became a traffic hazard. If the wingspan was a nuisance, the FH2's sheer bulk (fourteen tons at takeoff compared to the F9F's eight tons) made launches from *Essex*-class carriers' underpowered "short-throw" hydraulic catapults bone-jarring and adventurous at best.

***

In addition to VF-172, and Gray's VF-54, CVG-5 consisted of VF-51, a second jet squadron flying F9F-2s; VF-53, a Corsair attack squadron; two night-flying detachments (VC-3 Corsairs and VC-35 Skyraiders); a VC-11 Corsair antisubmarine detachment; and a helicopter detachment. Air Group 5's CAG was Cdr. Marshall U. Beebe of Anaheim, California, a Pacific-war veteran and, in his teens, a broad-shouldered star football player at Southern California's Occidental College.

Essex and CVG-5 were author and reporter James Michener's introduction to seagoing Navy aviation and its largely unsung role in the Korean conflict. It was also, in a way, Michener's reimmersion in a culture he'd sampled (albeit from the shores of a chain of backwater atolls) as a Navy officer a decade before in the South Pacific. Michener was onboard *Essex* for several stints of four to five weeks during her Korean deployment—stays interspersed with reporting from Korea itself and followed, at the end of *Essex*'s deployment, by stays on other carriers. It was a reunion, in other words, with a setting not altogether different from the one that had launched his writing career. Now clothed in journalistic stature and celebrity, Michener had more clout and ready access to the likes of Black Jack Perry—a trade-off, though, that meant correspondingly less day-to-day traffic with junior squadron officers and enlisted personnel. To most of them, Michener seemed a vague part of the background. VF-51 pilot Neil Armstrong, for one, recalled Michener as someone who sat around the wardroom in the evening or in the ready room in the daytime, listening to pilots talk—absorbing it all but rarely asking questions. Almost like a piece of Navy-issue furniture.

However, appearances notwithstanding, Michener was doing a good deal more than kibitzing. On *Essex* (and subsequently on *Valley Forge*), he was busily filling the pages of a series of lined notebooks. His hurried notes (some barely decipherable) were a disordered but purposeful accumulation of jargon, schedule and process sequences, statistics, place-names, and rudimentary diagrams.

Notebook entries read like the class notes of a diligent novice student. Michener was obviously trying, via this pileup of minutia, to master enough of combat aviation's patois, technology, and process to describe it coherently for his armchair readers back in the States. But he also seemed to be trying to parse the substance and spirit of its practitioners—not just how these men accomplished what they did but why.

During his tour in the South Pacific, Michener had experienced his own transformational flight-related epiphany.[2] Riding as a passenger on a routine hop to a remote island, Michener's plane had sputtered in the darkness over an empty stretch of the Pacific. The pilot somehow managed to nurse the aircraft to the vicinity of a small airstrip on the island of New Caledonia. Plunging toward the ground, the pilot pulled up at the last moment into a wheels-up crash landing. No one was seriously injured, but everyone was shaken.

Afterward, Michener felt numb and badly frightened. But as his nerves settled, Michener made a discovery: During the nerve-racking descent he'd been terrified of dying. But now he realized his death wouldn't have meant anything. The reality was sobering but also, in a way, liberating. If his life was important only to him, then he had to prove things only to himself—not to others. An internal voice told him he was a better man than his schools, the publishing business, or the Navy had known or would ever know. Michener had wanted to prove himself as a writer, and he didn't want to fail for lack of trying. He wondered if something analogous to his own near-death inspiration was at work here: motivating—though sometimes killing—these carrier pilots.

Michener was most interested in the experiences and mind-sets of the veteran pilots, many of them World War II veterans. For the air group rookies, however, men (though more nearly boys like VF-51's Armstrong and VF-831's George Schnitzer on *Antietam*, which joined Task Force 77 in mid-October), kept their foremost thoughts on simple practicalities—and attendant worries—of proving their mettle. When *Antietam* first reached station in the Sea of Japan, for example,

Schnitzer (who, though now a commissioned ensign, was still low man on *Antietam's* wardroom totem pole)* was more worried about carrier deck landings than facing enemy gunfire. "Landing back aboard" was real, he recalled, while the enemy, though somewhere out there, "wasn't real enough to get me all worked up." With only eighteen carrier jet landings, he was still "very wet behind the ears."

The same was true for Neil Armstrong: He was simply intent on doing the best job he could—and living to fly another day. He actually welcomed the combat experience, at least in the sense that he'd rather be flying than not. Still, because their lives were at stake, even rookie pilots like Armstrong and Schnitzer (at least within the ready room's fraternal sanctum) questioned everything: why, in particular, certain targets were available while others—especially those on, near, or north of the Yalu—weren't. They were just the sorts of questions military professionals exposed to the dangerous and absurd consequences of strategic decisions have asked, debated, and groused over for eons. For the most part they sloughed off the motivational "attaboy" blather piped into the ready rooms by ship captains or delivered to them in personal pep talks by touring dignitaries. Instead, they regimented time—and emotions—to the business at hand.

Much internal ready-room discourse centered on Task Force 77's mission. Against the backdrop of the peace talks (which, after their mid-July kickoff in Kaesong, dissolved in acrimony in late August, and then resumed in late October at Panmunjom), Task Force 77's operations were almost entirely devoted to interdiction. Regional responsibility then encompassed the territory from the bomb line 300 miles north to the Manchurian border and east of longitude 126°40'. To this was added the roadbed of a strategically vital cross-peninsula rail line; from an east coast railhead at Kowon (just north of Wonsan), the route pointed south only to pivot abruptly west on its way to a terminus at Yangdok.

In effect, Task Force 77 had road, rail, bridge, and tunnel responsibility for practically all of North Korea except the war's frontline trenches, the Yellow Sea coast, and "MiG Alley": a 3,250-square-mile

---

* Each of the wardroom's 256 officers was issued a numbered coffee cup. Schnitzer's was numbered 256.

trapezoidal patch in the Northwest bounded by the Yalu and Ch'ongch'on Rivers above which the swept-wing U.S. Air Force F-86s dueled Communist MiGs. Task Force 77 pilots were essentially shift workers in a destructive transit authority.

Although there was no lack of target opportunities within these boundaries, there were real differences in vulnerability and risk. The biggest target concentrations were along the narrow eastern coastal plain—most well within reach of coordinated air and coastal bombardment. Many key bridge and tunnel targets, however, lay farther west. Getting at them by air required flying greater distances, often through worse weather and over barren, inhospitable terrain. Because of their remoteness, both sides realized, the sites were particularly vulnerable; even with ready manpower, the Communists would be hard put to reroute, repair, or rebuild what American airpower could take out. To compensate, the enemy ringed them with elaborate antiaircraft defenses.

***

Soon enough, even the newest and least-experienced pilots took their turns in these flak shooting galleries. On September 3, while pulling up from a strafing run on railroad tracks near Wonsan, Neil Armstrong's Panther was abruptly jolted by flak. Armstrong regained control of his aircraft in time to avoid crashing, only to collide instead with one of the defensive "clothesline" cables now routinely strung between peaks overlooking target sites. This cable sheared a good six feet off the tip of his F9F's right wing, but Armstrong was once more able to regain control and even coaxed the plane into a climb.

Armstrong was flying this particular mission on the wing of John Carpenter, an Air Force major assigned to the Navy on a pilot exchange program. After talking it over—coolly and dispassionately in the way that perhaps only military aviators facing disaster can—both agreed that if Armstrong slowed for a ground approach, the damaged wing would stall ahead of the left wing, sending the Panther into an uncontrolled roll. All things considered, it was better to punch out, despite the fact that Armstrong had never before made even a practice jump.

With Carpenter flying close by, Armstrong kept the Panther aloft until they were well south of the bomb line, eventually punching out over Pohang—the site of a Marine Corps air base designated K-3. Just as Armstrong touched the ground on K-3's outskirts, a Marine Corps jeep trailing a huge plume of dust skidded to a stop right beside him. At the wheel was Goodell Warren, one of Armstrong's flight school roommates and now a Marine aviator based at K-3.

***

One of Michener's closest and most enduring relationships from his time aboard *Essex* was with CAG Marshall U. Beebe. A Pacific-war fighter ace with ten kills to his credit, Beebe, at the time CO of composite squadron VC-39, was one of 300 survivors of the 1943 nighttime torpedo sinking of carrier *Liscome Bay* (CVE-56)—a calamity in which more than 600 air crewmen and sailors perished. In "Snow White Is Down Again" (a draft of a profile eventually published in the *Saturday Evening Post* as "The Forgotten Heroes of Korea"), Michener extolled Beebe as a "red hot airman. . . . He is rugged, can fly any plane going, takes his men into the toughest targets, and fights for them against all the brass in the Navy." As one pilot told it to Michener, "He's the greatest of the follow-me boys."

Although Beebe was just thirty-eight ("handsome, gray haired, ruddy faced"), he looked older to Michener, "like a deeply worried, responsible man of fifty." A CAG like Beebe commanded the lives of 142 pilots; he also flew his share of combat strikes—in Beebe's case usually strapped into the cockpit of a Banshee. Beebe, Michener told his readers, could not afford to be sentimental about death. He was, after all, "engaged in a profession in which men must expect to die." Still, his passionate involvement in both the flight performance and the lives of his pilots had clearly exacted a physical and emotional price: "He flies every inch of the way with us," another pilot confided. "He makes every landing. This guy dies in every crash."

The exploits of VF-54's CO Paul Gray and his dwarves without doubt claimed a goodly portion of the price. Beebe was of two minds when it came to his AD squadron CO. Beebe was a combat pilot himself, of course, and he wanted veteran pilots like Gray to set the example when it came to leading others into combat and accomplishing their missions. At the same time he was responsible for preserving his air group—pilots and aircraft alike—for the duration of the deployment.

Having borne witness to the loss of so many squadron comrades in the fiery sinking of *Liscome Bay*, he now endured more. Already, by mid-October, still less than halfway through a Far East war cruise that would stretch until March 1952, the air group had lost nine pilots and one air crewman to a combination of enemy fire and flight accidents.

The group's first fatality—although officially still listed as missing in action—was a VF-53 Corsair pilot named Leo Franz. Franz was flying on instruments near Wonsan on August 23 when he lost contact with his flight leader; the twenty-four-year-old Kansan was neither heard from nor seen again. Just three days later, a VC-35 AD flown by Loren Smith, a twenty-three-year-old Oklahoman, unaccountably exploded and crashed at sea barely five minutes after launch. Lost along with Smith was his radarman, twenty-two-year-old Phillip "Peeb" Balch.

A bad August for casualties became a worse September—and got off to an early start. On September 3—the same day as Neil Armstrong's harrowing brush with death near Wonsan—Frank Sistrunk, one of Gray's VF-54 AD dwarves, was hit by ground fire during a bridge strike. Sistrunk, a twenty-nine-year-old Arkansan, married and the father of two girls, immediately pointed his aircraft toward the coast, but he was blessed with none of Snow White's good fortune. Instead, still feet dry, Sistrunk's aircraft dived suddenly, steeply, and uncontrollably before augering into the rocky slope of a North Korean hill. The very next day, two of Armstrong's VF-51 squadron mates, twenty-five-year-old Jim Ashford and twenty-six-year-old Ross Bramwell, were also lost to enemy ground fire, Ashford northwest of Sinp'yong and Bramwell over Haengsan.

That made three fatalities, and September was not finished; in fact, it had much worse in store. On September 16 (a "bright autumn day," as Michener would later describe it) a VF-172 Banshee piloted by John Kemp Keller collided with another aircraft during a high-elevation practice maneuver. The collision wasn't fatal, but its aftermath was.

Damage to his plane's tail section forced Keller to return to *Essex* for an emergency landing. Everything seemed normal during approach until Keller, perhaps shaken by the experience of the collision, neglected (or was unable) to lower his tailhook.

Keller's lapse was compounded by crewmen who failed to spot the still-retracted tailhook. By then it was too late. Fourteen tons of jet aircraft still heavy with fuel hit the deck, raced past the arresting wires, tore through the barriers, and smashed into a stack of planes parked forward. There was an explosion and a terrible blaze that instantly killed four crewmen. In the rush to prevent an even bigger calamity, Keller and his aircraft were pushed overboard. Meanwhile, five more *Essex* flight deck hands, each swathed in a curl of flame, jumped overboard. Two were fished out, severely burned but still alive, but the remains of Keller and the other three, like those of Franz, Smith, Balch, Sistrunk, Ashford, and Bramwell before them, were never recovered.

In his evening prayer, piped each day over *Essex's* internal radio circuit, the ship's Catholic chaplain, Commander Buzek, took note of the four men, as he did any day a pilot, air crewman, or sailor was killed or went missing: "O God, we humbly beseech thee for the soul of our shipmate John Keller [or Leo Franz, Loren Smith, Peeb Balch, Frank Sistrunk, Jim Ashford, or Ross Bramwell]." At the prayer's closing, for those such as Franz, Sistrunk, Ashford, and Bramwell believed down and likely dead in enemy territory, the chaplain had a further special plea: "Deliver him not into the hands of the enemy, but command that he may be received by the holy angels and conducted into paradise."

***

Other Task Force 77 carriers were hardly spared their own portions of sacrifice to combat, crashes, atomization in the trackless Korean landscape, or drowning in the eternal, depthless sea. *Bon Homme Richard's* Air Group 102 (whose acerbic verse had welcomed CVG-5 to the "Korean hills"), due to complete its deployment in early December, had lost six prop pilots, three each from VF-783 and VF-874, its two Corsair squadrons, and two from Skyraider squadron VA-923. VA-783, -874, and -923 were all activated reserve squadrons populated largely by recalled veterans with a sprinkling of youngsters. The demographics showed in the pilots' ages at death. The youngest (VF-874's William Henry Mero, plucked from the September 4 sky by flak) was just twenty-three; of the remaining five, however, the youngest was just shy of twenty-seven (VF-874's Fred Leslie Koch, whose Corsair exploded on August 11 as he leveled off from a bomb run on a bridge) and the oldest (VA-923's James Aloysius Savage, whose

Skyraider disintegrated in an explosion when he tried an emergency landing at K-18 with live ordnance still hung on a wing rail) just shy of thirty-one—"old" men no longer.

Carrier *Antietam*, meanwhile, not even a month into its deployment, experienced a flight deck accident that both mirrored and rivaled the mid-September carnage on *Essex*. In midmorning on November 4, a VF-837 F9F flown by twenty-nine-year-old lieutenant George Spencer Brainard made a deck landing so hard that his tailhook missed all the wires. Brainard pushed his nose down hard in an effort to stay on deck, but the nosewheel immediately blew, and the plane then zoomed past the barriers into a fiery collision with planes parked forward.

Brainard was killed instantly, as was one deckhand; two more deckhands died that same day, and ten other men were injured. The most seriously injured of these was Lt. George DePolo, a VF-831 pilot and squadron mate of George Schnitzer. Schnitzer's division was the last to touch down that morning, after first being diverted for a ground landing when one of its planes took damage. After their return, flight operations stood down for the balance of the day. For Schnitzer, the crash was one more reminder of the flight deck's sinister possibilities. In the end, he knew, each pilot "had to evaluate his own role in landing his aircraft in such a limited space."

The next afternoon, following scheduled morning replenishment, a funeral service was held on *Antietam's* lowered deck-edge elevator. It was a tearful, moving ceremony under a cold, gray, and rainy sky— this time replete with flag-draped, canvas-shrouded corpses. After the chaplain's words and the playing of taps—thereafter Schnitzer could never hear taps played without tears in his eyes—there was, for once, the finality of bodies splashing into the cold sea.

***

If there were a prevailing pattern or a logic to these fatalities—whether in time of day or stage of deployment; sea, wind, or weather conditions; target location or mission risk; pilot age (young or old); or pilot experience (extensive or slim)—it was that there existed no pattern or logic. The props took the brunt, likely because there were vastly more Corsairs and Skyraiders on sorties than Panthers and Banshees. What added risk the slower props might face over ground targets (witness

VF-54's Sistrunk and VF-874's Mero and Koch) was offset by the calamitous possibilities inherent in the jets' launches and recoveries (witness John Keller's runaway Banshee and Brainard's runaway Panther). What could be reliably expected seemed to be the unexpected: the wordless disappearance of VF-53's Franz, for example, or the anomalous midocean explosion of Smith's VC-35 AD. It was what manned flight had ever been through war and peace since its inception fifty or so years before: dangerous, unpredictable, and, if—as with Icarus—its odds were chanced too often, too far, or too high, fatal.

***

As September rolled into October, it was likely this cumulative heavy but imponderable weight of CVG-5's casualties that had already done most of the care wearing that Michener detected in Beebe's features. Yet more were still to die. The first two weeks claimed one, again from the ranks of Gray's daredevil dwarves: twenty-five-year-old Cordice "Tex" Teague, lost to ground fire on a road strike west of Wonsan. This was followed on October 16 by the loss of a second Banshee and with it one of Air Group 5's most experienced pilots. Lt. Cdr. Irad Blair Oxley, thirty years old and a 1943 Naval Academy graduate, crashed and died after his F2H was hit by radar-controlled ground fire over an extraordinarily well-defended railroad bridge near Majon-ri.

Compounding these two losses (to which would be added a third before the month was out: Richard Alan Bateman, a twenty-one-year-old VF-53 Corsair pilot) was yet another nail-biter from Gray himself. This was now his fourth and one that must have all but shattered the tenuous balance of Beebe's twin allegiances to mission and men. This time Gray's AD took a direct hit by a Communist 37mm antiaircraft round—a blow that set its Wright Cyclone engine afire and doomed the plane.

Gray had little choice but to venture his second ditching—now in icy October waters. Using his consummate repertoire of skills, Snow White made the sea and succeeded in settling his AD into the chop— although barely within reach of a rescue destroyer. By the time the tin can's gig crew hauled him in, Gray was near helpless with a pair of frozen hands and deep in hypothermia. Nevertheless, true to form, Gray was back in the VF-54 ready room the next day (the "caution" sign now taped to a bulkhead) and cleared by an overmatched group flight surgeon as fit to fly again.

After losing a fourth squadron aircraft, even Snow White must have realized that his odds were slipping in this race of luck against life. Despite this, Gray remained the odds-on choice to lead a special mission on October 30. Through anti-Communist guerrillas operating in North Korea's mountains and coastal areas, Eighth Army Intelligence learned that senior political, security, and military representatives of Chinese and North Korean forces would be meeting in a cluster of twelve buildings near Kapsan, a valley town high in the mountains of northeastern North Korea.

Eighth Army passed the information to Task Force 77 on October 29 (a day before the scheduled meeting), but mindful of the shadowy nature of this group and the often wild inaccuracy of its reports, confirmation awaited results of a VC-61 Panther high-altitude photo-reconnaissance flight that same day. When those came, a strike combining aircraft from *Essex* and *Antietam* was set for 7:30 A.M. on the thirtieth.

* * *

Forty aircraft—twenty each from *Essex* and *Antietam*—combined for the hush-hush mission. Gray led the *Essex* ground-strike package, two divisions of VF-54 Skyraiders, each equipped with two 1,000-pound bombs (one fused to explode on ground contact, the other to explode aboveground to take out antiaircraft emplacements), four small general-purpose bombs, and napalm. Four VF-172 Banshees and eight VF-53 Corsairs (with equal representation from *Antietam*) flew cover.

Approaching low to avoid North Korean ground radar, the aircraft reached Kapsan by nine o'clock but waited another quarter hour before climbing to 8,000 feet above the crest line of a ridge that overlooked the Communist compound. From this perch, the AD pilots watched F2Hs and F9Fs make flak-suppression sweeps before rolling in through the continuing rattle of ground fire to drop their proximity bombs. All eight bombs exploded and apparently on or near target: Flak was all but silent during subsequent runs.

The ADs climbed, circled, and swooped in next to pickle ground-contact bombs, followed by a third run to drop the smallest bombs and torch the remains with huge fiery dollops of napalm. By then the mission had devolved into a melee of rocket and strafing 20mm fire that reduced the compound to a mass of seared and smoking rubble. Above the ground, as the air armada's division leaders checked returning flocks, the results were best of all: every *Essex* and *Antietam* aircraft accounted for and all bound for home.

Poststrike reports from the anti-Communist guerrillas were effusive—though ultimately unverifiable: the deaths of some five hundred conference attendees and the destruction of virtually all North Korean Communist Party records. But the attack also ended up severing links with the guerrillas, as increased pressure from North Korean security forces either dismantled their units or drove them further into the shadows. For all the momentary acclaim, it would serve, in the months ahead, to make an already murky covert world (one on which pilots pegged their own hopes for rescue should they be downed over Communist territory) even murkier.

***

If the big Kapsan mission and the oncoming holidays presaged a welcome season of lower causalities—Group 5 grieved just two November losses: VF-54 pilots William Arnold Bryant Jr. and Eugene Brewer Hale, both to flight accidents and ocean graves—it wasn't for lack of trying. Strike operations continued unabated and, if anything, squared off against some of the thorniest and most resistant targets.

One evening in early December, Marshal Beebe, Paul Gray, and the three other CAG-5 squadron COs were assembled in Admiral Perry's cabin for dinner. Michener joined them, and afterward Perry asked each squadron commander to describe his experiences in flying over North Korea. When Gray got his turn, he detailed careful planning for the next day's strike against the railway bridges near Majon-ri, the same intensely defended site that had claimed the life of Banshee pilot Irad Blair Oxley weeks before.

The latest prestrike reconnaissance photos showed a hornet's nest of fifty-six antiaircraft guns surrounding the bridges—mostly 37mm sprinkled with a few even heavier caliber guns, many radar controlled, and all arranged to converge fire on the only route in and out of the river valley spanned by the narrow bridges. His pilots, Gray told Michener, knew it would be no walk in the park.

Success, Gray was convinced, would require longer, slower, and more vulnerable glide-bombing approaches, and to have a chance they first needed to suppress as many guns as possible. To do this, they'd settled on using the same heavier proximity-fused explosives employed at Kapsan. As at Kapsan, the shrapnel downpour from these "ugly bombs" stood the best chance of taking out the gun and radar crews so they could move on to the bridges.

***

After reaching the target area the next day, the twelve strike aircraft—eight Skyraiders and four Corsairs—circled at 15,000 feet, positioning for suppression runs on the guns and radars. Initially, the planes picked up some desultory flak, most of it high and astern, but then, as they separated and bore in, the volume and precision intensified. Gray went first and, after pickling his ugly bomb, pulled out south of the target area to watch the others. One Corsair got hit on the way down, forcing the pilot to abort; three other planes took minor flak damage, but all had apparently weathered the worst part.

After the join up, Gray detached and flew low over the area to flush any guns still operating. Sure enough, one opened up: 37mm fire from a surviving battery quickly chased Gray, forcing him to call in a reserve Skyraider. This last AD's ugly bomb exploded right over the holdout; suddenly, there were no more bursts from any of the big guns.

The planes took only sporadic machine-gun and small-arms fire as they swept in to take out the bridges. Mission accomplished; Oxley's loss avenged. After a final check of the target area, all twelve planes joined up, inspected their wingmen for damage, and headed home. Michener was a Vulture's Row spectator as LSO Doug Fannin brought all the returning aircraft safely back aboard.

***

Naturally enough, prop-pilot relief, elation, and pride followed the difficult Kapsan and Majon-ri missions; it was welcome evidence that, for now at least, they had a leg up on the Communist defenses. The casualty-free successes also set the stage for what looked to be an ideal year-end respite: *Essex* was due to stand down and sail for Yokosuka and ten days of Christmas R&R.

But if the fortunes of air combat defied prediction, the vagaries of brass bullshit apparently did not. Brass bullshit was widely understood to flourish inversely to the proximity of friendly shores. As *Essex* steamed up the coast of Japan, drawing close to Yokosuka, Marsh Beebe briefed his prop squadron COs, VF-53's Herman Trum and VF-54's Gray, on "Operation Pinwheel." Pinwheel was the brainstorm of *Essex* CO Austin W. Wheelock, a plan to use the *Essex's* ADs and F4Us to assist the ship in docking. The aircraft were to be "chocked down" along *Essex's* port side and, at a signal from the bridge, their engines revved to full power to "pull" as harbor tugs simultaneously "pushed" the carrier into her berth.

Both Trum and Gray were outraged at Pinwheel—a lamebrain stunt that could easily damage the engines of combat aircraft. When news of it hit the ready rooms, Operation Pinwheel became "Operation Pinhead" and Wheelock became "Wheelchock." Pilot resentment simmered. To Bob "Woody" Wood, a twenty-six-year-old VF-54 AD pilot now on his second Korean deployment who thought he'd seen everything, it was the height of absurdity.

Sensing a near mutiny on his hands, Paul Gray finally pulled Trum aside on the eve of *Essex's* arrival at Yokosuka. "I don't know what you're doing," Gray confided, "but I'm telling my pilots not to give them more than half power. If that engine temperature even begins to rise, cut back to idle." Trum agreed.

The next morning, half power was precisely what the AD and Corsair pilots gave. About an hour after the ship docked, an angry CAG ordered Gray and Trum to his office. Captain Wheelock had become outraged when he failed to get full power from the lashed-down props. Beebe got a tongue-lashing on the bridge, and, in turn, Gray and Trum got theirs in Beebe's cramped office. In the heat of the moment, Beebe ordered pilots from both squadrons put "in hack"— restricted to the ship until further notice, a heavy price to pay after a straight month of combat flying.

Hack, fortunately, lasted only three of the ten days in port, lifted in the end by the common sense of Black Jack Perry. Perry spent his own

R&R holding court—and buying free drinks—for visiting pilots in the bar of the Fujia Hotel, while he sipped Coca-Cola in penance for his own days of heavy drinking. Despite his fiery flag plot demeanor and the healthy fear he instilled in most pilots, Black Jack was actually a good listener who used this setting to keep his finger on the pulse of aviator morale. Pilots who worked up the nerve—the prospect of free drinks was often all it took—would take a seat and regale Black Jack with their latest death-defying escapades. After several days at the Fujia, Black Jack remarked to one of the jet pilots that he'd not yet seen any of the prop pilots. What were they up to? "Haven't you heard?" one pilot asked him. "CAG has all VF-53 and -54 pilots in hack."

After hearing a little more background, Black Jack blew his own gasket. "Get that idiot Beebe on the phone," Perry bellowed to his aide in a voice that boomed across the bar and into the hotel lobby. The next morning the restricted VF-53 and -54 pilots encountered a sub-dued Marsh Beebe who, it soon became clear, had again been whiplashed by both Perry and Wheelock—this time for restricting the men. "The hack is lifted," Marsh told them. "You're free to go ashore. Now get out of here and leave me alone." As they raced for the gang-planks and the delights of Yokosuka, the prop pilots had to feel sorry for a man whom they truly admired and respected but who, for now at least, could not win for losing.

10

FROM A COLD SEA

On January 22, 1952, *Essex* VF-53 pilot Lt. John Abbott was flying one of two Corsairs escorting a division of VF-54 ADs on a bridge and rail strike west of the remote northern port city of Chongjin. The six aircraft were still over North Korea when Abbott's engine quit and his cockpit flooded with smoke. Choking, his vision obscured, Abbott was barely able to reach the Sea of Japan before being forced to bail out. Lt. Ed Laney, Abbott's wingman and his friend since flight training, circled Abbott as his parachute canopy blossomed and he drifted down. Meanwhile, the four ADs, one of them piloted by Woody Wood, circled at higher altitude to coordinate communications.

Laney was worried and had reason to be. Abbott would land not only in freezing water but also in the middle of a coastal minefield, making the chances for a prompt rescue by destroyer slim at best. Moreover, given Group 5's recent string of fatalities, this looked to be one more in the making. Already, in the weeks since *Essex's* return from Yokosuka, Chaplain Buzek had beseeched for the souls of three more fallen aviators. In the January 6 evening prayer, his plea was for VF-51's Ens. Glen Howard Rickelton, a twenty-three-year-old pilot flying his fiftieth—and final—combat mission. Rickelton's F9F had disintegrated during a strafing run north of Kowon. Just three days later it was for another twenty-three-year-old: VF-54's Ens. Raymond Gene Kelly, whose AD had nosed over, crashed, and burned after being hit by antiaircraft fire. And then, on January 11, he interceded for another "dwarf": Joseph Henry Gollner, twenty-four, who, after reporting mechanical problems just minutes from launch, jettisoned his ordnance package only to disappear, as surely as his tons of bombs, into an unmarked, untraceable ocean grave.

In retrospect, neither Rickelton, nor Kelly, nor Gollner had much hope—for survival or the recovery of their mortal remains. But now, once he splashed down, John Abbott's prospects appeared at least a bit better. With what to Laney seemed practiced efficiency, Abbott unpacked and inflated his pararaft and looked ready to haul himself in.

Then the catch: Abbott's hands were already so numb he was unable to release his parachute harness straps. Acting like a sea anchor, the chute both kept him from getting into the raft and threatened to drown him. The most he could do was tether himself to the bobbing raft. After a hopeful start, Abbott's life-and-death stopwatch, Laney knew, had now begun ticking.

***

Twelve miles away, also within sight of the Korean coast, and just seconds after Abbott's first smoke-choked Mayday call, Duane Thorin and his crewman Ernie Crawford, the duty helicopter rescue crew aboard Navy cruiser *Rochester*, were already preparing to launch their Sikorsky from the ship's fantail. Earl Lanning, a strapping nineteen-year-old metalsmith in *Rochester*'s R (Repair) Division, did double duty supporting the helicopter detachment. Lanning, a rural North Carolina native and himself a pilot, had learned to fly crop-dusting biplanes at age thirteen. Like many *Rochester* sailors, Lanning deeply admired Duane Thorin, who, besides being a natural role model, was a mesmerizing shipboard raconteur and trusted confidant. Whenever "flight quarters" was piped through *Rochester*'s spaces, Lanning was quick to drop whatever he was doing and race topside to *Rochester*'s hangar and flight deck complex—spaces originally designed to store, catapult, and retrieve scout seaplanes but now used exclusively by the helo detachment.

Helicopter flight operations reminded Lanning of his backwoods biplane days: It was definitely seat-of-the-pants, a world apart from shipboard routine. One time he'd watched in awe as "Dewey" Thorin—trying to help young ensign Donal Hollis, the detachment's

other pilot and, by virtue of his rank, its OinC, touch down on a buck-
ing deck in a tricky wind—stood nonchalantly astern the hovering
Sikorsky, grabbed its whipsawing tail boom, and steadied it for landing. But through constant practice the operations—and especially the
launches—had also become quick and well synchronized. On this
bright, clear, frigid January morning, for example, it took just two
minutes and fifteen seconds to get the bird in the air. Lanning was on
hand to pull the Sikorsky's front chock—and to flash an encouraging
grin and a reciprocal "thumbs-up" to Thorin and Crawford as their
chopper lifted, wheeled, and thwacked shoreward to rescue Abbott.

Equipped with a vector from *Rochester*'s Combat Information Center (CIC), Thorin and Crawford were well en route by the time Ed
Laney reported the bailout. As Thorin's helicopter reached the scene,
Abbott, still attached to his parachute, was floating on his back waving
and smiling to the circling spectators.

* * *

The rescue of downed pilots like John Abbott was no small matter—
not only for the helicopter detachments but also for the escort "tin
cans" that raced like edgy sheepdogs about the outskirts of big ship
formations. Indeed, plane guarding—trailing in the boiling wake of a
carrier during flight ops, extra lookouts on heightened alert—more
and more edged out submarine screening as the escort destroyers'
most vital (and inestimably more gratifying) responsibility.

It certainly was important as far as the carrier aviators were concerned. Pilots who otherwise had little interest in the lives and fortunes
of men in the "black-shoe Navy" held deep personal affection and
enduring memories for the ships and sailors who pulled them (or a
buddy) alive from the clutches of a cold sea. During the last two weeks
in October—their first in the war zone—no fewer than three of *Antietam*'s CVG-15 aviators had been rescued by alert black shoes who,
in turn, were risking their own lives.

Two of the rescues were the especially tricky nighttime handiwork
of plane guards. The first, on October 22, by destroyer *Hanson* (DD-
832), extended the lives of a VC-11 pilot and his two air crewmen
when their AD lost power and ditched after a night landing wave
off. At the end of the month, another plane guard, this time *Eversole*

(DD-789), rescued a VC-3 night flyer who ditched with engine trouble just after launch. This recovery took longer—the distressed pilot lit off a flare and then fired a cylinder full of tracer rounds from his .38 revolver before he was finally spotted, tracked down, and hauled aboard—but was no less welcome.

***

Despite John Abbott's apparent calm as he waited for his rescue, every flyer in the vicinity knew well just how precarious his situation was. Abbott was likely already in hypothermal shock, and the chute canopy, should it fill with water instead of wind, could just as easily drown him as keep him afloat.

If any reminder was needed, there was the tragedy of Woody Wood's VF-54 division leader Bill Bryant. Bryant had launched during bad weather on November 17; within minutes his AD's engine quit, and he ditched hard in rough seas. *Essex's* angel was over the scene almost at once, ready to haul Bryant out of the drink. Despite the hard landing, Bryant, who was wearing a heavy winter flight suit instead of a poopy bag, had gotten out of his cockpit, but, as he waited for rescue, he was also apparently in a concussive daze. When the helo lowered its rescue sling, Bryant did little more than lean into it. As the sling cable was being reeled in, Bryant was already close to falling out, and soon he did, splashing back into the water. When rescue boats finally reached the scene, Bill Bryant was nowhere to be found.

Duane Thorin may or may not have known about Bryant's loss, but he had already experienced his share of rescue mix-ups and tragedies—and the helpless rage that went with them. Just a year before, well into his first Korean deployment aboard *Philippine Sea*, Thorin had witnessed the wrenching death of a sailor he'd been dispatched to save—and very nearly the compounding loss of Chester Todd, his air crewman at the time. That situation (unlike Bryant's in November or Abbott's now) was stamped with doom from the start: Although the sailor, a deckhand who had fallen off a supply ship during replenishment operations, was apparently still alive when Thorin and Todd reached the scene, he was already deep in hypothermal distress, blue-faced, and kept afloat only by the tenuous buoyancy of air pockets in the folds of his foul-weather gear.

"I can get him, Dewey," Todd had shouted as the helicopter hovered over the site that day, but Thorin was wary about sending Todd in after an unconscious man. Not until he spotted an approaching destroyer did Thorin finally let Todd jump in. It was a bad mistake. Todd couldn't get the rescue sling over the victim's bulky clothing, and the destroyer's whaleboat was out of commission with a frozen engine.

The inert sailor inevitably slipped from Todd's own weakening grasp, and the same gear that had kept him afloat now pulled him down and out of Todd's reach. Meanwhile, as Thorin simultaneously jockeyed his flight controls and the hoist apparatus to retrieve his crewman, Todd's hands grew too numb even to grasp the suspended rescue sling. Worse, Todd was now drifting into his own dreamy, slow-motion stupor. Todd's inflated life vest kept him afloat, but, unknown to Thorin, Todd's flimsy exposure suit had ripped and icy water already encased his legs.

That Todd lived to recount his piece in this harrowing tale was a credit to the quick response of the rescue destroyer CO and his crew. Unable to launch the whaleboat, the tin can's skipper had instead maneuvered upwind, stopped engines, and drifted downwind close enough for several volunteer swimmers tethered to safety lines to jump in and retrieve Todd.

Todd's rescue was a redeeming finale to an otherwise tragic event. But the tragedy—what Thorin believed was the needless death of one sailor and the near death of Todd—also gave him leverage to get two things he'd wanted all along. The first was a better exposure suit, something Thorin had coveted and lobbied for since the previous January and his time aboard icebreaker *Burton Island* in the Bering Sea. Within days, several frogman wet suits were flown in from the UDT (Underwater Demolition Team) training facility in Coronado, California.

The second, and ultimately more dramatic, was the opportunity and the resources to innovate better rescue gear. Helped by *Philippine Sea*'s air group parachute rigger, Thorin and Todd devised two simple but fundamental improvements. One was what they called a survivor's sling: a length of web strap that could be quickly hooked around the torso of a man in the water, drawn tight, and then snapped to the chopper hoist cable by another hook. The other was a strong shoulder harness for the helicopter crewman that could also be clipped easily to the hoist cable.

***

As it turned out, Duane Thorin and Chester Todd never got the opportunity to try out this new equipment—the hooded frogman suits were just on loan, and the survivor's sling and shoulder harness were onetime prototypes—before *Philippine Sea* ended its Far East deployment in March 1951 and returned to the States. However, six months later, when his helicopter detachment flew west out of northern California's Travis Air Force Base for its second tour, Thorin made sure to pack the sling and harness with his personal gear. He also managed to acquire—with the help and "backdoor requisitioning" of a friendly UDT chief petty officer—two frogman suits.

Although officially it was the detachment's second Korean tour, Thorin was one of its few experienced veterans. He had in Hollis (a greenhorn officer just graduated from Advanced Flight Training) a new OinC and, in Ernie Crawford (a rated petty officer and plane captain), a willing, dependable, but still novice in-flight crewman.

After fueling stops in Honolulu, Wake Island, and Iwo Jima, the detachment's air-transport flight touched down in Tokyo, where a connecting flight took them from Yokosuka to Sasebo. There they boarded a wood-hulled Japanese troop transport, a World War II remnant, for an overnight crossing to Pusan, South Korea. With the prospect of sleeping on a belowdecks bunk that was little more than a woven straw pallet, Thorin chose instead to spend the night topside. Beneath a temperate, moonlit sky, the ship's wooden prow seemed to glide effortlessly and in near silence across what proved to be a placid, nearly glass-top sea.

When the transport reached Pusan at dawn the next morning, it docked at a bustling quay directly astern of the detachment's new duty station, heavy cruiser USS *Toledo* (CA-23). *Toledo*—a derisive "Toodle-dee-Doo" to its ship's company—was not, as detachment personnel quickly learned, a happy ship. As Hollis's men embarked, personnel from the detachment being relieved had already scurried unceremoniously ashore (and onboard the soon-to-be-outbound

Japanese transport) without the customary formalities of a turnover meeting. The helicopter they left behind was desperately in need of major maintenance.

***

Toledo was then temporarily assigned to Task Force 95, an ever-changing dog's breakfast of U.S. Navy and ROK Navy vessels operating in coastal waters off North Korea as a bombardment, blockading, and screening force. With winter coming on, it was cold, unglamorous, monotonous, and often frustrating work, marked by dangers remarkably akin (in type if not in scale) to what the troops ashore encountered. In September 1950, for example, while bombarding shore positions off Tanchon, the bow of destroyer *Brush* (DD-745) triggered a submerged contact mine; the resulting explosion broke the ship's keel, killed thirteen sailors, and wounded thirty more. Six months later, ten officers and sailors from *St. Paul* (CA-73), a heavy cruiser like *Toledo*, were lost when their whaleboat was hit by enemy mortar fire in Inchon Harbor.* Then, on October 7, 1951, several weeks after Thorin's detachment boarded *Toledo*, destroyer *Ernest G. Small* (DD-838) suffered nine dead and eighteen wounded when it hit a mine just offshore from Hungnam.

Wartime casualties were not the cause of Toodle-dee-Doo's malaise. Instead, in Thorin's estimation at least, it was the grinding down of the ship's spirit and self-respect, in large part due to Task Force 95's grandstanding flag admiral. Thorin had first encountered him just after the Pacific war when Thorin was copiloting Navy cargo planes in the Far East. At that time the brass hat's specialty was displacing personnel from what were intended as passenger flights and filling the planes instead with contraband booty to be shipped back to the States for personal use or resale. His game now—much to detachment personnel's dismay and disgust—was to commandeer the Sikorsky for questionable "inspection" flights that turned out to be little more than sightseeing.

---

* In April 1952 thirty more *St. Paul* crewmen would die from an accidental powder explosion in a forward eight-inch gun turret during a shore-bombardment mission off Kojo, North Korea.

One such excursion flight, with Hollis at the controls, actually delayed rescue efforts for a Marine Corsair pilot who'd bailed out over the Yellow Sea south of Cho Do Island. The delay may well have cost the pilot's life; he was not found until the following day when his body, dragged by his parachute, washed ashore. Hollis and his air crewman had been the ones dispatched to extract the bloated, frozen corpse from a desolate strip of beach within sight of the North Korean coast. It was a dreadful task performed on an island that was code-named "Blood Stone" and under the baleful gaze of a few of the pilot's squadron mates circling overhead. Their silent stares weighed heavily on Hollis even though the situation was beyond his control.

Fortunately, circumstances steadily combined to relieve the tedium and frustration of the helicopter detachment's *Toledo* exile. Late October brought the first and biggest change. The cruiser's reassignment to Task Force 77 meant a welcome return to open waters and, more important, prompted the departure of the flag admiral and his staff. Soon there were also opportunities for temporary assignments on other Task Force 77 ships: Thorin, for example, enjoyed several days' duty aboard *Essex* while the carrier's own helicopter was being overhauled. The biggest change, however, came in November when *Toledo* ended its Far East deployment. The detachment then transferred to cruiser *Rochester*, newly arrived in the Far East.

***

Crawford was getting ready to lower the cable and rescue sling to the waiting Abbott until he realized the pilot's parachute was still attached. It didn't particularly worry Thorin. "Go ahead, Ernie," Thorin shouted. "If he can get in the sling we can pull him high enough for you to cut the shrouds." So Crawford triggered the hoist and lowered the sling. Abbott saw it coming and even hooked one arm into it when it dangled within reach. But that was it: He made no further effort. Instead, he just lay quietly, still smiling, his senses obviously dulled by the frigid water.

Thorin glanced back at Crawford who knew what was happening and was already adjusting the hood of his frogman suit and readying the survivor sling and harness. When Crawford nodded, Thorin lowered the chopper, dropping close enough to the water for Crawford to all but step into Abbott's pararaft. Then he raised it slightly, keeping it in a hover, but reducing the rotor wash. This enabled Crawford, athwart the raft, to scoot over to Abbott, loop the sling around Abbott's torso, and draw the loop tight.

This done, Crawford pulled out his survival knife and reached across Abbott to gather the parachute shrouds. However, as he did, the knife—it should have been attached to Crawford with a lanyard but inexplicably wasn't—dropped into the water and immediately sank. Crawford now had only his bare hands to work on the shrouds, and his fingers were practically paralyzed by the cold.

Crawford did somehow manage to hook the survival sling to the hoist cable and give Thorin a thumbs-up. The questions now: Could the chopper carry both Abbott and his water-weighted chute? And, if so, how soon could Thorin find a safe place to unload Abbott and return?

***

At this stage in his career, although still learning and still mastering the chopper's quirky subtleties, Thorin was largely unfazed by the things that could go wrong—and so often did—in these rescues, whether over water or on land behind enemy lines. Having learned to ride, rope, herd, hike, camp, hunt, fish, and otherwise survive in the open and still essentially wild spaces of Nebraska, Thorin was used to tough situations and unusually confident in his ability to improvise. Indeed, if Thorin had a personal flaw, it was his condescension for those who weren't as confident, clever, and resourceful.

Indeed, Thorin railed against entire classes of "fools," chief among them brass hats, bureaucrats, toadying staff officers, and rear-echelon "commandos." The latest and biggest of these classes, at least to this point, encompassed most U.S. Air Force personnel. Interservice rivalry was rarely put aside even in the war zone; for Thorin it often bordered on barely suppressed contempt.

In November, just days before *Toledo* left for Yokosuka and the States, Thorin had been called on to extract an Air Force F-51 pilot who had bailed out in the mountains west of Wonsan. Before crossing the coast-in point, Thorin, flying without a crewman but escorted by a flight of Marine Corsairs, climbed to 14,000 feet, both to avoid ground fire and to receive radar vectoring instructions from Air Force controllers. The controllers in turn were communicating with a pair of Air Force F-51 pilots said to be circling the mountain where their buddy had bailed out. During the thirty-minute flight, Thorin received a stream of eastward course corrections from the Air Force controllers—so many that he began to wonder if they (or the circling pilots) actually knew where to find the downed man.

Eventually, the controllers directed Thorin and his escorts to descend through a cloud layer. Emerging from the clouds, Thorin and his escorts immediately realized the rescue site was no mountain; rather, it was a broad valley rimmed with radar-controlled antiaircraft batteries protecting what looked to be a major North Korean supply route. Spotting Thorin's noisy and slow-moving chopper, battery gunners quickly drew a bead. Within moments Thorin was bracketed by flak; only a hasty climb and a reflex-quick intervention by the Corsairs saved him.

Afterward, the radio circuit fairly crackled with Marine and Navy invective and Air Force counterinvective. The problem got sorted out only when the Air Force pilots were finally pinpointed. The "mountain" they were circling turned out to be a thick cloud drifting eastward in the prevailing wind currents.

It would take a second day and another aborted rescue flight before Thorin (again flying alone because of the altitude) finally plucked the pilot, an Air Force captain named Waid, from a small clearing on an otherwise steep and jagged mountain slope. By then, however, Waid was expecting company. A small party of North Korean soldiers had spotted him and was closing in. Barely able to hover because of the elevation and lacking the help of a crewman, Thorin had no choice but to touch down. As the much relieved Waid (who'd abandoned his parachute and used flight charts as blankets during the night) ran to the idling chopper, climbed aboard, and buckled in, Thorin could hear rifle shots. During the climb there was even a "ping" as one bullet ricocheted off a wheel strut.

***

For the Abbott rescue, extra weight—not altitude or North Korean gunfire—was Thorin's biggest problem. But he also had in his favor a strong surface wind that gave the chopper an extra cushion of air. Thorin used the boost now to edge the chopper laterally until it hovered directly above Crawford and Abbott. He could see neither of them and wouldn't be able to until he had Abbott out of the water. Thorin then added power, being careful not to strain the chopper's engine or rupture the hoist motor as he hauled Abbott and his chute clear of the water.

There was a surge when the chute broke the surface and then another when a reservoir of water cascaded from its canopy. After each jerk, worried that Abbott might have toppled from the sling, Thorin tilted the chopper just enough to have a look. Sure enough, there was Abbott, still dangling and still connected to his chute. But, to Thorin's surprise, after a third, much smaller, surge, he spotted another item: Abbott's pararaft dangling like a yellow rubber boot at the end of an overloaded fishing line.

Crawford hadn't realized that Abbott was still tethered to the raft; once he found out, his hands were too numb to detach it. The pararaft's weight alone didn't make a substantial difference, but its removal left Crawford immersed in the water with only his frogman suit to protect him.

***

The first month of life aboard cruiser *Rochester* proved a major improvement over *Toledo*. It was what Thorin considered the "real Navy." Instead of being treated like recreational baubles, the helicopter and its detachment personnel were respected and put to intended use. The ship's CO and XO were explicit in valuing the unit as a search-and-rescue resource and were even willing to adapt shipboard schedules and procedures to accommodate airborne needs. Hollis and Thorin got what they needed most—more frequent and more realistic "flight quarter" drills. Getting the helo launched quickly and headed to the right location could make all the difference in the life or death of a downed flyer. They got the full cooperation of the ship's company, and especially the willing help of sailors like Earl Lanning and twenty-one-year-old Rulon V. Bird. Every man assigned had a specific role—Bird's was to race to the ship's armory to retrieve sidearms for the helicopter crew. By the time *Rochester* left (in company with carrier

Essex) for Christmas R&R in Yokosuka, the drills had clearly paid off; launch time went down, first to three minutes and then even lower.

In January, unfortunately, *Rochester*'s detachment to Task Force 95 meant the return of the troublesome flag officer. There was only so much *Rochester*'s skipper could do to shield the helo detachment from his schemes. Indeed, absent an equipment problem, a planned inspection of some coastal islands would have made the Abbott rescue flight impossible. Ironically, the problem—a broken weld cluster on a landing-gear strut—was almost certain to be the residual effect of the suspicious "ping" Thorin heard during the November mountain rescue. While of no concern aloft and not enough of a problem to preclude rescue flights, it gave the detachment a convenient excuse for pulling the chopper off-line.

***

Cautiously, Thorin triggered the hydraulic hoist to raise Abbott. Once the hoist cable spooled to the top he hoped to reach out and hang Abbott's survival sling to a door-mounted hook—maybe even sever the parachute shrouds and swing Abbott into the cockpit. The cable was still being reeled in when Thorin noticed Abbott's chute canopy again billowing in the wind, enough so that it risked fouling the tail rotor. Thorin had little choice but to lower the cable and leave Abbott dangling in the sling.

Thorin radioed VF-53's Laney that he would return to *Rochester* with Abbott as soon as he could drop another life raft to Crawford. Laney urged Thorin not to wait: He would jettison his own pararaft instead. Even as he said it, Laney knew he'd be taking a chance. Jettisoning a raft from the Corsair cockpit risked getting it caught in the slip stream and hitting the tail assembly. All pilots were warned about this, but Laney had twice before done it successfully.

Thorin rogered Laney and pointed the helicopter toward *Rochester*, applying full throttle. It was slow going: Fighting the wind resistance created by Abbott and all the dangling paraphernalia, the Sikorsky's airspeed was barely forty knots. Well aware that Abbott, out of the water but still suspended in frigid air, was running out of time, Thorin scanned the horizon for an alternative. The closest was destroyer *Collett* (DD-730)—already en route, but forced to pick its way cautiously through the minefield. Thorin radioed ahead to *Collett*, alerting the tin can's crew that he'd be depositing Abbott on her fantail.

Thorin came in high, being careful to stay well clear of *Collett's* superstructure and its maze of rigging. One of the ship's chief petty officers, positioned high enough to be at Thorin's eye level, flashed hand signals to help him maneuver, and, once Abbott was in reach, deck-level boatswain knives made quick work of severing the shrouds and harnesses.

With Abbott, his raft, and his parachute all aboard *Collett*, Thorin climbed and was poised to return for Crawford when he spotted another equipment problem. As he tried to reel in the hoist cable, the hoist engine suddenly stalled. The cable had somehow tangled in the landing struts. Thorin risked two possibilities: burning out the cable motor or tearing away the already damaged landing strut. He had no choice but to detour to *Rochester* to get it cleared.

It took a few more precious minutes, but as he hovered and deckhands freed the cable, a crew volunteer wearing one of the frogman suits jumped aboard to help with Crawford's retrieval.

***

Outbound once more, Thorin heard the radio circuits flood with excited chatter: "Lay it on 'em!" Then, "They're going back to their bunkers! Look at those rascals run!" Thorin switched to the guard channel and asked for details. Laney's Corsair, he found out, was in trouble. Before pushing the pararaft out of his cockpit, Laney had decided to pull its inflation lanyards. The blossoming pararaft had indeed gotten caught in the Corsair's slipstream and ripped off one of its stabilizers.

Now not only was Crawford still in the water without a raft, but Ed Laney had been forced to crash-land on the beach. Worse, as soon as he jumped from the cockpit, a North Korean patrol emerged from a concealed bunker to give chase. Laney had been hightailing it along the beach but was forced into the surf whenever his pursuers—and their bullets—got too close. He now faced three bad alternatives: freezing, being captured, or being shot. For the moment, Woody Wood and the other VF-54 pilots were cloverleafing just off the deck to strafe any NKPAs who tried to approach.

Crawford, meanwhile, despite having been in the water for more than a half hour, somehow managed—even with hands no more useful than clubs—to clip in when Thorin finally lowered the sling. As expected, Crawford was trembling and his hands were stone cold when they pulled him in; to help with that, the crewman unzipped the top of his own survival suit so Crawford could begin thawing against the other man's torso. Otherwise, though, Crawford seemed both conscious and coherent: worried most that *Rochester's* medical personnel might try to cut away the frogman suit that had saved him. "No way I'll let them do that!" he insisted, when Thorin kidded him.

***

Within minutes—the helicopter this time not much hampered by wind resistance—the reassuring bulk of *Rochester* hove into sight. After depositing Crawford on *Rochester's* fantail, Thorin, who by now had been airborne for well over an hour, set out along with his wide-eyed volunteer to try to pull Laney from the beach.

Thorin fully expected to find Laney in the water and was surprised instead to see him scurrying along the surf line. He positioned the helicopter upwind of Laney and readied for a crosswind approach. Seeing what was about to happen, one of the ADs swept in ahead, chewing up the beach behind Laney with 20mm fire. Thorin tilted the chopper to the left, and as it slipped down toward Laney, the volunteer crewman, leaning out of the cabin, did his part by expertly lassoing the pilot. Hovering momentarily, Thorin applied a touch of power to pull the cable taut and then more power to sweep them higher, out of bullet range, and seaward. They were well en route to *Rochester* by the time a breathless Laney was pulled into the cockpit.

***

It was, in all, a singularly proud moment for *Rochester's* helicopter detachment and, indeed, for every man in *Rochester's* and *Collett's* crews: a moment when each had reason to feel he'd contributed to something unique and tangible. It was a moment to put aside the effects of work that was mostly cold and dull, occasionally dangerous, and almost invariably thankless. Collectively, as a team, with Dewey Thorin as their chopper-flying avatar, they'd launched in record time, rescued two downed flyers, and saved one of their own.

Abbott had indeed arrived on *Collett* in bad shape—his mouth full of frigid seawater and a body temperature that dipped as low as ninety-two degrees. But the tin can's chief pharmacist's mate (an undertaker in civilian life) did all the right things to revive Abbott. Laney, although understandably shaky after his beach ordeal, was no worse for wear, and Ernie Crawford, thanks to his conditioning and the hooded frogman suit, had lost less than a degree of body temperature during all his time in the water. The recuperation for both men took little more than hot showers and shots of medicinal brandy. Especially gratifying to Thorin was the fact that the equipment and rescue techniques that he and Todd had devised and improvised fourteen months before aboard *Philippine Sea* had proved their value.

Recognition for everyone came that same afternoon when an announcement from the bridge invited all hands not on duty to go topside. After forming up for return to their respective carriers, the entire Task Force 77 afternoon strike force—sixty or more planes strung out in a series of small formations—staged an impromptu flyby for both *Rochester* and *Collett*. Passing to starboard of the two ships, each formation dipped its wings in unison in a salute signifying both gratitude and comradeship. For young sailors like Earl Lanning and Rulon Bird, who both stood on deck to witness it, it was an unforgettable, life-changing experience.

***

For his January 26 evening prayer, the *Essex* chaplain reserved a spot for Lt. (jg) Leonard Cheshire. Cheshire, a twenty-four-year-old VF-51 pilot from Albuquerque—recently married and a close friend of Neil Armstrong—had been hit by Communist gunfire near Wonsan. He shed his canopy and tried to punch out, only to have the explosive charge that propelled his ejection seat misfire. With his squadron mates screaming, "Jump! Jump!" over the radio circuit, Cheshire, still traveling at nearly three hundred knots, now had no choice but to risk a water landing in Wonsan Harbor. To everyone's amazement, he looked like he might succeed. Then, just moments before touching down, the explosive charge that had failed suddenly fired, sending Cheshire, still strapped to his heavy ejection seat, to a watery grave.

"O God," Chaplain Buzek intoned through the ship's crackling compartment speakers, "we humbly beseech thee for the soul of the pilot, our shipmate, Leonard Cheshire, who died this day. Deliver him not into the hands of the enemy, but command that he may be received by the holy angels and conducted into paradise."

In the two months of deployment that remained, the chaplain would have one more evening prayer elegy: on February 21, after VF-53 Corsair pilot Francis Gene Gergen, twenty-five, having become disoriented in a snowstorm, crashed into the sea. By that time, the chaplain had, all told, interceded for the souls of twenty-eight pilots, air crewmen, and sailors.

The toll was particularly heavy for VF-54. Twenty-four pilots were assigned to the squadron at the beginning of deployment in August. By the completion of the cruise, seven pilots, nearly one-third of the squadron, would be killed. Each squadron pilot, of course, looked at these losses individually, not collectively. They were lost friends, not statistics. During predeployment training at North Island, for example, VF-54 pilots Bill Bryant, Frank Sistrunk, Cordice Teague, and Woody Wood—each married and each, with the exception of bridegroom Teague, fathers of one or more children—had lived near each other in Imperial Beach. To enable their wives to have use of the family cars, the four pilots had carpooled. In the 1950s, it was a familiar ritual for many one-car suburbanite families. Now, however, Woody Wood, age twenty-six, was the lone survivor of his carpool.

Somewhat amazingly, the list of VF-54 fatalities did not include its CO, Paul Gray—though perhaps only because of another intercession from above. Into the closing weeks of the war cruise, after sweating through five separate "Snow White down" dramas—the last, a ditching, occurred on January 22, the very day of John Abbott's and Ed Laney's rescues—Black Jack Perry finally had enough. With the end of the deployment nearing and the war firmly mired in the twin stalemates of peace talks and endless combat, Perry finally ordered CAG Beebe to ground the Bald Eagle.

***

When "The Forgotten Heroes of Korea," Michener's *Saturday Evening Post* article, was published—at just about the time *Essex* finally left Point Oboe behind—it sadly included another elegy, this one for Duane Thorin. Concluding his account of the Abbott, Crawford, and Laney rescues, Michener wrote: "Out here it is not known what Duane Thorin has earned in the way of medals.* But one and all hope he will be recognized for what he was, the bravest of the brave. He is not among the living—he volunteered for a rescue mission more hazardous than the one described, and lost his life."

This portion of Michener's report to his readers made for a compelling, if somewhat abrupt, coda to the life of a remarkable hero. But, in the case of Duane Thorin, the epitaph also proved to be premature.

---

* Ernie Crawford was awarded a Navy Cross.

11
UNHAPPY VALLEYS

HARRY ETTINGER FLEW his first and only Korean combat mission—a night reconnaissance—on December 13, 1951, two weeks to the day after his twenty-fifth birthday. Night recco was a specialty for the radar-equipped AD-4NL models flown by *Valley Forge's* VC-35 detachment, and it would seem odd to Ettinger—when there was finally time and perspective to reflect on it—that after all the investment in training and operational preparation, his air combat career *over* Korea would come down to barely an hour's flight time.

After earning his commission and his wings in 1947 and qualifying to fly Skyraiders, Ettinger had hoped to stay in the Navy, only to be caught in the postwar manpower squeeze. After returning to civilian life—now a husband and father of two—Ettinger, like so many others, had been abruptly recalled to active duty in October 1950.

Ettinger along with radar operator Julian Gilliland and ECM specialist Jess McElroy had launched at sunset on a four-hour "dusk to dark" sortie that, in tandem with a "dark to sunrise" sortie to follow, stretched ATG-1's flight ops to a round-the-clock day. Ettinger this night was flying wing in a two-plane section scouring a triangular plot west of Wonsan for North Korean truck convoys moving under the cover of darkness. While his section leader, VC-35 detachment OinC Mel Schluter, skimmed the contours of area valleys and hills to uncover targets and draw fire, Ettinger flew behind and above, ready to pinpoint enemy ground fire and pounce.

Degrees of luck always shadowed pilots during air combat. For example, there was the indecent good luck that seemed to insulate pilots like VF-54's Paul Gray. However, even the best runs of good fortune were more than offset by more typical runs of good, indifferent, or bad luck that sooner or later claimed pilots who exposed themselves to combat too often or with too much reckless abandon. But what next happened to Ettinger, Gilliland, and McElroy somehow didn't fall along this spectrum. It was instead either a long-odds outlier or the product of an entirely different sort of probability: Call it "nonluck."

Nonluck came as a big bang and a sickening thump in the gathering darkness—a hit (well behind and below Ettinger's cockpit perch) so jolting that it could only have been the work of an antiaircraft gun. Probably a blind shot—but no less devastating for that.

Ettinger's first instinct was to climb and bank east toward the Sea of Japan. But already his fuel level was plunging, and the Skyraider's engine was cutting out. Instead of climbing, the plane was dropping. Craning his neck to port and starboard, Ettinger could see smoke and the flickering light that convinced him the plane was on fire. He transmitted a Mayday but had no way of knowing if it was heard.

Ettinger next tried the intercom to reach Gilliland and McElroy in the after compartment, but the line was dead. The three men had discussed circumstances when they should—or shouldn't—wait for the order to bail out. With so much gone wrong—the big hit and the fire, dead intercom, faltering engine, and loss of altitude that followed—they probably hadn't hesitated to jump. Whatever had happened to Gilliland and McElroy, it was time for Ettinger to look to his own survival.

***

On December 9, when Ray Edinger's COD aircraft rumbled onto *Valley Forge's* flight deck, he was, with two missions to his credit, the first VF-653 pilot with actual Korean air combat experience. Squadron CO Cook Cleland had dispatched Edinger to *Essex* three days before to get a taste of what lay ahead: a not-uncommon practice intended to smooth the way for untested squadrons like VF-653.

During the COD flight to *Essex*, Edinger got his first opportunity to wear a poopy suit aloft. The fit and feel, even on this short flight, lived up to lines from CVG-5's "welcoming poem" to ATG-1:

Of course the weather's cool out here
But in your poopy suit so dear
You'll find the sweat runs fast and free
From Antung down to Kono-ri.

Over the next two days, teamed with VF-53's CO Herman Trum, Edinger flew a strike against a railroad bridge and a gunfire-spotting mission for a battleship cruising off Tanchon. Although pestered by light flak during both missions, neither Corsair took hits. Trum even apologized afterward for not taking Edinger in close enough to get a bullet hole or two.

Coincidentally, Edinger returned to *Valley Forge* on the very day that VF-653 lost its first two pilots, twenty-seven-year-old lieutenant Donald London and twenty-nine-year-old lieutenant James Porterfield—both also from Cook Cleland's VF-653 "Flying Circus"—to an accidental midair collision on a "refresher flight." London (the law student) and Porterfield (the masonry contractor) were actually ATG 1's second and third deployment fatalities; the first, VF-111's skipper Frank Welch, was lost when his F9F-2 stalled and crashed during a carrier-landing approach off Hawaii in December.

Edinger's job was to refocus the minds of squadron personnel on the job ahead by relating what he'd learned about air warfare over Korea. The first thing they had to know was that despite exhaustive training in flying CAS, the air war, given the stalemate on the ground and the on-again, off-again negotiations at Panmunjom (where, in late November, although still well short of reaching a cease-fire, the parties had finally bargained a line of demarcation at the 38th Parallel), was now solely about interdiction and its unnerving counterpart: evading mobile, sometimes radar-controlled, flak.

None of them, not even experienced Pacific-war combat veterans like Cleland, had faced radar-controlled guns before. What big-bore flak they had been exposed to was predictable: rounds either with time-delay fuses or fuses "cut" for altitude—guesswork shooting that could usually be "outflown." Now, in addition to the small-bore 23mm machine guns and the midrange World War II–vintage 37mms, they would also have to dodge radar-guided 57mm guns. Up against the radar-aimed 57mms, pilots might have no warning before taking a direct hit.

Railroad locomotives were prize interdiction targets. However, not all targets of opportunity were big, fast moving, or even mechanized. They'd also be hunting for pack trains of Siberian ponies and even oxcarts or lone men shouldering big "A-packs." Sometimes, in order to distinguish the bad guys from the innocents, pilots would first have to make dummy runs without firing.

Such dry runs, in addition to being risky, were at best a crude means of making life-and-death decisions. "If it's a farmer, he'll be untying his ox and taking it with him—it's probably his entire life's savings." On the other hand, "if the guy just drops everything and runs, it's most likely a military target. Open fire on the next pass and look out for the explosion if he's hauling mortar rounds or grenades."

For aerial targeting purposes, North Korea and its coastal waters were segmented into a series of sector squares, each 10,000 meters (roughly 60 miles) on a side and each with a two-letter designation— CS (Charlie-Sierra), CT (Charlie-Tango), DT (Delta-Tango), and so forth. More exacting coordinates came by subdividing these squares into ten or even one hundred smaller segments.

The key railroad lines were further parceled into segments: each roughly 10 miles long and each labeled with female first names such as Birdie, Bonnie, Cindy, Dagmar, and Hazel. The names made convenient shorthand for establishing mission boundaries, but their lilt often belied the real danger they contained. One of the most dangerous was "Bonnie-Birdie"—a rail segment at the western extreme of the Kowon to Yangdok line coursing through North Korea's midriff.

Bonnie-Birdie ran—as did most rail lines in the mountainous interior—through a valley flanked by rocky and snow-covered hills. Hills near strategic targets such as bridges, tunnels, spurs, and depots typically concealed dozens of antiaircraft guns, all registered to cover target approaches. Perhaps the nastiest of these guns were the 37mms. The TNT-packed projectiles fired by the 37mms were about an inch and a half in diameter and five inches long. Although seldom radar controlled, they were more than capable of bringing down a plane on a low-level diving or strafing run with a single well-placed hit.*

---

* A generation later this weapon gained special media notoriety when actress Jane Fonda visited North Vietnam and was filmed sitting at the gunner's station of a 37mm antiaircraft installation targeting U.S. Air Force and Navy aircraft.

Taking out such targets required hit-and-run attacks through the crossfire gauntlet of their AA defenses. Targets along Kowon-Yangdok's far reaches were doubly formidable because of their remoteness. Any plane hit seriously during a strike would have a hard time reaching the Sea of Japan. By the same token, pilot rescue by helicopter would be chancy, both because of the distance to be flown and because of the high elevation.

***

Harry Ettinger considered bailing out, even though he had little sense of his altitude. He did know that in the dark and over this mountainous terrain, any crash landing would be blind—and probably fatal. When he slid back his cockpit canopy, Ettinger instantly felt the cold hard blast of wind; the wind ripped his helmet off and threatened to take his head with it. He used the new vantage to take another look around. He could see the fire now: ravenous tongues of flame licking up from the curve of the fuselage belly. The hit must have been to his fuel tank. The bright stabs of flame only made it that much harder to see beyond into the darkness. Looking to starboard, Ettinger noticed that the after compartment hatch had been jettisoned. There was no time now for procedures or checklists—it was leave now or never.

Using his cockpit seat as a platform, Ettinger tried to hoist himself enough to jump, but something held him back. Most likely one of the canvas straps of his parachute harness had gotten snared, but, buffeted by the fierce wind and consumed by the moment's urgency, he couldn't resist straining—using all of his 136 pounds to try muscling free rather than hunkering down to free the strap.

Just then Ettinger heard a big THWACK off to starboard. This new sound (he reasoned later that his wing had clipped tree branches in clearing a ridge crest) only stoked his determination. Bracing one foot on the Skyraider's control stick, he pushed up and back with all his might. That did the trick. In the next instant, Ettinger flew clear of the cockpit. Caught in the slipstream, he tumbled back, caroming off part of the Skyraider's tail section. There was no time to think—no time to judge his elevation nor hope of seeing the lay of the terrain below him. His hand found the parachute rip cord and instantly gave it a yank.

The parachute canopy deployed just in time: Ettinger dangled and swung just once in its cradle before hitting the ground hard but feet first. As the billowing chute collapsed, he tumbled and rolled clumsily through an inches-deep layer of powdery snow covering frozen ground. When he finally came to a stop and looked up, Ettinger sensed he had landed within yards of a village. Despite the darkness, he could discern the outlines of a handful of small huts and outbuildings.

As he caught his breath and considered what to do next, the choice was made for him. In an instant, hands were grabbing Ettinger from behind and pulling him roughly to his feet. He was surrounded by a half-dozen Korean men.

They looked to be civilians, but each brandished a rifle. As Ettinger, still encumbered by his chute, struggled to get his balance, the Koreans began pummeling him, a few with arms and fists, the rest with rifle butts. The layers of winter gear topped by the poopy suit cushioned most of the body blows, but Ettinger no longer had his flight helmet and one rifle butt came down squarely on his skull.

The beating was fierce but short—the sort of school-yard scrum where the assailants rise quickly to fury, then just as abruptly lose steam. The blow to the head was the worst part: It left Ettinger feeling dazed and woozy, and a trickle of blood coursed through his scalp and down the side of his face. But he was still conscious and able to stand, and the men apparently had no intention of doing him further harm, not yet at least. Instead, they stripped Ettinger of his knife and pistol, bound his hands in front of him, and, prodding him with rifles and bullying grunts, ordered their prisoner to march toward the village.

* * *

From his vantage as ATG-1's operations officer responsible for allocating squadrons to missions as well as an F9F pilot flying a share of those missions, Jim Holloway got his own hands-on indoctrination to the air and ground war's cat-and-mouse game. When destroying the North Korean railroad infrastructure became the primary strategic objective and "loco busting" its highest tactical priority (next came rolling stock, then bridges, and the tracks themselves), the North Koreans had adapted by concealing their trains by day in long mountain tunnels. Despite the daredevil tactics championed by the likes of VC-35's

Frank Metzner during *Princeton's* deployment the previous spring, "tunnel busting" had serious drawbacks as a long-term tactic. Success, for example, required a straight run of track leading into the tunnel and enough maneuvering room to enable the pilot—usually flying an AD—to pull out. There were only so many tunnels that met these requirements and, with the constant deployment turnover, only so many pilots with the skills, experience, and daring to pull it off.

Instead the efforts by night-flying VC-3 F4U-Ns and VC-35 AD-4Ns evolved to spot nocturnal trains, disable their locos with rockets and strafing, and then, when daylight arrived, launch flights of bomb-laden Corsairs and Skyraiders against the stranded loco and its tail of rolling stock. To counter this (and to ambush the daylight props' strikes) the Communists soon arranged to move in mobile flak batteries on flatbed cars, stationed either behind or ahead of the stalled train or even—if tracks adjoined—directly alongside.

Meanwhile, owing to their extra speed but limited bomb loads, VF-52's and VF-111's jets took the lead role in "route recce" armed reconnaissance, daylight missions over the often one-lane dirt-and-gravel roads that supplemented the rail lines as the Communists' lines of supply and communication. The most heavily trafficked roads were divided into numbered segments fifty to seventy-five miles long—about the length of road that could be covered effectively by a division of "short-legged" jets. Each carrier jet squadron normally flew two road recces daily—each division plane armed with HVARs, fragmentation bombs, and full magazines of 20mm.

The division would usually split over the target area: the two planes of one section guarding the flanks as the other made its runs—and then switching roles. There was also role rotation between the pilots of the attack pair: one soaring high to spot, the other skimming well below 1,000 feet to bomb and strafe. For the low man of the attacking section, jinking at 250 to 300 knots (4 to 5 miles per minute, slow for the jets but still faster than the props) to follow the contours and dodge a rat's maze of mountain defilades, it was a wild, unforgiving, physically exhausting ride requiring twitch-quick reflexes and flawless muscle memory, especially if the guns of flatbed flak trucks—camouflaged and tucked into a draw or just around a bend—suddenly unmasked and opened fire.

During attack runs, the low man—and often his high-altitude spotter as well—turned off his cockpit pressurization system: Absent the echoing pulse of his own breathing, he was more apt to hear the telltale sounds of small-arms fire signaling that ground troops were caught in the open and running for cover. AA machine-gun fire, meanwhile, would show up first as tracer streaks in the shadowy valley hollows.

Returning ground fire required another layer of awareness and concentration. More than a few pilots lost to "enemy flak" over Korea were instead victims of blasts from their own fragmentation bombs pickled too near the ground. A handful had even been known to select the wrong ordnance-rack toggle switch as they lined up a target to fire; flying low and flat intending to shoot rockets, they instead dropped bombs and paid the price.

***

ATG-1's first verified combat death came on December 18,* just four days after Harry Ettinger and his crew disappeared. VF-194's thirty-one-year-old XO Tom Pugh was on an interdiction mission near Wonsan when his Skyraider was hit by antiaircraft fire and he was forced to ditch. Pugh made a picture-perfect touchdown in choppy coastal waters, climbed effortlessly from his cockpit, stepped onto a wing, pulled the lanyards of his Mae West, and even waved confidently to the planes overhead. But then, to the circling pilots' astonishment and dismay, Pugh, rather than inflating his pararaft and climbing in, jumped (or accidentally slid) directly into the water.

Pugh was doomed. The day's two duty rescue helicopters, both based on coastal islands near Wonsan, were down with mechanical problems, and the cruisers and destroyers normally stationed in waters just minutes away were instead positioned fifty miles north. By the time a tin can finally reached the scene more than an hour later, Pugh was floating facedown and already dead. When his body was hauled aboard the destroyer, sailors found his poopy suit flooded with icy seawater all the way to his armpits.

---

* VF-194 pilot Alan W. Duck was killed on October 23, 1951, before *Valley Forge* joined Task Force 77.

Snow- and ice-covered flight deck of carrier *Valley Forge* (CV-45), 1952

Rear Adm. James L. Holloway Jr. and Secretary of the Navy James Forrestal

Ens. Jesse L. Brown, USN, September 1949

Aviation pilot Duane Thorin

VF-653 Commanding Officer Cook Cleland (left) with Executive Officer Ray Edinger

VF-831 F9F pilot George Schnitzer

VF-653 Corsair pilot Robert Balser

Official U.S. Navy photo, now in the collections of the National Archives

USS *Valley Forge* (CV-45) (foreground) and USS *Leyte* (CV-32) at Sasebo, Japan, 1950

AP photo courtesy of Robert Pigeon

September 1950: Corsair pilot winces in pain from burns as his survival raft is hoisted to the deck of an unidentified U.S. Navy destroyer off Wonsan

VF-32 Corsair pilot Bill Koenig

VF-32 Corsair pilot Tom Hudner

VF-112 F9F pilot
Edward D. Jackson Jr.

VF-112 F9F pilot Dayl Crow

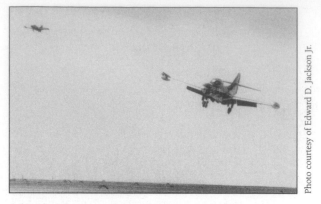

Ed Jackson approaching *Philippine Sea*'s flight deck.
Dayl Crow's F9F is visible in the background.

Ed Jackson's F9F immediately after touchdown on
Philippine Sea

Ed Jackson sitting in his cockpit as flight deck
personnel rush to assist him

Philippine Sea flight deck and medical personnel lift Ed Jackson from his cockpit

One of the thousands of marines and GIs who fought their way from Chosin to Hungam

Lt. Gen. Matthew B. Ridgway inspects frontline positions upon his arrival in Korea

Daisy Brown and Tom Hudner
at Medal of Honor ceremony

April 13, 1951: Tom Hudner being
congratulated by President Harry S.
Truman at Medal of Honor ceremony.
Hudner's parents are in the background.

Gen. Douglas MacArthur during an April 1951 ticker tape parade in New
York City

Essex VF-54 Division Six Skyraider pilots. From left to right: Cordice Isaac Teague, Lou Ahrentis, William Arnold Bryant Jr., Joseph Buford Parse Jr., Robert Wood. Teague, Bryant, and Parse were all fatalities of the 1951–1952 deployment.

December 1951: Destroyer Division 91 crews crowd the decks of their ships [from background to foreground: USS *De Haven* (DD-727), *Mansfield* (DD-728), *Lyman K. Swenson* (DD-729), and *Collett* (DD-730)] in Sasebo, Japan, to receive Navy Unit Commendations

Photo courtesy of Earl Lanning

Duane Thorin (left) with ship's crewmember aboard
USS *Rochester* (CA 124)

Photo courtesy of Earl Lanning

Rochester crewman Earl Lanning (left) with shipmate

Photo courtesy of Rulon V. Bird

Rochester crewman Rulon V. Bird

Rochester detachment helicopter touching down with rescued aviator

Casket of unidentified aviator being transferred from *Rochester* to destroyer

Essex VF-53 pilot John Abbott being lowered to deck of USS *Collett* (DD-730) from rescue helicopter flown by Duane Thorin

In Memoriam

Phillip K. Balch	ATAN	26 AUG.
Loren D. Smith	LTJG	26 AUG.
James J. Ashford	LTJG	4 SEPT.
Ross K. Bramwell	LTJG	4 SEPT.
Frank Sistrunk	LT	4 SEPT.
Joseph B. Parse	LTJG	8 SEPT.
Wade H. Burfield	AD 3	16 SEPT.
Charles L. Harrell	AA	16 SEPT.
John K. Keller	LTJG	16 SEPT.
Earl K. Neifer	AOC	16 SEPT.
Vernon Netolicky	AN	16 SEPT.
Sidney M. Sanders	AA	16 SEPT.
William J. Stewart	ADC	16 SEPT.
Samuel R. Marker	AN	3 OCT.
Cordice I. Teague	LTJG	6 OCT.
Roger C. Hammond	AA	7 OCT.
Irad B. Oxley	LCDR	16 OCT.
Richard A. Bateman	ENS	28 OCT.
Lawrence B. Jackson	AN	7 NOV.
William A. Bryant	LTJG	17 NOV.

Frank Sistrunk
VF-54 4 September 1951

Cordice Isaac Teague
VF-54 6 October 1951
VF-54

Joseph Buford Parse
VF-54 8 September

William Arnold Bryant
VF-54 17 November 1951

Eugene Brewer Hale
VF-54 27 November 1951

Raymond Gene Kelly
VF-54 9 January 1952

Joseph Henry Gollner
VF-54 11 January 1952

Photo collage courtesy of Robert Wood

VF-54 pilot and air crew casualties from 1951–1952 Korean War deployment aboard *Essex* (CV-9)

VF-194 Skyraider pilot
Howard Thayer

VF-194 Skyraider pilot
Dick Kaufman

VF-194 Skyraider pilot Joe Akagi

Reconnaissance photo of North Korean railroad complex taken in March 1952 by VF-194 Skyraider pilot Oren Peterson

VF-653 pilot Ray Edinger lands his crippled Corsair aboard *Valley Forge*. Edinger landed without flaps and with an armed rocket still hung on his port wing.

Ray Edinger's Corsair catches an early wire. Note collapsed landing gear and bent propeller. Hung rocket has been dislodged and disposed of by flight deck personnel.

VF-653 pilot group photo, July 1952. Back row (left to right): Dave Robertson, Ed Kearns, Bill Clarke, Bob Balser, Cook Cleland, Ray Edinger, Nip Wilson, Ross Rohleder, R. Smith (replacement pilot); front row: Bob Jesswine, Roy Johnson, John Gray, Bill Hartman, Tommy Davis, Bob Geffel, Guy Dunn, Sam McKee, Ralph Evans.

VF-781 pilot Royce Williams points out the damage to his aircraft following a harrowing multi-MiG dogfight east of Chongjin.

Photo courtesy of E. Royce Williams

VF-194 AD pilots Howard Thayer (left) and Kenneth Schechter reunite aboard *Valley Forge* at completion of ATG-1's Korean War deployment.

Lt. Cdr. James L. Holloway III, USN, on board USS *Boxer* (CVA-21) in 1952, as executive officer and then commanding officer of VF-52

VF-194's Joe Akagi receiving Distinguished Flying Cross from Vice Adm. J. J. (Jocko) Clark while aboard USS *Boxer* (CVA-21)

Gen. Mark Clark signs Korean War Armistice documents.

August 1953: Officers and men of USS *Boxer* (CVA-21) uncover to pay tribute to shipmates who gave their lives during the Korean War.

September 5, 1953: Harry E. Ettinger is greeted by Marine Major Gen. Randolph Pate upon Ettinger's release from Communist captivity.

Dayl Crow as member of Blue Angels

One of the helpless spectators to Pugh's loss was Ens. Joe Akagi, then on just his second combat mission. (Returning from the first, a December 11 rail strike north of Hungnam, he'd found his dive brakes—what the AD pilots called "barn doors"—thoroughly peppered with fist-sized shrapnel holes.) Pugh and Porterfield were both World War II combat veterans, while London and Ettinger were not. Neither Porterfield nor London had flown a Korean combat sortie, while Ettinger had been flying his first and Pugh (like Akagi) just his second. The cumulative impacts of the eight quick aircrew losses (or nine, if the December death of VF-111's Welch was included) were proof that the most dangerous period at Point Oboe was early on: sometimes on the first missions, sometimes even before a round had been fired, a rocket launched, or a bomb dropped.

***

As a senior pilot, but also because (as staff operations officer) he was not directly in ATG-1's squadron command chain, Jim Holloway was often privy to the personal concerns, misgivings, and hardships of the younger pilots. Sometimes he even played the role of counselor or priestly confessor. The "nuggets," fresh out of flight training and steeped in black-and-white checklists and procedures, had an especially hard time coping with the choices they were now facing over hostile territory   the decision, for example, whether to strafe what might be an innocent farmer with a produce-filled oxcart or, alternatively, a Communist operative driving a cartload of explosives. This was not a concern new to this or any other war, but it was blurred by altitude, speed, and, not least, speculation about the peace talks at Panmunjom. It was a war that neither side was apt to win outright. And this made what should be quick decisions agonizing and problematic. Who wanted to fire the war's last shot or drop its last bomb, only to find it blew away an innocent peasant?

Clearly, the Korean War was unlike the last war, an all-out affair that Holloway had experienced on the decks of a combat destroyer in the Southwest Pacific. Because of distance, the ever-advancing front lines, spotty mail (often arriving months late), and few means of direct communication or transport, everyone, from top to bottom, like it or not, seemed to have his head fully in the war—if only for getting through alive and in one piece.

By contrast, circumstances, even mind-sets, were radically different on Point Oboe. Day by day, Task Force 77 combat pilots actually flew more missions than had their Pacific-war counterparts. On the other hand, they also got shorter, usually date-certain, deployments and, within those deployments, scheduled R&R breaks in Japan. During R&R, a few even wangled flights to Hawaii to rendezvous with wives or sweethearts.

And the differences didn't end there. There was also more ready access to news from home and with it the means to return there quickly if circumstances compelled. As one example, there was the case of VF-194 pilot Ens. Marvin S. Broomhead. No sooner had *Valley Forge* reached the forward area than Broomhead learned via a Red Cross telegram that his wife, Beatrice, had been severely injured in a car accident. Almost immediately Broomhead took emergency leave and returned to San Diego, where he found Beatrice in Balboa Naval Hospital in critical condition, and, so word had it, a permanent paraplegic. While everyone felt empathy for Broomhead's predicament and no one begrudged his swift departure, the event had the feel of Broomhead's being called home from the office. Equally strange was news that, once Beatrice's medical situation stabilized, Broomhead was set to return in late January for the balance of the deployment.

The link to people and circumstances back in the States was actually a two-way mirror. Pretty much lifted was the patriotic veil of secrecy and stoic acceptance that had shrouded World War II frontline events. If the general public and national media avoided or played down the news from Korea, this lack of interest didn't hold for the local press, especially when it came to scrutinizing the fortunes and sacrifices of hometown boys.

Ever since the reservists of VF-653's Flying Circus had gone off to war, CO Cook Cleland had been under everyone's microscope. The first and most meaningful scrutiny came from the Navy and its career aviators. There was, truth be told, almost an inbred suspicion of Cleland's "weekend warriors" (a suspicion that held for all of Task Force 77's reserve squadrons, including VF-831 on *Antietam*), the sense that because Korea was not "their war" and could end at any moment with a truce, the reservists would just go through the motions and avoid taking chances.

Jim Holloway had befriended Cook Cleland; they were about the same age, and Cleland, whose squadron was short on administrative savvy, sought out Holloway's help in complying with administrative routines and procedures. As far as Holloway could see, Cleland had developed great squadron camaraderie. His pilots admired Cleland and tried to emulate his daring flying style—although not all could match his skill or luck, VF-653's esprit and Cleland's leadership and dedication eventually showed themselves in tangible statistical results. In the tricky and dangerous business of cutting railroad lines, for example, post-mission photo analysis over the long haul showed VF-653's aviators were getting an average of 1.3 cuts per sortie while results for some Air Force F-51 squadrons dipped as low as 0.1 cuts per sortie. Cleland also pushed to get maximum use of his planes and pilots. This meant, for example, that squadron landing signal officer Bob Herman, himself a naval aviator, maintained his operational qualification and that many VF-653 pilots were qualified for night carrier landings.

Back home, meanwhile, the "boosterism" of the Pittsburgh and Cleveland press coverage when Cleland and his Flying Circus left for war was turning dour and critical. After all, the first news items out of the war zone were the deaths of young London and Porterfield. These were followed two weeks later by VF-653's first combat fatality: thirty-three-year-old Bob Sobey, the Pittsburgh steel company engineer. Sobey's death—his Corsair disintegrated without a trace east of Yonghung after being hit by flak—made it three for December. The next was not far away: On January 9, 1952, chemical engineer Frank Frankovich's Corsair lost oil pressure and disappeared, also without a trace, while on patrol northwest of Yodo-ri.

This added up to four squadron deaths in exactly thirty days: about one a week. If the pattern continued at this pace, it didn't take much of a mathematician to calculate that none of VF-653's pilots could reasonably expect to emerge alive. While VF-653's patriotic sendoff turned to a subdued vigil for some families back home, for others the toll triggered anguished pleas to reporters and congressmen. Was Cook Cleland leading their loved ones in a systematic massacre, flying ancient, outmoded, and dangerous aircraft in a lost cause?

***

James Michener, whose job it was to sort through the complexity and frustration of this lost (or at least uncertain) cause for his reading audience back home, had relocated his reporting vantage to ATG-1, following carrier division commander John "Black Jack" Perry as he shifted his flag to *Valley Forge*. Michener went about acquainting himself with the new group—hanging around the wardroom and squadron ready rooms, continuing to interview pilots, scribble notes, and build his understanding of how such men did what they did and why.

Atop one page of notes written soon after relocating to *Valley Forge*, Michener scrawled THINKING, and below this heading he listed (in part based on an interview with VF-194's recently promoted XO and Denver native Donald S. Brubaker) the thoughts, concerns, and fears that coursed through a pilot's mind during a strike mission.

There were, he noted, two overarching considerations for a division leader such as Brubaker (who, at age twenty-nine, was known as "Pappy" to younger squadron pilots) during the one hundred minutes aloft. "Destroy the bridge" was first, but fast on its heels was this: "3 men (Brubaker's division pilots) depending on him to lead them through & get them out."

Below these two imperatives, Michener ticked off—much like a flight checklist—the sequence of events leading up to the target run: rendezvous, check fuel, navigate by dead reckoning (here a direct quote from Brubaker: "I know North Korea better than I know Denver"), evaluate AA, say a prayer on the turn and approach, concentrate on the target, pickle the bomb, determine how the others made out, check for damage.

Embodied in these steps were two baseline mantras used to hold the mission—and pilot—together: "Regiment time to the job at hand" and "Stop projecting flight ahead to target."

***

The village militiamen who first captured Harry Ettinger had marched him the next day to an NKPA camp where, after being rewarded with a cash bounty, they handed their prize over to an NKPA officer. The bounty, Ettinger realized, probably explained his survival. At any rate, he was now officially a North Korean POW.

In the days that followed, Ettinger was kept on the move as NKPA authorities decided—and then reconsidered—what exactly to do with him. Each night—and for occasional longer intervals of a day or so— he was confined in a different dirt-floored house or barn or subterranean bunker, sometimes with civilians, other times with soldiers. Ettinger was escorted now by ever-changing teams of two or three NKPA guards. Ettinger's diet was sparse and irregular, but he ate no less and no less often than did his warders or hosts.

Although the weather was brutally cold, often with snow falling, and the sheltered interiors were scarcely warmer than the outdoors, Ettinger was well enough insulated by his winter gear. The only layer he had shed—and this by his own choice—was the poopy suit. It was a matter of practical necessity. Ettinger and his guards usually traveled by foot through rugged terrain. Wearing the poopy suit only reduced Ettinger's mobility (on one lonely stretch of road he and his entourage had to dodge a strafing F-51) and increased his exertion while burning up precious calories.

During these marches (mostly, it seemed, pointing either south or southeast, presumably closer to the front lines) Ettinger and his NKPA guards passed through areas heavily occupied by Chinese Communist troops. The Chinese had commandeered nearly all the available houses, barns, stables, and outbuildings, and there were few civilians to be seen.

The Chinese soldiers Ettinger encountered—either gawking at him from the doorways of commandeered houses or from the edges of small groups loitering in village communal areas—seemed remarkably cheerful and friendly. They greeted his passing with warm grins, and some even approached him to proffer cigarettes. If the Chinese had any ill will, it seemed directed toward the NKPA guards.

Within the first two days, much to his relief, Ettinger crossed paths with both of his crewmen—first Gilliland and then McElroy. Gilliland was being treated in a Chinese aid station that Ettinger and his guards visited during the first day's march. Ettinger's radar operator had been raked by shrapnel when the Skyraider was hit. That wound was serious:

a long raw gash stretching from under his right arm to his chest. Gilliland also had a bullet wound clear through his right leg—a rifle shot from a Chinese soldier as Gilliland still dangled from his parachute.

As one of the Chinese medics cleaned Ettinger's scalp laceration, another offered him a cigarette and pieces of hard candy. "I have a brother living in New York City," the medic, who spoke good English, confided to Ettinger.

The first sign of Jess McElroy came the next day when Ettinger was ushered into an NKPA bunker adjacent to some 37mm antiaircraft emplacements. One of the soldiers inside pointed to a shoulder holster containing a .38-caliber pistol, and Ettinger assumed it once belonged to McElroy.

Ettinger didn't have long to wonder or worry further about McElroy's fate. A guard escorted him to a nearby building—perhaps a barn or a stable—packed with an audience of North Korean soldiers. An NKPA officer standing on a small dais at one end of the building was orchestrating a shouting, fist-shaking revival or pep rally. Sitting on a stool atop the dais near the officer was the object of the unintelligible harangue: Jess McElroy.

* * *

Harry Ettinger's reunion with his ECM operator—like Ettinger, McElroy had been captured by Korean villagers, ransomed to the NKPA, and even passed through the same aid station where Gilliland was being treated—also marked the start of their interrogations. After a night spent in the bunker near the antiaircraft batteries, the two men were kept marching all the next day before finally reaching a farm compound that served as a crude frontline interrogation center.

The NKPA inquisitors may well have been neophytes in the curious methods of their allies. If the Koreans had modeled their initial treatment of POWs after the blunt brutality displayed by the Japanese (their occupiers during World War II), they now were apparently trying to augment them with the more subtle "reeducation" techniques favored by their Russian and Chinese sponsors.

The resulting "blend" was a harsh, largely homegrown regimen of intimidation, deprivation, and isolation. After a preliminary round of

questioning in one of the camp buildings, Ettinger was marched outside and told to begin digging. Even if he'd been handed a shovel, Ettinger knew there was no way he could pierce the frozen ground. As
it was, he'd barely cleared away some snow before the guards ordered
him to stop. As Ettinger stood near the shallow depression he had just
created, one of the guards ceremoniously cocked a pistol and put the
barrel to Ettinger's head. There was angry shouting and, for Ettinger,
an agonizing, breath-stopping pause at eternity's doorstep before the
guard finally pulled the trigger and the hammer clicked sharply on
an empty chamber. Ettinger shuddered and opened his eyes, momentarily uncertain if he was alive or dead.

***

Following this unnerving "execution," Ettinger joined McElroy and a
handful of other POWs in the prison quarters—little more than a live-
stock stable with straw scattered across mud floors. Among their fellow POWs was a U.S. Army sergeant named William Arnold who had
a bizarre and cautionary account of his own capture: He'd been kid-
napped by ROK troops, smuggled across the lines, and ransomed to
the North Koreans.

The mud-walled stable was not much of a prison, at least in a traditional sense. Its small exterior window openings lacked barricades,
bars, or even panes: Winter winds whistled through, carrying with
them sprays of powdery snow that settled in small drifts along the inside walls.

The structure was partitioned into separate rooms, but none of the
interior walls extended from floor to ceiling, and most were flimsy.
Indeed, breaking into a room or, for that matter, breaking out of the
stable building itself would take little more than bulling through brit-
tle masonry. Yet despite this and the fact that there were few guards
and no fenced perimeter, little realistic thought was given to escape.
The compound's real barrier—the merciless North Korean winter—
was all but impenetrable.

Winter was also the NKPA warders' best all-purpose tool for punishment and coercion. Its use on Ettinger began a day or so later
when, without warning, he was removed from communal confinement and hauled before one of the camp interrogators. Boiling with

anger, the English-speaking interrogator abruptly launched into a loud, rambling, and fist-pumping tirade, accusing Ettinger of lying, conspiring to escape, and being ungrateful for the NKPA's patience and humanitarian treatment. Then he ordered Ettinger to remove his clothes.

Prodded by guards, Ettinger reluctantly shed the protective layers that thus far had kept him from freezing—his flight suit, wool pants, wool shirt, and long underwear—until he stood naked and shivering before his captors. The glowering interrogator and impassive guards watched in silence as Ettinger shook almost uncontrollably. Finally, after about ten minutes, Ettinger was handed his new outfit: a thin pair of pants, a sleeveless shirt, and a pair of canvas sneakers. He was then taken to an empty stable cubicle where, except for being served a small daily portion of millet and occasional forays to an outdoor latrine, he was kept in isolation.

Given the limits of the quarters, Ettinger's isolation was never total. The compound's other POWs, it turned out, were just next door, and Arnold and McElroy kept up a stream of encouraging chatter. Arnold even arranged to slip cigarettes through a gap in the wall even though cigarettes were the last thing Ettinger needed: Starved and now ill-clothed, he soon contracted pneumonia. He also began to feel excruciating pain in his feet—the first signs of frostbite.

***

Ettinger's solitary confinement lasted about a week, during which time his captors gave no clue as to what they wanted from him or how this punishment figured to coerce his compliance. (It was as if they were familiar with just the "stimulus" half of Pavlov's stimulus-response formulation.) By the time he rejoined the other prisoners, Ettinger's pneumonia had fully settled, and he lacked the resiliency to shake it. While in solitary, he had set what he thought was a modest morale-preservation goal of somehow cadging and smoking a cigarette a day, but soon, coughing uncontrollably and even spitting blood, he gave up smoking altogether. On the rare occasions when he dared remove his canvas shoes to inspect his feet, he noticed his toenails were gone and the skin color of his toes was deepening to a bruised black.

Sensing Ettinger's precarious condition and perhaps concerned about killing a prisoner with long-term value, compound authorities grudgingly relaxed Ettinger's deprivation. Just before Christmas he was given a light jacket to cover his sleeveless shirt; then, after a visit by a doctor and an injection of penicillin, Ettinger received a North Korean army uniform.

During this holiday period there were even a couple of fleeting—and most likely staged—thaws in captor-captive relations. On Christmas Day, for example, the captives received a "holiday feast" consisting of a supply of apples and cigarettes and extra rice portions. A few days later a North Korean officer brought them a pack of playing cards, and, in exchange, the prisoners showed him how to play blackjack.

Year's end brought a few additions to the compound's POW population, including a bandaged and hobbling Julian Gilliland and a newly captured U.S. Marine private named Les Ribbick. And it also brought rumors of a change in scenery—at least for a select number of prisoners who were to be relocated to more permanent facilities near Pyongyang.

When the transferees—Ettinger, Arnold, and Ribbick—were finally designated, the choices seemed neither logical nor surprising. Was it because one represented the Navy, another the Army, and the third the Marine Corps? Did the NKPA interrogators spot long-term potential in these three men? Or was it perhaps that, at least in Ettinger's case, the captors wanted to absolve themselves of responsibility for a prisoner whom their own medical personal advised should be hospitalized? None of the POWs (and least of all the men chosen) had a clue.

***

The three prisoners and their guard detail set out January 4 on a punishing journey—first backtracking to Wonsan and then heading west to Pyongyang—that would take the better part of five days. For the most part they went on foot, their progress largely set by Ettinger's slow pace. Occasionally, they hitched rides on the cargo beds of supply trucks, but these rides (always by night) were unpredictable, often circuitous, and nearly always short-lived. In fact, their last ride, in a Russian-made truck whose cargo bed was stacked with fifty-gallon fuel drums, nearly proved fatal. The truck—part of a convoy strafed and napalmed by Air Force F-51s—careened off an icy road and toppled upside down in a snow-packed ditch. Tossed about amid flying fuel drums, the men were lucky not to have been crushed. As it was, Ribbick's back was badly injured, leaving him, like Ettinger, barely able to walk.

The truck accident occurred on January 8. The balance of the journey was made on foot, the last miles through drifting snow into the teeth of a ferocious blizzard. When they finally reached their destination, a large L-shaped building dominated by a towering cylindrical brick chimney, their faces and beards were caked with ice and their frozen feet were moving less from will than unconscious memory.

Under the circumstances, the three captives' immediate impression of the building, an NKPA interrogation center northwest of Pyongyang, was more of shelter and relative comfort than uncertainty and dread: They were inside, out of the snow and biting wind; it was comparatively warm; best of all, for the time being at least, they were done walking.

***

The facility, the three men soon learned, was run by a North Korean colonel named Pak. Although some POWs called it the "Brickyard," to most it was simply known as "Pak's Palace." Pak's prisoners (for the most part U.S. Air Force jet and bomber pilots) were held in a communal room, a combination sleeping quarters and holding tank from which they were removed—either individually or collectively—for interrogation.

The new arrivals were "interrogated"—first as a group—by being ordered to respond to a long list of handwritten questions. It was a slow-moving, bureaucratic process that actually worked, at least at first, to the prisoners' advantage. Whatever they scribbled in English required translation into Korean and then into Russian or Chinese. It would be several days before they learned their answers had been "useless lies" and the cycle would begin again. All the while, though, Ettinger's perilous condition worsened.

Finally, on the last day of January, Ettinger was removed from interrogation and introduced to someone who looked by his uniform to be a ranking NKPA officer—a colonel, maybe even a general. The "Junior General," who spoke no English, signaled Ettinger to follow him. Leaving Pak's Palace, Junior General took Ettinger to a first aid station and then to a nearby farmhouse—apparently the general's billet—where Ettinger received his first full meal in weeks.

While still at the farmhouse, Ettinger met two more North Koreans: a sergeant (Ettinger never learned his name, but his distinctive saucer-shaped eyes led Ettinger to refer to him as "Banjo Eyes") and a civilian who introduced himself as John Chun. While Banjo Eyes spoke a little English, Chun was fluent and acted as Junior General's interpreter. Chun told Ettinger somewhat cryptically that the general's contacts on Nan-Do had been "asking for him."

That same night the three men boarded a jeep,* which sped back east toward Wonsan. They spent the next day in a Wonsan bunker, where Chun informed Ettinger that arrangements were being made to smuggle him out. Chun then gave Ettinger a pencil and a piece of paper, asking him to compose and sign a pledge that, until final details were arranged, he wouldn't try to escape.

The men next traveled twenty miles south by jeep to another farmhouse. It was there that Ettinger briefly encountered yet another North Korean. Tall (he towered a head above each of the other Koreans) and well groomed, he was dressed in a gabardine suit and looked as if he'd just stepped out of a business meeting. Whoever he was he was clearly in charge of whatever was brewing.

Soon Junior General and the mysterious official went their separate ways, leaving Chun, Banjo Eyes, and Ettinger in the farmhouse that turned out to be well stocked with food, including American C-rations and cartons of Lucky Strike cigarettes. Chun told Ettinger that the general had arranged many other escapes, though always on the ground through the front lines. This time, though, Junior General wanted to arrange for rescue by a Navy helicopter to see how it would work.

They were to wait several more days at the farmhouse during which time Ettinger, too weary and sick to contemplate the prospect of freedom, mostly slept.

---

* Russian-made like the trucks used by the North Koreans, it nonetheless had some distinctly American touches, including a dashboard that was, according to Ettinger's recollection, an exact duplicate of the Ford Model T dashboards he'd seen growing up.

PART 3

THE BRIDGES
AT SAMDONG-NI

12

EPICS IN FAILURE

February 7, 1952, Off Wonsan

The actual plan to rescue VC-35 pilot Harry Ettinger was the brainchild of CCRAK, a joint Army Intelligence/CIA enterprise; the initials stood for Combined Command Reconnaissance Activities, Korea. CCRAK had been hatched in January 1952 in an effort to stem military-civilian rivalry over Korean War intelligence and psychological operations. With mission tactical support to be drawn as needed from the U.S. Navy and Air Force, one of CCRAK's primary responsibilities was to coordinate the activities of guerrilla agents working behind the lines in North Korea.

But CCRAK stood as well for Covert, Clandestine, and Related Activities—Korea: a classified designation hinting at a more diverse and secretive mandate as well as a duplicitous mind-set. If Korea was the emerging model of armed conflict for the Cold War, it was also the testing ground for the competing schemes and shifting alliances of a thick alphabet soup of overt, covert, quasi-independent, and rogue groups (OPC, OPO, FEAF/TAG, FECOM, JACK)—and the odd collection of "spooks" who filled their ranks.

Hundreds of undercover Korean agents trained and organized into operational brigades with names like Yellow Dragon, Blue Dragon, White Tiger, and Owl had been infiltrated into North Korea in the spring of 1951.* Agents from these brigades ranged widely in skill and

---

* It was an operative named Choe Che Bu, the commander of the Blue Dragon and White Tiger Brigades, for example, who had instigated the October 1951 air strike on Kapsan flown by pilots from *Essex* and *Antietam*. Soon thereafter, the NKPA reportedly caught up with and killed Choe and his coterie of agents.

value. Most were expendable "footers," low-level Korean soldiers or civilians who, after being taught the rudiments of sabotage and espionage, were dropped a few miles behind enemy lines with instructions to walk back to the front, on the way spreading disinformation and observing enemy installations and activities; for one reason or another, most never returned. But at the high-value end, brigade members also included a handful of North Korean army officers who, after being co-opted, vetted, and more thoroughly prepared, were "injected" to rejoin their units as "moles"; if the ploy succeeded, each was to remain incommunicado but ready to be activated as circumstances required. After infiltration, it was up to CCRAK operatives to keep tabs on these covert cadres, communicating with them when possible, supplying them when expedient, and extracting them when necessary.

One CCRAK unit was stationed on Nan-Do, a small UN-held island (in truth not much more than a reef outcropping) three miles off the North Korean coast about forty miles south of Wonsan. And it was from Nan-Do that a CCRAK emissary, twenty-four-year-old U.S. Army captain Joseph R. Ulatoski, flew by helicopter to cruiser *Rochester* on the morning of February 7. When the helicopter touched down on *Rochester's* fantail, its pilot, Ens. Donal Hollis, OinC of the ship's HU-1 detachment, escorted his passenger to the command bridge. Waiting for them there were *Rochester's* skipper, Capt. Charles F. Chillingsworth, and detachment CPO Duane Thorin, just then rousted from the chiefs' coffee mess.

***

Ulatoski explained to Chillingsworth, Hollis, and Thorin how in late January one of his agent teams had rescued Harry Ettinger from North Korean captivity and had since managed to smuggle him to the coast. The agents' intention had been to extract the downed aviator by boat to Nan-Do, only to conclude that such a plan was too risky. Ulatoski had been warned that Ettinger was suffering from pneumonia and severe frostbite; he was in such bad shape agents weren't certain he could survive much longer. Ulatoski now wanted instead to arrange a helicopter pickup. The mission, Chillingsworth assured Hollis and Thorin, had been cleared by commander Seventh Fleet, subject to the agreement of tactical units involved.

Ulatoski then spread out a map on one of the bridge's chart tables and outlined his plan: a night extraction, with *Rochester's* helicopter pulling Ettinger from a fire-lit clearing atop a ridgeline about four miles in from the coast. After listening to Ulatoski's plan, Hollis and Thorin explained why a night mission was impossible. The HO3S1 wasn't equipped with night-flying instrumentation; even if it were, the flare from its exhaust port would make an inviting target should enemy soldiers be near.

Ceding the point, Ulatoski produced additional charts and recent aerial photos for Hollis and Thorin to study. The two pilots quickly spotted several better sites in the same area. They proposed that Ulatoski review these sites with his agents and have them select one. The pickup could be scheduled for early the next morning, February 8.

Then Chillingsworth voiced a concern: What if Ulatoski's "agents" were actually North Korean spies, and this was all a setup to bag a helo? Ulatoski admitted the outside possibility but assured them he was in the process of sorting that out. Anyway, he argued, it wouldn't matter as far as the particular mission was concerned; whatever their allegiance, the Koreans would be out to demonstrate their value, using Ettinger's rescue as proof. Thorin, who thus far had been impressed by the young Army captain's poise and professionalism, wasn't won over by this logic—especially if he and Ernie Crawford were to be the bait for a North Korean trap.

Still, suspicions aside, they had a tentative plan: Ulatoski would cross-check his agents and work out the final site and extraction schedule while Chillingsworth arranged Task Force 77 air cover. *Rochester*—code-named "Above Board"—would control the mission. But then Ulatoski threw in a wrench: He wanted one of his own men to go along on the rescue. This meant replacing Crawford with an Army man, a prospect neither Hollis nor Thorin liked. A helicopter rescue behind enemy lines was no place for amateurs.

But Ulatoski pressed his case. It was important for his mainland agents to see that the Army men on Nan-Do took risks too. And Army lieutenant Bill Naylor-Foote, the man Ulatoski proposed to send, had impressive credentials: He spoke Chinese. During World War II, he'd parachuted behind Japanese lines to rescue downed airmen. He was thoroughly familiar with the rescue area. Most important, Naylor-Foote had been working tirelessly on arrangements to rescue Ettinger and had thereby earned the chance to be in on the extraction.

Though still reluctant, Hollis and Thorin agreed, but only if, as Ulatoski said, Ettinger was in such bad shape that Ettinger would have to be carried aboard the chopper. If so, no one would need to operate the hydraulic hoist or be lowered from the helicopter. A final decision, they agreed, would await final confirmation from Ulatoski on Ettinger's exact condition.

***

Once *Rochester* CO Chillingsworth's ResCAP request wound its way through channels, three VC-3 Corsairs and three VC-35 ADs—Task Force 77's contribution to the Ettinger extraction mission—were added to *Valley Forge's* February 8 morning launch schedule. With no bad weather threatening, the six-plane ResCAP (set for launch at 6:00 A.M.) was an incidental sideshow to what otherwise would be a typical flight day.

ATG-1's midmorning centerpiece was to be a coordinated flak-suppression and bombing mission against three key railroad bridges along Bonnie-Birdie, the western stretch of the Kowon-Yangdok rail line. The flight, to be led by VF-194 CO Lt. Cdr. Robert Schreiber, consisted of four VF-194 Skyraiders supplemented by a section of VF-653 Corsairs. Each Skyraider would carry (in addition to full magazines of 20mm) three 1,000-pound delay-fused bridge busters (one racked centerline, the other two inboard on either wing) and eight 250-pounders. The Corsairs would join the bomb runs, armed with wing racks of 250-pounders.

A World War II combat veteran, fearless and famously disdainful of flak (much in the mold of VF-54's Paul Gray), Bob Schreiber was known as "Iron Pants Schreiber" to his pilots. Schreiber usually led the charge on bombing runs and often insisted that the bigger bombs be dropped one at a time. The logic was to increase accuracy while reducing the risk that one of his low-flying ADs would be blasted out of the sky by its own ordnance. Of course, the edict came with a trade-off: To deliver the same bomb load, strike pilots might have to double or triple their target runs and their exposure to enemy gunners.

The other VF-194 pilots scheduled to fly with Schreiber were Dick Kaufman, Bob Komoroff (leading the other AD section), and Marvin Broomhead. Kaufman (a twenty-three-year-old Holloway product via San Jose State College) normally flew on his CO's wing and would for this strike. For Broomhead, who had only recently returned from Stateside emergency leave, this would be just the third combat sortie since rejoining the squadron.

The Bonnie-Birdie rail segment being targeted coursed through a narrow valley floor past a string of nondescript villages with names like Poko-ri, Toko-san, and Samdong-ni. Suspended across a riverbed that paralleled Bonnie-Birdie near Samdong-ni (the most westerly of the three villages and closest to Yangdok) was a trio of bridges. Reconnaissance photos from earlier inconclusive strikes revealed more detail, both familiar and disquieting: Each of the three bridges at Samdong-ni carried a rail line as well as an adjoining road for vehicle and pedestrian traffic. Each span was supported by tall stone and masonry pilings, and each lay athwart the valley's east-west approaches—making bombing runs along the bridge-span axes dicey.

Perched in the hills on either side of the valley were obstacles that presented the greatest challenge of all: concentrations of dozens of antiaircraft batteries, most of them 37mm. The hills the guns were dug into were hardly majestic; elevations ranged from roughly 1,000 to 1,200 feet above the valley floor. This meant that Iron Pants Schreiber's Skyraiders and Corsairs would end up pickling their bombs about level with the hill summits. It also meant the enfilading flak and machine-gun batteries, positioned around the bridges and midway up the hill slopes, would have ideal shots as planes ran the gauntlet.

The circumstances and terrain ordained hit-and-run approaches from the east. The AD pilots would need to be particularly careful in dropping their 1,000-pounders: low enough and close enough for accuracy—but not so low and close as to be ripped apart by the explosions or end up dead-ended in the valley. And, as much as ever, it was important that the strike's opening act—flak-suppression runs by a separate flight of F9Fs—come off without a hitch.

February 8, Inland from Wonsan

As Duane Thorin's helicopter approached the Ettinger rescue site after first light the next morning, Thorin beheld a steep series of terraced paddies tucked in a valley bounded by a string of mountain ridgelines.[1] The valley was covered in fresh snow under a brightening, near-cloudless sky. From high altitude it made a beautiful, albeit misleading, calendar-quality picture: a peaceful winter in Korea.

As he descended in a tight spiral into the valley, Thorin noticed for the first time just how narrow its paddy terraces were—a feature neither the reconnaissance photos nor Ulatoski's maps had revealed. While Ettinger might be waiting for rescue on one terrace, Thorin could well have to land on another, either above or below. It would be a tricky approach requiring extra caution, leaving Thorin to regret more than ever that Bill Naylor-Foote, not Ernie Crawford, was sitting behind him in the cockpit.

Thorin had been wary of Naylor-Foote from the moment he first saw him the day before, waiting on the ground at Nan-Do when Thorin ferried Ulatoski back from *Rochester*. While Thorin knew that looks could be deceiving, Naylor-Foote hardly resembled the daring operative whose exploits Ulatoski had extolled. Beneath a bulky winter parka and green army fatigues, Naylor-Foote was of average height and build. He sported a beard but also a pair of glasses with thick lenses, and his face was framed, almost compressed, by the pile-lined earflaps of one of the Army's familiar cold-weather field caps. If Ulatoski, with his bearing, dress, and chest full of campaign ribbons, looked regulation U.S. Army, Naylor-Foote appeared anything but.

After loading a radio transceiver and some boxes of unspecified equipment into the back, Naylor-Foote climbed aboard the chopper for the return shuttle to *Rochester*. There was a second passenger as well—a wounded GI who had apparently just shot himself in the foot. Weighed down by the two passengers and the boxes, the helo strained to get airborne. During the return flight Thorin occasionally glanced at his passengers: If Naylor-Foote and the man with the self-inflicted gunshot wound were any indication, CCRAK was some strange outfit.

Once they touched down on *Rochester* and the wounded man was hustled off to sick bay, Naylor-Foote unloaded his boxes and set up his transceiver topside to await final instructions from Ulatoski.

Thorin and Hollis meanwhile completed other mission details. Helicopter launch from *Rochester* would be after daybreak, allowing *Valley Forge* ResCAP aircraft enough time to arrive overhead. Once they rendezvoused, the chopper with its escorts would coast in at 10,000 feet: high enough both to avoid AA while also giving the impression they were flying farther inland than actually planned. As winter darkness fell on the eve of the mission, all the pieces were in place except one: final word on the condition of Harry Ettinger and, with it, the decision on whether Crawford or Naylor-Foote would accompany Thorin on the mission.

Later that night Earl Lanning, the *Rochester* R Division crewman who helped out during helicopter launches, spotted Thorin sitting alone in the crew mess hall, drinking coffee and writing letters. Thorin seemed to be as cordial as ever as he set aside his letter and Lanning sat down to chat. Mostly they traded ship scuttlebutt and shoptalk, but at one point Thorin confided to Lanning that he had a bad feeling about the upcoming daylight rescue mission. He really didn't trust the Army "spooks" responsible for setting it up.

***

The column of signal smoke curling up from the rescue site was thicker, blacker, and more conspicuous than Thorin had expected. Suspicious of it as well, the ResCAP leader dipped down to investigate. After making a pass, he reported three people adjacent to a signal fire—what turned out to be the smoldering thatched roof of some sort of small hut. On a second pass two of the three were gone. Still, it didn't look to be a trap: There were only the few sets of foot tracks around the site and no sign of suspicious activity. In the distance, however, a handful of figures—enemy troops perhaps—were trudging uphill through the snow toward the site. It would take them about thirty minutes to arrive; most likely they were coming to investigate the column of smoke.

Thorin had by then scoped out his exit route: Over a ridge just a mile south of the pickup site was a narrow valley extending all the way east to the coast. They would fly "on the deck" all the way back with ResCAP planes in the lead—using firepower to suppress any troublemakers. The approach to the site had given Thorin an excellent view of the situation. The nearest unexplained intruders were at some distance. In the worst case (and despite the tricky terrain) there was enough time, Thorin figured, to touch down, idle the helicopter, retrieve Ettinger himself, and be on their way. He wouldn't be looking for any help from Naylor-Foote.

*　*　*

The final decision to include Naylor-Foote had not been made until well past midnight when Naylor-Foote at last heard from Ulatoski. "The man's a stretcher case," Naylor-Foote assured Hollis and Thorin; he had seemed excited, almost happy, about Ettinger's plight. "The Koreans had to carry him out to where they set up the radio to contact Nan-Do."

It was, as Thorin expected, just the opening Naylor-Foote needed to press home his case for going: After carrying Ettinger by stretcher to the rescue site, CCRAK operatives (who knew Naylor-Foote and could spot his distinctive beard and glasses) would be hiding nearby, ready to light a signal fire when the planes approached. Naylor-Foote could even bring his transceiver to communicate with them.

Thorin still didn't like the look of it, and as pilot of the aircraft he had the absolute right to decide who if anyone was to accompany him. Thorin prided himself on his common sense and his ability to see through human facades. But in this case, much to his everlasting regret, he gave in: Naylor-Foote was allowed to go instead of Ernie Crawford. After a couple of hours of fitful sleep, Thorin was up early and topside on the fantail well before flight stations were sounded.

It was there that Naylor-Foote threw in a final wrench—showing up just moments from launch, a sailor on either side of him holding one of the boxes Naylor-Foote had brought from Nan-Do. CCRAK, he shouted to Thorin amid the flight deck bustle and noise, also wanted to drop off some desperately needed supplies for its agents— medicine and canned goods, but also a supply of whiskey and cigarettes for bartering.

Thorin was furious, but now, so close to launch and so intent on readying the helicopter and sticking to the schedule, all he felt he could do was contain the risk. Naylor-Foote could bring his supplies, but he was to drop them before Ettinger was carried aboard.

***

During the inbound flight, Thorin's disgust and suspicion festered, fueled by Naylor-Foote's greenhorn naïveté, the presence of the transceiver and supply boxes, and his own faulty judgment. It reminded Thorin a bit of the Far East airlift flights he'd flown between the wars: where contraband goodies like the ones in Naylor-Foote's boxes took up the space intended for people and where commissioned know-it-alls like Naylor-Foote could spell disaster.

Then, just a few hundred feet above the site—literally moments away from touching down—Thorin saw something startling. On the terrace adjacent to the burning building was a lone figure: It looked to be Harry Ettinger, and, far from being strapped to a stretcher, he was on his feet.

"Dump that stuff out right now!" Thorin screamed over his shoulder to Naylor-Foote. The landing and extraction were going to be tricky enough without the added weight of the boxes. Although Ettinger was no stretcher case, Thorin decided to land. Naylor-Foote had fed him bad information about Ettinger, and he saw no reason to trust Naylor-Foote to operate the rescue hoist.

As Thorin turned away from Naylor-Foote and concentrated on the approach, he realized the terrace where Ettinger stood was too narrow for a touchdown. The adjacent plot lay a bit lower and looked more promising; even so it was barely wider than the helicopter's tricycle undercarriage. In particular, Thorin had to be sure his starboard wheel didn't extend beyond the lip of the terrace—something that required Ernie Crawford's eyes, judgment, and experience.

Almost at once things began going wrong, if not under the exact conditions they had when Thorin crashed *Philippine Sea*'s helo outside Sasebo Harbor, then at least at the same pace: slowly at first, but then cascading out of control. First, Thorin momentarily lost sight of Ettinger. Rather than staying put for instructions, Ettinger had instead hobbled his way toward the helicopter. Even before the wheels touched down, Ettinger was at the cockpit door, trying to clamber aboard. The move apparently surprised Naylor-Foote who was still strapped into his seat, an M1 carbine firmly in his grasp. Somehow Naylor-Foote did manage to reach over, grab Ettinger's flimsy jacket at the nape of the neck, and grapple him partway inside. Ettinger ended up sprawled facedown on the cabin floor, his feet and lower legs still hanging outside. After nearly two months in North Korean captivity, Ettinger weighed scarcely a hundred pounds. Still, the sudden surge of extra weight was enough to pitch the helicopter's nose down, threatening to drive the rotor tips into the wall of an adjacent terrace.

Thorin knew he'd have to pull up or crash, but engine rpms were already low, and a sudden pull-up could well reduce them to the "coning point," where the main rotors invert like the spines of a cheap umbrella. Thorin pumped the pitch control to boost rpms, but the chopper was still too nose heavy. There was simply too much weight onboard.

Nose down with Ettinger's legs still outside the cabin, the helicopter now also began to sideslip off the landing terrace. When the rotors reached the terrace edge, the helo abruptly lost its vital air cushion. Now the chopper could only go down. Listing to the right, it skidded into the ravine, the main rotors buzzing into the ice, snow, and dirt of the opposite bank like a runaway circular saw.

February 8, Mid-Morning, Near Yangdok

It had taken an hour's flight time for Bob Schreiber's four Skyraiders and two Corsairs to reach Samdong-ni. The two-hour round-trip left them just a small window to complete their strike runs. As it was they were late, their launch schedule disrupted—as were the entire morning's ops—by the scramble to put more ResCAP over a helo crash site inland from the coast near Wonsan.

In the valley below there was no evidence of the flak-suppression aircraft that were to have preceded them. Perhaps they'd arrived early, made their own time-pressed runs, and departed—or perhaps they'd not shown up at all. Schreiber's flight would find out soon enough.

The six props climbed to 12,000 feet, dispersing to set intervals for a counterclockwise racetrack pattern beyond the range of the AA batteries. Then, following Schreiber's lead, each peeled off in turn for initial runs westward into the valley: ADs first (Dick Kaufman after Schreiber, then Bob Komoroff and Marv Broomhead), followed by the two Corsairs.

As he angled to begin his own run, Dick Kaufman watched Schreiber take his AD down—barn doors closed to increase speed and avoid flak—in a forty-degree dive. Almost at once, heavy crossfire erupted from the valley flanks. At higher elevation, the most visible and effective flak was from the time-fused 37mm rounds: ragged, sooty puffs of exploding shrapnel. The 23mm machine gunners had opened up, and Kaufman could already see the bright arcs of their tracers. For the moment, because of Schreiber's altitude, they were only wasting rounds. But then, as Schreiber kept descending, the tracer patterns intensified—at first into bright, random cross-hatchings and then into a thicker, almost fabriclike weave. Kaufman suspected either the F9Fs had never shown up—or their work had merely stirred up the valley's hornet's nest. It was the heaviest flak he'd seen in more than thirty prior combat strikes over Korea.

Kaufman neared his nose-over point as Schreiber completed his run and was poised to pull up. There was no time now to observe how (or whether) Schreiber actually escaped the valley—and, in an odd way, at least for the moment, little interest. Kaufman, like Schreiber before him and those to follow, had to regiment time (and with it emotion) to the job at hand.

To keep his concentration fully on the primary target bridge during this first run, Kaufman decided to hold his 20mm fire and pickle just his centerline 1,000-pounder. He flicked the toggles on the three centerline bomb stations. Then, as his altimeter steadily unwound, Kaufman scanned the other gauges (fifteen inches of manifold pressure, 2,400 engine rpm, airspeed crowding three hundred knots) before locking his eyes on the bridge as it loomed ever bigger through the sight pipper.

It was the dive-bomber's job to ignore enemy AA fire as he entered the target crucible. Pulling this off was a feat somehow conjured from a mingling of circumstances and factors unique to each pilot: It might be innate—an audacious confidence, an unusual power of concentration, or an unflappable composure. It might be muscle memory built of intense training and countless practice runs. Or, in the end, it might simply be a young man's blissful aura of invincibility.

In truth, if Kaufman tried to maneuver through AA fire as thick as this, he was just as apt to run into it as avoid it. Still, Kaufman couldn't stifle his senses entirely. Their peripheries took in the gun-muzzle winks below and to either side, the arcs of the rounds passing closest, and even—despite the sealed Plexiglas enclosure—the whiff of cordite and the sound of insistent, murderous whistles. The sensory evidence was unmistakable: On the valley floor and its adjacent slopes were men as intent on shooting him out of the sky as he was on destroying these bridges.

Thorin Crash Site, Inland from Wonsan

Duane Thorin was still sitting in the cockpit of the downed helicopter trying to radio the ResCAP flight leader when he heard a short burst of burp-gun fire from behind. He looked back to see three soldiers emerge from the nearby woods. Naylor-Foote had already been scrambling up the slope of the ravine with Ettinger hobbling close behind, but now he stopped and dropped his carbine and both men raised their hands.

Thorin considered slipping from the cockpit and taking off on his own, but the soldiers had already spotted him. All three were dressed in NKPA uniforms; two were young, barely teenagers, but the third was older and his uniform showed sergeant's stripes. Once all three Americans were rounded up, the sergeant pointed them toward the woods. As they moved away from the wreckage and into the tree line, Ettinger told Thorin and Naylor-Foote he'd never seen these men before. Once they reached the trees the sergeant pointed them downstream, apparently toward the same village Thorin had seen during the ill-fated approach. They'd not gotten very far before they had to dive for cover. There were bursts of small-arms fire, apparently from other soldiers nearby, and the ResCAP aircraft were moving in to strafe.

Near Yangdok

Dick Kaufman's first run through Samdong-ni's flak and machine-gun gallery lasted all of about fifteen seconds, but to him it was an eternity. After pickling his bomb, bottoming out just past the bridges, angling to the left to disrupt the ground gunners' aim, and two-blocking into a climb, he could feel his heart racing and a fresh rush of sweat pooling beneath his layers of flight gear. He was absolutely astonished to still be in one piece.

Even more astonishing, the others had apparently survived in good shape, too. After joining up, and taking turns inspecting each other for damage, all six pilots wheeled back to the high-altitude carousel, tidied up their intervals, and awaited further instructions from Schreiber.

Of course, they all could see the same thing Schreiber saw, and, having seen it, they all knew the inescapable verdict. At other times, in other places, and for other people—the IO (intelligence officer) debriefings, for example, or over drinks with pilots from another squadron at the Fujia—they might fudge, embellish, or even (for the benefit of rival squadrons) lie like feckless schoolboys. But they couldn't do that here—not now and not in company with each other. Schreiber's assessment and his orders were already playing in their heads before he was back on the circuit: With two bridges down but one still standing, they were going back down to get the third span.

Late Morning, En Route to the Thorin Crash Site

The four-plane pickup ResCAP consisting of VF-653's Ray Edinger, Roland "Rollo" Busch, and Dick "Ensign" Jensen along with VF-194's Joe Akagi was still short of the coast-in point on its way to relieve a *Philippine Sea* ResCAP when word came of a second ResCAP crisis: the downing of a VF-194 aircraft well inland near Yangdok.

By Edinger's reckoning, his was the third TF 77 flight dispatched to the Thorin crash site. That one situation alone must be using up a lot of pilots, airplanes, ordnance, and fuel. No doubt this second crash would stretch resources even thinner, might even exhaust them. Still, if it was him down there at the business end of a Communist manhunt, he'd want the whole air group overhead.

From preflight, Edinger knew that Thorin and his Army passenger had survived the crash, both apparently uninjured. Before fleeing the site Thorin had even managed to radio VC-3 ResCAP flight leader Lt. Bob Taylor that the three men (Thorin, his passenger, and apparently Ettinger) were bound for a wooded patch adjoining the frozen creek and ravine where the bird had settled.

Bob Taylor's call for a second helicopter was answered by the arrival of the HO3A-1 from *Greer County* (LST [landing ship, tank]-799), an amphibious ship stationed off Wonsan. The *Greer County* helo made two approaches to the crash site only to run into small-arms fire each time—clear proof that NKPA were skulking about. Peppered with bullet holes, the stricken angel finally fled the scene on its way to an emergency landing aboard cruiser *St. Paul*.

As the six ResCAP aircraft continued to sweep and strafe, the VC-3 Corsair piloted by Lt. John McKenna was the next to be hit. Bullets ignited a fire in the Corsair's engine, and flames quickly spread to the cockpit. McKenna was last reported making a solo dash for the sea where, as far as anyone knew, he was still unaccounted for. Soon the VC-35 AD flown by Mel Schluter was also disabled by ground fire; Schluter left the area bound for an emergency landing at K-50. That left four covering aircraft, although not for very long; all but drained of fuel, the two F4-Us and two ADs were routed to emergency landings at K-18.

To replace them *Philippine Sea* had dispatched a division of VF-113 Corsairs; it was this ResCAP that Edinger's division was en route to relieve when the Yangdok situation flared. With two rescue missions now under way—and both sites behind enemy lines—TF 77's CAGs, including ATG-1's Fritz Crabill, were desperately shorthanded. One of Crabill's remaining options was to divert aircraft already aloft; accordingly, Edinger was ordered to detach his second section and send it north to Yangdok. Edinger chose Joe Akagi and Dick Jensen, and, as those two peeled off and vectored northwest with Akagi in the lead, Ray Edinger and Rollo Busch flew on to the Thorin site.

Near Yangdok

One of the trailing Corsairs was the first to call out that Marvin Broomhead's AD had been hit. By that time Dick Kaufman had already completed his second run—this time strafing to suppress ground fire as he lined up to pickle his two inboard bombs—and was climbing back to 12,000 feet. Over his shoulder he could see that Komoroff was through as well and beginning his own climb. Then he saw that the odds had caught up with Marv Broomhead. His engine must have taken a 37mm round; already at low altitude, his AD was trailing a thick funnel of smoke.

Soon Broomhead came on the circuit. His voice was calm and matter-of-fact, but his prospects were bad: "I'm losing rpms and manifold's below twenty inches."

Bob Schreiber cut in, his voice laced with urgency: "Bail out."

"I'm already too low," Broomhead responded, still calm but this time more edgy and insistent. "I have to find some place to set down."

Marvin Broomhead's plight put an end to the strikes. For the moment the high-altitude ADs were helpless spectators. Flying lower, the two Corsairs were closest to Broomhead as he fled east through the valley, trailing smoke and looking for a spot to land.

Under the circumstances Broomhead had little time to be choosy, and he soon picked a spot: a sloped but relatively flat snow-covered clearing. Nearby was a road descending into a valley village maybe a half mile distant. With no time for a checklist, he readied for a wheels-up landing. From Dick Kaufman's remote vantage, Broomhead's approach looked good, but he still hit the clearing hard—more crash than landing. It was some minutes before he was reported emerging from the cockpit. As the ADs neared the scene, Broomhead could be seen sitting at the trailing edge of a wing, his feet in the snow.

While Bob Schreiber kept altitude to call for a helicopter, Kaufman and Komoroff swept down to join the Corsair pilots. Troops or militia would doubtless soon be advancing up the road toward the crash site, and help would be needed to keep them at bay. Schreiber meanwhile learned that for now there were no choppers to be had: *Rochester's* had crashed near Wonsan, and *Greer County's*, after being dispatched to that site, had taken ground fire and was now out of commission.

With an hour's return flight still ahead of them Schreiber's aircraft were in no position to linger. Both Corsairs, perilously low on fuel, were already on their way back to *Valley Forge*. Schreiber got confirmation that two aircraft were then en route but knew his ADs would have to leave before they showed up.

Early Afternoon, Above the Thorin Crash Site

When a division of Phil Sea Corsairs arrived to relieve Ray Edinger and Rollo Busch at the Thorin crash site, there was no real way to tell whether the rescue was over or just beginning. Busch's airplane had caught a round of ground fire during one early pass, and so, with nothing visible to fire back at and doubly wary of shooting friendlies and getting hit again, the two pilots opted to climb, circle, and wait.

Whenever one or both spotted suspicious movement, they swooped down to have a look and unload some ordnance. In the space of two hours they did it often enough to use up most of their .50-caliber and virtually all their wing ordnance—Edinger still carried a lone HVAR on his port wing, but only because it had failed to fire.

Even under a bright, cloudless sky, the downed helo was tricky to spot. It was camouflaged by a combination of snow and what Edinger thought might be a draped parachute canopy. Perhaps Thorin had tried to hide it from the NKPA or the NKPA was trying to conceal it from any would-be rescuers. Realizing the wreckage would be even more difficult to find in the afternoon's shadows, Edinger decided to help the newly arrived Phil Sea pilots get their bearings. Leaving Busch and three of the relief planes at high altitude, Edinger radioed the Phil Sea division leader to follow him down.

The two airplanes flew just off the deck, roughly tracing the line of the frozen creek bed with Edinger poised to holler "Mark!" when he crossed the spot. It required two passes to pinpoint the site; going in the second time Edinger heard—and felt—a hollow metallic thump on his left wing. It was the kind of seemingly inconsequential sound a motorist might ignore as he cruised down a lonesome highway, re-membering it ruefully only when his car finally broke down. Intent on handing off the mission and heading feet wet for *Valley Forge*, Edinger ignored it for the moment, flew on, crossed the site, and yelled out "Mark!" to the Corsair on his tail.

"Roger," the Phil Sea pilot responded. "See target." But then, just as they pulled up, he was back on the circuit to warn Edinger: "You've been hit. Your port wing's leaking oil."

Early Afternoon, Above the Broomhead Crash Site

Marvin Broomhead was still close to his wrecked AD when Joe Akagi and Dick Jensen arrived at the scene. Schreiber, it turned out, need not have worried, at least about leaving the site without cover. Already there were other planes overhead. Some had shown up unbidden, breaking off from secondary targets or route recces to fly cover as long as their fuel and ordnance permitted. No surprise, a downed aviator was everybody's concern.

One AD had apparently dropped a "survival bomb," a canister packing food, water, sleeping bag, cold-weather clothing, and a carbine. It had landed maybe twenty or thirty yards from the wreckage, and Broomhead was now crawling slowly—undoubtedly in great pain—in its direction. Behind him was a telltale trail that looked to be fresh blood.

For the moment, Akagi saw no sign of Communist troops, but experience told him that didn't mean they weren't around. He'd not spotted any during a previous successful ResCAP near another small village, but the rescued pilot later assured him they were there. Clothed in white camouflage and lying prostrate on snow-covered roofs or crouching in village alleys, the Communists popped up to fire whenever ResCAP planes swooped by.

There was still no helicopter in the vicinity, though one had finally been located. It was *Manchester's* (CL-83) detachment helo in use that day for coastal bombardment up near Songjin. *Manchester* was still steaming south, but already detachment pilot Navy lieutenant Edward Moore had set out, carrying his Marine spotter with him. It would take Moore the better part of an hour to arrive.

Outbound from the Thorin Crash Site
When Ray Edinger first saw oil streaming across the top of his port wing, he instinctively turned off the wing's oil air cooler. With the engine oil heating up, he estimated forty-five seconds more at full power before the engine seized up. He poured on full throttle and, with Rollo Busch trailing, pointed toward the Sea of Japan, hoping at least to make it to the water. Edinger also established communications with Above Board to get a range and bearing. The cruiser already had a gig in the water, standing by to pull him out of the drink. He ran through the ditching process in his mind. He'd have to tighten his shoulder harness, keep the Corsair's long nose up, head into the wind, and keep a close watch on the height and intervals of the wave tops. Once on the water he'd have to disconnect seat harness, G-suit hose, and radio-headset wire before reaching for the life-raft lanyard under his seat. Sequence, speed, and efficiency were crucial: The aircraft would stay afloat for maybe a minute.

Edinger was already over water, keeping an anxious eye on his gauges and his punctured wing, when he realized, much to his relief, he was losing hydraulic fluid, not engine oil. This meant a problem with his flaps, landing gear, or both, but not necessarily his engine. He might still end up in the drink but not here and not now. Edinger thanked Above Board for their rescue offer, and accelerated seaward with renewed hopes of landing on *Valley Forge*.

***

Forty minutes later, when Ray Edinger and Rollo Busch reached Point Oboe, flight control reminded Edinger of the hung rocket on his port wing. At first they advised Edinger to turn around, head for the beach, and land at King-18, but Edinger wanted no part of that; so, for the moment, he ignored the transmission—acting as if he'd not heard it. He was either going to touch down on Happy Valley or take an ice bath right nearby.

Resigned to the fact that Edinger would try to land, Air Boss Blackie Weinell radioed him to keep circling while other aircraft recovered. Meanwhile, deck crews were alerted to respot the stack, ready crash barriers, and even position a line of donkeys—tow vehicles—in anticipation of the worst.

Edinger already knew his flaps were gone, which meant a straight-on, high-speed run with little or no margin for fine-tuning his approach. His tailhook was down, but hydraulic pressure was also needed to lock it; the hook might well just bounce over the wires. The biggest problem, though, would be lowering and locking his landing gear. The wheels had an emergency backup system—a small CO_2 bottle used to pump the wheel struts into place when hydraulics failed. When Edinger activated this backup, however, the wheels still failed to lock. The crash landing would be wheels-up—perhaps without a tailhook—with a HVAR hung on his wing.

Still, Edinger was committed. During the approach, he could see the flight deck was clear—everyone was in back of something. He sensed everyone on Point Oboe was waiting. Until his fate was settled, carriers and screening destroyers would have to steam into the wind burning up fuel. Airdales would have to stay at flight quarters and sailors at GQ. All for his sake. He could only half-hear the circuit chatter but knew it must be about him. He imagined that none of it was too complimentary—especially after he aborted his first approach (too fast) and made a wide circle to prepare for another.

This second try, Edinger knew, was now or never. This time his approach was slower, closer to stall. In the groove he leaned his head out the cockpit and into the slipstream—his eye on the LSO. Whatever was about to happen—failed landing gear, useless tailhook, exploding HVAR—was up to the Good Lord.

When he got the cut Edinger dropped the U-Bird's long nose and dipped his starboard wing slightly so his port wing—the one with the hung rocket—wouldn't take the full brunt. As he touched down, he learned later, the rocket broke loose and skidded across the flight deck. Two young deckhands—each apparently cloaked in his own mantle of invincibility—managed to corral it and heave it over the side.

Once the Corsair scraped to a stop, a firefighter ran out to pull Edinger from the cockpit ahead of any possible fire. There was none, and as soon as Edinger was clear the Corsair was hauled to a flight deck elevator and lowered to the hangar level. Both would fly another day.

Late Afternoon, Above the Broomhead Crash Site

VF-653's Bobby Balser and wingman Harold "Ed" Sterrett were among the day's last ResCAP contingents diverted to the Broomhead crash site. The two Corsair pilots were flying route reconnaissance at the tail end of a rail strike when they were tapped to escort an Air Force helo to the site.

It was close to sunset by now, making it a race against time—but that was just part of the problem. It was a hot site: Aircraft providing cover were invariably taking ground fire, and one, a *Philippine Sea* AD, was reported down, its pilot missing. Worst of all, a rescue mission whose initial objective was to extract one man now had three to pull out: In addition to Marvin Broomhead, Navy helicopter pilot Ed Moore and his spotter Marine Corps first lieutenant Kenneth Henry.

As anticipated, it had taken Moore's HO3S-1 more than an hour to reach the scene from the coast. Henry, the CO of *Manchester*'s Marine detachment, had reportedly volunteered for the artillery-spotting mission to get a front row view of Korean ground combat. He ended up with more than he bargained for.

No sooner had Moore begun his approach than he took blistering ground fire, intense and accurate enough to disable the helo. The HO3S-1 settled gently to the ground close to the AD wreckage only to lose its footing and topple on its side. Both Moore and Henry were seen jumping from the crew compartment, although Henry appeared to be hobbling. After making their way over to Broomhead the two men improvised a crude sleigh to haul him farther from the wreckage.

An Army helo was the next to try. Its pilot managed to land on solid ground perhaps two hundred yards from the men, but Moore and Henry adamantly waved him off. The small chopper could take only two passengers, Broomhead was now unconscious, and neither Moore nor Henry would leave without him.

***

The bigger Air Force chopper Balser and Sterrett were escorting thus became the day's last hope. But while the bird's power and size seemed to bolster the chances of success, the realities at ground level quickly erased them.

As was so often the case in this terrain, late-afternoon crosswinds were lashing the site. The Air Force pilot reported sixty-knot gusts. He fought the winds only to come under heavy ground fire. The pilot pulled back but was game to give it another try, leaving the choice to Balser. Surveying the shadowy terrain, Balser could see it was no use: They'd only end up with another bird on the ground. He told him not to, even though he knew that once they left the scene there was little to stop the Communists from capturing or killing Broomhead, Henry, and Moore.

Late Afternoon, the Thorin Crash Site

The ResCAP aircraft that had been circling the Thorin crash site off and on for the better part of the day were gone before sunset. They'd been more aggressive in the morning; any burst of ground fire or sign of movement from the twenty or so troops scattered about the area was answered by strafing or rocket fire. To the men concealed in the woods just downstream from the wreckage, the gun rounds sounded like popping corn whenever they hit the branches overhead. Sizzling shrapnel pieces occasionally dropped to the ground nearby.

After midday the intensity of rocket and cannon fire eased. At one point, a North Korean noncom Harry Ettinger called Banjo Eyes ran up the line of the creek bed. Banjo Eyes was camouflaged in white; he spoke briefly with the guards but signaled no recognition of Ettinger.

Twice during the lengthening afternoon they also heard the distinctive "flop-flop" sounds of approaching helicopters. The first was a Navy chopper that came so close that Duane Thorin could recognize the crew chief peering through the open door of the Plexiglas greenhouse. This first helicopter drew some burp-gun rounds; as it retreated, Thorin heard the metallic "plink" of a bullet striking its fuselage.

The second chopper, arriving close to sunset, was a large Marine HO4S. Harry Ettinger had never seen a craft like it before, and he watched with fascination as it paused directly overhead before lumbering downhill. After hovering above one of the terraced paddies, the big chopper turned and flew once more overhead, this time so low that Ettinger could feel the backwash of its rotors. Ettinger and Thorin both stood up, their hands raised to signal that they'd been captured. After the Marine chopper left, a hush settled over the scene.

Finally, once the winter sun was well down, the NKPA sergeant pointed his captives toward the clearing where two men soon approached them. One looked to Thorin to be a ranking NKPA officer; he kept back while the other man, apparently a Korean civilian, sidled up to Ettinger. Gesturing deferentially toward the NKPA officer and speaking translator's English, the civilian expressed "the general's deep regret" that the rescue mission had failed. He told him not to worry: They would return to the village and plan what to do next. Then he turned to Thorin: "Why did you crash?"

As they walked, Ettinger told Thorin that it was the "general," his civilian aide Chun, and Banjo Eyes who had arranged his release from a Pyongyang interrogation center a week before, stashed him in a house near the village, and eventually marched him uphill to another house closer to the actual rescue site. Two more Koreans described by Chun as UN agents joined them there. These two men came equipped with American radio gear that they used to contact Nan-Do.

Ettinger explained that he had actually spoken three times with Nan-Do personnel: first—briefly—with an officer named "Ski"; next with Naylor-Foote, who broke off the conversation when he learned "one of his boys" had just shot himself in the foot; then finally, just the night before, with Ski. Ski had asked about Ettinger's mobility: Could he make it on foot to the helicopter once it approached? Were his arms strong enough to be pulled out using a survival sling?

Ettinger assured Ski that despite pneumonia and frostbitten feet, he could still reach the helo and manage the sling. They'd agreed on a signal fire at the extraction site. Ettinger would also draw a triangle in the snow. Finally, he would be on his feet if things were okay and lie down if he sensed danger.

Ettinger had been caught off guard when the chopper landed instead of lowering a sling. Apparently, the bigger-than-expected signal fire (Banjo Eyes had torched the thatched roof of a small pagoda near the site) had attracted other NKPA troops who weren't in on the plan. The more Thorin heard, the angrier he got.

February 9, Aboard *Valley Forge*

Sitting in *Valley Forge's* flag plot through most of the previous day, James Michener overheard nearly all the message traffic coming from the Thorin and Broomhead crash sites. When night fell, both rescue efforts looked to have ended in disaster. At first light, when planes winged over the two sites, there was little more to report. At the Thorin crash site there was no sign, other than the bulge of the wreckage under the snow and the burned-out hut nearby, that Thorin, Naylor-Foote, or Ettinger had ever been there.

At the Broomhead crash site near Yangdok there was little more to see and none of it encouraging. To Joe Akagi, one of the pilots dispatched to inspect the site, it was clear the Communists had done their best to camouflage the two wreckages with snow and brush. They'd even been careful to wipe away footprints. Akagi's flight blasted the concealed aircraft with rockets and cannon fire. The pilots considered working over the village downhill but finally decided not to. If Broomhead, Moore, or Henry were still alive, the Communists were likely holding them there.

Michener was then taking notes for "An Epic in Failure," a UPI news dispatch that would later appear in expanded form in the July 1952 edition of *Reader's Digest*. "Here was complete failure," one paragraph in the *Reader's Digest* version began, "a heartbreaking tragedy."

"Helicopter, planes and men were lost in the futile tragedy," it went on (focusing on the Broomhead incident). "The enemy had a field day and we had nothing."

But Michener's article also had a compensatory coda: "But as you watched you did not know it was failure. For there was a spirit of ex-ultation among the flyers involved." All day he had been listening in on radio traffic as pilots flew cover over the crashes and, once they returned, volunteered to rearm, refuel, and head back.

Michener then reached to convey succinctly to his readers what he knew to be a deeply imbedded reciprocal bond among these combat pilots: "'We don't desert our men,' they said."

***

Separately but simultaneously, Ray Edinger was mulling his own thoughts on the day—thoughts finally composed in a letter to his fa-ther, Emory, back in Pittsburgh. "I have been intending to write this for a long time," the letter (dated February 12) began. "As tomorrow is replenishment day with the mail being picked up I thought I'd get it done tonight."

Edinger's handwritten letter was ten pages long—and apparently long overdue—much of it taken up explaining VF-653's flight-ops routine, detailing, for example, how one typical morning strike mis-sion against railroad targets stretched from six to noon. Only mid-way through did Edinger recount the "rough day several days ago," cautioning his dad: "I don't know whether Mom should read all this . . ."

After describing the circumstances of Ettinger's downing in Decem-ber, his botched rescue, and the near-coincident crash—and failed rescue—of Marvin Broomhead, Edinger touched on his own role and, self-deprecatingly, his close-call landing aboard *Valley Forge*: "I didn't get a scratch and was flying the next day."

He then tried to wind up the letter—"This is starting to become a book instead of a letter"—only to spill into a chronicle of the facts and underlying emotions of wartime loss, both cumulative and personal.

It began with a sobering aside. Just the day before ("on the same RR strike I was using as an example"), Dick Jensen had been killed when his Corsair took a hit, crashed, and exploded on impact. "I felt badly as he was just a kid and a very likeable one." Dick Jensen, moreover, was Rollo Busch's closest friend: "They went through training together and we got them at the same time."

In two months' time, Edinger calculated, VF-653 had lost six pilots, VF-194 and the two jet squadrons another five. "From one Air Group of approx. 100 pilots, that's a high attrition rate." There were still four months of combat air operations ahead for ATG-1 and VF-653. But, closing his letter with son-to-father candor, Edinger admitted a big part of him was already "ready to come home. I'm not getting nervous or going to pieces, it's just a damn hard job out here and I don't like killing people."

"I'M BLIND! FOR God's sake, help me; I'm blind!"

As soon as VF-194 pilot Howard Thayer heard the scream on the circuit, he looked around and above him for a plane in trouble. He was sure he spotted one: at ten-o'clock, another Yellow Devil AD climbing straight toward solid overcast at 10,000 feet. "Plane in trouble, rock your wings," Thayer called over the circuit. "Plane in trouble, rock your wings."

For a second or more the plane still climbed toward the cloud layer. But then Thayer saw the wings move—rocking back and forth, again and again.

"Put your nose down—put your nose down," Thayer called insistently, trying to keep his voice calm though his heart was pounding. "Push over. I'm coming up."

Thayer climbed at full throttle, knowing if the other pilot was hurt or unconscious and disappeared into the overcast there'd be no finding him. He was almost there.

"This is Thayer—this is Thayer!" he barked into his mic, desperate to get the pilot's attention. "Put your nose down quick! Get it over!"

***

The other pilot was Ken Schechter, one of Thayer's *Valley Forge* roommates. Both held a Southern California upbringing in common—Schechter as a transplant from New York, Thayer as a native. Both had also been 1949 University of California undergrads: Schechter for two years at UCLA, Howie Thayer at Cal-Berkeley where as a senior he played first-string center for the Golden Bears in the 1949 Rose Bowl.

Ken Schechter had not been scheduled to fly this particular mission, an eight-plane March 22 strike on marshaling yards near Pachungjang. Instead, he'd been on standby, his AD warmed and waiting on *Valley Forge's* flight deck should another aircraft get scratched. Then, sure enough, squadron mate Charlie Brown's AD lost its hydraulics and Schechter took off in his place.

Schechter and his wingman, Lou Stoakes, had been making a target run through intense flak when suddenly something exploded in Schechter's cockpit. Instinctively, Schechter pulled back on his stick before passing out. Though he regained consciousness just moments later, Schechter had no idea what had happened, only that he couldn't see, that his face and head were throbbing, and that wind and engine noise were heavy and close.

When the pilot who heard his cry came on the circuit, Schechter could barely make out the voice above the noise. At first he had no idea it was Thayer; it was almost too much to unravel what he was being told to do: "Rock . . . your . . . wings."

When Schechter figured this out and moved his stick side to side, his buzzing brain and wavering consciousness were challenged by another instruction puzzle: "Put . . . your . . . nose . . . down . . . put . . . your . . . nose . . . down."

When the gears in the puzzle machine that was Schechter's brain finally engaged, he realized that Howie Thayer was on the circuit. Schechter pushed his control stick forward. From the angle of his body he could tell he was heading down, but was it the right angle? Schechter had no idea. That was up to Howie Thayer to decide.

Ettinger and Thorin

For Ken Schechter and Howard Thayer whose war in that hour had telescoped into desperate action in an unbounded sky, it would have been impossible to fathom the drawn out, circumscribed, but no less desperate circumstances of flyers like Henry Ettinger and Duane Thorin. For Thorin, who by then had been held captive by North Koreans for little more than a month, the reversal of fortune still rankled:

Instead of plucking Ettinger from Communist clutches, he had instead tumbled down a sort of rabbit's hole into the outskirts of Hell.

On this same March day Thorin, Ettinger, and a coterie of other "uncooperative" POWs—fourteen in all: six officers (including Ettinger) and eight enlisted men (including Thorin, Mark Gilliland, and Les Ribbick)—were imprisoned in mud-walled buildings within a larger compound they called the "Slave Camp." Located on the western side of a ridge separating it from a railroad marshaling yard, the Slave Camp was in truth a supply center for NKPA military installations in and around Pyongyang. Although situated just a few miles from Pak's Palace, the interrogation center where Thorin and Naylor-Foote had been delivered within days of the failed helicopter rescue, and where Thorin had his first exposure to life as a Communist POW, the Slave Camp presented an altogether different regimen for testing the will and humanity of its captives.

There were no more interrogations or periods of isolation from other prisoners. Instead, there was an unsparing schedule of forced labor administered by an NKPA officer and carried out by a chubby and officious corporal of the guard. The officer (dubbed "Idle Hands" by the prisoners because "idle hands cause discontent" was one of his few intelligible English expressions) and the noncom martinet ("Little Commie" to the prisoners because of his impromptu lectures on Communist doctrine) kept the POWs either working or on-call. Completed tasks almost invariably triggered more tasks; any individual resistance was met by deprivation, mock executions, and beatings.

The Slave Camp's physical living conditions were not appreciably worse than Pak's Palace, and the POWs' immediate taskmasters—North Korean supply sergeants and truck drivers—were not particularly cruel, just indifferent. However, the work regimen bred horrid circumstances: The wear and tear of nonstop heavy labor reduced prisoner clothing to little more than rags. Without opportunities to bathe, prisoner bodies produced bumper crops of parasitic lice. Whatever periods of sleep the prisoners managed to cadge were spent without bedding in a cold room on a hard clay floor. Worst of all, food and water rations never kept pace with the prisoners' level of exertion.

Harry Ettinger (whose well-established reputation for stubborn "noncooperation" predestined his transfer to the Slave Camp) had arrived at the compound in relatively decent shape—the beneficiary of a two-week respite of sleep and regular meals in Wonsan before his internment. That was March 1; under the Slave Camp regimen Ettinger had since succumbed, first to diarrhea and then to the bloody, mucous feces that signaled the onset of dysentery. As a result—in a pattern that held for each new arrival—his body's futile efforts to counter exertion with rest and sustenance were all but lost.

Schechter and Thayer

"You're doing all right now," Howie Thayer assured Ken Schechter. "Pull back a little; we can level off now."

As the damaged Skyraider leveled off, Thayer steadied his own plane about a hundred feet off its starboard quarter. He could tell it was Ken Schechter. The plane's canopy was all but blown away; the rim of the cockpit and portions of the after fuselage bore crimson splashes—Schechter's blood flash-frozen onto the deep navy blue of the AD's fuselage. Schechter's face was a mess—caked in dried blood with fresh streams coursing from his eyes and forehead. It was a wonder Schechter was alive—a bigger wonder he was conscious and speaking. "Get me down, Howie," Thayer heard him say in a way that was serious but also had about it the familiar tone of Ken Schechter's ready-room banter and bluster. "Get me down."

"Roger." First things first—regiment time to the job at hand: Thayer dipped a wing momentarily to inspect Schechter's undercarriage and saw Schechter still carried a partial bomb load. "Drop your ordnance," he told Schechter, and when the released bombs fell away, Thayer dipped once more to be sure none were left hanging.

"We're heading south, Ken. Push over a little more . . . That's the boy."

Ken Schechter fumbled for the canteen in his survival pack, found it, and somehow got the cap off. He held it close to his face and tipped it, letting the water splash into his eyes and then shaking his head. The water stung, but for a tantalizing moment Schechter could see the cockpit control panel swimming into view. Then, just as quickly, he was blind again.

Schechter splashed more water onto his face: the same stinging, and with it the same momentary red-rimmed sight of the control panel followed by utter darkness. This time, though, Schechter sensed something was wrong with his face. Probing with a gloved hand, he found a long flap of flesh, what must be his upper lip, dangling from the right side of his face across his mouth and over his lower lip. It hurt, and the thought of it sickened Schechter. He wondered if anything he said could be understood.

Then, Thayer's voice again: "We're headed for Wonsan, Ken. Not too long now."

Though he heard what Thayer said, Schechter was suddenly overwhelmed by the darkness, by the pounding in his head, by pain radiating from his groin, by nausea at the thought of his butchered face and the blood choking his throat. He had barely enough resolve for a few words: "Get me down, Howie."

Ettinger and Thorin

It had been near nightfall several days after their capture when the jeep carrying Duane Thorin and Bill Naylor-Foote west from Wonsan crested the mountain pass leading into Pyongyang. It was a moonless night, and the jeep traveled without headlights, but the sky was clear and the stars were brilliant, illuminating the snow-covered woods on either side of the road. The night air was bracingly cold, and the jeep's tires rode a surface of packed snow that made what otherwise would have been a rough ride smooth—almost, Thorin thought, like a winter sleigh ride in Nebraska.

Rounding a curve the jeep encountered three Soviet-made tanks clanking east toward Wonsan. As the heavy-footed slaps of their track treads retreated, the quiet ride resumed momentarily only to be broken by the sharp bark of a rifle shot close by; immediately, the driver swerved the jeep and braked to a stop under the canopy of the roadside trees. Thorin heard several more shots—apparently some kind of signal—before a night-heckling AD, its belly profile silhouetted by the constellations of stars, swooped overhead, firing a burst of 20mm as it passed. Next he heard a bomb burst coming from the direction of Pyongyang.

A few minutes later the jeep reached the site of the blast, a flat clearing apparently used as a rest stop on the mountain road. Thorin saw several trucks and a scattering of fires, but beyond that there wasn't much to see. Thorin realized, though, that if the heckler had arrived a few minutes earlier, the Soviet tanks might have been crossing the clearing; a few minutes later and the jeep would have been in its sights.

By the time they reached the outskirts of Pyongyang it was sunup. Under heavier traffic below the frost line the road had turned rough. Both Thorin and Naylor-Foote sat on a hard bench directly over the jeep's rear wheels and had to hold onto the vehicle's frame to keep from sliding off. The temperature rose slightly, but Thorin's frogman suit kept any moisture on his skin from evaporating, allowing the soggy cold to penetrate clear to the bone.

***

Thorin and Naylor-Foote's trip to Pyongyang dashed any illusions that the two of them, along with Harry Ettinger, might yet be rescued. For two days—the first spent in the village near the crash site, the next in a bunker carved into a hillside above Wonsan—the three men had waited hopefully while Junior General (the interpreter, Chun assured them) cooked up a new plan to get them out.

On the second day, after a breakfast of rice and soup, a haircut for Ettinger, and an involuntary shave for Naylor-Foote, the Americans waited nervously until finally, late in the afternoon, Chun pulled Thorin aside, the sound of genuine regret and resignation tempering his voice. "A jeep will be here soon to take you and Naylor-Foote to Pyongyang."

Chun shook his head. "I am very sorry other arrangements could not be made. We will get Ettinger as good medical treatment as our limited resources can provide. I'm afraid there will likely be unpleasant times ahead for you. I am sure, though, that you will be able to endure them." It was the following evening when, after a day spent shuttling between NKPA and Chinese Communist outposts in and around Pyongyang, the jeep finally reached a clearing some miles northwest of the capital. Despite the darkness, Thorin could make out the lines of a building Harry Ettinger had already described to him. It was Pak's Palace.

Schechter and Thayer

VF-194's Howard Thayer had been telling himself: Wonsan's the ticket. If Ken can get over Wonsan, maybe he can bail out and get picked up by one of the destroyers.

But then, after letting Schechter know where they were headed, there'd been silence. Maybe Schechter hadn't heard him. Thayer stared apprehensively at Schechter's blood-rimmed cockpit, worried he might have blacked out. Knowing if he had it was curtains.

"Roger me," Thayer shouted to be sure Schechter could hear—to keep him from losing hope, to keep him from blacking out. "We're approaching Wonsan now. Get ready to bail out."

Only then did Ken Schechter finally come on the circuit, his words blurred but insistent: "Negative! Negative! Not going to bail out! Get—me—down!"

Schechter's transmission startled Thayer. It was almost as if Schechter had snapped back to life. It also made Thayer realize how, rather than acting in the moment as both pilots had been trained to do, he'd instead been projecting ahead—as if the mission were somehow over once they were over water.

Thayer thoroughly understood Schechter's refusal to bail out. Ending up in the icy, mine-strewn waters of Wonsan Harbor was every pilot's worst nightmare, especially after witnessing the loss of XO Tom Pugh. Parachuting blind and wounded was almost certain death. Schechter could get trapped in his parachute harness and be pulled under. The friendly ships down there might not see him or be able to get to him in time. If Howie Thayer was in Ken Schechter's fix he'd be thinking the same thing: I'll ride this plane down somehow—or die trying.

Thorin

During their first night at Pak's Palace, Thorin and Naylor-Foote were confined to a cold, windowless, unlit, and mud-floored communal cell that held a dozen other American and South Korean prisoners. Although instinctively wary about striking up acquaintances with other prisoners, Thorin nevertheless began a whispered conversation with an Air Force pilot named Joe Green who at once confirmed the importance of circumspection.

"Anything you don't want the enemy to know about you, Chief," the lieutenant cautioned, "don't mention to anyone in here." The Korean prisoners, Green told Thorin, might well be informants, and several American prisoners were compulsive talkers, heedless of the fact the enemy was listening in. They and others (here Thorin thought immediately of Naylor-Foote) might also be talking freely to interrogators both about themselves and also about others. As important, Green warned, any "cooperation" with the North Koreans, no matter how small or seemingly inconsequential, would only lead to aggressive, endless demands for more. There would be threats, some of them dire, for "not cooperating," but the real punishments were isolation, the withholding of food, water, and the chance to bathe—simple, but amazingly effective.

***

For Duane Thorin, the proving ground of Green's cautionary precepts began the very next day. Every UN POW, including Thorin, brought aspects of themselves into the mystery-cloaked arena of Communist captivity and interrogation: degrees of strength, resilience, resourcefulness, worldliness, wariness, resolve, patience, self-respect, and equanimity. Each also was driven by human needs: for sustenance and sleep, of course, but also for companionship and approval.

Few POWs (whatever their internal makeup and needs) had received much guidance on how to behave in the face of what the Chinese Communists styled as *xi-nao* (reformative "mind cleanse") and the American press hyped as brainwashing. The previous summer, Thorin recalled, *Life* had published an article titled "How We Fooled the Communists." The article pictured a group of Americans captured and subsequently released by Chinese Communists. The essence of the captives' story was that, after listening to lectures on Capitalism's evils and Communism's virtues—neither arguing nor disagreeing with their captors—they were released with instructions simply to "tell what they had learned."

The incident had evidently prompted a new, somewhat ambiguous directive on U.S. POW behavior—a version of which had been disseminated prior to Thorin's September deployment.[1] The timeless rule about giving enemy captors no more information than name, rank, serial number, and date of birth still held. But, as Thorin remembered the gist of the directive, if the enemy started talking about politics, it was possible and permissible to "pretend to go along" in hopes of being released.

* * *

Duane Thorin's principal interrogator at Pak's Palace was an NKPA officer known—because of his spectacles—as Four Eyes.* During the sessions Thorin was confined to a small windowless room, barren save for a small table and chair, and lit by a soybean-oil lamp that Four Eyes carried with him. Four Eyes's approach was to order Thorin to "write all you know" about broad subjects such as guns, planes, and ships. Incensed each time he returned to the room to find that Thorin had scribbled: "I don't know anything important enough to write," Four Eyes warned of dire consequences for not cooperating. Another "uncooperative" prisoner, an American colonel named Black, had died in this very room.

Each night Thorin was left alone in the locked interrogation room, absent the chair, the table, and the soybean lamp. At the time Thorin still wore his flight suit and his lined flying boots and, beneath them, the frogman suit. Still, it was unbelievably frigid; fearing the onset of frostbite, Thorin stayed mostly awake, pacing in a circle. He occasionally got food (usually thin soup), water, and access to the latrine (*benjo*), but only when he pleaded.

Lack of sleep inevitably caused Thorin to doze during Four Eyes's marathon interrogations. Each time, Four Eyes yelled for him to "sit at attention!" and launched into another tirade about the importance of cooperation.

Four Eyes seemed less interested in what Thorin might have to tell him than he was in convincing his subject that he, not Thorin, ultimately controlled Thorin's fate. "You must change your attitude!" Four Eyes repeatedly insisted. "If you will only learn to cooperate and do the things I ask, then you will be entitled to lenient treatment. Then you can be with the others, for company to talk with and to be warm."

---

* The interrogators frequently used different names with different prisoners. It was easier for prisoners to keep track of interrogators by using such nicknames.

After about a week of this, Thorin's resolve began to crack. It happened in stages. At first there was a deep enraging hatred for Four Eyes, enough to kill the North Korean if the opportunity—and Thorin's ebbing strength—permitted. However, this soon gave way to stages of self-pity and then despair. He thought most of his mother back in Nebraska who had lost a husband, another son during World War II, and now—soon—him.

It was a perilous time for a self-reliant maverick like Thorin. He had made his way in the world on his wits, his physical capabilities, and his jaundiced eye for the foibles and shortcomings of others. Now, after uncharacteristic lapses in judgment (trusting Ulatoski and being cajoled into taking Naylor-Foote along on the rescue mission), Thorin risked succumbing to the drip-drip-drip of Four Eyes's intimidation.

Remarkably, Thorin was able to regain his emotional footing. When things seemed worst he found himself drawing on a hitherto untapped source of inner energy. At first it was just a flickering ember at the core. It was as if the North Koreans had all but doused the fire of Thorin's resistance only to have missed this final, irreducible, spark. Now, with each hour and day, the ember seemed to intensify and grow.

Instead of losing himself in self-pity, Thorin came to realize the immediate source of his pain and distress was not Four Eyes. Rather, he was fighting an inner battle—a test of his own strength, endurance, and sanity. Thorin had almost been persuaded that Four Eyes was superhuman when the truth was that he had no unusual powers. Instead, Four Eyes was relying on Thorin's internal collapse to do it for him. Thorin's desperation receded, replaced by a new energy and assurance. While none of his physical circumstances had changed, Thorin's determination to prevail in the contest within himself had grown stronger.

Thorin had also learned—or at least confirmed—another important lesson: In a society as severe and starved as North Korea, everyone depended on deceit for survival. They might mouth Communist precepts or the importance of cooperation, but everyone (the POWs, the guards, Four Eyes, even Pak himself) was looking out for himself. They had no choice: Reduced to such desperate circumstances, duplicity (whether to get information, clothing, food, sleep, or anything else) was the essence of survival. Thorin realized this was, in a very real way, like existing on the unforgiving American frontier—and he'd already learned to be very good at that.

Schechter and Thayer

Knowing they had to find a landing field fast, Howard Thayer scanned the shoreline ahead looking for a Navy warship on the "bomb line" demarcating UN ground-force operations.* That would provide the surest marker they were flying over friendly ground. A few minutes later he saw one: a big cruiser, its guns blasting away at Communist troop positions to the north. That was it. Thayer knew that K-18, a Marine base, was about thirty miles due south. The worst was still ahead, but at least they had a destination.

Thayer was almost giddy with the news: "We're at the bomb line now, Ken, heading for K-18. Can you hear me, Ken? Will head for K-18. Over."

"Roger." Schechter's voice was tired and barely audible.

"Can you make it, Ken?"

"Get me down, you miserable son-of-a-bitch." Again, Thayer sensed a flash of resolve—Schechter's ready-room banter. But how long could he last?

Thayer ordered Schechter to bank right. Thayer turned inside Schechter's path and got them both steadied on a course toward K-18. Then he saw Schechter's head flop forward, then straighten, only to flop over again, this time to the side. Thayer quickly became convinced he'd never get him to K-18. He had to get Schechter down now. Somewhere, anywhere, any flat piece of real estate, even a rice paddy. Then he saw something ahead—a clear spot that looked worth a try.

"Ken, we're going down. Push your nose over, drop your right wing."

Schechter complied. Good: He was still listening and reacting to instructions. As they got closer to the clear spot, Thayer remembered what it was: Jersey Bounce.

***

---

* North of the bomb line, UN air and sea forces could attack targets without having to coordinate strikes with ground commanders. Conversely, below the bomb line, pilots could be reasonably certain that territory was in UN hands.

Jersey Bounce was a dirt airstrip just south of the bomb line once used by Army light planes for artillery-spotting flights. Its name reflected its character—just a few small buildings fronting a short north-south gravel runway scarred with wheel ruts and potholes—but also apparently the wiseass attitude of whoever named it. Jersey Bounce was largely abandoned now, but, as the two ADs converged on it from the east, Thayer spotted a jeep and a small group of men looking up at them.

"We're approaching Jersey Bounce, Ken. Will make a two seven zero turn and set you down."

"Roger, Howie. Let's go," Schechter replied and then repeated it, though the second time more faintly. He was ready to try it, but he was running out of steam.

"Left wing down slowly," Schechter heard Thayer say. "Nose over easy. Little more." The two planes banked into a turn that brought them to the north end of Jersey Bounce's runway. Thayer positioned his plane just feet from Schechter's port wing.

Ken Schechter remembered Jersey Bounce from earlier missions. He could picture it in his mind's eye: rough and short. Weak as he was, Schechter knew he was heading to the do-or-die moment. Flying blind was one thing; landing blind on a dirt strip was unimaginable. He had to put the pain in the background and focus on following Howie's instructions. He had to believe he would make it.

Thorin

If the Soviets and their Asian clients had indeed mastered techniques of mind cleansing or brainwashing, it provided a ready-made—and disturbing—explanation (at least for Americans) for the alarming behavior of a handful of American POWs.

On March 16, 1952, China's foreign minister, Chou En-lai, announced to the world press that Kenneth L. Enoch and John S. Quinn, two USAF B-26 pilots who were shot down over North Korea in mid-January, had confessed to Chinese interrogators that their planes had been armed with biological weapons, including anthrax, typhus, cholera, and plague.

"I was forced," Quinn stated in a taped statement broadcast on Peking Radio, "to be the tool of these warmongers and made to . . . do this awful crime against the people of Korea and the Chinese volunteers." The Chinese had been lenient, Quinn said. "They issued me with warm clothing against the cold, gave me excellent food, bedding and a warm place to sleep. I am eternally grateful for their kind treatment. At last, after much patience on the part of the Volunteers, I realized my crime."

***

The origin of Chinese accusations—and worldwide speculation—that UN forces were engaging in biological warfare had been a secret March 1951 mission behind enemy lines to investigate the possibility (raised by a North Korean CIA agent) that Chinese and North Korean troops might have fallen victim to a strain of the bubonic plague. Called the "Black Death," the bubonic plague was a bacterial disease that had scourged Europe during the Middle Ages and was still endemic to Manchuria. If Chinese troops had indeed brought the plague with them to Korea, it could wipe out UN troops who were not immunized.

Acting on this concern, a small (and hastily immunized) Army and Navy contingent led by Brig. Gen. Crawford W. Sams (then Douglas MacArthur's public health aide) landed ashore near Chilbro-ri in a rubber raft embarked from the whaleboat of destroyer *Wallace L. Lind* (DD-703). Sams returned from the dangerous foray (he spent his time ashore holed up in a shoreside cave interviewing agents while others in the party slipped into a local hospital to make detailed observations of Chinese army patients) convinced that North Korean doctors were treating smallpox, not plague.

The crisis might have ended there, had the results of what was intended as a hush-hush mission not somehow leaked to the press. A United Press headline that blared US GENERAL RISKS LIFE BEHIND RED LINES TO PROBE DEADLY EPIDEMIC gave the Communist world (and its many external sympathizers) all they needed to launch their case that America was engaging in germ warfare.[2]

If the Sams expedition was the grist for this campaign, the Enoch and Quinn confessions a year later furnished proof. Although, to most Western listeners, Quinn's stilted language and emotionless voice had the earmarks of a Communist script read under duress, the confession set off a global backlash and immediately compromised the United Nations' position in the Panmunjom truce talks. Confessions seemed to snowball as three Air Force officer crewmen in another B-26 chimed in with their own.

U.S. military brass were understandably alarmed that none of these five men were young, naive, and ill-trained recruits; instead, they were all commissioned officers and well-trained aviation professionals. If men such as these couldn't resist Communist pressures, who could?

***

Pak's Palace POWs had learned of the Enoch and Quinn confessions well over a week before they were announced to the world. Four Eyes had convened a group session during which, barely concealing his glee, he told the POWs that two U.S. Air Force pilots at another facility nearby had confessed to dropping "germ bombs" on North Korea.[*]

Afterward, Duane Thorin noticed that another POW, an Air Force captain and B-26 pilot named Byron Dobbs, looked unusually shaken and distraught. Dobbs, a large man who towered over each of the guards and interrogators, had, since his arrival at Pak's Palace, gone out of his way to express gratitude to the North Koreans—almost, Thorin felt, to the point of groveling. Pak's Palace's interrogators had seized the opportunity to cultivate Dobbs. They treated him gently, and he had reciprocated by listening earnestly. Interrogators had even supplied Dobbs with a bundle of "captured U.S. documents" allegedly proving U.S. and South Korean complicity in launching the invasion of North Korea.

Dobbs might just have been "going along," but, to Thorin's mind, he seemed headed for deep waters. Now, in the aftermath of Four Eyes's stunning announcement, Dobbs looked ashen faced. "Oh my God," Dobbs finally whispered quietly. "They're both from my outfit. Johnny Quinn was my roommate before he was shot down."

***

---

[*] In late February, when Harry Ettinger, accompanied by Banjo Eyes, had been sent to the Slave Camp after a brief stop at Pak's Palace, he had been marched past a compound controlled (according to Banjo Eyes) by the Chinese Communists. Banjo Eyes told Ettinger that one of the compound buildings housed two very important Air Force POWs. When he later learned of the confessions, Ettinger assumed those two important prisoners were Enoch and Quinn.

Heightened interest in "germ warfare" followed, with Pak's Palace interrogators intent on exploiting any glimmer of potential cooperation on the issue. They seemed not so much interested in obtaining direct confessions as they were in getting expressions of distress and concern that America might be engaged in such heinous acts. And they wanted to record these expressions.

Thorin, who was questioned about germ warfare by no less than Colonel Pak himself, denied any knowledge or opinion and was never asked again, but the North Koreans continued to bait other prisoners, especially those who were young, wounded, or ill. Coupling better treatment (in a hospital) with being "allowed" to tape-record a statement seemed to be the most common ploy. While most declined the offer, some agreed; those who did rationalized that it was a chance to have their families hear from them.

Taking the lead in this seductive effort was the Professor, a stocky, well-dressed North Korean interrogator who described himself as a former instructor at Pyongyang University. Duane Thorin had been questioned by the Professor on a few occasions, sessions the Professor styled as "conversations," staged in a heated room supplied with tea and rice cakes. During these sessions, the Professor had calmly described the virtues of Communism and the inequities of Capitalism to Thorin, probing for some glimmer of "cooperation." Thorin had by then already concluded that any level of "pretending to go along" was a sure trap. Thorin's "conversations" with the Professor were short-lived.

The Professor was now staging these "conversations" for groups of prisoners. One of his common ploys with Air Force and Navy pilots and crews was to probe repeatedly for information about the ordnance loads their aircraft carried—with the not-so-subtle intimation that some of the loads could contain things other than explosives. Once, when Thorin spoke up during one of these group interrogations to warn about this, he was quickly expelled from the session.

His expulsion was to mark the end of Thorin's idyll at Pak's Palace. Colonel Pak had apparently concluded that Thorin and other POWs such as William Arnold, Julian Gilliland, and a young GI medic named J. W. Rambo were beyond the pale of cooperation. Late that same day the four were summarily packed into the back of a waiting trunk that transported them to an undisclosed location.

After sundown, once the four alighted from the back of the truck and were marched to a mud-walled building, Thorin could pick out several familiar, if somewhat reduced, forms sitting atop bundles of rags. One was Harry Ettinger; another was Joe Green. "Welcome to the Slave Camp!" a voice hailed faintly from somewhere in the darkened room. Thorin, Arnold, Gilliland, and Rambo exchanged glances. Conditions looked bad. Still, as ragged and emaciated as these men seemed, Thorin felt somehow that the four new arrivals had been ushered into the presence of an elite and exclusive brotherhood.

Schechter and Thayer

"Wheels down," Schechter heard Thayer say. Instinctively, from some hidden reserve of determination he found himself shouting back, almost screaming: "To hell with that!"

Wheels down on a runway like this could be a disaster. He could rip off a wing or do a nose over. Schechter knew he had a better chance on the belly with wheels up.

"Roger, gear up," Thayer said.

A moment of silence as they came out of the turn, and then Thayer's voice again, still calm: "We're heading straight. Flaps down. Hundred yards to the runway. You're fifty feet off the ground. Pull back a little."

Schechter followed each step but made no effort to acknowledge Thayer's commands. Above them and listening in, Schechter's wingman, Lou Stoakes, who had been trailing Thayer and Schechter throughout, watched as the two ADs approached the strip in tandem. Thayer flew just feet from Schechter's port wing, duplicating each adjustment he coached Schechter to make.

"Easy. Easy. That's good. You're level. You're O.K. You're O.K. Thirty feet off the ground now. You're O.K. You're over the runway. Twenty feet. Kill it a little. You're setting down. O.K. O.K. O.K. Cut."

Ken Schechter tensed, waiting for the plane to hit. When it came it was not as bad as he expected. The Skyraider hit, lurched a bit, then slid on its belly along the gravel runway. It finally came to rest, all in one piece. No smoke, no fire. Just the ticking of hot metal and a settling blanket of dust.

"You're on the ground," he heard Thayer say, almost as if Schechter had no way of knowing that. Yes. Yes. On the ground.

Howie Thayer circled Jersey Bounce, almost at once putting aside those unnecessary words. He saw Schechter climb out of the cockpit and ease himself to the ground, leaning against the fuselage with one hand to his face. The jeep that Thayer had spotted had by then raced down the runway trailing a cloud of dust and pulled up alongside the plane. A man leaped out, ran over to Schechter, and helped him limp to the jeep. With Schechter inside, the jeep sped back through the dust cloud to the cluster of buildings.

Thayer meanwhile formed up with Stoakes, and the two pointed east toward a landing on *Valley Forge*. When they touched down Thayer found the ship was buzzing about his and Ken Schechter's escapade. All through the ordeal the radio speakers in Air Operations had been tuned into their transmissions. Many pilots, ship's officers, and crewmen had sneaked in to hear all or portions of the exchanges. In fact, a recording had been made, and that night it was piped in its entirety over the *Valley*'s intraship radio system.

14

IMPLACABLE ENEMIES AND UNFORGIVING ELEMENTS

ON APRIL 20, 1952, six VF-194 ADs flew late-morning strikes on tracks and marshaling yards south of Hungnam—a mission advertised (as always seemed to be the case) as a "gravy run." During his first pass, flying number two, Dick Kaufman dropped two delayed-fuse bombs that severed a section of rail a half mile from where squadron CO and flight leader Bob Schreiber's ordnance hit.

All six ADs survived that first run, but as they climbed, circled, and lined up for the next, Kaufman noticed that Jack Workman's AD was in trouble. While swooping low to investigate what looked to be a camouflaged locomotive, Workman had taken small-arms fire. Now his AD was trailing a thick plume of engine smoke and struggling to hold altitude.

Kaufman was closest to Workman, so he lowered his dive brakes, dropped altitude, and joined on Workman's wing. Workman's hand signals told Kaufman he could receive radio traffic but not transmit; Kaufman rogered, reminded Workman to drop his remaining ordnance, and then stayed close as the crippled AD struggled seaward.

Once they went feet wet, Kaufman thought Workman had a good chance of ditching near one of the coastal ships. Then without warning Workman's airplane nosed into a steep dive. Kaufman followed, hollering for Workman to bail. At about four hundred feet Workman finally did—much too low for his parachute to deploy. Kaufman saw Workman hit the water in free fall just a moment after his airplane splashed.

Kaufman immediately dropped flaps and circled the spot where Workman floated facedown and motionless. Cruiser *St. Paul*, the nearest ship, was then five miles away, but it had a radar fix on Kaufman's airplane and was closing at full speed. Soon its helicopter was over the scene. Kaufman continued circling as the chopper crewman jumped in the water and wrestled Workman into the survival sling. It didn't look good. Workman dangled like a collapsed marionette as the pilot retracted the sling cable. Flown immediately to a medical facility at Yodo-ri, Workman was pronounced dead on arrival.[1]

***

Jack Workman was ATG-1's fourteenth confirmed deployment fatality—though possibly as high as its eighteenth pending the fates of Harry Ettinger, Julian Gilliland, Jess McElroy, and Marvin Broomhead. Workman was VF-194's second confirmed pilot loss (XO Tom Pugh had been the first back in December), leaving V-194 in third place (behind VF-52, with three pilot losses) in the unenviable tally of air group fatalities. Flight ops had claimed one VF-111 aviator (its CO, Frank Welch) as well as one each from two of the composite detachments (VC-3's John McKenna on February 8 and VC-61's Alan N. Hoff during a March 11 photo-recco mission west of Yangdok). *Essex*'s Air Group 5 had completed its TF 77 deployment with seventeen aircrew fatalities, compounded by the loss of five flight deck personnel. Now ATG-1 was positioned to equal or eclipse that total.

ATG-1's death tote-board leader was VF-653: By late March, with more than two months of war deployment remaining, Cook Cleland's Flying Circus had already lost six pilots. The latest, on March 11, had been twenty-nine-year-old Hull Wright. The Pittsburgh reservist and steel company lab professional had bailed out of his flak-damaged Corsair during a reconnaissance mission east of Pungsan. Unlike VF-194's Workman, Wright cleared his aircraft at high-enough altitude. But his parachute caught fire, and it too failed to deploy.[2] Wright's remains were never recovered.

VF-653's casualty record earned it special attention from Secretary of the Navy Dan A. Kimball during a two-day visit to *Valley Forge* at the end of March. Kimball, a cigar-wielding former Army Air Service pilot and defense-industry executive, expressly wanted to witness an entire VF-653 mission cycle: from briefing and launch through recovery and debriefing. It had all the earmarks of administration and congressional oversight sparked by hometown hand-wringing.

The showcase mission, a sixteen-plane (eight VF-653 F4Us led by Ray Edinger and eight VF-194 ADs led by Pappy Brubaker) bomb, rocket, and napalm strike on rails, gun emplacements, and troop barracks along Dottie, was orchestrated with fanatical detail—and some thought overkill—under the doubly piercing scrutiny of Kimball and Task Force 77 commander Black Jack Perry. Yet despite risky low-level napalm drops in the face of intense ground fire (six planes were hit), the mission went off without a major hitch; *Valley Forge* recovered fourteen aircraft, and another landed at K-18. The sixteenth, a VF-653 Corsair, was lost to ground fire; its pilot, Ed Sterrett, however, was retrieved unharmed by the helo from LST-799 after he ditched in Wonsan Harbor.

Total rail cuts for *Valley Forge's* entire day of flight ops—144 from 89 combined sorties—were claimed as a record for "cuts scored by one carrier for one day's operations,"[3] prompting SecNav Kimball to dispense kudos for all hands on his departure the next day. Kimball's return to the States, aviators in Cleland's Flying Circus hoped, spelled an end to home-front second-guessing about their capabilities. Freed from the distractions of any more trick-pony performances, they turned their focus to completing the final weeks of the cruise.

***

Kimball's tour coincided with significant changes in the Far East command structure—dominoes tripped by Gen. Dwight Eisenhower's decision to leave his European NATO command and return to the United States to launch a political career. In May, when Matthew Ridgway was summoned to succeed Eisenhower, SCAP command fell to Army general Mark W. Clark. Clark, fifty-six, another of the Army's World War II wunderkind, had skipped the rank of colonel altogether during his ascent and had been among the Army's youngest-ever three-star generals when he commanded U.S. forces in Italy during World War II.

The Italian campaign was a successful but costly grind during which Clark solidified a reputation for being short-tempered and aloof, with touches of arrogance and vanity. One staff officer from the time remembered that "conceit wrapped around [Clark] like a halo," and the general was known to instruct photographers to snap his "facially best" left side.[4] Still, because of his command experience in Italy, Clark was intimately familiar with the problems of peninsular warfare. Afterward, in Austria, Clark had also been among the first to come to grips with the guileless negotiation style of the Communists.

Seventh Fleet, meanwhile, got a commanding "Clark" of its own: fifty-eight-year-old vice admiral Joseph J. "Jocko" Clark. Clark's aquiline nose, broad face, copper-burnished complexion, and outwardly placid countenance revealed his Cherokee heritage (born in 1893 in Oklahoma's Pryor Indian Territory, in 1917 he became the first Native American to graduate from the Naval Academy) while masking a Halsey-like combativeness that was to make him the Korean War's most aggressive fleet commander.

From the start, Clark never hesitated to inject himself among Task Force 77 pilots and crews. Chauffeured to the scene of the action by his flagship *Iowa* to learn firsthand about their difficulties and insights, Clark used pilot input as the basis for new air combat initiatives. Notwithstanding the rail-cutting statistics touted by Task Force 77, Clark publicly bemoaned the strategic shortcomings of the interdiction and rail-cutting campaigns. Despite piles of elaborately tracked damage assessments, the Chinese and North Koreans seemed pretty much undeterred in dragging out the war.

Clark's criticism came at a watershed juncture: By May 1952 Navy and Marine pilots had expended as much aviation ordnance as they had in the entire air war against Japan. In addition to bombs, rockets, bullets, and fuel, Clark saw the effort as needlessly burning up pilots and airplanes. Clark pushed for more effective tactical approaches. For example, after a frontline aerial inspection convinced him Communist supplies were being stockpiled north of the main line of resistance (MLR), just beyond artillery range, Clark ordered what came to be known (in deference to his Native American heritage) as Cherokee Strikes. Meanwhile, the brakes were applied—officially at least—to some of the more egregious tactical excesses: Pull-out altitudes were raised, and limits were set on the maximum number of target passes during a mission.[5]

***

Sometime that same May, James Michener received a letter from Ken Schechter's father, George, the president of a lace and embroidery firm in Southern California. Schechter's son was then an outpatient at San Diego's Balboa Naval Hospital under the care of its highly respected eye specialists. After surgery and periods of hospitalization, the vision in Ken Schechter's left eye had returned and continued to improve, but there was no realistic possibility of regaining sight in his right eye. Eventually, a cosmetic lens was to be fashioned and installed. And while the biggest, sharpest, and most threatening shards had been removed (Schechter explicitly remembered the metallic rattling as Navy surgeons aboard hospital ship *Consolation* [AH-15] tossed the shards into a steel bowl), other pieces of shrapnel would remain forever embedded elsewhere in his face.

Praising Michener's United Press article "Epic in Failure" ("That story was a journalistic gem. . . . The names of Broomhead, Moore, Henry, Thayer and Schechter will be forgotten but their valor and gallantry in combat during the KOREAN campaign will be remembered for a long, long time"), and remarking that his son was in a "wonderful frame of mind," George Schechter informed Michener, "It might interest you to know that in December 1951 Ensign Marvin Broomhead's wife Beatrice was bedridden at the Naval Hospital, San Diego as a result of an auto accident. She is still in critical condition there."[6] The "first thing" his son Ken did when he checked in at the same hospital, Schechter wrote, "was to visit Mrs. Broomhead down the hall."

"Isn't it wonderful," Ken told us. "Mrs. Broomhead can now move her fingers and arms. She is even allowed to sit up an hour or so each day." And after a pause, he continued, "You know what, she really believes that Marvin is alive." A sudden chill ran through Mrs. Schechter and myself. "Some nights she watches and waits for familiar footsteps to come through the door of her room," Ken said as he shook his head. To us, Ken regretted profoundly he could not share her optimism and hinted that he would pray for another miracle. Ken thinks it's a miracle that he is alive today. "Beatrice hopes," Ken concluded, "someone will take her close to see the Valley Forge approaching our shores perhaps in July." She clings to the faith and hope that Marvin will be on the "Rusty Bucket" as the Valley is affectionately tabbed.

***

While it is impossible to know what if any impact news of Beatrice Broomhead's circumstances and poignantly reported hopes affected Michener, he was then dealing with his own personal crisis. His wife, Evangeline (Vange), had traveled with him to the Far East, remaining in Japan as he went on to Korea and shipboard stays in the Sea of Japan. Correspondence from the time hinted heavily at a foundering marriage.

Michener confided to one acquaintance that he was feeling fine but that "Vange, on the other hand, has had something of a nervous breakdown and is recovering with her brother in Rome." In a letter to a different correspondent, Michener lifted the veil a bit more: "My charming wife had what I hope is a nervous breakdown—if it isn't that, it's something much more gruesome—and is on her way home under her own steam. I hope that a spell of rest will right the ship."[7] It was at once a submerging of emotions and an understatement of what was likely the unwinding of his relationship with Vange.

***

Despite this "spell" of domestic turmoil, Michener soon returned to Korea, this time to interview frontline GIs and marines near the 38th Parallel. One evening a courier from *Life's* Tokyo office reached the front lines with a package for Michener—what turned out to be the advance galleys for Ernest Hemingway's *The Old Man and the Sea.* Hemingway was the famous, near-iconic, author of books such as *For Whom the Bell Tolls* and *A Farewell to Arms.* He was a novelist, as Michener aspired to be, but also, during World War II, a journalist, as Michener now was in Korea.

Hemingway's spare but powerful prose had brought him acclaim, while his expatriate lifestyle, along with the sense that Hemingway's heroes were his alter egos, had brought him equal measures of fame and notoriety. However, in the postwar years, Hemingway's fame had dwindled along with his literary production. Now he hoped for a comeback with *The Old Man and the Sea*, which was to be published in full in the pages of *Life*. The editors had tracked down Michener to solicit his comments on the manuscript for publicity purposes.

Although he was then on assignment for *Reader's Digest*, Michener read Hemingway's short novella (just 26,000 words) with deep interest. The old man of Hemingway's tale was Santiago, an aging and luckless Cuban fisherman who, while fishing alone, snares a giant marlin that pulls his skiff far out to sea. Santiago finally harpoons the fish and lashes it to the skiff, only to begin an epic four-day battle with sharks trying to savage his catch. In the end, with the predators still circling the small boat and Santiago himself exhausted and half crazed, the head and tail, connected by "a great long white spine," are all that remain of the great fish. The old man finally steers his battered skiff back to the shore—the marlin's carcass still lashed to its side as evidence of his epic failure.

The Old Man and the Sea is told from the perspective of a simple man with pride in his endurance who realizes, fatalistically, that he has gone too far out to sea but must battle to the end, in part because of his reverence for the adversary he has subdued. It represented Hemingway's—and Michener's—ideal of manhood: fighting implacable enemies and the unforgiving elements to achieve personal (though virtually anonymous) vindication.

After reading the manuscript, Michener was convinced that Hemingway had written an "incandescent" masterpiece. His laudatory comments—"No one reading my words could doubt that here was a book worth immediately reading"—were among those heralding the September 1952 publication of Hemingway's novella in *Life*. That edition of the magazine (then a weekly) sold more than 5 million copies. The best-selling book version that followed returned Hemingway to the top rank (he would win the Nobel Prize in Literature in 1954) and solidified his position as an important American literary figure.

***

Santiago's forlorn and washed-up condition, lying exhausted in the bilges of a battered skiff on a deserted Cuban beach, resembled, though under much different circumstances, the physical and emotional desperation of the fourteen U.S. POWs interred in the Slave Camp, the NKPA supply center near Pyongyang. Squalor and round-the-clock exertion were taking their tolls on even the camp's newest arrivals— Duane Thorin, Bill Arnold, Julian Gilliland, and J. W. Rambo—while systematically wringing the final reserves of energy and human dignity from longer-term residents like Harry Ettinger and Joe Green. Still, in the midst of its mundane horrors, the Slave Camp offered its occupants two salvations.

The first—hardly appreciated by spectral men who were slowed by untreated wounds, exhausted by diarrhea or dysentery, reduced to wearing rags, plagued by lice, and starved for food, water, sanitation, and sleep—was that North Korean wartime logistics could not afford to spare any hands, legs, or backs. Had this not been so (due in no small part to the unrelenting Task Force 77 air strikes), the "uncooperative" Pak's Palace exiles might well have been subject to peremptory executions instead of lingering deaths.

The second grace, a true and indisputable lifesaver considering the Slave Camp's grueling conditions, was group cohesion. If Pak's Palace had been enormously successful in discouraging camaraderie and in pitting groups (the "cooperative" and "noncooperative") and even individuals against each other, the Slave Camp's collective squalor and forced labor had just the opposite effect.

All fourteen men were subjected to the same relentless work and heartless supervision, and so all fourteen learned to focus their hatred toward their North Korean oppressors. Despite differences in age (the oldest, a Marine Corps Mustang lieutenant named Felix Ferranto, was forty, while several of the youngest, among them Les Ribbick, were not yet twenty), rank, and background, the prisoners coalesced around the simple imperative of keeping each other alive. Indeed, the importance of collective leverage was the one positive lesson any would take from Communist captivity.

Perhaps the biggest test of their cohesion came in April when, after a full night of backbreaking work, Little Commie (the Slave Camp's officious corporal of the guard) took it on his own initiative to rouse the sleepless, unfed POWs for a full day of chores. During the grueling detail Little Commie even cracked down on "banjo" breaks, despite the fact that virtually all his charges suffered some degree of intestinal distress. Eventually, one and then another POW soiled themselves.

It was the last straw: Abruptly and collectively, the prisoners decided enough was enough. Someone called out, "Everyone sit down!"—and all fourteen did. The rebellion momentarily subdued Little Commie; he brusquely agreed to a rest break, but when he tried to rouse them a few minutes later, the POWs refused and instead demanded to be fed. This reignited the standoff: "He who doesn't work doesn't eat!" Little Commie shouted (parroting one of his stock doctrinaire phrases), leaving the strikers to the guards as he raced off to alert his boss, Idle Hands.

Hurrying from his office, Idle Hands confronted the prisoners with the threat of withholding food entirely until they resumed work. To make his point, Idle Hands made a show of sending all the compound personnel—save the POWs and their guards—off for an extended lunch break. "At least," Harry Ettinger muttered stoically to the seated group as they awaited their fate, "we lose so little when they take it away."

Despite Idle Hands's ultimatum, the POWs realized they had some leverage: It was not as though the North Koreans had some huge army of replacements. And trying to work now was as sure a way to collapse as never eating again.

When Idle Hands returned an hour later to once more confront the strikers, Joe Green, the group's acknowledged master of diplomacy, began to reason with the North Korean: "We understand your situation," Green explained through a translator. "You've got work that needs to be done. We'll do it, but we simply need some reasonable rest and food."

Not entirely to the POWs' surprise, the combination of the sit-down and Joe Green's words and demeanor seemed to register with Idle Hands. Green and the other older POWs realized, however, the North Korean was in a bind; before he could concede anything, he would somehow need to save face. They waited anxiously until a mollified Idle Hands finally seemed to decide on a way: The work that Little Commie had set for them to do was important, Idle Hands insisted, and needed to be finished. But there was also some important unloading to be done the same night, so the men would have more opportunity to rest and the chance to eat now and before the night work.

***

The symbolic "revolt" marked the end of Little Commie's direct supervision. The POWs' diet continued as meager as ever, but there were no more threats of withholding food entirely, and Slave Camp overseers gradually allowed more reasonable intervals of sleep and rest breaks. The harsh work regimen largely continued, but with a slackening in gratuitous threats and outbursts of violence. And, out from under Little Commie's imperious thumb, the POWs learned to work the margins of the system—using collective and well-timed deceit to pilfer, hide, and distribute (as did most of the North Koreans working in the compound) items of food (rice and soybeans in particular) and small luxuries like soap and cigarettes. Though they possessed no significant trade surplus, the POWs also managed to husband their resources for bartering with the compound's noncoms, the civilians who hung around its margins and even the Chinese workers who'd been brought in to upgrade the area's defenses.

Among the positive side effects of the POWs' chicanery and subversive commerce was the sense that they were gaining an element of control, however small, over their miserable and otherwise subhuman existences. The intricacies of commerce encouraged ingenuity, scheming, and, to some degree, renewed self-respect and planning for the future.

One of the most cherished by-products from bartering proved to be information gleaned from the POWs' trading partners. Although the information might be spotty, ill-informed, even outright bogus, it was a welcome antidote to the systematic disinformation spewed by their Communist captors. Much of this black-market news understandably centered on the prospects of the peace talks in Panmunjom, but other bits of information closer to home crept in as well. In mid-May, for example, Chinese workers brought news that the Slave Camp prisoners were soon be transferred to a Chinese prison camp up near the Yalu River. Americans already there, they said, had better rice and more of it, played games, and enjoyed music and dancing. Asked with whom the POWs danced, the answer was "with each other."

***

For James Michener, neither Hemingway's Gulf Stream nor the Sea of Japan off North Korea was remotely like the landscape he surveyed during his final frontline tour of Korea. It was instead a barren trench line extending—virtually uninterrupted—140 miles "right across the Middle of Korea." It was, taken together, known as the MLR—the "main line of resistance."

The American trenches were close to the Communists' own lines—on average, separated by about 400 yards. Despite this proximity and the fact that the excavations themselves were just shoulder deep, troops occupying the trenches eventually grew indifferent to the threat of Communist machine-gun and rifle fire. "Few men are killed that way," Michener learned. "It's the mortars and the big shells that do the damage."

To counter this threat, troops dug deep bunkers into the banks of the trench line, shored up by logs and roofed by more logs and sand-bags. Each bunker measured roughly twelve by twelve and housed four to six men. The bunkers were in some ways like "underground apartment houses," warm in winter and cool in summer, wood floored in many cases, some even elaborately decorated—"Marilyn Monroe being the favorite wallpaper." Still, the environment could be gloomy and claustrophobic, "a place for moles, not men."

The elaborate dugouts and the proximity of opposing trench lines separated by a barbed-wire-strung no-man's-land seeded with high-powered microphones, land mines, and even drums of napalm rigged to detonate during any enemy approach were clear markers of a pro-longed siege. Not that there weren't skirmishes and losses on both sides. For their part, the U.S. troops sent out two kinds of patrols—one type to snatch individual prisoners, the other, called mousetraps, to lure Communist patrols into V-shaped tactical culs-de-sac where they could be captured or killed in groups. But mostly, the troops hunkered down and improved their positions. The war might end any day or go on forever.

For their part, the brass had no illusions as to what might happen if the Chinese and Koreans decided to stage an all-out assault on the trench lines. The United Nations' 600,000 combined troop level faced more than 1 million Communists across the line. If the Communists hit the trench lines with massed power, they would undoubtedly break through and push the defenders back. Michener had witnessed the interrogation of newly captured Communist prisoners. The Chinese troops in particular were well fed and clothed. They also brimmed with confidence. "They remember that they licked us at the Yalu River and they feel they can do it again."

UN ground forces—still headed by U.S. Army general James Van Fleet who, though hawkish and irritated by the limits imposed on him, was resigned (at least for now) to the political realities of the stalemate—counted on the belief that, for lack of good logistics, any massed Communist offensive would inevitably run out of steam. "They'll never be able to sustain their drive for more than six days," Van Fleet assured Michener. "Then their supplies will give out and we'll chop them to pieces."

Another possibility for the Communists was to unlimber their many huge artillery batteries to fire massed barrages to literally wipe out the trenches. To do this, however, would require access to unlimited ammunition supplies while exposing their gun positions to aerial attack. To counter this, UN forces coupled air strikes against Communist supply lines and stockpiles with their own artillery barrages—using fewer guns but with vast ammunition stores and, thanks to aerial spotting, much greater accuracy.

***

During this time Michener also visited Panmunjom, a bleak, outwardly peaceful but nonetheless fiercely contested battleground of the protracted stalemate. Panmunjom, the locus of the peace talks since October 1951, was, Michener told readers in the first of six newspaper dispatches bannered as "The Real Story of Korea," "so incredible a place that the daily goings on which occur there seem entirely fitting. I cannot recall anything in world history that remotely resembles the fairy tale of Panmunjom."[8]

Michener accompanied UN support personnel in a convoy of twenty battered jeeps that left the UN headquarters at Munsan early each morning and traveled dusty, nearly trackless, roads north to the negotiation compound. "You do not see picturesque Korean villages," Michener reported. Instead, "you see great empty deserted highlands. . . . This is the great upland tundra of Asia, cruel and barren and unforgiving."

Panmunjom itself, reached by crossing a bridge and rumbling over a final dusty straightaway, proved to be a "doleful, dismal stopping place" containing "exactly four mud huts, side by side." Across the road from the deserted huts, pitched on a plot of rising ground, were the truce-talk tents—"not large and not particularly well set up."

Negotiators from the two sides arrived precisely at 10:00 A.M., the UN principals by dust-stirring helicopters from the south, the Chinese and North Koreans from the north "in four Russian jeeps, two captured Fords and a Buick." From opposite sides of the compound both sets of principals—UN negotiators were led by Vice Adm. Turner C. Joy, head of Far East Naval forces; the Communists' main delegate was Lt. Gen. Nam Il, the NKPA's young, dapper, yet dour chief of staff—eventually entered the windblown main tent where, amid a "severely plain" interior furnished with "green covered tables, folding chairs, oil stoves," and flags (the North Korean flag "slightly bigger and taller than the U.N. flag"), they "hammer[ed] away at the great problems involved in a truce."

***

After reaching agreement in late November 1951 to use the 38th Parallel as the official demarcation of the "line of contact," the negotiations had resumed their slow, acrimonious pace, what UN delegates had taken to calling "Operation Quagmire." The truce problem of greatest dispute into the spring and summer of 1952 was the status of POWs. The Communists, who were not signatories to the Geneva Convention, at first refused to provide any POW data or to open their camps for Red Cross inspections. On the UN side, some U.S. brass publicly alleged that the Communists were responsible for the "butchering" of more than 6,000 GI captives.*

---

* In total, 7,245 U.S. personnel were captured or interned during the Korean War. Of these, 2,806 died in captivity, 4,418 were returned to military control, and 21 refused repatriation (http://korea50.army.mil/welcome.shtml).

This contentious logjam finally broke at year's end, first when an AP photographer imprisoned by the Chinese was allowed use of a camera to take snapshots of GI prisoners in his camp, and then in December, when the Communists finally agreed to furnish POW data.

After a year-end recess to allow both sides to check their information, UN negotiators returned with a proposal that POWs on both sides (132,000 were in UN custody) be allowed to repatriate voluntarily— without being forced to return to their country of origin. It was an idea abhorrent to the Communists, who immediately labeled it a "shameful proposition."[9]

The deadlock on the cease-fire and the repatriation of POWs continued well into April. Finally, on the morning of April 28, 1952, UN negotiators presented a package proposal to the Communists that encompassed the three major obstacles to completing negotiations: restrictions of the construction of military airfields, the POW exchanges, and the selection of neutral nations for a commission to oversee the final peace. After a brief recess to consider the proposal the Communist principals returned to the table—but only to reject the package in its entirety. "We are losing men at the front every day," a distraught Admiral Joy afterward confided to one of his interpreters, "because I can't negotiate this damned truce."[10]

Ironically, things were made only worse by comparative images and reports about the plight of each side's POWs. While photos of American POWs eating with chopsticks, playing chess with their guards, and playing basketball and football continued to find their way into the pages of U.S. newspapers, UN forces were battling hunger strikes, riots, and even bloody camp-level civil wars between staunchly Communist POWs and those (as many as a third or more) favoring repatriation in South Korea or Nationalist China.

On May 7 the United States suffered the huge embarrassment of having Brig. Gen. Francis Dodd, its newly appointed commandant of the UN prison camp on Koje Island, captured and held hostage by Communist POW hard-liners. Dodd emerged, disgraced but unharmed, three days later but only after authorities agreed to halt further POW repatriation screening, conceded in writing that "there have been instances of bloodshed where many PW have been killed and wounded by UN forces," and promised that "in the future the PW can expect humane treatment . . . according to the principles of International Law."[11] It was, to say the least, a stunning psychological and propaganda coup for the Communists.

On June 2, as he left for the United States and his new job as Naval Academy superintendent, Turner Joy (who was being succeeded as lead UN delegate by Army major general William K. Harrison) delivered a blistering farewell to the Panmunjom Communists. "Apparently," said Joy, "you cannot comprehend that strong and proud and free nations can make costly sacrifices for principles because they are strong, can be dignified in the face of abuse and deceit because they are proud, and can speak honestly because they are free, and do not fear the truth."

As to his successor, Joy concluded: "May God be with him."

***

"Flak over North Korea has increased 400%" read the lead-in to an above-the-fold section 2 article in the *Pittsburgh Press*'s July 6 edition. Headlined: "Pittsburgh's Fliers Back from Korea's Flak Alley," the story hailed the Stateside arrival of "the All-Pittsburgh Squadron VF-653."

Pittsburgh Press staff writer Waldo L. Russell, the same reporter who covered VF-653's departure for the front lines, had once more flown cross-country accompanied by a staff photographer to capture the emotional scene when *Valley Forge* docked in San Diego. Sandwiched between four top- and bottom-page homecoming photos ("Lt. and Mrs. John R. Rohleder hug in a burst of happiness . . . Cook Cleland crouches to embrace his two children while Ray Edinger and his wife meet . . . a group of gobs beam at the realization they got home"), Russell's article described the exploits of "the heroes of 'Flak Alley'": "From December until Mid-June, they drove their Corsairs virtually at tree-top levels to knock out anti-aircraft batteries, transportation lines and railroad marshalling yards."

Noting that the antiaircraft "robot" guns the VF-653 pilots battled were "radar controlled . . . automatically computed and aimed by some of the latest developments in warfare," Russell detailed (in bold type) that "flak accounted for most of the squadron's heavy losses, 13 pilots. Nine were killed in action, two are missing and believed dead, and two were burned too badly to get back into the fracas." Operations in North Korea were "a nightmare," according to the once gung-ho chief aviation machinist mate Wallace J. Zielinski.

***

Russell's parochial attention to VF-653's losses failed to see the forest: Of ATG-1's combined deployment complement of 112 pilots, roughly a third were either killed, wounded, or missing—aviation casualty rates not experienced by the U.S. Navy since the Battle of Midway.[12] But Russell also managed to miss the trees: With three pilots killed and two more presumed dead, no one month was more deadly for VF-653 than May—and no one single stretch more ill-starred than the first week of ATG-1's fifth and final tour on the line.

May's first VF-653 confirmed fatality*—thirty-one-year-old Joe Sanko on a May 13 rail strike north of Munchon—closed out a particularly intense mid-April to mid-May tour that racked up more than three hundred ATG-1 Corsair combat sorties. But if anyone believed the upcoming Yokosuka R&R respite signaled the end of the worst, those hopes lasted no longer than May 26's resumption of flight ops and the downing of Ed Sterrett's Corsair during a late-afternoon rail strike near Hapsu.

Sterrett pulled out of a bomb run trailing fluid from a broadside 37mm hit: "It's oil, I can smell it," Sterrett radioed. "I'm heading for the beach." Flight leader Ray Edinger saw black smoke pouring from Sterrett's Corsair just before it rolled into a diving spin. "Bail out! Bail out!" Edinger heard Bob Balser, Sterrett's wingman, scream over the circuit. Almost simultaneously he saw a parachute blossom. Sterrett landed successfully, but he was stranded in steep and inaccessible terrain where determined efforts to find him in the next days only compounded losses.

The first came the very next day when Roland Busch's Corsair slammed into a ridgetop. At first, flying low to inspect the crash site, Edinger and Balser saw only flaming wreckage and exploding wing ammo—what looked to Edinger like a giant napalm drop. Making a

---

* ATG-1's first May loss was VF-52's John Zachary (Jack) Carros, thirty-two, whose F9F-2 crashed after apparently being hit by small-arms fire on a rail-cutting mission near the Chosin Reservoir.

second pass, however, the pilots saw something more: a smoke flare forward of the Busch wreckage and a man wearing a Mae West and waving a scarf—it had to be Sterrett.

On May 28—task force replenishment day—two borrowed Marine HRS-1 helicopters (bigger craft with better endurance and high-elevation capabilities) reached *Valley Forge* to augment the search. One was put to use the next morning, but not before another VF-653 tragedy: the death of Channing Gardner, whose Corsair cartwheeled into the water, broke up, and sank after losing power during takeoff. Screening ships were still combing the waters in a futile search for Gardner's remains when word came that one of the Marine choppers had crashed while trying to hover at the Sterrett site. All three Marine crewmen had survived, but now four men were down in the so far empty-handed search for a fifth.

It would take a bold improvisational stroke to bring some closure to this increasingly quixotic affair. After a day's foul-weather delay, the second Marine helo and its Corsair escorts returned to Hapsu, but this time with no thought of hovering. Instead, trailing a long rope ladder—a "Jacob's ladder" manufactured by *Valley Forge* boatswains—the big HRS-1 made three separate passes over the pickup site, each time adding an eagerly waiting marine to the rungs of its dangling ladder.

It was a redemptive but ultimately bittersweet coda: Although the HRS-1 safely extracted all three marines, it could find no sign of Sterrett or Busch. Meanwhile, on the preceding day when task force sorties were limited to test hops and coastal strikes, VF-653 had suffered its thirteenth loss (and ninth confirmed fatality): Ens. Gordon O. Galloway, twenty-eight, a recent replacement pilot, was killed when his Corsair unexpectedly crashed near a screen destroyer.

It was, to Black Jack Perry at least, one more instance of the "Bald Eagle of the *Essex*," this time on a squadron-level scale. With the home stretch within reach, Cook Cleland's Flying Circus was ordered to stand down.

***

While *Pittsburgh Press* photos captured the unfettered joy of reuniting families, two different snapshots perhaps better memorialized *Valley Forge* and ATG-1's proud but casualty-strewn Korean deployment. The first, a group flight deck portrait taken by a Navy photographer (using Bob Balser's personal camera) a day or so after ATG-1's closing combat sorties on June 10, 1952,* shows two rows (the front crouching, the back standing) of eighteen flight-jacketed pilots, seventeen of whom had flown with Cleland's Flying Circus for the entire TF 77 deployment.** Arrayed on the flight deck at their feet are thirteen of the Flying Circus's tricked-out helmets, emblematic of the thirteen squadron losses. With good reason, the photo has the most resonance for the men pictured—only those present could reliably recall the absent.

The second snapshot (also by a Navy photographer) was taken aboard *Valley Forge* the very day it docked in San Diego. It shows two beaming, handshaking comrades: Howard Thayer and Ken Schechter in their first reunion since Schechter's miraculous landing in March.

Though this photo records a happy occasion, it too has a missing element. Prior to coming aboard, Schechter had parked his car dockside just as *Valley Forge*—the "Rusty Bucket"—pulled into its berth. To fulfill a promise, Schechter had made arrangements with the staff at Balboa Naval Hospital to bring Marvin Broomhead's wife along. Unable even with assistance to navigate *Valley Forge's* gangplank, passageways, and ladders, Beatrice instead remained in the Schechters' car, held fast by an arrangement of cushioning pillows and restraining straps.

***

As returning ATG-1 personnel basked in their welcome home (Squadron 653 personnel, the *Pittsburgh Press's* Russell reported, were slated to return to Pittsburgh "for a big ovation and luncheon celebration at the Hotel William Penn"), most of its reservist pilots and crewmen also looked forward to imminent returns to civilian life. For many Navy squadrons it would prove to be, ironically, the flip side of the disruption experienced by reservists when they were yanked precipitously from jobs, homes, and families. The "weekend warriors" now

---

* VF-653 resumed flight operations in the tour's final days; on June 10 Cook Cleland's Corsair ditched in Wonsan Harbor where he was quickly rescued by a waiting ship.
** The eighteenth, standing in the second row at the far right, is a replacement pilot whose name VF-653 veterans remember only as "R. Smith."

took with them much of the leadership skills, professional expertise, and combat experience built up over Korea, leaving a void and a real challenge for those who remained.*

In May, for example, when *Antietam* returned to NAS Alameda from its Korean deployment and Air Group 15 transferred to NAS Moffett Field at the south end of San Francisco Bay, all but eight VF-831 squadron pilots and a few enlisted crewmen were gone, most back to civilian life—an attrition pattern that held for all CVG-15 squadrons. To young career navy aviators like George Schnitzer, for whom the Korean deployment had been an incredible bonding experience, it was unsettling to see so many trusted comrades depart.

However, to more seasoned veterans like Jim Holloway, now XO of VF-52, then undergoing a similar postdeployment reshuffling, turnover was now the new way of naval aviation. In contrast to World War II, where carrier deployments were for "the duration," interrupted only by overhaul (or sinking), the new way was six- to nine-month "forward-deployment" cycles with Stateside intervals of overhaul, up-keep, and wholesale personnel changes in between. To complicate things further, because of the continuing shortage of aircraft carriers there were no longer permanent air group assignments to specific carriers. Schnitzer's CVG-15, for example, would next deploy on *Princeton*, while VF-52, part of CVG-5, would next deploy on *Boxer*.

Changes in squadrons were analogous to complete ship overhauls: They went from full to zero readiness. Most long-term combat aviators and experienced petty officers transferred out while squadron aircraft were assigned to the AirPac fleet pool. The squadron then embarked on a workup cycle of a half year or more.

To young squadron holdovers like George Schnitzer, this restart was equally disruptive: Having already witnessed the departure of close buddies, they now had to watch their own hard-won skills atrophy for lack of practice. But older veterans like Jim Holloway knew the downtime interval also meant ultimately an influx of new energy and the opportunity for those who had already shown their mettle to step into more decisive roles.

---

* In February 1953, VF-653 would trade in its Corsairs for Panthers. Reconstituted as VF-151, the squadron would deploy to Korea aboard carrier *Boxer*.

15

COUNTERING AT
THE RIGHT MOMENTS

EARLY IN THE afternoon of November 18, 1952, as carriers *Essex*, *Kearsarge* (CV-33), and *Oriskany* (CV-34) cruised southeast of Chongjin and their squadrons pounded industrial targets around Hoeryong south across the Yalu-Tumen River from the Soviet base at Vladivostok, *Oriskany's* CIC air controllers vectored VF-781 pilots Lt. Royce Williams and his wingman, LTJG David Rowlands, toward a cluster of incoming bogies. It was the day's second hop for Williams (he'd flown a morning bomb strike) but the first for Rowlands: a hastily assembled division-size CAP formation that, in addition to Williams and Rowlands, included flight leader Claire Elwood, a Detroit reservist, with John Middleton as his number two.[1]

At 1:40 P.M., as Williams's and Rowlands's Panthers climbed through snow at 12,000 feet, they spotted approaching contrails—white vapor strokes against a clear sky. Williams tallyhoed the bogies: seven shiny swept-winged Soviet-made MiG-15s flying abreast in a loose formation at 45,000 feet. Inbound from the north—almost certainly originating at Vladivostok—the aircraft were screaming in at 450 knots, now less than 50 miles from the task force.[2]

It looked to be the U.S. Navy's worst-case scenario: a sudden onslaught of MiGs streaking in to strafe Task Force 77 carrier flight decks, setting them up for a devastating follow-on attack by bombs and torpedoes. In the larger moment, potentially at least, it also threatened a head-on confrontation with the Soviets.

***

The specter of just such an escalating confrontation had been at the back of planners' minds all that summer and fall as Task Force 77 ships ranged far north into the Sea of Japan to strike bigger, more strategic targets. Up to then all of North Korea's power grid and much of its industrial infrastructure (with the notable exception of the Wonsan Oil Refining Factory) had remained off-limits—on the premise that these resources should stay intact for the time when the Communists were expelled from the North. Now, with the uprooting of Communists no longer likely, the Chinese fully embroiled in the war, and the Panmunjom peace talks in acrimonious "recess," these core targets became fair game. Hitting them, Air Force and Navy planners argued, would at last tip the Communists toward a negotiated peace.*

In pursuit of this broadened aerial campaign, Task Force 77 carriers and aircraft operated—for the first time since 1950—within easy striking range of targets as far north as the Yalu. Joint Navy and Air Force attacks on North Korea's power grid would in time knock out 90 percent of North Korea's electrical generating capacity; level military concentrations in and around the capital, Pyongyang; and devastate its mining, milling, refining, and manufacturing capacity.

As it progressed into the fall, however, the campaign also risked inadvertently baiting both the Chinese Tiger and the Soviet Bear. As early as October, Mao Zedong had signaled China's interest in "peaceful coexistence." And Task Force 77's continued operations so far north in the Sea of Japan could backfire, tempting Kremlin leader Joseph Stalin (who then represented, on the Communist side at least, the toughest obstacle to peace) to unleash counterstrikes from air bases in and around Vladivostok.

***

In mid-November *Oriskany* was less than a month into its first Korean War deployment. Combat flight operations had begun on November 1, but storm threats and heavy seas had often delayed, curtailed, or altogether canceled air strikes. Already, however, Air Group 102 (now

---

* Even more provocative strategies were being advocated at this juncture. In mid-October Mark Clark petitioned the Pentagon to begin planning for the use of atomic weapons, specifically in the bombing of Manchuria and North China. The Pentagon brass demurred, although President Truman himself had considered the possibility.

on its second war deployment) had lost two pilots. The first, Ens. A. L. Riker of VA-923, was reported missing in action on November 4 when his AD went down south of Wonsan. The second, just three days before, was Lt. George Aloysius Gaudette Jr., thirty-one, a VA-923 veteran whose flak-crippled AD spun out of control and crashed during a rail strike near Majon-ri.

The aviators of VF-781, one of *Oriskany's* two jet squadrons, were a blend of regulars and reservists: some "nuggets," some second-tour veterans, and some "retreads" (prop pilots stepping up to jets).* Royce Williams, who'd earned his wings in 1945 and was now a full lieutenant, was by any reasonable measure still a combat novice. At the outbreak of the war Williams was enrolled at the University of Minnesota—assigned there by the Navy to complete his undergraduate degree. It was not until after graduation and a postgraduate stint in Monterey, California, that Williams finally received orders to join VF-781.

VF-781's pilots flew F9F-5s, the first of the new, bigger, and more powerful Grumman series to reach the front lines. The new model had a thinner wing that simultaneously increased its maximum speed and stall threshold.[3] The F9F-5 was also equipped with a radar-ranging gun sight that—at least in tests—dramatically increased the pilot's chance for an aerial kill provided he could get into firing position.

That proviso, of course, largely depended on crucial pilot variables— reflexes, skills, luck, and, above all, experience. For Navy pilots in Korea—for good or ill—air-to-air combat experience was a conspicuously missing ingredient. In the war's first weeks Navy aviators had played a predominant role in wiping out the nascent North Korean air force, but mostly by means of bombing and strafing ground-bound aircraft. Since then (given the shortcomings of the Navy's carrier-configured jets), the rigors of air-to-air combat with Communist jets had been all but ceded to Air Force F-86 pilots, with MiG Alley—the skies above northwesternmost North Korea—as their exclusive hunting ground.

---

* During VF-781's first Korean deployment (aboard *Bon Homme Richard* from May to December 1951), Navy publicists touted squadron aviators as the "Pacemakers": West Coast reservists who had, to a man, volunteered for active duty when war first broke out.

For their part, Communist aircraft—jet or prop—rarely ventured south or east of MiG Alley. One reason was the proximity to Manchuria, just across the Yalu River—a ready safe haven when the going got rough. But another reason involved the credible suspicion that veteran Soviet pilots (Air Force pilots called the Russians "honchos," their Chinese and North Korean acolytes "tyros") flew some of the MiGs: Staying close to China reduced the potential embarrassment of having "neutral" Soviet pilot personnel fall into UN hands.

The disparity of air-to-air combat experience was such that since November 1950, when VF-111 squadron CO Lt. Cdr. W. T. Amen shot down a MiG-15 during a Yalu bridge strike (one of three MiG kills scored by Navy F9Fs in the space of a week), Navy pilots had splashed barely fifty enemy aircraft, jet or prop. In scoring these rare kills, Navy aviators relied more on skill, training, and savvy—better formation discipline, maneuvering, and marksmanship—than airplane characteristics. But even these advantages had their limits when the Communists purposely dispatched MiGs in formation strength to counter the bombing of North Korea's infrastructure. In October, for example, at the height of the strategic bombing campaign, MiGs claimed kills on Corsairs from both *Kearsarge* and *Princeton*.[4]

***

When VF-781's Williams and Rowlands tallyhoed the oncoming bogeys, the odds (should there be a dustup) were already seven to two. Flight Leader Elwood's F9F-5 had reported a warning light on his fuel-boost pump, and he, along with wingman John Middleton, was directed to stay at 13,000 feet.

If anything, circumstances pointed to even worse odds for Williams and Rowlands. No matter the mission and the capabilities of the aircraft being flown, section leader and wingman should be like practiced, longtime tennis doubles partners who know intimately each other's strengths, weaknesses, and instincts. Williams and Rowlands lacked this tandem experience: Though squadron mates and friends, they had never flown together before.

Considering the circumstances, neither pilot ached to tangle with the MiGs. And, as they edged closer, it appeared they might not have to: For whatever reason, the seven MiGs abruptly reversed course as if to return to Vladivostok. Relieved but wary, Williams and Rowlands continued to climb and pursue the retreating contrails.

Then, as suddenly as before, the bogeys broke back again, this time diving and splitting into two groups—of three and four—as if to outflank Williams and Rowlands and come back on their tails. As the MiGs descended into warmer air, their vapor trails vanished. Without visual contact, Williams and Rowlands had to rely on *Oriskany's* CIC for directions.

"Will set you up to maintain position between last contact and task force," a controller promised, but moments later CIC had lost contact as well. It was a fighter pilot's worst nightmare: an infinite sky with bogeys skulking about but nothing to be seen by eye or radar. However, as he flew level at 26,000 feet and turned to a new CIC-ordered vector, Williams spotted four of the MiGs, now loosely abreast and already lined up for a flat-side firing attack.

***

Pilots use the circumference of a clock face and the hour hand to measure other aircraft's relative position. The MiGs were at ten o'clock high, maybe eleven, their cannons (two 23mm and one 37mm) already blazing. Orange-lit 23mm tracers—one of every four rounds fired—already filled the sky. Rounds of 37mm (the same caliber as NKPA flak guns) were no doubt flying, too; although not betrayed by tracers, the 37mm projectiles were big enough to spot if they got close—assuming they missed.

Reflexively, Royce Williams did what he'd been taught: Rather than try to run or elude, he and Rowlands instead broke hard to challenge the MiGs. The four MiGs reacted by breaking right, creating a strung-out formation.

Williams and Rowlands "wrapped" their turn, bringing them in for a stern shot on Tail End Charlie. Using the F9F-5's new gun sight, Williams lined up a shot just a few degrees off the MiG's tail. A short burst from his four 20mm nose cannons put the enemy jet into a smoking descent.

***

It was a good start: an opening odds-leveling gambit that would give the other MiGs pause—provided Williams and Rowlands stuck together and played tenacious defense. Instead, Rowlands surprised Williams: Rather than staying on Williams's wing he nosed over to hurtle after the crippled MiG, his gun camera whirring but meanwhile leaving his section leader facing three-to-one odds.

For the moment, these three MiGs had accelerated into a climbing turn that easily distanced them from Williams's gun range. But then—perhaps having seen Rowlands's departure—they split once more (into a pair and one) and made head-on passes. Williams went nose-to-nose with the MiG twosome, getting in short bursts as they passed.

Meanwhile, the three "missing" MiGs had returned, taking up positions to pounce. In the thirty-minute melee that followed, all the MiG pilots seemed reluctant, despite the odds, to engage Williams head-on. Instead, like matadors, they used their better acceleration and agility to get out of range and set up more passes. Williams, meanwhile, had little choice but to play the bull: Staying at full throttle, doggedly countering to keep his six o'clock clear, firing short bursts whenever he could—and keeping his poise should another MiG pilot make a mistake. Moments later it happened: Another wrapped turn brought Williams dead astern of an overshooting MiG long enough to trigger a sustained burst. The MiG at once disintegrated, so close that Williams had to dodge debris with a G-heavy pull-up.

***

By now, having broken off pursuit of the first doomed MiG after his guns failed, Rowlands was climbing to rejoin his section leader. Middleton had also been vectored toward the melee, and both reported facing head-on attacks by MiGs. After spotting a smoking MiG already on its way down, Middleton got in a long-range deflection shot and saw the pilot eject.

Royce Williams, meanwhile, was lining up for a kill shot on a smoking MiG when another slipped in on his six. Spotting him, Williams broke sharply but too late—a jarring explosion, a 37mm hit, convulsed his airplane, severing control cables and hydraulics. All at once the F9F-5 lost all rudder control and nearly all aileron control, leaving Williams little more than speed and elevation with which to maneuver.

Realizing he was now out of the fight, but with orange tracers still streaking past, Williams dove for the cloud tops, using elevators to "porpoise" his aircraft. The plunge through overcast shook off the pursuing MiGs, but as Williams broke below the low cloud ceiling into swirling snow squalls, another danger loomed. Mistaking the F9F-5 for a MiG, edgy task force gun crews were lining up Williams in their sights and throwing up a blanket of flak. Out of one frying pan but about to land in another, Williams looked to be a sitting duck until cooler heads prevailed and the shooting stopped.

North of Williams's position, *Oriskany* was maneuvering into the wind and clearing its flight deck; it was Williams's call to eject, ditch, or come in. Already much too low to punch out (the cloud ceiling was barely 400 feet), muscling his stick to keep his aircraft in some sort of trim, and keeping speed high to avoid stalling, Williams could conceive of only one thing hairier than a carrier deck landing right now—a water landing under the same circumstances.

Williams lined up as best he could, leaving it to the LSO to adjust for *Oriskany*'s roll and pitch and the bridge helmsman (the ship's CO was patched into the LSO's radio circuit) to compensate for the crippled Panther's horizontal drift. He had one factor in his favor: Stiff surface winds were keeping relative deck wind high, allowing for an early cut—and with it more chances to grab a wire.

During the final seconds of his approach Williams experienced the same bowstring tension, the same fierce concentration and adrenaline rush of the high-odds dogfight with the MiGs. As surely as these sensations sustained him up there, he had to believe they would now help him get back aboard in one piece.

Williams kept his alignment, and, just as expected, the LSO's early cut brought him down fast and hard. The F9F-5's hook caught the number-two wire, wrenching plane and pilot to a jolting stop.

After taxiing forward, Williams found himself sitting longer than usual in the open cockpit, laboring to catch his breath and listening to the plaintive wind down of the jet's turbine even as the plane captain clambered onto the fuselage behind him. While the brown shirt hovered, releasing straps and detaching umbilical connections, Williams kept inhaling and exhaling: quickly and forcibly at first but then ever more slowly and calmly. He could almost sense, with each exhalation, the escaping vapors of tension, concentration, and adrenaline.

***

In his action report, Air Group 102 CAG G. P. Chase attributed VF-781's November 18 air-to-air combat success to "countering at the right moment," "sound look-out doctrine," pilot ability to fly the F9F-5 "to the maximum," the "excellent performance" of guns and radar-ranging gun sights, and, last, "the seeming inexperience of these particular Communist pilots." The report, which jointly credited Williams and Middleton with downing two MiGs and Rowlands with damaging another,* also ventured that the incident was "believed to be the Navy's first jet dogfight with MiG-15s."[5] That it was not was a small but telling sign that the Navy's aviation corps—given so much pilot turnover and the unrelenting pressure to keep the war-deployment carousel moving—could neither fully digest nor quickly disseminate even its most singular combat lessons.

That very same November, for example, as Air Group 15 pilots (on the far side of the deployment carousel) moved into final preparations for their January 1953 deployment, it seemed (at least to some young veteran pilots like George Schnitzer) that key lessons somehow weren't filtering through. There was, he remembered, "still no information given to us about what tactic to use if North Korean MiGs intercepted any of us."[6]

***

The uphill work of rebuilding Air Group 15's jet squadrons had begun the previous June using a nucleus of veteran pilots and a few borrowed F9F-2s. With most reservists gone, squadron designations

---

* Upon *Oriskany's* subsequent arrival in Yokosuka, Royce Williams was briefed in secret by Vice Adm. Robert Briscoe, then Commander Naval Forces, Far East, who informed Williams that he had shot down at least three of the MiGs. MiG pilot transmissions had been secretly monitored throughout the engagement, and all pilots were believed to be Russian.

were changed: VF-153 (formerly VF-831) and VF-154 for the two jet squadrons, VF-152 for the Corsairs, and VF-155 for the Skyraiders. That summer the pace accelerated: In mid-July fourteen pilots (seven veterans and an equal number of "nuggets": ensigns fresh from the training command) joined VF-153, and in September the squadron received its first F9F-5 aircraft.

Squadron leaders (all veterans, but not of combat in Korea), in Schnitzer's recollection at least, seemed to base little predeployment training on the missions actually flown during the *Antietam* cruise. There was scant practice in ground-support intercepts, for example, or use of dead-reckoning navigation. Although Schnitzer was among eight Korean combat veterans parceled out so that each division had at least one, he remained an ensign—one with a reputation for pushing his airplane hard—who carried little weight in squadron training decisions.

That December Schnitzer's predeployment preparations did include a foray into groundbreaking person-to-person tactics: a quick trip east to propose marriage to Beverly Greensides, then a Pan American Airways stewardess. Newly engaged, Schnitzer returned to Moffett in time for the squadron's New Year's Eve party (doubling as a deployment send-off bash) during which XO Jerry Miller announced that both Schnitzer and his buddy Larry Quiel were being promoted to LTJG. As initiation, Quiel and Schnitzer were each given a water tumbler half filled with Scotch. Their new silver JG pins rested at the bottom of the glasses, and both men set about "drinking their way" to promotion.

***

"The Way It Is in Korea," the lead article in the January 1953 edition of *Reader's Digest*, was the culmination of James Michener's summer and fall reporting from Korea. In it, Michener outlined what might eventually happen in Korea. "The following observations are my own," he cautioned his readers. "No doubt every military man would support some of these ideas, but I know of no one who supports them all."

A continued stalemate was likely. "No military leader anywhere, United Nations or Communist," relished the costs of an all-out offensive, or the full-scale war that would follow. The Communists had incentives to keep peace talks bogged down—the stalemate hand-cuffed U.S. military strength while eroding America's reputation in Asia. When peace, or something like it, eventually came, occupation costs would at once supplant war costs. Otherwise, South Korea would be quickly overrun.

Any attempt at a decisive victory, Michener reasoned, would have to avoid a slugfest on the Korean peninsula and instead use flanking amphibious assaults, massive air strikes, and blockades to knock China out of the war. This, of course, had been MacArthur's agenda—though absent the use of nuclear weapons. The plan's flaws were, Michener acknowledged, uncertainty about Soviet Union intervention and the near inevitability of World War III.

Michener assured his readers that individual soldier, sailor, and air-man morale was "extraordinarily high." That wasn't to say there was no resentment over the perceived favoritism that resulted in some being called to combat duty while others stayed home—prospering in their careers and safe with their families. Perhaps the worst mis-treatment was of the "unorganized reserves from the last war." They'd been shocked to be called first to war while many in the organized reserves stayed home. It was, Michener felt, "one of the most inexcus-able military injustices in our history."

Had the effort, the nagging injustices, and the steep losses been worth it? Yes, Michener concluded: As infuriating, wearying, and draining as the conflict had been, it had galvanized U.S. preparedness, spurred a regional defense pact with Japan, and, most important, con-fronted Communist aggression in Asia with the "world's first collective security action."

***

Michener's writing career was continuing to flourish, but his plan for a novel based on what he'd seen of the air war over Korea had stalled. Earlier in 1952 he had written an outline based on Marvin Broom-head's crash during the February 8 attack on the bridges at Samdong-ni. To navigate the hastily scribbled pages of his notebook from the time, Michener had anchored his outline with typewritten topical cross-references. The cross-references reminded him, for example, that notebook page 6 contained "Brubaker age and data," that page 110 contained "the strike," and that page 136 described "how Korea looks."

Meanwhile, the cross-reference to page 118 identified "the opening scene" of the project. Page 118 (spilling onto page 119) sketched a picture (from a carrier force commander's perspective) of flight operations edging close to the 100-fathom curve ("a busy day of launches and recoveries put him always closer to land") and task force ships forced to point into a wind that has "veered suddenly," in effect luring them even closer. "The bridges at Toko-ri," reads the topical entry for notebook page 106. "Red-6" is the title heading across the actual page, and below it are a bare-bones map and other notations for a target "80 miles inland" described as "Samdong-ni—Yangdock R.R. + Trucking route." Its scope condensed, the outline was used in the July 1952 *Reader's Digest* article "All for One: A Story from Korea."* He revisited it several times, only to again set it aside.

Then that fall, mindful of Hemingway's September *Life* success with *The Old Man and the Sea*, Michener's literary agent, Helen Strauss, nudged Michener to follow through on the story in novella form. Michener undoubtedly had Hemingway's "incandescent" masterpiece in mind as well. Its basic theme—fighting both enemies and elements to achieve personal vindication—aligned with his own feelings for the "forgotten heroes" of Korea. *The Old Man and the Sea*'s compactness and uncluttered narrative also fit. Although James Michener could not pretend to be Ernest Hemingway, "Papa" had shown him a way to capture the mettle of the troops, sailors, and especially the naval aviators he'd observed. Strauss lined up *Life*, asked Michener for a work of about 30,000 words, and gave him a May 1953 deadline.

By Michener's account, he sat down and wrote without pause. "The story I told them that day," he said later, "wasn't changed by so much as a comma when I came to put it down."[7] That was, of course, not entirely true. There was a first typescript (titled "Original Notes") that Michener roughed out between January and mid-March 1953. Though it contained nearly all the elements of the final novella, it was self-consciously polemical, overly strident, and stilted. There followed

---

* Michener reported incorrectly that Broomhead's first name was Norman.

several more drafts in which his ideas, language, and narrative discipline adhered ever more closely to an artist's equivalent of the aviator's twin edicts: Regiment time to the job at hand. Stop projecting flight ahead to target.

Years later Michener warmly recalled the novella's writing, in part because of what he'd done "to make myself competent": checking out aircraft, attending pre- and poststrike briefings, and even going out on several missions. He had worked diligently, not only to "get it right" but also to tease out the illusive qualities that somehow made these men so singular. He proudly remembered Black Jack Perry's reaction to the prospects of his involvement: "He said he wanted to be one of us. If he's game, I'm game."[8]

***

By January 1953, when "The Way It Is in Korea" was finally published, the American public was by and large fed up with the interminable war and its apparently fruitless peace negotiations. There was no bigger evidence of this than the November quadrennial elections. Republican candidate Dwight Eisenhower won the presidency in a landslide. Now in control of both the executive and the legislative branches, the Republicans were poised and eager to undo the foreign policy programs of the Democrats. As he had pointedly promised during the campaign, President-elect Eisenhower went to Korea in December for three days of briefings, inspection tours, and meetings. Before returning he even conferred with President Rhee—a boost to Rhee's credibility (and, it turned out, to his obstinacy and self-preservation instincts).

During his January 20 inauguration speech, Eisenhower tried to walk a fine line between war hard-liners (Truman, who had openly criticized Ike's Korea visit as "a piece of demagoguery," listened to the speech in stony, tight-lipped silence before departing for his home in Independence, Missouri) and those demanding peace at any cost. Eisenhower stressed that people of the free world had to accept sacrifices in the cause of peace. Those who valued their privileges over their principles, he argued, soon lost both. While many Americans may have agreed with this lofty notion—at least in the abstract—most were preoccupied with something more pressing: How soon could Ike actually end the war so that their boys could come home?

***

If the peace stampede needed further impetus it got some the day after Eisenhower's inauguration when the Chinese Communists produced a devastating germ-warfare "confession" from U.S. Marine colonel Frank H. Schwable, chief of staff of First Marine Air Wing.[9] In his statement, Schwable (a captive since being shot down while on an errant administrative flight the previous July) echoed allegations made by Air Force pilot POWs Kenneth L. Enoch and John S. Quinn nine months before. But he also added specific details: the program code name (SUBPROP), initiation date (October 1951), aircraft used (B-29 bombers, but also Skyraiders, Corsairs, and Panthers), and even squadron numbers and the names and ranks of senior officers involved.

Schwable's abject confession was at once a painful reminder that thousands of U.S. POWs languished in Communist camps and yet another withering blow to America's increasingly shaky reputation in the court of global public opinion. Coming as it did from the lips of a senior U.S. Marine Corps officer, the confession (no matter how it was extracted) added a new, almost exponential level of outward veracity to Communist biological warfare claims. If this wasn't enough, Marine Corps major Roy Bley—Schwable's passenger on the ill-fated flight—also confessed, enabling the Chinese Communists to circulate the text of both confessions among UN delegates when the General Assembly convened on January 23. Within the month, the Chinese produced confirming admissions from an additional thirty-five POWs.

***

It was undoubtedly Schwable's confession that brought Henry Ettinger under renewed scrutiny by his Chinese Communist prison camp warders that same January. Since the previous August, when he and Air Force C-46 cargo pilot John Dick had been marched the five miles from Camp 2 to new quarters—a small mud-walled, dirt-floored building just north of a satellite POW facility called "Camp 2 Annex," Ettinger had largely been ignored.*

Ettinger particularly recalled August 8, 1952—the second day in their new quarters—when he and Dick were told they could use a nearby stream to bathe. The stream wasn't much (a mere trickle that ultimately fed into a main stream used by POWs at Camp 2 Annex), and they had no soap (they substituted streambed sand), but it was a momentous event—the first opportunity to wash since just before Ettinger's one and only *Valley Forge* combat sortie some twenty months before.

After that landmark day (it proved a turning point in his ongoing battles with lice and dysentery), Ettinger and his housemate had settled for a time into their new, tightly guarded, but largely interrogation-free mode of existence. They had been issued two sets of clothes (canvas sneakers, cotton underwear, blue prisoner trousers, and jackets—another plus for hygiene) and a steady if monotonous twice-daily diet of rice and thin cabbage soup (prepared by annex prisoners), a distinct improvement over the meager low-nutrient sorghum and millet rations used on occasion as punishment.

While there were no letters or packages from home—and no prospect that any would arrive—Ettinger and Dick at least shared the company of another like-minded human being. They also had ground-level seats to the high-altitude drama of MiG Alley, as hundreds of MiG and F-86 contrails streaked across—and occasionally tumbled from—the morning and afternoon skies right above them.

***

That fall there was a shuffling of personnel and housing. First Dick was removed from the one-room hut, replaced by an Air Force navi- .

---

* Together, Camp 2 and its annex composed one of eight permanent numerically designated Chinese Communist POW camps stretching over a fifty-mile sector (spaced roughly five miles apart) in North Korea along the Yalu River. In 1951, after the Chinese established several temporary camps, POW death rates—owing more to cold, starvation, and lack of medical treatment than outright brutality—soared as high as 40 percent. Finally, alarmed by the appalling death rates and realizing that American POWs were important peace-bargaining chips, the Chinese took steps to establish more permanent facilities and drastically improve conditions. In the case of Harry Ettinger and other U.S. aviation POWs, however, the "permanent" Chinese prison camps were usually little more than commandeered civilian villages.

gator named Guy King (a member of Dick's C-46 crew); then, in late October, two more Air Force pilots (Byron Dobbs and Vern Wright) were added. Finally, in December, these four were marched to a new facility south of (but relatively close to) Camp 2 Annex—a bigger three-room building that already housed ten prisoners.

Among the fourteen POWs (mostly Air Force officers) were familiar faces from Pak's Palace, the Slave Camp, or both: John Beers, Byron Dobbs, Norman Duquette, and Joe Green (the Slave Camp diplomat). But there were also new faces, including Marine first lieutenant Kenneth Henry, the *Manchester* Marine-detachment CO who'd been the spotter on the helo dispatched to rescue VF-194 AD pilot Marvin Broomhead. Henry supplied Ettinger with the details of the failed rescue (which occurred on the very same day as Ettinger's and Duane Thorin's debacle)—and the subsequent captures of Broomhead, Henry, and helo pilot Edward Moore. Broomhead, who was still hobbled by two broken ankles sustained in the crash, was confined in Camp 2 Annex, while Moore was believed still held in Camp 2.

Each of the POWs—new or familiar—had a unique story of career, capture, and captivity. Vern Wright, for example, was an F-86 Sabre pilot shot down over MiG Alley, while Norm Duquette (an F-80 Shooting Star photo-reconnaissance pilot) had begun his aviation career in the U.S. Navy and even been in the same Basic Flight Training class as Harry Ettinger.

Perhaps the oddest collective experience was that of the Air Force C-46 crew: pilots John Dick, Dennis Haley, and Gene Layer; navigator Guy King; and David Harrison, an Army sergeant and jumpmaster. During a low-level mission to drop Chinese and North Korean agents behind enemy lines, one of the supposedly friendly "spooks" aboard the C-46 tossed a live grenade into the cargo hold before parachuting free. The resulting explosion killed two others aboard, severed control cables, and sent the two-engine aircraft to the ground and its surviving crew into Communist hands.

Despite their divergent backgrounds and paths into and through captivity, the commune of fourteen POWs shared a common virtue.*

---

* There were similar communes elsewhere in Camp 2 and throughout the Communist Chinese POW gulag.

Despite constant psychological, emotional, and physical pressure; despite wearying isolation, cold, heat, lack of sleep, untreated wounds, and near starvation; despite dire threats or blandishments of better, more "lenient" treatment; and despite month-on-month stints of relentless questioning by batteries of skilled Chinese Communist interrogators at Camp 2, each had stubbornly, persistently, unflinchingly—and evidently successfully—resisted all their captors' efforts to coerce them into writing, speaking, or signing confessions to falsely implicate, discredit, vilify, or betray their country.* This was no minor accomplishment. Their resilience stands among the highest (and least-heralded) acts of American courage during the entire war—a magnificent counterweight to alarmist speculation about wholesale "brainwashing" and the sharp, denigrating sting of a handful of "confessions."

***

For their part, whether motivated by true belief or cynicism, Chinese Communist interrogators were singularly committed to producing a nonstop cavalcade of germ-warfare confessions. Ettinger's own exposure to this Communist Grand Guignol commenced just days after his May transfer from the Pyongyang Slave Camp to Pyoktong and Chinese Communist custody.

The immediate change in surroundings and atmosphere at Camp 2—dramatic improvements in facilities, hygiene, food, medical care, even guard demeanor—were both welcome and, for highly prized aviator prisoners like Ettinger, illusory. Within hours of completing a "registration" form, Ettinger was separated from the other new arrivals and installed in a small, windowless interrogation room. Confined to the room for the balance of May, through all of June, and well into July, Ettinger was worked over by a tag team of Chinese interrogators, including a lead interrogator named Yen.

Yen, who spoke fluent English, used his first sessions with Ettinger to extol the "lenient policy of the Chinese people" and to constantly remind Ettinger how it would "pay to tell the truth." When the actual questioning began—Ettinger perched atop a stool in the windowless

---

* The resistors included Byron Dobbs, whom Duane Thorin worried was "going along" with the North Koreans at Pak's Palace.

room while Yen alternately sat behind a small table or stood and paced—Yen seemed particularly interested in naval and aviation matters: names and numbers of ships, naval bases in Japan and the United States, squadron organizations, rank and pay scales, pilot training, and so forth.

Because he knew virtually nothing about ships, Ettinger either pled ignorance or, when Yen turned up the heat, simply made up answers. Although he had to be more circumspect about aviation matters, Ettinger invented here as well—sensing that Yen had neither any way of cross-checking nor any real interest in doing so. Instead, Ettinger believed, Yen was just loosening him up, paving the way for the real questions and the real ordeal to come.

Those questions came after about a week; in substance: What was the purpose of Ettinger's last mission? And what exactly was in the bombs his airplane carried?

Each of the days that followed was a repetitive journey—sixteen- to eighteen-hour interrogation marathons interspersed with "banjo" breaks (their frequency necessitated by Ettinger's then near-intractable diarrhea and the interrogator's aversion to fouling the room) and infrequent feedings, and punctuated by inadequate spells of sleep on the floor. While Yen's long interrogation shifts had their own rigors—extended lectures that were sometimes soothing, other times strident and even furious; having to endlessly rephrase essentially the same questions; having to keep close eye on what he assumed would be the eventual prize of Ettinger's psychological collapse—he at least had the luxury of being spelled by other interrogators.

To Yen's mounting frustration, Ettinger never came close to caving under pressure. It was hard to tell precisely why he held out—or for that matter, why, in late July 1952, Yen and his superiors gave up trying to break him.

For Ettinger, part of it may have been that his earlier more brutal (albeit less sustained) treatment during his first days of North Korean captivity had, so to speak, inoculated him. Perhaps as important, Ettinger could also take strength in knowing that others were enduring the same regimen and not caving. The Camp 2 facilities, structurally at least, were hardly high security. During his frequent latrine visits, Ettinger inevitably crossed paths with other POWs and could trade reassuring glances and greetings. (Guy King, for example, was being questioned in a room wallpapered with old English-language newspapers. Interrogators punished King by having him stand nose to the wall for extended periods. King quickly learned to memorize what he was staring at and shared fleeting bits of this "news" to whomever he saw at the latrine.) A final factor, oddly enough, was that refusal to confess (aside from the blatant falseness of whatever he was coerced to confess) was the one challenge that animated Ettinger's life now that he'd been robbed of freedom and the opportunity to fly.

Camp 2 authorities, meanwhile, may have simply concluded that, given limited time, space, and interrogator resources, it was best to turn the spotlight on newer and perhaps more promising POW arrivals. On July 23, after Yen abruptly and unceremoniously ended Ettinger's interrogation, Ettinger was slapped into solitary confinement for two weeks (sustained only by sorghum and millet rations) before being released into more workaday POW captivity at the outskirts of Camp 2 Annex.

***

"It is not nice to lie" were the Communist interrogator's first words to Harry Ettinger when his interrogation resumed the following January. The interrogator held in his hand the written summaries of Ettinger's answers in the earlier sessions, waving them in front of Ettinger's face as if the very ink on the pages was incriminating.

This time, instead of being returned to Camp 2, Ettinger was confined somewhere in the annex compound. Ettinger never learned the name of this new interrogator or the underlying reason for the new sessions.

There was a sense this time that the Chinese interrogators were just going through the motions—as if they had been prompted from on high to give it one more go. Each of the fourteen POWs in the house south of the annex got his "turn in the barrel," and each turn seemed to last about a week. Witnessing this predictable pattern instilled two kinds of hope: The prisoners questioned later in the cycle knew what to expect, and all who went through got the sense that the slow clock of captivity was now accelerating—and perhaps moving on its way to a new day of freedom.

***

In truth, aside from the nagging matter of prisoner repatriation, the pressure toward peace was two-sided, lacking, it seemed, only a game-changing event to clear the way. That game changer finally came on March 5, 1953, when the death of Joseph Stalin—the implacable Red Czar—seemed to set off an opportunistic chain of promising, even conciliatory, moves.

First, Kim Il Sung, in response to Gen. Mark Clark's request for an exchange of sick and wounded prisoners—what was to be called "Little Switch"—agreed that such an exchange could proceed under the provisions of the Geneva Convention. Next, the North Koreans proposed a resumption of peace negotiations.

Finally, taking his cue from U.S. reluctance to resume full-scale talks unless the Communists advanced a constructive proposal package, China's Chou En-lai offered an important conciliation: After the cessation of hostilities, there could be an immediate exchange of prisoners who insisted on repatriation; simultaneously, remaining POWs could be place in neutral state custody for final disposition. On April 1, when new Soviet leader Georgy Malenkov signaled concurrence with Chou's idea, the way was open to resume peace talks.

During the last week of April, the parties finally returned to dusty Panmunjom for high-level "plenary sessions." In May, with the Communists convinced their opponents would not back down on voluntary repatriation and U.S. negotiators conceding that release of all North and South Korean POWs need not immediately coincide with an armistice, the parties agreed to the formation of a Neutral Nations Repatriation Committee (NNPC). NNPC representatives from India, Poland, Czechoslovakia, Sweden, and Switzerland would determine and administer the POWs' actual repatriation preferences once the armistice was set.

June 1953—the war's third anniversary—arrived with the thorny repatriation issue largely resolved. Now it seemed, absent any unforeseen events to derail the process, the fundamental requirements for achieving "something like peace" were in place at last.

16

SOMETHING LIKE PEACE

VF-194's JOE AKAGI learned about "Johnny" Johnson's crash at the 7:00 A.M. launch briefing. During a predawn takeoff the AD piloted by VC-11's detachment OinC had hurtled directly off *Boxer*'s flight deck into the drink. In the darkness, with his plane sinking fast, Johnson had barely enough time to extricate himself and save one of his two crewmen.

A plane lost and an air crewman with it: Akagi supposed it was the price to be paid for the hurry-up rigors of Task Force 77's summer flight operations. When *Boxer* rejoined Task Force 77 on Independence Day 1953, operational sorties were moved up to July 5 (Johnson's ill-fated launch was one of the very first), sidestepping the normal protocol: a day of "shakedown" to clear the post-R&R cobwebs, kinks, and bugs from crewmen and aircraft.

Akagi—now a "second tour" and section leader—nevertheless shrugged off the mishap. This would be his eighty-first combat mission, and experience told him there was no reason another's bad fortune should bear on his. Better to focus on the job at hand: a big morning strike involving Panthers, Skyraiders, and Corsairs—twenty-four planes in all, including two divisions of VF-194 ADs.

***

During the spring and oncoming summer of 1953, amid the swirl of events that seemed to point at long last to an armistice, South Korea's stubborn, mercurial president, Syngman Rhee, had perceived the ground shifting beneath him. To Rhee, armistice would mean a still-divided Korea with Communists firmly entrenched in the North: "a death sentence," he complained in a letter to Dwight Eisenhower, "without protest."[1]

Feeling cornered, Rhee threatened to fight on, going it alone without U.S. help if need be. On June 7, the eve of reaching a subsidiary agreement to finally resolve the repatriation obstacle and resume full-scale Panmunjom talks, Rhee abruptly declared martial law in South Korea. He recalled or rescinded trips to Washington, D.C., by his generals, canceled all military leaves, and appealed to his people to support his "life or death" decision.

Then, on the eighteenth, with a surprise midmonth Communist assault on ROK forces faltering under withering aerial bombing, and a final armistice agreement rumored to be in the offing for June 20, Rhee triggered a plan that he and a tight coterie of South Korean insiders had been secretly plotting: the release of all North Korean POWs held in South Korean custody. Within a matter of hours, some 27,000 North Koreans poured through open gates, most melting forever into South Korean cities and countryside—likely taking with them any near-term hope for a negotiated peace.

Rhee's peremptory action—piled atop his threat to go it alone with the prosecution of the war—once more threw talks at Panmunjom into upheaval, leaving both sides little choice but to escalate hostilities on the ground and aloft.

* * *

Joe Akagi's AD was among the last aircraft in *Boxer's* full-scale morning launch. When he taxied to fly one, set his brakes, and throttled up, everything seemed fine: the same full-throated roar of the AD's Wright Cyclone engine, the same instrument readings, and the same taut shivering of metal and flesh just prior to launch.

It was only after the launch officer pointed him off the deck and the ten-ton AD rumbled forward, struggling to gather momentum, that Akagi realized things weren't right. Acceleration was sluggish: Instead of soaring, the AD lifted briefly, only to touch down again with all its weight still on the wheels. Akagi knew then he was not going to make it.

To avoid the slipstream of the plane launched before his, Akagi had angled his deck run to starboard. But now, as its wheels lost the flight deck's underpinning, the AD's left wing dipped, and the entire plane rolled to port, tumbling just feet ahead of the forward rounddown and barely avoiding being knifed by *Boxer's* prow. From Akagi's inverted and disoriented vantage, the Sea of Japan looked to be falling on his head. Instinctively, he chopped power, yanked the emergency bomb-release lanyard, and prayed.

The impact of nearly top-down water entry ripped off Akagi's helmet and pinned his torso to his shoulder harness and his chin to his chest. Impact and propeller spin also tore away the plane's engine, sending seawater thick with oil, hydraulic fluid, and the pungent smell of avgas into the open cockpit. The airplane was almost certain to break up, but for a precious moment it righted itself, giving Akagi enough time to escape his seatbelt and shoulder harness, stand, and step onto the port-wing root.

Akagi barely noticed *Boxer's* towering hull as the last of it slid past to starboard; and he was still fixated on unhitching his parachute pack when *Boxer's* wake turbulence sucked him off the wing into a seething vortex. Choking back gulps of polluted seawater, Akagi panicked for an instant, still fumbling with his parachute while entirely forgetting to inflate his Mae West. Fortunately, *Boxer's* rescue helo had already wheeled overhead, and its pilot, John Monday, was lowering the horse collar—Akagi's first hope that he might somehow escape this disaster.

When the collar reached him, Akagi inserted one arm. He continued to work the chute with his free hand until a sudden, sharp upward tug brought him to his senses. Realizing he was too weak to cling to the collar with just one arm, Akagi at last gave up on the chute, wedged his other arm into the collar, and held on as he was hoisted.

Praying now that his chute canopy would not deploy, fill with water, and pull them all into the drink, Akagi looked up to gauge the distance to the refuge of the open chopper door. As he did he saw, stenciled in large white block letters across the chopper's blue belly: "ABANDON CHUTE." God knew how hard he had tried.

***

Akagi's recovery from the dunking consisted of a hot shower in sick bay topped off with a beaker of "medicinal" brandy laced with mineral oil. The shower didn't fully rinse away the feel of oil or the odor of avgas, and the doctored brandy had the twin effects of bracing him while nearly making him vomit. Within days, though, Akagi would be cleared to fly again. A July 12 CAS strike was his next sortie, and he would add six more hops in short order—each carrying with it the prospect of being among the war's last casualties.

Such a possibility (for Akagi and all other Task Force 77 flyers as well as frontline GIs and marines) added a disquieting new dimension to fighting a war that seemed on the brink of resolution one moment, of perpetuity the next. During this July, while leaders on both sides maneuvered to cool the hot war, they were ever ready to use any suspected deception or provocation as a trigger to press their advantage in battle or global diplomacy.

After Rhee's bold display of defiance, it was not until July 8 that the Communists agreed to return to the table. And even as talks resumed on the tenth—the second full anniversary of their inception—Chinese forces were poised to kick off the first of two stages of a massive retaliatory offensive aimed at punishing ROK units and demonstrating the North's implacability.

On the evening of July 13 and on into the morning of the fourteenth, the Chinese pressed the offensive's second stage, six of their divisions all but crushing four ROK divisions on the eastern front. As ROK lines collapsed, the U.S. Army's 3d Division pulled back to avoid being outflanked, finally setting up a support position behind the ROK 1st Army. With the Chinese salient swollen into a twenty-mile bulge,[2] disorganized streams of southbound ROK troops and armored equipment clogged main UN supply routes.

To make matters worse for frontline GIs and marines, monsoon weather took hold. Unstable masses of moist air topped by towering cumulus pushed into the mountain valleys of central Korea, generating banks of low clouds and thick fog. The clouds and fog benefited the Communists, concealing their troop movements while grounding land-based aircraft.

In an effort to close the gap in air cover, four Task Force 77 carriers were kept continuously on station at Point Oboe, their air groups tasked with both CAS and interdiction. In the midst of weather that was only marginally better at sea, flight schedules were stepped up to two daily hops for each pilot.

Despite these ambitious plans, however, flights often had to be diverted, delayed, or canceled due to foul weather and unpredictable surface winds. Sometimes, when the soup was particularly thick or widespread, tactical aircraft formations were even commandeered for high-altitude bombing missions.

When *Princeton's* Air Group 15 returned to the line after an extended layoff, for example, VF-153's George Schnitzer led several division-size "big bomber" sorties: First, coasting in at 18,000 feet south of the MLR, Schnitzer established radio contact with an Air Force radar controller on the ground. Then, once things were set, the division turned right to a specified northbound heading at a specified airspeed. Finally, after a controller countdown ("three, two, one") and command ("drop"), the four F9F-5s simultaneously released bombs. The blind drop, the abrupt loss of weight—nearly a ton—and the sudden lift were, Schnitzer recalled, "weird, to say the least."[3]

***

Not being a war-ending casualty—especially through some boneheaded mistake—was an obsession with Schnitzer and his squadron buddies as they accumulated combat sorties during *Princeton's* tours on the line. Ever since his second-deployment combat baptismal in mid-March (a "Cherokee Strike" against a North Korean supply dump), Schnitzer had paid strict attention to the lessons of his first war cruise: making sure, for example, to execute evasive maneuvers going into and coming out of each attack run. He also challenged himself with a goal: Having begun the deployment with 114 consecutive accident-free deck landings, Schnitzer bet air group LSO David Rose that he'd reach 200 without an accident.

Still, despite the collective focus and discipline of its aviators, Air Group 15 had absorbed a painful string of pilot losses. The first, which occurred within days of CVG-15's inaugural tour, was followed by a late-April pileup of three deaths. Two of these three were VF-154 pilots Schnitzer scarcely knew, but sandwiched in between was a fatality—

VF-153's second of the deployment—that shook Schnitzer to the core. Larry Quiel, Schnitzer's roommate and buddy of four years who so recently had celebrated with Schnitzer their simultaneous promotions, was killed when his F9F-5 stalled off the catapult, hit the water left wing down, and cartwheeled into complete disintegration. A few aircraft parts and pieces of Quiel's flight gear were the only things retrieved.

Then, on May 13, while returning from an afternoon recce flight west of Wonsan, Schnitzer looked on dumbfounded as Dick Clinite, another good friend and roommate, suddenly and inexplicably punched out of his aircraft over the harbor. There was nothing to explain it: no fire, no smoke or trailing fluid, no Mayday from Clinite.

Schnitzer jumped on the circuit: "Mayday, Mayday, Mayday, Blue 3 has ejected!" Clinite had punched out at 8,000 feet into clear skies and a strong west-to-east wind. His parachute opened, and, as Schnitzer followed him down, flying big figure eights around the billowing chute canopy, Clinite waved to him. The wind was carrying him out of enemy reach but also out over a turbulent sea. The duty helicopter, launched from an LST stationed up the coast from Wonsan, was on its way. But would it arrive in time?

Clinite hit the water hard; the offshore wind at once caught his chute canopy and dragged him along through the chop. Schnitzer continued flying figure eights over the spot so as to give the helicopter a target area to head for. It seemed to take ages, but when the helo finally arrived, its pilot wasted no time: He used rotor downwash to collapse the chute canopy and then sent his crewman into the water to help Clinite.

There was nothing more that Schnitzer could do. As it was, his own aircraft was extremely low on fuel, and he was barely able to make it back to *Princeton*. Schnitzer was physically exhausted and emotionally spent when he finally touched down; he staggered down to the ready room and planted himself, scared but hopeful, in front of the ready-room Teletype. Soon the machine clacked out a message from *Samuel N. Moore* (DD-747), the destroyer dispatched to aid the rescue. The message was brief and blunt: "Pilot was picked up, pilot dead, drown."[4]

***

During July 1953 the most intense maneuvering toward an eventual armistice occurred away from the tents and baize-covered tables at Panmunjom. Part of it involved diplomatic arm twisting—another part vengeful last-licks bloodletting.

On the UN side, Dwight Eisenhower had dispatched a special emissary to Korea to deal with Syngman Rhee. Having proved to his own satisfaction that he was no American puppet (Eisenhower's envoy had come to him, not vice versa), Rhee was persuaded not to upset the implementation of an armistice. In exchange he was promised a mutual security pact and long-term economic aid for South Korea.

With Rhee finally mollified, the UN commission led by U.S. Army general William K. Harrison was then made to mark time as the Communist delegation's front man, Nam Il, stalled to await the results of the Communists' valedictory offensive. At the prospect of this stonewalling Harrison was prepared to walk away from the table—a signal to the other side there would be no further concessions—only to have the Communists beat him to the punch: A recess was called until July 19.

***

In mid-July perhaps no one, in VF-52 XO Jim Holloway's estimation, was feeling the pressure more than his squadron skipper and friend, Lt. Cdr. James Kinsella.[5] Kinsella, son of a Navy chief boatswain's mate and a much decorated World War II Hellcat veteran, had taken command of VF-52 when skipper Herb Baslee, a Naval Academy contemporary of Holloway's, had been shot down and killed during the 1952 *Valley Forge* cruise. Kinsella had eventually handpicked Holloway to be his XO for the next deployment, and the two had teamed to staff and retrain VF-52 using a combination of "second tours," retreads (including former VF-194 pilot Howard Thayer), and nuggets. It was hard and challenging work hampered near its end when the squadron's new F9F-5-series aircraft had to be traded in for older F9F-3s and F9F-2s: VF-52, it turned out, would be deploying with *Boxer*, still equipped with older short-throw hydraulic cats unable to handle the heavier 5-series Panthers.

Kinsella came away from his first Korean War cruise convinced that, given enough training and flight-formation discipline, VF-52 (which, in addition to CO Baslee, had lost three aviators during the *Valley Forge* deployment) could survive the *Boxer* cruise intact. That was the goal—implicit or explicit—of many a squadron CO and CAG going into a second cruise. (It also seemed to be the prevailing—if tin-eared—mood of Navy brass: Holloway had blanched when one visiting two star told a group of pilots prior to a strike launch that there was no target in Korea worth the life of *his* pilots.)[6]

But, while some brass and frontline leaders might avoid casualties by raising bomb-release altitudes or routinely using marginal weather conditions as an excuse to "abort" and retreat to easier "weather-divert" targets, Kinsella would never permit himself or his flight leaders to do so. Imbued with his father's values, he well knew the consequences for imperiled frontline GIs and marines. Now, however, his ambitious, perhaps irreconcilable, goals were being put to a real test. With the month far from over, VF-52 had already lost seven F9F-2s to enemy flak. It was some sort of miracle—one that couldn't possibly last—that all of their pilots had been rescued alive (though several with serious deployment-ending injuries).

Stress was only heightened by the imperative to blunt this latest Communist offensive. It was an atmosphere reminiscent of frantic efforts to support the Marine Corps during their December 1950 break out from Chosin Reservoir. On July 21, after being briefed for a morning CAS mission near Kumhwa, Holloway happened to cross paths with the skipper—then about to lead his own flight against a reported southbound truck column in the same sector.

"Go get 'em!" Kinsella said as the two left the ready room. "We'll do our best," Holloway responded offhandedly, only to be stunned by what Kinsella said next: "You won't know you've tried your hardest until you start losing pilots."

As Holloway returned from that morning strike—with the help of a frontline FAC not fifty yards from the Chinese positions, Holloway's six aircraft had penetrated a perilous combination of clouds and mountain crags to pound Chinese positions with bombs, rockets, and 20mm—he reflected on Kinsella's words. It was the only time he'd seen Kinsella lose his cool, expressing something they undoubtedly both felt but dared not utter. It was as if he'd jettisoned his supreme goal for the cruise.

All six aircraft in Holloway's flight were recovered intact, but after Holloway taxied and climbed sweat soaked and disheveled from his cockpit, VF-52's maintenance crew chief approached him with bad news: "The Skipper's down! Just been shot down."

Holloway rushed to the catwalk and down to the ready room where he grabbed the squadron duty officer for information on Kinsella. "Well, Triple Sticks, looks like you're the Skipper now!" the SDO began. "First report was no survivor." The gallows humor stung, even though Holloway knew the SDO, like everyone else, employed it as a coping mechanism, a way to deal with the daily dice roll of combat flying: It wasn't you or me today, but it easily could have been—and might well be tomorrow.

Holloway could now only wait for the rest of Kinsella's flight to return. When Bill Brook, one of Kinsella's veteran section leaders, finally entered the ready room, Holloway approached him, and the two sat down. Still in the middle of his own postmission decompression, Brook described how, after reaching the target area and milling around at higher altitude, Kinsella had finally spotted the enemy column through a momentary break in the clouds.

He immediately led his flight into a steep dive. Hurtling down in a loose column with brakes out, none of them could be entirely certain the thick veil wouldn't carry them straight into a mountain. As it was, each pilot had to pull heavy Gs just to escape crashing. Then, as the F9Fs overtook the southbound line of cargo trucks interspersed with gun-bristling "flak wagons," passing within feet of their cabs and canopies, strafing with 20mm fire and lining up HVAR shots, there was a terrific explosion just beneath Kinsella's airplane.

Brook saw the skipper's F9F wreathed in engine-compartment smoke as Kinsella pulled up and hightailed it south to escape the mountains and reach the front. The skipper, Holloway and Brook both knew, had vowed never to eject over enemy lines. By the time he reached the flat "no-man's-land" of the MLR, his smoking aircraft, now low off the deck, was sprouting flames. Over no-man's-land Kinsella's F9F slowed, its canopy blew off, and the plane abruptly bellied in through a field, leaving behind it a twenty-foot swath one hundred yards long before exploding. Convinced Kinsella could not possibly have survived the inferno, Brook joined up with the flight, called TACC to report the crash coordinates, and got ready to return to *Boxer*.

***

The Communist contingent Harrison and his UN team faced across the tables at Panmunjom on July 21 was now prepared to make a deal. Although there'd been staggering casualties on both sides (estimates of UN casualties for June and July were upward of 50,000—mostly ROK—with Communist losses estimated to be double that),[7] and fighting still raged in godforsaken terrain pockets with names like the Punch Bowl, Pork Chop Hill, Little Berlin, and Sniper's Ridge,[8] the MLR was once more stabilizing. Just the day before, subdelegates had convened separately to hammer out the final details of the demarcation line. This dickering process took three more days, with each side jockeying for more chunks of territory than either had earned by dint of blood or diplomacy, but, by July 25, both sides had signed off on final armistice maps. Interpreters at once began work on drafting final copies of the armistice agreement itself.

It was also agreed that these truce documents would be signed on the twenty-seventh, first at 10:00 A.M. by Harrison and Nam Il in a newly constructed "Peace Pagoda" in Panmunjom, and then, hours later and separately, by Peng (for China), Kim (for North Korea), and Mark Clark. The cease-fire itself would occur at 10:00 P.M. that same day.

The final hurdle to the long-sought but tenuous peace came, not surprisingly, as an emblematic footnote to the illogical litany of the entire conflict. The Communists, who had constructed the T-shaped Peace Pagoda, had placed two giant blue and white "peace doves"— symbolism copied from a famous painting by Pablo Picasso—over the building entrance. Adamant that the doves represented a stroke of Communist propaganda, the UN commissioners demanded that they be removed.[9]

By the time both sides arrived for the July 27 morning signing— the UN and Chinese representatives wearing drab uniforms, while the North Koreans sported crisp military tunics "with gold shoulder-boards and blue trousers with red stripes" down the inseams—the Picasso doves had been painted over.[10]

***

While VF-52 CO James Kinsella was the eighth VF-52 aviator downed by the enemy in July 1953 and indeed was among the final naval aviation casualties of the Korean War, he was by no means the last casualty, nor, it turned out, was he a fatality.*

Before finally going feet wet on July 21, VF-52 section leader Bill Brook had led three aircraft in a "final salute" pass over Kinsella's wreckage. As he zoomed low, Brook saw that the fuselage of Kinsella's plane had broken at the cockpit. While the engine and after fuselage had erupted in a flaming mass, the cockpit and nose section had been tossed clear of the inferno.

To Brook's astonishment, he also saw Kinsella climbing out of his ejection seat and the open cockpit and moving toward the cover of a small hill. Several hours later, along with news of his field promotion to squadron CO (the first unit command in a career that would eventually lead to his becoming CNO), VF-52's James Holloway learned that Kinsella, although badly burned, had somehow negotiated a perilous minefield and been picked up by Army 2d Infantry Division GIs.

Holloway also learned that the veteran skipper had nearly been undone by what first looked to be a mistake high up in the pantheon of bonehead pilot moves: Intending to fire rockets on his strafing pass, Kinsella had mistakenly dropped bombs that blew him out of the sky. (Only later did an astute maintenance officer discover that several 3-series Panthers converted to 2-series had—apparently like Kinsella's—crossed wiring on their bomb and rocket weapon stations.)

Whether it was a case of pilot or material failure, Kinsella was lucky not to have been killed. Nevertheless, as of July 27, Kinsella's ambition for the cruise still held. And, although none of the pilots, even air group and squadron leaders, realized it with any precision, the Korean War was within hours of ending.

---

* Ship and air group action and casualty reports seem to narrow the Korean War's last U.S. Naval aviation fatalities down to three, all on July 26, 1953: *Lake Champlain* (CVA-39) VF-22 Banshee pilot Ens. Edwin Nash Broyles Jr. during a strike against North Korea's Hoeryong Air Field; VF-151 Panther pilot Ens. Thomas Franklin Ledford to a sea crash forward of carrier *Boxer* while on a combat mission; and *Princeton* VF-152 Corsair pilot Lt. William Charles Blackford Jr., shot down by antiaircraft fire while on a reconnaissance mission over North Korea.

For Holloway, the clearest sign that the fight was at last winding down came during a July 27 afternoon mission northwest of Hung-nam. The North Korean coastal city had long before been devastated, but as Holloway's flight skirted its barren ruins, an unprecedented barrage of flak was being thrown up. Ground weapons of every caliber and ordnance of every type were sent their way. It didn't seem to matter that Holloway's flight was soaring well out of range. For once, there seemed no constraints on the ground gunners' expenditure of ammunition.

July 27, meanwhile, began as another "maximum effort" day for Air Group 15: *Princeton* was marking its fifty-sixth consecutive day on the line. George Schnitzer's eleventh mission in six days was a morning CAP, his twelfth a strike south of Wonsan against supply trucks heading for the front.[11]

A little over two weeks earlier, Schnitzer's string of unblemished deck recoveries had finally been broken. On the morning of the seventeenth, as he returned from a morning CAP and made his initial approach, his instruments warned of a landing-gear hydraulics failure. As a precaution, Schnitzer took a wave off so maintenance personnel could visually inspect his gear.

The wheels were reported down, so Schnitzer was cleared for a second and final approach. When he got the "cut" and touched down, his tailhook caught the number-two wire. Almost at once, however, his wing wheels—but not his nose wheel—began to fold. By the time the airplane stopped, the rear of the fuselage was on the deck. It was Schnitzer's 191st carrier landing. He had lost his bet but had walked away, and his wartime carrier deck landings would soon total 216. Meanwhile, so depleted was the squadron's supply of operational aircraft that after the hydraulic problem (a ruptured hydraulic hose) was fixed and its inboard wing flap replaced, the plane was flown in the very next launch cycle.

Now, in the war's final afternoon, Schnitzer was a Vulture's Row observer as the Air Group's last combat flight returned from a strike against a North Korean airfield. Knowing now it was to be their final combat sortie, division pilots jockeyed to be the last to touch down. Time and again they took voluntary wave offs until the air boss caught wind of what was happening and ordered all of them to get aboard, "NOW!"[12]

***

As of August 6 Harry Ettinger and the thirteen other American POWs confined to the three-room house across the stream from Camp 2 Annex in northwestern North Korea still hadn't learned that a truce had been signed. As late as June (while, unknown to the POWs—as were virtually all matters beyond the bounds of Camp 2 Annex— "Rhee's Rebellion" nearly derailed the outbreak of peace), Ettinger and seven cohorts had been planning a breakout, something conceivable only in the summer months that far north.

But the unanticipated arrival of letters from home—the first any had received since the beginning of their captivity (now nearing two years for Ettinger)—quickly quelled the POWs' fugitive ardor. While three would make the attempt (and almost at once be recaptured), the rest, including Ettinger, took it as a sign that peace and release might actually be at hand. There was no sense plunging needlessly into even more hardship.

If the distribution of letters and Red Cross packages was a Chinese tactic to mollify the POWs—first as the truce approached and then as the machinery of prisoner exchanges geared up—it both worked and backfired. POWs used the receipt of mail (a minimum require-ment for POW treatment under the Geneva Convention) as an open-ing to assert themselves and to agitate for additional concessions big and immaterial. Indeed, on July 30, when an interrogator named Shai (chief among the camp interrogators when it came to pressing for germ-warfare confessions) accompanied by several guards assembled the eleven remaining "uncooperatives" in front of their quarters, the men all but read him the riot act over camp conditions and rules.

Only later did Ettinger surmise that Shai had originally set out to inform the POWs that fighting had indeed ended. Instead, flustered and angered by the POWs' litany of complaints, Shai and the guards left in a snit. They took a different approach. Over the course of the next week, the POWs were mysteriously summoned in ones or twos to "final interrogations" from which they mysteriously failed to return. By this means the house eventually emptied out; on August 6 only Ettinger and Kenneth Henry were left, and neither knew with any cer-tainty what was in store for them.

***

That April during Operation Little Switch—the prearmistice human-itarian exchange of about 700 American, UN, and ROK prisoners (among them VF-194's Marvin Broomhead)* for nearly ten times as many Chinese and North Korean POWs—Western officials had ex-pected to be overwhelmed with sordid, gripping tales of mistreatment once these most seriously sick and wounded POWs were released. They were surprised, almost stunned, at how subdued and reticent the 149 American returnees were.

Already in bad condition, and now besieged by reporters and flash-ing banks of cameras, most were reluctant to talk at all. Others would speak only of comrades left behind. There were few claims of delib-erate mistreatment, and a handful even praised their captors for pro-viding medical treatment, blankets, and clothing.**

To some observers it was proof that brainwashing was actually more insidiously effective than suspected. The docile behavior displayed by this first returning contingent (most, it turned out, were only trying to protect those still in captivity), combined with confessions by men such as Enoch, Quinn, and Schwable, served to stoke concerns about the far-reaching implications of conditions for hundreds more still in captivity. Were they being hypnotized or drugged?*** Were they vic-tims of systematic reprogramming being conditioned to return as sub-versive "sleepers" or slowly ticking "time bombs"?[13]

The Communists, meanwhile, used the thirty days of Operation Big Switch (set to begin August 5) to release its 3,404 UN POWs (in-cluding 944 Americans) in ways that best suited their agenda. One centerpiece of the monthlong pageant, during which an average of

---

* There were a total of 11 U.S. Navy POWs repatriated as part of Little Switch. The 10 others were hospital corpsmen serving as medics with Marine Corps combat units.

** After screening and debriefing in Japan, however, at least one group of POWs suspected of being victims of Communist propaganda was airlifted to Valley Forge Army Hospital for psychiatric treatment.

*** Several prisoners released later actually reported being drugged on the train returning from Manchuria—apparently to black them out as they passed through militarily sensitive areas. Specu-lation about this was among the inspirations for *The Manchurian Candidate*, a 1959 novel about a brainwashed POW returning from the war as a "sleeper" assassin controlled by the Chinese Communists.

400 returning UN POWs were processed each day, was the September 4 release of U.S. Army general William Dean. Dean, the highest-ranking POW on either side, had been captured in August 1950. He had been in North Korean custody ever since and occasionally showcased as a glowing exemplar of the Communists' humane regard for POWs.

Dean's repatriation was set to occur just two days shy of Big Switch's scheduled conclusion. After its completion, the remaining 22,604 North Korean and Chinese POWs being held in South Korea's island prisons—the majority of them thought to be anti-Communists— would be loaded on LSTs and shipped up the coast to the new De-militarized Zone (DMZ), where, along with 35 South Korean and 24 UN POWs who had initially refused repatriation and were housed in a separate DMZ compound, they would be screened by the NNPC.[14]

Dean's release therefore represented Big Switch's grand public finale. Other POWs would follow, but, the Communists hoped, he would be their poster boy. Yet even as they prepped Dean for his appearance— putting him through an orgy of photographs, showering him with gifts, and supplying him with a fresh, if oddly matched, set of clothes— they continued to work behind the scenes to produce as many POW confessions as possible. One high-ranking American prisoner, a USAF colonel and deputy wing commander named Andrew Evans Jr., finally signed a confession on September 3, a day before Dean, dressed in blue denim pants, a pink shirt, tennis shoes, and a coat from a tailor-made suit, stepped down from the seat of a brand-new Russian jeep at Panmunjom.[15]

***

Success in extracting any last-minute confessions depended—as it always had—on the skill, duplicity, and "true-believer" tenacity of the Communist captors pitted against the eroding physical condition, outward obstinacy, and inner resiliency of the POWs. Harry Ettinger's final reckoning came on August 6 when he was brought to a one-room interrogation hut within the confines of Camp 2 Annex. It was hot and dark inside the hut, which was furnished with a small table, a dim oil lamp, and a single chair.

An interrogator ordered Ettinger to sit and, after a pause, told him this was his "last chance to go home." Arranged before Ettinger on the table, lit by the unsteady glow of the oil lamp, was a display of newspaper clippings, magazine spreads, and POW confessions, all supporting the Communist contention that America had practiced germ warfare.

In order to go home, the interrogator insisted, Ettinger would have to prepare a statement. He could write it to "suit himself" using the material on the table for reference, but in it he would have to admit he'd been lying all along. He'd also have to apologize to camp authorities, thanking them for their humane treatment and for the good food and clothing he'd received. The interrogator then set paper and pencil before Ettinger and left the room.

Ettinger stared at the blank paper until his eye picked out some writing scratched onto the table's surface itself. In the dim light, it took him some minutes to decipher what it said: "War over. Denny Haley's gone home. Duquette."

Norm Duquette's scrawl was the first credible news Ettinger had that the war was indeed over—that Haley, presumably Duquette, and even he were at last going home.

* * *

Encouraged, Ettinger then turned to crafting his statement. It took hours, and he never got it right, at least in the interrogator's eyes. Ettinger worked all the variations: He apologized for the war being over. He thanked the authorities for not lying about food and clothing. He apologized for lying about not receiving food and clothes. It went on and on in unsatisfactory revision after revision, until the interrogator's anger and frustration blended into obvious fatigue.

Finally—by now it was well into the night—the guards took him across the creek to the Camp 2 Annex headquarters where he was, the interrogator told him, to apologize to the camp commandant in person. The commandant, it turned out, wasn't there. He'd long since gone to sleep. In his place was the commandant's deputy, a hunchback who was apparently heading up an impromptu three-man tribunal. The tribunal members were tired, too, apparently exhausted after an endless progression of these minitrials.

Ettinger's session may well have been the very last of the day. His statement was submitted but barely scrutinized. (He never heard anything further about it.) Instead, before adjourning, the sleepy judges ordered Ettinger escorted to Camp 2 where, he learned the next day, he was to begin processing for repatriation.

Clean, newly clothed, and beefed up (though still frail and rail thin), Harry Ettinger finally emerged from Communist captivity on September 5, 1953. His crewmen Mark Gilliland and Jess McElroy, he was to learn, had been released before him.

THREE EPILOGUES

1. The Bridges at Toko-ri

In February 1954 an odd formation of five aircraft flew over the peaks of the Chocolate Mountain Aerial Gunnery Range (CMAGR). Four of them—a division of F9F-2-series Panthers—trailed a fifth: a modified World War II B-25, the type of two-engine light bomber used by Jimmy Doolittle in the 1942 bombing raid on Tokyo. The F9Fs flew just above stall speed, their pace constrained by the lumbering B-25's maximum velocity, about 175 knots.

The guns and Plexiglas had long since been removed from the surplus B-25's tail turret, replaced by a camera pedestal. Behind an enormous swiveling camera in the exposed turret, standing waist-high in the plane's slipstream, wearing a leather jacket and the cloth helmet and goggles of a World War II aviator, stood Paul Mantz, the stunt and racing pilot hired by Paramount Pictures to direct the aerial filming for James Michener's book-turned-movie *The Bridges at Toko-ri*.

Over the course of two days, using the CMAGR (a half-million-acre U.S. Navy aerial bombing and gunnery preserve east of California's Salton Sea) as a double for the rugged terrain of North Korea's interior, the fifty-year-old Mantz (who as a stunt pilot had been at the controls of a four-engine B-17 during a crash landing staged for the film *Twelve O'Clock High*)* ran his government-paid stunt pilots through their paces: joining up, dive-bombing, strafing, and even simulating crashes.

---

* Mantz would die in an air crash during the 1965 filming of *The Flight of the Phoenix*.

Afterward, the VF-52 jet pilots, detached for temporary duty from NAS Miramar—among them squadron CO James Holloway and "first tours" Grant Dean, Art Labelle, and Bill Thompson—got a tour of the special-effects set used for the film's climactic combat sequences. Primitive by today's digital-effects standards, it was a miniaturized panorama, roughly fifty feet on a side, of mountains, valleys, buildings, roads, tracks, and bridges positioned to blend into the backdrop of the Chocolate Mountains for visual continuity. For the visitors' benefit, film technicians demonstrated the set's crude but ingenious special effects: aircraft models swooping along wires with timed pyrotechnics used to simulate flak fire and ground explosions. To Holloway it was fascinating, even remarkable, albeit in a hobby enthusiast's train-set sort of way.

***

James Michener's novella *The Bridges at Toko-ri* appeared complete in the July 6, 1953, issue of *Life*—just three weeks before the Korean War armistice. "This novel tries to explain our experience in Korea," Michener told *Life*'s readers in a short preface. "I believe that often in the years to come our nation will face problems similar to those we met for the first time in Korea." Random House published a hardcover version simultaneously—and Michener dedicated the book "To Marshall U. Beebe, fighter pilot." *The Bridges at Toko-ri* achieved immediate sales success, quickly prompting Paramount to buy the film rights.

The book itself got mixed critical reviews, but, in the end (as was always the case with Michener's subsequent best-sellers), its many readers passed the final judgment. Michener's story was engrossing and captured the poignancy of human triumph in the midst of hostile conflict. He placed readers inside the war and allowed them to experience the emotions of men (and women) before, during, and after the stress of battle. War was unfortunate and stupid and put innocent people (including reluctant reservists) in precarious circumstances. Still, men and women could perform heroically in the face of fear and even death. The slender book remains in print to this day.

At the time the book was also a tremendous hit with the U.S. Navy. For the filming CNO Arleigh Burke agreed to lend planes and pilots (not to mention access to nineteen ships)* at no charge to Paramount. (The film producers reciprocated in part by treating the Navy stunt pilots and their spouses to a Hollywood tour, including a visit to the set—where filming continued—and a star-studded nightclub bash.) And when the film version premiered in Washington, D.C., in 1955, Burke lauded it as a meticulously accurate depiction of the naval air war in Korea and the best Navy war film ever.[1]

Solid box-office receipts demonstrated the moviegoing public's enthusiasm for the film as well. Even the Motion Picture Academy of Arts and Sciences chimed in: The film was nominated for Best Film Editing and won an Academy Award for Best Special Effects.**

Book and movie vaulted Michener's literary success to another level. By 1954 seven foreign-language versions of *The Bridges at Toko-ri* were in distribution worldwide (including, oddly enough, a version circulating in the People's Republic of China). However, despite the pride and satisfaction that accompanied this resounding, multilayered triumph, *Bridges* also contributed to a personal setback for Michener. His extended stays with Task Force 77 and on the ground in Korea only seemed to accelerate the collapse of an already tottering marriage.

Michener and his wife, Vange, finally divorced in 1955, and afterward he wrote her a letter that accused her of drunkenness, adultery, and abuse during their time in Asia. Once, Michener complained, he'd returned to Tokyo to find her "in pretty dreadful shape": drunk, disorderly, and in need of hospitalization. "I did my best to bring you around," he continued, "but in the end you ran off to Korea and traveled about with various men. While I was working at sea, you were thrown out of the Correspondent's Club."[2]

It was an all too familiar tale played out both overseas and back in the United States. Though Michener had underscored the love between Harry and Nancy Brubaker to heighten the tragic finale of *The*

---

* During filming USS *Oriskany* stood in for the fictional *Savo Island*, although when *Oriskany* went out of service for repairs during filming, sister carrier *Kearsarge* took over. (For continuity *Kearsarge's* hull number, 33, was painted out and replaced with a 34.) The squadron depicted in the film is VF-192, the "Golden Dragons."

** The film competed in the Special Effects category with *The Dam Busters*, a British film depicting the Royal Air Force World War II "bouncing bomb" attack on the Ruhr dams in Germany.

Bridges at Toko-ri, casualties in human relationships were as much war legacies as physical wounds, mental trauma, and even death.

***

Because he flew the lead aircraft in many of the crucial aerial shots for *The Bridges at Toko-ri*, James Holloway in effect portrayed (though often behind goggles and an oxygen mask and always under a flight helmet and at a distance) Michener's lead character, Harry Brubaker. Although Holloway didn't speculate (then or after) as to who might be the real-life model for Brubaker—Michener's fictive twenty-nine-year-old Denver lawyer, aviator, and reluctant reservist killed after crash-landing behind enemy lines—many others did.

Perhaps an earlier movie (based in part on Michener material) that was more explicit in its depictions set the tone. *Men of the Fighting Lady* (which blended accounts from Michener's "The Forgotten Heroes of Korea" with Cdr. Harry A. Burns's "The Case of the Blind Pilot") used actual names—Van Johnson starred as Howard Thayer, Dewey Martin as Kenneth Schechter, and Frank Lovejoy as Paul Gray—but then went on to substantially modify (and perhaps even misrepresent) details. Bowing to the public's new fascination with carrier jet aircraft, Gray's, Thayer's, and Schechter's VF-194 Skyraiders were changed to Panther jets,* and the drama of Thayer's blind landing on Jersey Bounce was recast as a carrier deck landing. (Details like this gave VF-112's Ed Jackson and Dayl Crow good reason to feel that parts of *Men of the Fighting Lady* were just as rightfully about them.)

Speculation therefore may have only flared when *The Bridges at Toko-ri* premiered and Hollywood stars fleshed out and glamorized its key roles: William Holden as Harry Brubaker, Grace Kelly as Nancy Brubaker, Fredric March as George Tarrant, and Mickey Rooney as Mike Forney. Some of this speculation was played up by the popular press. William Holden's younger brother, Robert Beedle, for example, was a Navy fighter pilot killed in action in World War II. Beedle's former squadron mates, the press reported, remembered him as having been very much like the Harry Brubaker character.

---

* VF-192 F9F Panther jets were also used in this film. Afterward, the "Golden Dragons" styled themselves as the "World Famous Golden Dragons."

Beyond such tabloid ruminations, some character and real-life parallels are compelling and indisputable. Adm. George Tarrant's passion, demeanor, and physical appearance are an undeniable fit for Rear Adm. John Perry. Likewise, *Savo Island* CAG Lee was modeled after Air Group 5 CAG Cdr. Marshall U. Beebe (who served as a technical adviser for the film version). For other characters and situations, however, either the fits are looser or composites sneak in. Duane Thorin's failed effort to rescue Harry Ettinger, for example, was almost certainly the inspiration for Mike Forney's valiant, doomed attempt to retrieve Harry Brubaker. Duane Thorin himself may well have been the inspiration for roustabout chopper pilot Mike Forney (and Thorin's crewman Ernie Crawford the inspiration for Nester Gamidge): Both were enlisted pilots and staunch anti-Communists, although in real life Duane Thorin neither dressed, drank, nor caroused with Mike Forney's (or Mickey Rooney's) Gaelic flamboyance.

Harry Brubaker's real-life identity remains the most problematic and elusive. There was for certain a VF-194 prop pilot (and later XO) named Donald S. (Pappy) Brubaker aboard carrier *Valley Forge* whose less-than-regulation looks and easygoing demeanor may have loosely coalesced into the model for Michener's Harry Brubaker. Brubaker was USNR—a reservist—but Michener's notes also indicate that after a postwar try at civilian life, he voluntarily returned to active duty in 1948, well before the Korean War. (Donald Brubaker reportedly stayed in the Navy until retirement as a captain.)

Brubaker's civilian profession and Colorado origins were likely a blend of story-driven conceits (the reservist yanked unexpectedly from family and job who nevertheless performs dependably, even heroically) and Michener's own history: He'd been a professor near Denver who volunteered for Pacific-war duty.

Many would claim to see themselves or others in the personality or exploits of Harry Brubaker. In a very real way all these claims have merit. Michener was—and always would be—meticulous in his writing of realistic fiction. When it came to characters and situations, however, he felt free to borrow, transpose, and build compelling composites to suit his novels. By contrast, the naval aviators he observed and admiringly documented are people of certainty, competitiveness, and all-or-nothing decisive action. If they saw themselves (to the exclusion of others) in certain heroic characters and daring situations, they had every right to—and Michener the artist would not have been one to deny any of them.

For his part, beyond the acclaim and celebrity that followed from *The Bridges at Toko-ri*, James Michener was ultimately to reap rewards few other authors (including Hemingway) could hope to experience in their lifetime.* His later books—among them *Hawaii, Centennial, The Source, Chesapeake, Caribbean, Space, Alaska, Texas,* and *Poland*— were almost always audience favorites. Prepublication announcements were often enough to guarantee best-seller status.

Reviewers, however, weren't always as receptive. They often pounced on Michener's overcrowded plots, two-dimensional characters, and wooden dialogue. There was a sense—both among the critics and in Michener's own assessment—that his earliest, most passionate, and least-cluttered works (*Tales of the South Pacific* and *The Bridges at Toko-ri*) were by far his best. As Michener told his agent, Helen Strauss (whom he credited as the driving force behind the book's completion), in a letter, *The Bridges at Toko-ri* was his "best single piece of writing."

2. The Biderman Principles

In January 1954 Lt. Harry Ettinger was attending an instrument training course at NAS North Island and awaiting shore-duty assignment to NAS Miramar when he was ordered to present himself at the San Diego headquarters of the Eleventh Naval District. Navy Intelligence wanted a detailed statement from him about his experiences as a North Korean and Chinese POW, including the circumstances surrounding the ill-fated February 1952 attempt to rescue him by helicopter.

Ettinger had a sense right away that some if not most of this had to do with the Navy-Army-CIA interservice turmoil prompted by Duane Thorin. Thorin (who was now also stationed in San Diego) had preceded Ettinger by a week or so in being repatriated at Panmunjom. Since his first footsteps into freedom Thorin had been intent on ensuring that Ulatoski (at the time he knew him only as "Ski"), the

---

* Michener died in 1997; his birth date is listed as February 3, 1907. However, having been raised by an adoptive mother, Michener professed uncertainty about the actual date and year.

Army spook who arranged for Naylor-Foote to participate in the botched rescue, was called to task.

Thorin had first told his story to Randolph Pate, the U.S. Marine Corps general who welcomed many of the returning POWs when they reached Panmunjom. Pate had directed that Thorin go home via Tokyo, giving him the opportunity to report details directly to the Army's Far East Command.[3]

Ettinger had already told his story once to U.S. Army debriefing specialists. This was back in September while he and other repatriated U.S. POWs were en route to San Francisco from Inchon aboard an Army troop transport. The questioning then had been hasty and perfunctory (the Army interrogators had hundreds of POWs to process during the eleven-day passage) with no particular attention paid to the matter of Thorin, Naylor-Foote, and Ulatoski.

This time, though, when he settled into a chair in an office at the Naval District, it was for two full days of questioning. In attendance were a Navy yeoman taking dictation on a stenographic machine, a full Navy commander named Bartlett (who let it slip that there was indeed "bad blood" flowing over the Thorin situation), and an agent named Neurberg from Navy Intelligence. The results of the questioning were ultimately reduced to a twenty-eight-page single-spaced transcript, a copy of which Ettinger finally managed to obtain in 1980. The contents covered Ettinger's life history from World War II to the present—with special attention paid to the fateful day of February 8, 1952. However, as far as Harry Ettinger knew, aside from the collection of exhaustive statements, nothing further ever came from the matter.

***

The fallout associated with American POWs' captivity, treatment, and behavior during the Korean War echoed for years within the military establishment; the halls of academe; the reports from the media; the fears, concerns, and lingering suspicions of many U.S. citizens; and, of course, the dreams and postwar neuroses of POWs themselves. The concern that there has never been a full accounting of the disposition of every American POW and MIA remains to this day. And, although the years since have eased (though by no means completely erased) fears about brainwashing as a specific irresistible and pervasive mind-altering technique, the brainwashing controversy has smoldered and periodically flared—sometimes in unanticipated, unintended ways.

In a 1954 *New York Times Magazine* article Dutch psychologist Joost A. M. Merloo described the direst fears about the long-term impacts of Communist brainwashing: "The totalitarians," Merloo argued, "have applied the Pavlovian technique . . . to produce the reflex of mental and political submission of the humans in their power." In a way Merloo's Orwellian assessment marked the high-water mark of concerns that brainwashing might somehow systematically undermine global freedom.*

From there, in light of new findings and revelations, hysteria about brainwashing receded. First there was evidence that even successful "brainwashing" rarely stuck. Almost to a man, the Americans who had made such damaging statements recanted their confessions as soon as they were repatriated. (The confessions, of course, made front-page headlines, the recantations seldom did, and the men bore the stigma of enemy collaboration ever after.) Soon enough, new questions and systematic doubts emerged: about the credibility of so-called brainwashing experts, and about just how unprecedented brainwashing techniques actually were.

Among the first experts to be discredited was Edward Hunter: The "journalist" who helped coin the very term *brainwashing* was revealed to be a propagandist on the CIA payroll. Experienced agency insiders, meanwhile, suspected all along there were actually no "secret techniques" involved. One 1953 CIA memo concluded that techniques the Communists employed to induce personality changes and produce confessions had been used by police states across the centuries. Doubtless, some combinations of techniques were particularly creative and effective. (One U.S. POW described—according to Hunter—how Chinese interrogators so often brought him "to death's door" that he ultimately credited them with saving his life and was ready to do anything they asked.)[4] Still, they amounted to little more than manipulative threats and age-old brutality.[5]

---

* George Orwell's *1984* was first published in 1949.

Three years later, in a medical journal article titled "Communist Attempts to Elicit False Confessions from Air Force Prisoners of War," Alfred D. Biderman, a sociologist working for the Air Force who interviewed 235 Air Force Korean War POWs, listed the distinct techniques actually used by the Communists. While the techniques— isolation, monopolization of perception, exhaustion, threats, occasional indulgences, demonstration of omnipotence, degradation, trivial demands, semistarvation, exploitation of wounds, and filthy surroundings—are punitive, perverse, even diabolical, none was particularly new.

In fact, some of the so called techniques may have been little more than exploitation—perhaps intentional, perhaps inadvertent—of cultural differences. For example, during postwar debriefings, some returning POWs pointed to the prison diet and the forced use of open latrines as instances of "fiendish torture." It turned out that public defecation was customary in rural China and that Chinese Communist captors usually provided a diet equivalent to what they themselves were eating.[6]

***

Rationalizing the techniques, however, did not fully remove the pain and acrimony over American POW collaborations and confessions (or, for that matter, erase questions about the sincerity of their recantations). Some argued that American confessions were just the visible tip of a large iceberg. One postwar study concluded that as many as 70 percent of U.S. POWs had, to one degree or other, caved into pressure: symptomatic, the study said, of collective "give-up-itis."[7] The concept of "brainwashing" was a way of "papering over" this inconvenient and embarrassing reality.

The confessions by Enoch, Quinn, Schwable, and Bley (all of whom returned with their military careers in ruins) were the most difficult to account for, not only because of the degree of their compliance but also because of the obstacles the Communists faced in orchestrating their statements. Each had to describe criminal acts (convincingly and in great detail) and simultaneously portray themselves as helpless pawns in a big conspiracy, all the while expressing remorse and thanks to their captors.

The transformation required rigorous teaching and dedicated learning. As instructors, some Communists had the "advantage" of being true believers: They were living the Big Lie rather than cynically perpetrating it. (For their part, the relative handful of POWs who produced outright confessions became "true believers" as well, adopting—however fleetingly—the worldview espoused by the Communists.)

Whether true believers or cynics, the Communists also knew they had a ripe propaganda issue: "germ warfare." Because of the nature of the air war, they also benefited from a substantial crop of aviation officer POWs (predominantly USAF) on whom to apply pressure techniques. They knew that confessions from any of these men could have a multiplier impact on world opinion; even if most held out (as did Ettinger and his many cohorts), they still had a good chance of bagging a few. They were right.

***

Even absent final conclusions about the nature, substance, and long-term implications of brainwashing, U.S. military and intelligence communities knew they had a big problem on their hands. "There was deep concern over the issue of brainwashing," former CIA director Richard Helms admitted years later. "We felt it was our responsibility not to lag behind the Russians or the Chinese in this field, and the only way to find out what the risks were was to test things such as L.S.D. and other drugs that could be used to control human behavior. These experiments went on for many years."

Having fought one Asia-based limited war and on the cusp of being embroiled in another, policy analysts and military brass also mobilized to transform what they'd learned into training programs to "inoculate" future prisoners. The result was SERE—for "survival, evasion, resistance, escape"—a program that became a training staple for soldiers, sailors, and especially airmen deployed to overseas conflicts, beginning with the Vietnam War.

The training—though much more extensive than any received by American troops prior to Korean War deployment—was too often outmatched by the special rigors of captivity, intense interrogation, and willful, depraved brutality practiced by the North Vietnamese, especially against U.S. Air Force, Navy, and Marine Corps pilots. SERE training might well have benefited some of those who survived these crucibles. For many, if not most, though, it was inner character and fiercely resilient "band of brothers" camaraderie that apparently made the difference—much as they had in Korea.

***

Most recently, dramatically, and somewhat ironically, the tables seemed to have turned on the use of these interrogation techniques. Inoculation, in effect, was transformed to venom.

In the wake of 9/11 and the capture of al Qaeda operatives, the CIA outsourced interrogations to organizations and countries with few qualms about the use of manipulation and brutality. In one instance, an accused al Qaeda commander handed over by the CIA to Egyptian security forces for interrogation produced a confession replete with claims about Saddam Hussein's chemical and biological weapons of mass destruction (WMD) and close links between al Qaeda and Iraq. The claims were later used by President George W. Bush and other administration officials in the run-up to the war in Iraq. Asked by FBI agents after the postinvasion WMD debacle why he had testified as he had, the suspect replied, "They were killing me. I had to tell them something."

In December 2002 when military trainers went to Guantánamo Bay to conduct a class in "coercive management techniques" for possible use on terrorism suspects, their curriculum was built on a SERE foundation. In a follow-up e-mail report, trainers summarized their approach as "the theory and application of the physical pressures utilized in our training."[8] The sessions, they reported, included "an in-depth class on Biderman's Principles." They even used the original chart of techniques from Biderman's 1957 article, although the article's explicit title had been dropped.

The training, at least in part, became the basis for interrogations by military personnel at Guantánamo Bay until 2005, when coercive practices were banned by Congress. The U.S. military, it seemed to many critics, had made a 180-degree turn, using techniques it had once denounced as torture and that, its own research indicated, produced false and fleeting results. As one knowledgeable critic, Albert J. Mora, the U.S. Navy's general counsel from 2001 to 2006, phrased it in testimony before a congressional hearing (where use of the Biderman chart was revealed): "Our nation's policy decision to use so-called 'harsh' interrogation techniques during the war on terror was a mistake of massive proportions."[9]

3. Such Men as These

On Monday, July 27, 1955, George Schnitzer, now a flight instructor with the Navy's Advance Training Command in Kingsville, Texas, was assigned to fly-check rides with a student who had failed his instrument qualification and was back for one final try.

The student's anxiety (he'd been recommended for dismissal by Kingsville's flight-disposition review board and staff from the Advance Training Command) was palpable during their first of two days of check rides in a TV-2—essentially a lengthened dual-control version of the Air Force's straight-wing F-80 Shooting Star.

George Schnitzer had long since chosen naval aviation as a career. Flying jet aircraft (with its attendant thrills and risks) was as much a passion as a vocation. Proof of that—for Schnitzer and many others—was evidenced in his willingness to undertake assignments in far-off, often unglamorous places (Kingsville, Texas, was a prime example), and to instruct and mentor those who displayed much less skill and promise.

In truth, concern that 1946 legislation laying the groundwork for the Holloway Program would waste taxpayer money—opening a quick path to a free college education and equally quick exit from a military-service obligation for "flying midshipmen" like Schnitzer—had no basis in fact. Hundreds of Holloway Plan naval aviators flew aerial combat during the Korean War. Many (like Ed Jackson and Ken Schechter) sustained life-threatening wounds, and some (like Jesse Brown) even made the ultimate sacrifice. The vast majority (Joe Akagi, Neil Armstrong, Dayl Crow, Ed Jackson, Dick Kaufman, George Schnitzer, and Howard Thayer, to name just a few) who took the "Holloway" met their full obligation, often served well beyond it, and, in many cases, ended up making U.S. Navy aviation their adult careers. It proved a sound investment for the Navy—though not always so for individuals.

***

During the first of what were to be two check rides on two consecutive days, with his student "under the hood" (the retractable opaque canvas canopy used to simulate "flying blind") and at the controls, Schnitzer quickly understood the problem. While his student might be a marginal flyer in a clear sky, he was terrible on instruments. He was amazed the kid had gotten this far.

Once they'd completed the first day's check flight and landed on the Kingsville duty runway, Schnitzer took some time to brief his shaky student on the things they'd be doing the next day. Although Schnitzer realized it might have only the opposite effect, he stressed the importance of being relaxed, not tense.

The next morning the student seemed in remarkably good spirits as Schnitzer fired up the TV-2 engine and, just before seven o'clock, rolled the aircraft onto the duty runway. After moving into takeoff position and setting the brakes, Schnitzer turned over the controls to the student pilot, who added throttle, released the brakes, and rolled the aircraft smoothly down the runway. When groundspeed reached 90 knots he lifted the nosewheel, letting the main gear carry the weight until they reached takeoff speed. Then, just as the main gear lifted from the runway, the student abruptly pulled back the control stick, at the same time inexplicably reducing throttle. The aircraft—now just feet from the ground—was about to stall.

Schnitzer screamed for him to release the controls. In an instant he pushed both stick and throttle forward, yanked the landing-gear handle up, and reached for the emergency tip-tank jettison button.

The full tanks weighed more than a ton. Had Schnitzer been able to jettison them in time, the faltering aircraft might have stayed aloft. Instead, the plane hit the ground at the end of the runway, skidding on its belly into the surrounding brush for another five hundred feet before it stopped with its engine still surging.

Crash trucks and emergency personnel were at the scene within minutes. The student—flight career finished though little the worse for wear—was lifted easily from the backseat. But it took an hour more and a huge dose of morphine to painstakingly extract Schnitzer.

The flight surgeon at the scene knew that Schnitzer's spinal column was critically damaged—if not altogether severed.

X-rays showed that Schnitzer's first lumbar vertebrae had been smashed and that bone fragments had penetrated his spinal column, causing extensive nerve damage and paralyzing him from the waist down. After an operation to remove bone fragments and fuse the spine around the shattered vertebrae, Schnitzer spent the next months bound to a Stryker frame that permitted his limp body to be rotated; he subsisted during that time on a diet of liquids and narcotic painkillers.

***

Given time and the logging of enough flight hours, the odds implicit in envelope-pushing flight—even outside the murderous confines of war—were bound to overtake a handful of even the best aviators, among them Frank Metzner, Roland Busch, and, not least, Howard Thayer.

After he returned Stateside from *Princeton*'s Korean deployment, VC-35's Frank Metzner—formerly a civilian adman—published a feature article titled "I Fly the Night Skies over Korea" in the December 1952 edition of the *Saturday Evening Post*. A picture accompanying the article shows Metzner perched on an Officers' Club barstool, using his hands (wreathed by the smoke from a cigarette propped in one of them) to demonstrate an intricate maneuver. He looked to be in his element. Although Madison Avenue may have beckoned, Metzner was back in naval aviation to stay. Just a few years later, though, he was killed (along with his backseat student) when the wings of his prop training aircraft sheared off during a practice loop.

Even ratcheting down the risks of flight didn't always stave off tragedy. Rollo Busch, for example, the VF-653 Corsair pilot who himself crashed while flying ResCAP above the Ed Sterrett crash site in North Korea (both survived and were captured, imprisoned, and repatriated together; after the war Busch would meet and marry Ed Sterrett's twin sister), chose to trade in the rigors of full operational flying in order to become a landing signal officer. During LSO training, however, while being checked out to fly an A-4 Skyhawk jet, Busch was killed during a catapult "cold shot."

There was, of course, no comparative measure for the irony or cosmic injustice of such peacetime tragedies as these. However, had there been such a scale, then the tragic fate of Howard Thayer would have registered near the top.

In 1961, then a lieutenant commander, Thayer was an A4D-2 Skyhawk squadron operations officer flying from the USS *Independence* (CV-62) in the Mediterranean. On a night mission, Thayer's CO suffered a disastrous in-flight casualty to his aircraft—the complete loss of electrical power, depriving him of all lights and communications. Sensing his skipper's critical predicament (and perhaps as well registering a jolt of déjà vu), Thayer was guiding the crippled aircraft and its "blind" pilot to a carrier landing when both planes crashed at sea on the final approach.[10] All that was ever found of either of the two Skyhawks was one tip tank.

***

It was not until September 1955 that George Schnitzer, still miserably encased in a Stryker frame, experienced the first spark of hope— the twitching of the big toe on his right foot. By month's end he was able to sit up in bed (though painfully) and even ease himself into a wheelchair.

Exhaustive physical therapy to restore some movement to his legs followed. It was slow, excruciating work with only partial success: Permanent nerve damage had irremediably affected key muscles in the back of his legs. Still, by November Schnitzer reached a once unthinkable milestone: He was able to walk, supporting himself on crutches.

The following May, when he retired from the Navy on full disability, George Schnitzer was fully mobile on crutches, set to return to college— this time to Stanford. After completing graduate work, he embarked on a career in computer systems, a nascent field that seemed as promising and limitless as naval aviation had once been.

NOTES

Prologue: Mariners

1. David Halberstam, *The Fifties*, 70.
2. James Michener Papers, letter dated September 12, 1951.
3. James A. Michener, *The World Is My Home: A Memoir*, 365, 367.
4. Ibid., 366; James A. Michener, "With Fast Carrier USS *Essex* in Korean Waters," 2.
5. James A. Michener, "'Old Men' in Antique Planes Fighting Reds."
6. James A. Michener, "The Forgotten Heroes of Korea."
7. James A. Michener, "Snow White Is Down Again," 6.
8. George Schnitzer, *Panthers over Korea*, 111.
9. Michener, *World Is My Home*, 365.

1. The Holloway

1. James L. Holloway III, *Aircraft Carriers at War: A Personal Retrospective of Korea, Vietnam, and the Soviet Confrontation*, 13.

2. Disturbing the Peace

1. Richard P. Hallion, *The Naval Air War in Korea*, 22.
2. Ibid.
3. Ibid., 291.

3. The Pittsburgh Corsairs, the Long Island Panthers

1. Halberstam, *The Fifties*, 134.
2. Jonathan Brent, *Inside the Stalin Archives: Discovering the New Russia*, quoted in Martin Walker, "Paper Trail: An American Publisher Gains Access to the Soviet Archives."
3. John Toland, *In Mortal Combat: Korea, 1950–1953*, 125.
4. Schnitzer, *Panthers over Korea*, 64.

4. Onionskin Angel
1. Hallion, *Naval Air War in Korea*, 114.

5. Other Everests
1. John W. Dower, *Embracing Defeat: Japan in the Wake of World War II*, 214.
2. Ibid., 132.
3. Ibid.
4. Ibid., 133.
5. Ibid., 111.

6. Iroquois Flight
1. Toland, *In Mortal Combat*, 236.
2. David Halberstam, *The Coldest Winter: America and the Korean War*, 427.
3. Ibid., 470.
4. Toland, *In Mortal Combat*, 307.
5. Ibid., 282.
6. Ibid., 346.
7. Ibid., 356.
8. Ibid., 362.
9. Ibid., 341.
10. Ibid., 373.

7. The Ridgway
1. Hallion, *Naval Air War in Korea*, 141.
2. Toland, *In Mortal Combat*, 376.
3. Rick Atkinson, *The Day of Battle: The War in Sicily and Italy, 1943–1944*, 107.
4. "The Airborne Grenadier."
5. William Manchester, *American Caesar: Douglas MacArthur, 1880–1964*, 752.
6. Ibid., 760.

8. Roads, Rails, Bridges, Tunnels, Dams
1. Manchester, *American Caesar*, 764.
2. Ibid., 776.
3. One vestige of the Medal of Honor's formative history is that each military branch—Navy (including U.S. Marines and Coast Guard), Army, and now Air Force—has its own unique medal design.
4. Toland, *In Mortal Combat*, 436.
5. Ibid., 462.

9. Oh! Welcome to Korea Hills
1. Hallion, *Naval Air War in Korea*, 165.
2. John P. Hayes, *James Michener: A Biography*, 65.

12. Epics in Failure

1. Letter with accompanying map from Duane Thorin to Harry Ettinger dated July 20, 2000.

13. Jersey Bounce

1. Duane Thorin, "Perils of Pegasus," 246.
2. Toland, *In Mortal Combat*, 416–419.

14. Implacable Enemies and Unforgiving Elements

1. *Valley Forge Action Report*, April 14, 1952, to May 16, 1952, 13.
2. Warren Thompson, "Down in the Dirt," 499.
3. *Valley Forge Action Report*, March 8, 1952, to April 4, 1952, 4.
4. Atkinson, *Day of Battle*, 183–184.
5. James A. Field Jr., *History of United States Naval Operations: Korea*, 377.
6. Letter from George Schechter to James A. Michener, Michener Papers.
7. Michener Papers, Container I:61, Folders 1–8.
8. James A. Michener, "Panmunjom Setting Weird as 'The Talks.'"
9. Toland, *In Mortal Combat*, 518, 502.
10. Ibid., 519.
11. Ibid., 524.
12. Remarks by Adm. James L. Holloway III, USN (Ret.), at the ceremony for the posthumous award of the Distinguished Flying Cross to Lt. (jg) J. Howard Thayer, USN, May 5, 2009.

15. Countering at the Right Moments

1. The account of the actual engagement recounted in this chapter is based on two primary sources: contemporary interviews with E. Royce Williams and CVG-102 Action Report, October 28–November 22, 1952.
2. Barrett Tillman, "Where Are They Now? Royce Williams."
3. Oral History Excerpts: Adm. James L. Holloway III, USN (Ret.), III-129.
4. Hallion, *Naval Air War in Korea*, 116–117, 241.
5. CVG-102 Action Report, October 28–November 22, 1952, VI-3–VI-4, II-3, VI-4.
6. Schnitzer, *Panthers over Korea*, 167.
7. Stephen J. May, *Michener: A Writer's Journey*, 110.
8. Michener, *The World Is My Home*, 364.
9. Toland, *In Mortal Combat*, 551–553.

16. Something Like Peace

1. Toland, *In Mortal Combat*, 565.
2. Ibid., 574.
3. Schnitzer, *Panthers over Korea*, 230.
4. Ibid., 224.
5. This account combines interviews with Adm. James L. Holloway III with separate coverage of the same events in his book *Aircraft Carriers at War* and typed portions of his oral history.
6. "Deployment Cycles," III-146.

7. Toland, *In Mortal Combat*, 574.

8. Holloway, *Aircraft Carriers at War*, 128.

9. Toland, *In Mortal Combat*, 574.

10. Ibid., 575.

11. Schnitzer, *Panthers over Korea*, 254.

12. Ibid.

13. Dominic Streatfeild, *Brainwash: The Secret History of Mind Control*, 22.

14. Toland, *In Mortal Combat*, 590.

15. Ibid., 584.

Three Epilogues

1. Holloway, *Aircraft Carriers at War*, 129.

2. May, *Michener*, 114.

3. Toland, *In Mortal Combat*, 582.

4. Kathleen Taylor, *Brainwashing: The Science of Thought Control*, 212.

5. Streatfeild, *Brainwash*, 338.

6. K. Taylor, *Brainwashing*, 90–91.

7. Streatfeild, *Brainwash*, 340.

8. Scott Shane, "China Inspired Interrogations at Guantanamo."

9. Time Weiner, "Remembering Brainwashing."

10. James L. Holloway III, "Remarks at the 5 May 2009 ceremony for the posthumous award of the Distinguished Flying Cross to Lieutenant (jg) J. Howard Thayer, USN."

GLOSSARY

Able Dog	Nickname for the Douglas AD Skyraider attack aircraft
AD-4	Propeller-driven Skyraider attack aircraft designed and manufactured by Douglas Aircraft
Airdales	Aircraft carrier aviation and flight deck personnel
Banshee	McDonnell Aircraft's F2H fighter-bomber
BB-	Letter designation (supplemented by hull number) for U.S. Navy battleship
Ben-jo	Latrine (Korean)
Bingo	Minimum fuel level required for a carrier based aircraft to return for a safe deck landing
Bogey	Unidentified and potentially hostile aircraft
Bomb line	A line established to demarcate UN ground-force operations
CA-	Letter designation (supplemented by hull number) for U.S. Navy heavy cruiser
Cat	Carrier flight deck catapult
Coast-in point	Geographic point where seaborne aircraft reach landfall
Corsair	U.S. Navy propeller-driven fighter-bomber aircraft; letter-number designation: F4U
CV-	Letter designation (supplemented by hull number) for U.S. Navy aircraft carrier; additional letter (e.g., *A* for Attack, *E* for Escort, *L* for Light) specifies use
CVA	Chinese Volunteer Army
CVG-	Letter designation (supplemented by a number) signifying a U.S. Navy carrier air group
DD-	Letter designation (supplemented by hull number) for U.S. Navy destroyer
F-51	Mustang fighter-bomber propeller aircraft
F-80	Shooting Star jet fighter aircraft
F2H	Banshee fighter-bomber twin-jet aircraft
F4F	Wildcat fighter-bomber propeller aircraft
F4U	Corsair fighter-bomber propeller aircraft
F6F	Hellcat fighter-bomber propeller aircraft

F7F	Tigercat fighter-bomber aircraft
F8F	Bearcat fighter-bomber propeller aircraft
F9F	Panther fighter-bomber jet aircraft
Feet wet (feet dry)	Status designation used in radio transmissions indicating whether a naval aviator is flying over water (or land)
Fly one	Takeoff position on aircraft carrier flight deck
Fox flag	Naval signal flag representing the letter *F*, indicating the start of flight operations
G-suit	Flight apparatus to protect pilot from extreme in-flight gravity (G) forces
HO3S	U.S. Navy helicopter
In Min Gun	North Korean People's Army; also NKPA
LOC	Line of communications
Mae West	Inflatable water survival vest
MiG	Letter designation for Soviet fighter aircraft; the letters refer to Artem Mikoyan and Mikhail Gurevich, lead designers of the Soviet "MiG" bureau
MiG Alley	Northwestern portion of North Korea above which there were numerous dogfights between U.S. Air Force fighter jets and Communist MiGs
Mustang	Commissioned military officer who began his career as an enlisted man
Nuggets	Rookie aviators
Panpan	Term for Japanese prostitutes
Panther	F9F fighter-bomber jet aircraft
Pickle	To drop a bomb from an aircraft
Pinwheel	Helicopter
Plane guard	Helicopter or ship assigned to rescue carrier aviators in the event of a crash or water landing
Point Oboe	Geographical reference point in the Sea of Japan, 125 miles east of Wonsan, from which Task Force 77 conducted flight operations over North Korea
Poopy suit	Water-tight survival suit worn by naval aviators; also called poopy bag or poofy suit
Prop	Propeller-powered aircraft
Punch out	Bail out of an aircraft using an ejection seat
R4D	U.S. Navy version of the Douglas DC-3 twin-engine propeller cargo aircraft
Ready deck	Status of an aircraft carrier flight deck when it is cleared of obstacles and ready for aircraft to land
Retreads	Propeller aircraft pilots trained to fly jet aircraft
The River	Informal name for the U.S. Naval Test Center, Patuxent, Maryland
Rounddown	Leading and trailing edges of a carrier flight deck
Shooting Star	Air Force F-80 straight-wing jet fighter aircraft
Short-legged	Description of Korean War era jets (both Navy/Marine and Air Force) whose fuel-consumption and ordnance-load constraints limited both their time over target and their effectiveness in ground-support and interdiction missions
Skyraider	U.S. Navy propeller-driven attack aircraft; letter designation is AD
SNJ	Propellor-driven Basic Flight Training aircraft

Survival bomb	Canister containing survival gear dropped by aircraft over the scene of a pilot rescue
TAD	Temporary additional duty
Tail End Charlie	The trailing aircraft in a flight formation
TarCAP	Target combat air patrol
Tip tanks	Fighter aircraft auxiliary fuel tanks mounted on the tips of the aircraft's wings
Top cover	*See* TarCAP
Torp	Torpedo
TV-2	Navy two-seat jet training aircraft, a version of the Air Force's straight-wing F-80 Shooting Star
U-bird	Nickname for Corsair
VA-	Letter designation (supplemented by a number) for a U.S. Navy "Attack" squadron
VC-	Letter designation (supplemented by a number) for a U.S. Navy "Composite" squadron
VF-	Letter designation (supplemented by a number) for a U.S. Navy "Fighter" squadron
Vulture's Row	Observation station on inboard side of aircraft carrier superstructure (island)

BIBLIOGRAPHY

Interviews

Jesse LeRoy Brown family: Daisy Brown Thorne (widow)

Howard Thayer family: Shirley Thayer (widow), Ann Frohlich (sister)

Duane Thorin family: Darrel Thorin (nephew)

HU-1: Bill Dixon, Doug Froling

USS *Boxer*, VF-52: James L. Holloway III; VF-194: Joe L. Akagi, Dewitt F. (Dewey) Ferrell Jr., Buddy Jordan

USS *Essex*, VF-51: Neil Armstrong; VF-54: Robert Wood

USS *Leyte*, VF-32: Thomas J. Hudner Jr., William Koenig

USS *Oriskany*, VF-781: E. Royce Williams

USS *Philippine Sea*, VF-112: Dayl E. Crow, Edward D. Jackson

USS *Rochester*: Rulon V. Bird, Earl Lanning

USS *Valley Forge*: James L. Holloway III; VC-35: Henry E. Ettinger; ATG-1: James L. Holloway III; VF-194: Joe Akagi, Richard Kaufman, Ken Matson, Kenneth A. Schechter, Lou Stoakes; VF-653: Bobby G. Balser, Ray Edinger, David W. Robertson

Books

Atkinson, Rick. *The Day of Battle: The War in Sicily and Italy, 1943–1944*. Henry Holt, 2007.

Dower, John W. *Embracing Defeat: Japan in the Wake of World War II*. W. W. Norton/New Press, 1999.

Edwards, Paul M. *Korean War Almanac*. Facts on File, 2006.

Field, James A., Jr. *History of United States Naval Operations: Korea*. U.S. Government Printing Office, 1962.

Halberstam, David. *The Coldest Winter: America and the Korean War*. Hyperion, 2007.

———. *The Fifties*. Villard Books, 1993.

Hallion, Richard P. *The Naval Air War in Korea*. Kensington, 1986.

Hayes, John P. *James Michener: A Biography*. Bobbs-Merrill, 1984.

Hemingway, Ernest. *For Whom the Bell Tolls*. Charles Scribner's Sons, 1940.

———. *The Old Man and the Sea*. Charles Scribner's Sons, 1952.

Higgins, Marguerite. *War in Korea: The Report of a Woman Combat Correspondent*. Doubleday, 1951.

Holloway, James L., III. *Aircraft Carriers at War: A Personal Retrospective of Korea, Vietnam, and the Soviet Confrontation.* Naval Institute Press, 2007.

Manchester, William. *American Caesar: Douglas MacArthur, 1880–1964.* Dell, 1979.

May, Stephen J. *Michener: A Writer's Journey.* University of Oklahoma Press, 2005.

Michener, James A. *The Bridges at Toko-ri.* Random House, 1953.

———. *The World Is My Home: A Memoir.* Random House, 1992.

Schnitzer, George. *Panthers over Korea.* Publish America, 2007.

Streatfeild, Dominic. *Brainwash: The Secret History of Mind Control.* Thomas Dunne Books, 2007.

Taylor, Kathleen. *Brainwashing: The Science of Thought Control.* Oxford University Press, 2006.

Taylor, Theodore. *The Flight of Jesse Leroy Brown.* William Morrow, 1998.

Thorin, Duane. *A Ride to Panmunjom.* Henry Regnery, 1956.

Toland, John. *In Mortal Combat: Korea, 1950–1953.* William Morrow, 1991.

———. *The Rising Sun: The Decline and Fall of the Japanese Empire, 1936–1945.* Modern Library, 1970.

Magazine and Newspaper Articles

"The Airborne Grenadier." *Time*, March 5, 1951.

Atkinson, Cdr. K. W. "Tex," USN (Ret.). "The Plan Was to Drop a Large Bomb with a Delayed Fuse into the Mouth of a Railroad Tunnel." *Naval Aviation News* (January–February 2001).

Barringer, Felicity. "A Press Divided: Disputed Accounts of a Korean War Massacre." *New York Times*, May 22, 2000.

Biderman, Albert D. "Communist Attempts to Elicit False Confessions from Air Force Prisoners of War." *Bulletin of the New York Academy of Medicine* 33, no. 9 (September 1957): 616–625.

Burns, Cdr. Harry A., USN. "The Case of the Blind Pilot." *Saturday Evening Post*, November 29, 1952.

Cooper, Lt. Col. James L., USMCR (Ret.). "Flying the Early-Early." *Naval History* (February 2009).

"Epilogue." *Time*, June 2, 1952.

Evans, Mark L., and C. Ross Bloodsworth. "The Dambusters at Hwachon." *Naval Aviation News* (May 1, 2001).

"The Fighting Phil Sea." *Tailhook* (Fall 1988).

Gawande, Atul. "Hellhole." *New Yorker*, March 30, 2009.

Gittings, John, and Martin Kettle. "US and S Korea Accused of War Atrocities: Inquiry Uncovers Secret of Series of Attacks by South on North." *The Guardian*, January 18, 2000.

Gray, Paul N. "The Bridges at Toko-ri: The Real Story." *Shipmate* (July–August 1997).

Jackson, Lt. Edward, USN, as told to Theodore Taylor. "Wingman! Fly Me Down!" *Argosy* (July 1952).

Kaufman, Richard F., Ph.D. "Behind the Bridges at Toko-ri." *Naval Aviation News* (March–April 2002).

Krebs, Albin. "James Michener, Author of Novels That Sweep Through the History of Places, Is Dead." *New York Times,* October 17, 1997.

Lacouture, Capt. John. "Bridges and Dams: The Swede Carlson Way." *Shipmate* (2000).

Metzner, Lt. Comdr. Frank, USN. "I Fly the Night Skies over Korea." *Saturday Evening Post*, December 27, 1952.

Michener, James A. "The Bridges at Toko-ri." *Life,* July 6, 1953.
———. "Fairy Tale at Panmunjom." International News Service, 1952.
———. "The Forgotten Heroes of Korea." *Saturday Evening Post,* May 10, 1952.
———. "The Front Lines." International News Service, 1952.
———. "Navy Cages 'Bald Eagle' So Vultures Can Rest." *Stars and Stripes,* February 15, 1952.
———. "Night Riders Blast the Daylights out of Foe." *New York World Telegram and Sun,* February 26, 1952.
———. "'Old Men' in Antique Planes Fighting Reds." International News Service, 1952.
———. "Panmunjom Setting Weird as 'The Talks.'" May 25, 1952.
———. "The Way It Is in Korea." *Reader's Digest,* January 1953.
"The Navy in the Hills." *Time,* May 14, 1951.
"Official Reports of the Day's Operations in Korea." *New York Times,* February 7, 1952.
Pearce, Jeremy. "Earl H. Wood Is Dead at 97; Helped Invent G-Suit." *New York Times,* March 27, 2009.
"Restrained Power." *Time,* August 4, 1958.
Rich, Frank. "The Real-Life '24' of Summer 2008." *New York Times,* July 13, 2008.
Roberts, Sam. "Figure in Rosenberg Case Admits to Soviet Spying." *New York Times,* September 12, 2008.
Russell, W. L. "Pittsburgh Fliers Back from Korea's Flak Alley." *Pittsburgh Press,* July 6, 1952.
———. "Thousands of Reserves Ready Here for Quick Plunge into Battle." *Pittsburgh Press,* July 24, 1950.
Schechter, Kenneth A. "Blind and Alone over North Korea." *Naval Aviation News* (September–October 2004).
Shane, Scott. "China Inspired Interrogations at Guantanamo." *New York Times,* July 2, 2008.
Thompson, Warren. "Down in the Dirt." *Combat Aircraft* (January 2000): 496–500.
———. "The Reality Behind Toko-ri." *Military Officer* (June 2003).
Thorin, Lt. Duane, USN (Ret.). "Chilling Rescue at Sea." *Foundation* (Spring 1994).
Tillman, Barrett. "Where Are They Now? Harry Ettinger." *Hook* (Winter 1999).
———. "Where Are They Now? Royce Williams." *Hook* (Winter 2010).
Traub, James. "What a Naval Officer Now Knows." *New York Times Magazine,* September 21, 2008, 40–50.
"Truman Presents Top Medal to Navy Flier Who Landed in Enemy Area in Rescue Try." *New York Times,* April 14, 1951.
Walker, Martin. "Paper Trail: An American Publisher Gains Access to the Soviet Archives." *New York Times Book Review,* January 25, 2009.
Weiner, Time. "Remembering Brainwashing." *New York Times,* July 6, 2008.
White, William S. "G.O.P. Threatens Impeachment Step." *New York Times,* April 12, 1951.

Official Documents (Declassified)

Action report of Carrier Air Group 102 for the period 28 October through 22 November 1952.
Action report of Carrier Air Group 102 for the period 2 December through 27 December 1952.

Other Sources

"Biography of Rear Admiral Joseph James 'Jocko' Clark." http://www.jacklummus.com/Files/Files_R/rear_admiral_joseph_james_jocko_clark.htm.

"Carrier, Carrier-Based Squadrons and Non-Carrier-Based Squadron Deployments During the Korean War." http://www.history.navy.mil/branches/koreaob.htm.

Cathcart, Donald E. "Lieutenant Royce Williams US Navy—Fighter Pilot." http://www.mofak.com/F9F-5_Panther_Pilot_Bags_3_Migs.htm.

Coleridge, Samuel Taylor. "The Rime of the Ancient Mariner."

"Deployment Cycles." Excerpts from Adm. James L. Holloway III's oral history.

Edinger, Ray. Unpublished wartime journal.

Essex Daily News (ship's newspaper), August 23, 1951.

Friedman, Sgt. Maj. Herbert A., (Ret.). "The American Psyop Organization During the Korean War." http://www.psywarrior.com/KoreaPSYOPHist.html.

Hauser, George R. "V-1/6 Naval Pre-Flight History." http://www.vpnavy.com/v5_1941.html.

Jordan, C. C. "Panthers Prevail." http://home.att.net/~historyworld/VF-781.html.

McCallum, Bunny. "Nice Day for a Swim." http://www.abledogs.com/Stories/swim.htm.

Michener, James A. Papers. Library of Congress MS 22,485. Container I:4, Folders 1–13.

———. Container I:61, Folders 1–8.

———. "Snow White Is Down Again." Unpublished typed article from papers of James A. Michener.

———. "With Fast Carrier USS *Essex* in Korean Waters." Typed story dated February 25, 1952, and addressed to Commander Naval Forces, Far East.

Oral History Excerpts: Admiral James L. Holloway III, USN (Ret.), covering the Korean War workup chronology of carrier squadrons.

Oral History Transcript: Neil A. Armstrong interviewed by Dr. Stephen E. Ambrose and Dr. Douglas Brinkley, NASA Johnson Space Center Oral History Project, Houston, Texas, September 19, 2001.

Parker, George A. "Blind Carrier Pilot." http://www.abledogs.com/Stories/blind.htm.

"Remarks prepared by Admiral James L. Holloway III, USN (Ret), and delivered by VADM Robert F. Dunn, USN (Ret.) at the 5 May 2009 ceremony for the posthumous award of the Distinguished Flying Cross to Lieutenant (jg) J. Howard Thayer, USN, for his exceptional actions during Korean War combat on 22 March 1952."

———. "Perils of Pegasus." Unpublished memoir. Letter with accompanying map sketch. Thorin, Duane to Harry Ettinger dated July 20, 2000.

ACKNOWLEDGMENTS

My aim in this book has been to tell human stories against the backdrop of history. Because of war's cruel circumstances and the passage of intervening decades, I embarked with the near certainty that many of the people I would have wished to interview would not be accessible. This sad reality was made all the more certain because the lives of my Navy aviator subjects were always at risk, whether in combat or intervals of peace.

Despite this, I was more than fortunate in locating and talking extensively with those whose accounts proved essential to the fabric of this book. Along the way I also encountered "undiscovered heroes," men and women who could find a place in anyone's pantheon. Foremost in this roster are:

- The two "blind pilots," VF-112's Ed Jackson (along with his indispensable wingman Dayl Crow) and VF-194's Ken Schechter who shared their separate, but equally amazing stories of professionalism and perseverance.
- VF-32's Tom Hudner who shared the details of his instinctive, daring, and selfless efforts to rescue downed squadron-mate Jesse Brown.
- VC-35's Harry Ettinger who was particularly generous with his time in recounting each painful step of his POW sojourn in North Korea. His humor and equanimity served him well during his extended ordeal and still do.
- George Schnitzer who supplemented the contents of his terrific book *Panthers over Korea* (Publish America 2007) with detailed interviews. A fledgling aviator at the beginning of the Korean War, George—as so many did—quickly became a veteran. His fortitude in surmounting the trauma and trials of his horrific postwar crash is an inspiration.
- E. Royce Williams who recounted his harrowing—and to date largely unacknowledged—aerial battle with a gang of MiGs flown by Soviet combat veterans.

For stories where key individuals (Jesse Brown, Duane Thorin, and Howard Thayer, among others) were missing, I was fortunate in being able to talk with others who knew them, witnessed their exploits or both.

- In the case of VF-32's Jesse Brown: his widow Daisy Brown Thorne and squadron mates Tom Hudner and Bill Koenig.

- In the case of HU-1's Duane Thorin: his nephew Darrel Thorin; Harry Ettinger who encountered Thorin both during the failed rescue and later during North Korean captivity; Lynn Waterman, a friend who arranged to post his unpublished memoirs on the Internet; and Earl Lanning and Rulon V. Bird who served as impromptu "ground crew" for Thorin during his tour aboard cruiser *Rochester*.
- In the case of Howard Thayer: Shirley Thayer (she and Daisy Brown Thorne are both living exemplars of the spirit, determination, grace, and quiet heroism of generations of naval aviation spouses), Ken Schechter, and many other squadron mates.

Big portions of the book center on *Essex* and *Valley Forge* flight operations during the fall, winter, and spring of 1952—roughly the period where James A. Michener reported on the air war over Korea and simultaneously laid the groundwork for *The Bridges at Toko-ri*. The contributions of many CVG-5 and ATG-1 aviators added greatly to the authenticity of these portions. Foremost among them were: VF-194's Joe Akagi (himself a "barrier breaker" in U.S. Navy aviation); VF-653's Bob Balser; Ray Edinger, VF-653's executive officer; Jim Holloway, who was instrumental in devising the air task group concept and served as ATG-1 operations officer; VF-194's Dick Kaufman; VF-653's Dave Robertson; and VF-54's Robert Wood. During the time I was wrapping up *Such Men as These* I was honored to attend (at Jim Holloway's invitation), a posthumous award ceremony for Howard Thayer. There I had the pleasure of meeting and talking with a number of Thayer's VF-194's squadron mates who each contributed insights: Dewey Ferrell, Buddy Jordan, Ken Matson, and Lou Stoakes.

My hope is that the individual and collective exploits of such men as these will have an enduring impact on readers. A "forgotten war" need not mean "forgotten heroes."

I also want to thank a number of people who provided essential behind-the-scenes assistance, in particular:

- Barrett Tillman whose books and articles on military aviation have earned him wide, long-standing, and much-deserved acclaim. Though fascinated with aviation, I am not a pilot; while my aviator interviewees were more than helpful in supplying aircraft and flight details, Barrett was most generous in reviewing portions of the manuscript to help shed gaffes and close gaps. (Those that remain are solely mine, not his!)
- Former *Today* host Jim Hartz and NBC colleague Jay Barbree who arranged access to VF-51's Neil Armstrong. While carrying enduring affection for his Navy service and his VF-51 squadron mates, Neil is modest and understandably cautious when it comes to inquiring authors. Jim's and Jay's assurances made the inclusion of Neil's Korean War exploits possible.
- Cheryl Glogovsky of Morris County Library who negotiated hurdles to gain me interlibrary access to the Library of Congress's collection of James A. Michener letters, manuscripts, and notes. Thanks to her efforts I had the leisure to review and hone in on the background material I so much needed.

Final rounds of thanks go to three individuals who in different but important ways were instrumental in bringing this book to print, book shelves, and readers: my astute and indefatigable agent Jim McCarthy of Dystel & Goderich; my knowledgeable and collegial editor Robert Pigeon; and my wife, Mary, whose support and forbearance during these projects flows from her own considerable experience with being "under the gun" of a manuscript deadline.

APPENDIX 1: READY ROOMS

For many hours the admiral remained alone. Then toward morning he heard the anti-submarine patrol go out and as the engines roared he asked, "Where does America get such men?"

—JAMES A. MICHENER, *The Bridges at Toko-Ri*

Joseph Akagi (VF-194): After his final Korean War deployment, Joe Akagi served as a flight instructor until 1954, when he left the Navy and returned to Texas A&M to complete his undergraduate education. After graduation in 1957, Akagi worked briefly for Lockheed Aircraft before rejoining the Navy. He retired from the U.S. Navy in 1977 and subsequently worked as a flight simulator instructor at Whiting Field near Pensacola. Akagi, now a widower, resides in Florida.

Neil A. Armstrong (VF-51) was 22 when he completed active duty and returned to Purdue University to complete his degree. Armstrong then joined the National Advisory Committee for Aeronautics (NACA), the predecessor to NASA, as a research pilot and engineer. Armstrong would eventually fly the X-15 and other experimental aircraft before joining the NASA astronaut corps as part of the Gemini and Apollo Space Programs. Armstrong's second and last spaceflight

was as mission commander of the Apollo 11 moon landing mission on July 20, 1969.

B.G. (Bob) Balser (VF-653): Following war deployment with VF-653, Balser left Navy active duty (he continued as a reservist, retiring as a Commander) in 1953 to embark on a new career with Trans World Airlines (TWA). During his thirty-one years with TWA (initially piloting a prop DC-3 and ultimately captaining a Boeing 747S), Balser flew destination routes to Europe, Asia and Africa. (At age 85 he still pilots his 177 Cardinal RG, single engine Cessna.) Balser and his wife Jacqueline raised two sons and have four grandsons.

Jesse L. Brown (VF-32) was posthumously awarded the Distinguished Flying Cross. The destroyer escort Jesse L. Brown (DE-1089) was named in his honor during launching ceremonies at Avondale Shipyards, Westwego, Louisiana on March 18, 1972. Attending the ceremonies were

Brown's remarried widow Daisy Thorne and Captain Thomas J. Hudner, USN. Daisy Thorne eventually earned a master's degree from Southern Mississippi State, the capstone of a long career in secondary education that ended, fittingly enough, with her retirement from Hattiesburg High School in 1990. Jesse and Daisy's daughter Pamela Knight supervises elder care services for forty-one Mississippi counties. Their grandson Jamal is a mechanical engineer living with his wife and three children in Houston. And their granddaughter Jessica, a political science graduate from Millsap College, is a staff director for the Congressional Black Caucus in Washington, D.C.

Cook Cleland's pace in the 1949 Thompson Trophy Race remained the record for the class until the late 1960s. Cleland (VF-653) remained in the Navy following the Korean War, retiring in 1967 while stationed in Kodiak, Alaska. He then moved to Pensacola and opened an antiques store. A specialist in Early American furniture, Cook Cleland died at age 90 in 2007.

Dayl Crow (VF-112) flew combat missions in a subsequent Korean War deployment, this time with VF-821 aboard carrier *Essex*. Prior to leaving the Navy he flew as a member of the Blue Angels from 1953 to 1956. Crow next flew as a civilian test pilot for Chance Vought Aircraft, testing what became the F8-U Crusader. Crow joined Merrill Lynch in 1960, beginning a thirty year investment advisory career. He opened his own investment firm in 1990. He and his wife Marion raised three children and have two grandchildren. The couple resides in Northern California near Lake Tahoe.

Ray Edinger (VF-653): Following his deployment on *Valley Forge*, Edinger continued in the Navy; after receiving helicopter flight training, he served as a flight instructor, public relations officer and transport plane commander. In 1958, Edinger returned once more to civilian life, this time for a Lockheed missile and

space subsidiary. He continued to fly and maintain his Navy reserve affiliation, finally retiring in 1973. He and his wife Margery raised three children. They recently celebrated their sixty-ninth wedding anniversary.

Harry E. Ettinger (VC-35): After his release from Chinese Communist captivity, Ettinger was assigned to shore duty followed by flight duty with VA-56 and sea duty as *Lexington* (CVA-16) First Lieutenant. (During this period, Ettinger recalled, he removed the final piece of metal shrapnel from the leg wound received when his Skyraider was shot down over North Korea.) In 1965 he commanded VA-25 during its first Vietnam War cruise aboard carrier *Midway* (CVA-41). After two subsequent war cruises assigned to Carrier Division Nine and attendance at the Naval War College, Ettinger was assigned to the Joint Chiefs of Staff. He retired as a Captain in 1974 and moved to coastal California. He and his late wife Jean raised three children; he has four grandchildren and one great grandchild.

James L. Holloway III (VF-52): Following two tours of duty in Korea, Holloway went on to command the USS *Enterprise* (CVN-65), a Sixth Fleet Carrier Striking Force, and the Seventh Fleet. Admiral Holloway served as Chief of Naval Operations from 1974 to 1978 and as Chairman of the Joint Chiefs of Staff (JCS). He retired from the Navy in 1978 and more recently retired as Chairman of the Board of the Naval Historical Foundation and the Naval Aviation Foundation.

Thomas J. Hudner Jr. (VF-32): Hudner's was the first Navy Medal of Honor awarded for actions in the Korean War. When Hudner returned to Fall River, the city proclaimed "Thomas Hudner Day," presenting him with a check for $1,000. Hudner endorsed the check and sent it to Daisy Brown who by then had returned to school. Following his tour with VF-32, Hudner held a variety of training, operational and staff assignments, including service as Executive Officer of USS *Kitty Hawk* (CVA-63), exchange pilot flying Air Force interceptors, and with the Joint Chiefs of Staff at the Pentagon. He retired from the Navy in 1973 with the rank of Captain. He currently serves as vice president of Battleship Cove, the USS *Massachusetts* war memorial and museum complex in Fall River.

Ed Jackson (VF-112): Following the Korean War, Ed Jackson served initially as a military test pilot attached to McDonnell Douglas in St. Louis. Following subsequent squadron assignments, he completed his undergraduate schooling at the University of Mississippi and went on for additional education at the Naval Postgraduate School (where he would later serve as an instructor). After a ship's company tour aboard carrier *Bennington* (CV-20), Jackson served as XO of VF-141 from 1963 to 1965. He retired from the Navy in 1974 after heading up maintenance operations at Cecil Field, Jacksonville. He and his wife Mary Grace have two children and a granddaughter; they reside in the Jacksonville area.

Richard Kaufman (VF-194): During the balance of his 24-year Naval career Dick flew the F9F Panther, FJ-2 Fury, and other jet aircraft from twelve different carriers. He also served as the Guided Missile Officer aboard the carrier *Shangri-La*, and served with the Bureau of Naval Weapons during the Vietnam Era, shepherding the production of the OV-10 aircraft. He retired in 1970 and later received his PhD from the University of Texas. He has taught Economics and Finance at Texas Christian University, Ball State University, and, most recently, at California State University. Retired now from teaching, he lives in Northern California with his wife Norma Anglum Kaufman. They have four children, eleven grandchildren, and four great-grandchildren.

William Koenig (VF-32) continued flying with VF-32 through December 1952 when he joined the Naval Air Basic Train-

ing Command as a flight and air to air gunnery instructor. Following additional squadron assignments, Koenig was assigned to the Naval Aviation Safety Center specializing in flight escape systems and protective equipment. From 1964 to 1967 he commanded the Naval Aerospace Recovery Facility, El Centro, California, where he personally qualified as a master naval parachutist. Commander Koenig retired from active duty with the Navy in 1969. In 1985 he retired from a subsequent civilian career with the Travelers Insurance as a specialist in the insurer's Engineering and Loss Control Division. Koenig and his wife Dorothy, who have two children, recently celebrated their fifty-third wedding anniversary.

Kenneth A. Schechter (VF-194) was awarded the Distinguished Flying Cross, Purple Heart, and Air Medal. Physically retired from the Navy, Ken went on to receive an A.B. in Economics from Stanford and an M.B.A. from Harvard. After a long and varied business career, he retired from the insurance industry. Schechter and wife Sue live in Southern California.

George Schnitzer (VF-831): After graduation from Stanford in 1958, Schnitzer began a forty-two year computer engineering career, specializing in both military and commercial applications for firms such as Lockheed, Computer Sciences Corporation (CSC) and Science Application International (SAIC). In Washington, D.C., Schnitzer served as Deputy Division Manager for the Nation Photographic Interpretation Center (NPIC), part of the CIA. He later founded Ternary Corporation, a business he eventually sold in 1995. After retirement Schnitzer volunteered for the National Air and Space Museum and, encouraged by a former squadron commander, began researching and writing an account of his naval aviation experience. Beverly, Schnitzer's wife of fifty-two years, died in January 2005 after a long illness. In March 2006 he married Joan M. Brazier and the two subsequently moved to North Carolina.

Schnitzer's account of his 161 air combat missions—*Panthers Over Korea*—was published in 2007.

Duane Thorin (HU-1): After his release from captivity, Thorin lived for a time in Southern California. Thorin eventually worked at the National Security Agency and lived in the suburbs of Washington D.C. During that time, he and his wife Lillian—nicknamed Lee—separated, although they never divorced. In retirement, Thorin returned to Nebraska, eventually settling in Chambers, not far from his boyhood home in Ewing. He spent his last years working to restore old homes and operating a small lumber mill. He died in 2002.

E. Royce Williams (VF-781) remained in the Navy until his retirement as a Captain in 1980. During his career he served as an exchange pilot with the USAF flying the F-86 and F-100. He also served as XO and CO of VF-33 on board the USS *Enterprise* (CVN-65), flying the F8-E Crusader, and later on board the USS *America* (CV-66) flying the F-4 Phantom

11. During the Vietnam War he also served as an Air Wing Commander and later as commanding officer of the USS *Eldorado* (LCC-11). He married his hometown sweetheart, Cam, in 1947. They have three sons and currently reside in Southern California.

Robert "Woody" Wood (VF-54): Following his tour with VF-54 aboard *Essex*, Wood completed a B.S. and M.S. in Aeronautical Engineering. He then served as an aircraft commander and squadron maintenance officer flying twin-engine A3D Skywarriors, the heaviest aircraft ever flown from an aircraft carrier. Subsequent assignments involved training, aircraft maintenance, weapons systems and ground support equipment both on the West Coast and in Washington D.C. After retiring from the Navy as Captain in 1971, Wood served as assistant director for an educational institute at Brigham Young University. He and Marva, his wife of sixty-three years, raised a daughter and three sons; they have thirty-two grandchildren and thirty-eight great-grandchildren.

Carrier, air group, and carrier-based squadron deployments during the Korean War [*] *with partial listings of air group and squadron personnel* [**]

Valley Forge (CV-45) with CVG-5 (May 1, 1950–December 1, 1950)

- Harvey P. Lanham, CAG

VF-51 (F9F-3)
- E. W. Brown
- John Henry Nyhuis (KIA—August 12, 1950)
- Leonard Plog
- Edward Dominquez (squadron deck crew; KIA—September 12, 1950)

VF-52 (F9F-3)
VF-53 (F4U-4B)
- John Richard Brinkley (KIA—December 23, 1950)
- William Edmund Brown (KIA—September 25, 1950)
- Keith Edward Thomson (Lost—July 25, 1950; died later in POW captivity)

VF-54 (F4U-4B)
- Arthur Wesly Hanton (KIA—August 10, 1950)

---

* Adapted from "Carrier, carrier-based squadrons and non-carrier-based squadron deployments during the Korean War, " Naval Historical Center online document
** Squadron personnel listings compiled from interviewee records and official U.S. Navy documents. Fatality listings and dates derived in part from Korean War Project (http://www.koreanwar.org/) online documentation

- Robert Wood

VA-55 (AD-4/Q)
- Don Richard Stephens (KIA—
  July 22, 1950)

VC-3 (Detachment C; F4U-5N/AD-3N)
VC-11(Detachment; AD-3W)
HedRon-1 (Detachment; F4U-5P)
HU-1 (Detachment; HO3S-1)

Badoeng Strait (CVE-116)
(July 1950–February 1951)

VMF-323 (F4U-4B)
- Vivian Moses (KIA—August 11, 1950)

HU-1 (Detachment; HO3S-1)

Sicily (CVE-118) (July 1950–
February 1951)

VMF-214 (F4U-4B; aboard August–
November)
VS-21 (TBM-3E/S; aboard to December)
HU-1 (Detachment; HO3S-1)

Boxer (CV-21) with CVG-2 (August
24, 1950–November 11, 1950)

VF-23 (F4U-4)
VF-63 (F4U-4)
- Franklin Smith Jr. (KIA—September
  19, 1950)

VF-64 (F4U-4)
VF-24 (F4U-4)
- Claude C. Howell Jr. (September 29,
  1950; died in captivity)

VA-65 (AD-2)
- Clifford Eugene Seeman (KIA—
  September 20, 1950)

VC-3 (Detachment; F4U-5N)
VC-11 (Detachment A; AD-3W)
VC-33 (Detachment; AD-4N)
VC-61 (Detachment; F4U-4P)
HU-1 (Detachment; HO3S-1)

Bairoko (CVE-115) (November 1950–
August 1951)

VS-21 (TBM-3S/W; aboard December–
February)
VS-23 (TBM-3E/S/W; aboard February–
August)
HU-1 (Detachment; HO3S-1)

Bataan (CVL-29) (November 1950–
June 1951)

VMF-212 (F4U-4; aboard December–
March)
VMF-312 (F4U-4; aboard March–June)
HU-1 (Detachment 8; HO3S-1)

Valley Forge (CV-45) with CVG-2
(December 6, 1950–April 7, 1951*)

VF-64 (F4U-4)
VF-63 (F4U-4)
VF-24 (F4U-4)
- Richard Charles Loomer (KIA—
  March 19, 1951)

VA-65 (F4U-4)
VC-3 (Detachment; F4U-5N)
- David Allen McCoskrie (KIA—
  February 13, 1951)

VC-11 (Detachment; AD-4W)
VC-35 (Detachment 4; AD-4N)
VC-61 (Detachment F; F4U-4P)
HU-1 (Detachment; HO3S-1)

---

*CVG-2 *Boxer* (CV-21) crossdecked with
CVG-11 from *Philippine Sea* (CV-47) on 28
March 1951 and *Valley Forge* returned to San
Diego, California, April 7 with CVG-11.

Philippine Sea (CV-47) with CVG-11
(July 1950–March, 1951*)

CVG-11
- Raymond William (Sully) Vogel Jr.,
  CO (KIA—August 19, 1950)
- L. K. Bruestle, LSO

VF-111 (F9F-2)**
- W. T. Amen, CO
- R. S. Bates
- L. R. Brewer
- D. J. Brimm
- H. E. Camp
- Leonard Ray Cheshire
- Carl E. Dace
- C. A. Dallard
- J. W. Eash
- J. R. M. Fisher
- U. L. Fretwell
- R. M. Gerdes
- R. A. Guyer
- W. L. Hall
- H. L. Haro
- A. Hengl
- G. H. Holloman
- W. P. Johnson
- C. B. Jones
- R. M. Killingsworth
- R. C. Knight
- G. A. Martin
- J. E. Nicklin
- J. D. Omvig
- J. V. Polosky
- E. R. Reimers
- E. M. Tollgard
- J. W. Waggoner
- C. W. Walker
- R. R. Yount

VF-112 (F9F-2)
- Ralph Weymouth, CO, later CO, CVG-11
- John L. Butts, CO
- R. E. Aslund
- Dayl E. Crow
- Doug Haywood
- Edward D. Jackson Jr.
- Curtis Latham Smith, (KIA—August 20, 1950)

VF-113 (F4U-4B)
- John Frederick Kail, (KIA—August 5, 1950)
- Bunny McCallum

VF-114 (F4U-4B)
VA-115 (AD-4/Q)
- William Donald Noonan, (KIA—November 27, 1950)

VC-3 (Detachment 3; F4U-5N/AD-4N)
VC-11 (Detachment; AD-4W)
VC-61 (Detachment 3; F4U-4P)
HU-1 (Detachment 3; HO3S-1)
- Harry Sundberg, CO
- Duane Thorin
- Chester Todd

---

*CVG-11 crossdecked with CVG-2 from *Valley Forge*; *Philippine Sea* returned to San Diego, California, June 9 with CVG-2.
** Roster from June 1950 from VF-111 historian Hank "Omar" van der Lugt.

Philippine Sea (CV-47) with CVG-2 (March 2, 1951–June 9, 1951)

VF-64 (F4U-4)
- James Blanding Dick Jr. (KIA—May 29, 1951)
- Raymond William Murphy (KIA—May 29, 1951)

VF-63 (F4U-4)
- William Robert Ball Jr. (KIA—May 19, 1951)
- Maurice Alfred Tuthill (KIA—April 5, 1951)
- Clarence Edward West (KIA—April 24, 1951)

VF-24 (F4U-4)
- Emory Ronald Coffman (KIA—April 20, 1951)

VA-65 (AD-2/Q)
- Elwood Earl Brey (KIA—April 16, 1951)

VC-3 (Detachment; F4U-5N)
VC-11 (Detachment; AD-4W)
VC-35 (Detachment 4; AD-4N)
VC-61 (Detachment; F4U-4P)
HU-1 (Detachment; HO3S-1)

Leyte (CV-32) with CVG-3 (September 1950–February 1951)

CVG-3
- Walter Madden, CAG
- George Hudson (LSO)

VA-35
- Ralph Bagwell, CO
- Roland Russell Batson Jr. (KIA—November 11, 1950)

VF-31 (F9F-2)
- George C. Simmons, CO

VF-32 (F4U-4)
- Dugald (Doug) T. Neill, CO
- Dick Cevoli, XO
- Jesse Leroy Brown (KIA—December 4, 1950)
- E. W. Byron
- J. J. Cotchen (Mediterranean deployment only)
- F. J. Cronin
- W. G. Ferris
- R. E. Fowler
- W. G. Gelonek (Mediterranean deployment only)
- M. Goode
- Thomas J. Hudner Jr.
- R. H. Jester
- H. N. Key
- Bill Koenig
- C. M. Lane
- Ralph McQueen
- A. A. Miller
- C. R. Mohring (Mediterranean deployment only)
- L. E. Nelson
- R. Roth
- B. C. Rudy
- H. A. Sargent
- F. H. Shefield
- R. A. Stack
- J. R. Stevens (Mediterranean deployment only)
- W. F. Whalen
- W. Wilkinson

VF-33 (F4U-4)
- Horace H. Epes Jr., CO

VC-4 (Detachment 3; F4U-5N)
- O. E. McCutcheon, OinC

VC-33 (Detachment 3; AD-4N)
- E. W. Silverthorne, OinC

VC-62 (Detachment 3; F4U-5P)
- L. B. Cornell, OinC
- Mike Alexatos
- William George Wagner (KIA—November 28, 1950)

HU-2 (Detachment 3; HO3S-1)
- A. E. Al Monahan, OinC

Princeton (CV-37) with CVG-19 (November 1950–May 1951*)

- Richard C. Merrick, CAG
- George A. Parker
- Charles Ramsay Stapler (KIA—June 10, 1951)

VF-191 (F9F-2)
- John Joseph Magda, CO (KIA—March 8, 1951)
- Lowell Ray Brewer (KIA—May 7, 1951)
- Pat Murphy
- Florian "Sober" Soberski
- Gerald James Sullivan (KIA—May 6, 1951)

VF-192 (F4U-4)
- Marcus Paul Merner (KIA—January 28, 1951)
- William Ernest Patton (KIA—March 10, 1951)
- Richard Marshall Ruppenthal (KIA—April 21, 1951)

VF-193 (F4U-4)
- Clement Craig, CO
- Thomas Clarence Biesterveld (April 29, 1951; died in POW captivity)
- Ronald Eugene Paris (KIA—December 15, 1950)

- E. A. Parker
- Hugo Verner Scarsheim (KIA—December 24, 1950)
- Harold Trolle (KIA—February 10, 1951)

VA-195 (AD-4)
- Harold G. "Swede" Carlson, CO
- K. W. "Tex" Atkinson
- Robert E. Bennett
- Evan Charles Harris (KIA—January 28, 1951)

VC-3 (Detachment F; F4U-5N)
- Baxter Hughes Cook (KIA—March 9, 1951)
- Albert Rowe Tiffany (KIA—April 22, 1951)

VC-11 (Detachment; AD-4W)
VC-35 (Detachment 3; AD-4N)
Pilots:
- Frank Metzner, OinC
- Atlee F. Clapp
- Addison R. English
- John Ness

Air Crewmen:
- Kenneth Alred
- Richard K. Green

VC-61 (Detachment; F9F-2P)
HU-1 (Detachment; HO3S-1)

———

*Air Group transferred at Yokosuka, Japan, CV-37 remained in WestPac.

Princeton (CV-37) with CVG-19X (May 1951–August 1951)

VF-23 (F9F-2)
- Bruce Bowen Lloyd (KIA—July 28, 1951)
- Philip Sprague Randolph Jr. (KIA)

VF-821(F4U-4)
- Royce M Carruth (KIA—June 20, 1951)

- James Charles Hughes Jr. (KIA—August 9, 1951)
- Donald Vaughan Ray (KIA—July 30, 1951)

VF-871 (F4U-4)
- Horace Melvin Hawkins (KIA—May 18, 1951)
- Frank Martin III (KIA—July 18, 1951)
- John Peter Moody Jr. (KIA—July 22, 1951)

VA-55 (AD-4)
- Harley Stafford Harris Jr. (KIA—June 28, 1951)

VC-3 (Detachment; F4U-5N)
VC-11 (Detachment; AD-4W)
VC-35 (Detachment; AD-4N)
- David Arthur Arrivee (KIA—June 21, 1951)

VC-61 (Detachment; F9F-2P)
HU-1 (Detachment; HO3S-1)

Boxer (CV-21) with CVG-101 (March 2, 1951–October 24, 1951)

VF-721 (F9F-2B)
VF-791 (F4U-4)
VF-884 (F4U-4)
- Glenn Frye Carmichael, CO (KIA—May 24, 1951)
- Marion Thomas Dragastin (KIA—May 18, 1951)
- Charles Garrison (Lost—May 18, 1951; later died in POW captivity)
- Harold Roosevelt Podorson (KIA—September 18, 1951)
- Henry Brownell Rathbone (KIA—September 13, 1951)
- Paul Laverne Schaefer (KIA—June 20, 1951)
- Alfred William Clement Thomas (KIA—April 18, 1951)

VA-702 (AD-2/4Q)
- Fenton B. Robbins (KIA—May 7, 1951)

VC-3 (Detachment F; F4U-5NL)
VC-11 (Detachment F; AD-4W)
VC-35 (Detachment F; AD-4N)
VC-61 (Detachment F; F9F-2P)
HU-1 (Detachment; HO3S-1)

**Bon Homme Richard (CV-31) with
CVG-102 (May 1951–December 1951)**

VF-781 (VF-122) (F9F-2B)
- Ralph Nelson Mew (KIA—
  March 22, 1953)
- Roy Taylor (KIA—April 13, 1953)

VF-783 (F4U-4)
- Arthur Lionel Dixon (KIA—
  July 4, 1951)
- Leonard Arlo Gundert (KIA—
  October 3, 1951)
- Eugene Daniel Redmond (KIA—
  June 3, 1951)

VF-874 (F4U-4)
- Fred Leslie Koch (KIA—
  August 11, 1951)
- William Henry Mero (KIA—
  September 4, 1951)
- James Joseph Venes (KIA—
  August 11, 1951)

VA-923 (AD-3/4Q)
- Orville Melvin Cook (KIA—
  July 18, 1951)
- James Aloysius Savage (KIA—
  July 6, 1951)

VC-3 (Detachment G; F4U-5NL)
VC-11 (Detachment G; AD-4W)
VC-35 (Detachment G; AD-4N)
VC-61 (Detachment G; F9F-2P)
HU-1 (Detachment; HO3S-1)

**Sicily (CVE-118) (May 1951–October
1951)**

VMF-323 (F4U-4; aboard June–
  September)
VS-892 (TBM-3S/W; aboard until
  mid-July)
HU-1 (Detachment; HO3S-1)

**Essex (CV-9) with CVG-5 (June 26,
1951–March 25, 1952)**

- Marshall U. Beebe, CVG-5 CO

VF-51 (F9F-2)
- Ernest M. Beauchamp, CO
- Bernard Sevilla, XO
- Neil A. Armstrong
- James Joseph Ashford (KIA—
  September 4, 1951)
- William W. Bowers
- Ross Kay Bramwell (KIA—
  September 4, 1951)
- John W. Carpenter
- Leonard Ray Cheshire (KIA—
  January 26, 1952)
- Herschel L. Gott
- Herbert A. Graham
- Thomas B. Hayward
- Francis N. Jones
- Robert J. Kaps
- Kenneth C. Kramer
- William A. Mackey
- Daniel V. Marshall
- Donald C. McNaught
- John M. Moore
- Robert E. Rostine
- George E. Russell
- Glen Howard Rickelton (KIA—
  January 6, 1952)
- Wiley A. Scott
- Harold C. Schwan
- Richard M. Wenzell
- Kenneth I. Danneberg, Intelligence
  Officer
- Howard C. Zehetner, Maintenance
  Officer

VF-172 (F2H-2)
- M. E. Barnett, CO
- Andrew Brtis
- Otho Crowl
- John Kemp Keller (KIA—
  September 16, 1951)
- Irad Blair Oxley, (KIA—
  October 16, 1951)

VF-53 (F4U-4/B)
- Herman Trum, CO

- John Abbott
- Richard Alan Bateman (KIA—
  October 28, 1951)
- Leonard Doss
- Eugene Leo Franz (KIA—
  August 23, 1951)
- Francis Gene Gergen (KIA—
  February 21, 1952)
- Ed Laney

VF-54 (AD-2/4/L/Q)
- Paul N. Gray, CO
- Lou Ahrendts
- William Arnold Bryant Jr. (KIA—
  November 17, 1951)
- Sam Ellison
- Joseph Henry Gollner (KIA—
  January 11, 1952)
- Eugene Brewer Hale (KIA—
  November 27, 1951)
- Raymond Gene Kelly (KIA—
  January 9, 1952)
- Thomas Lewis
- Ted Martin
- Bert Masson
- Boyd Muncie
- Joseph Buford Parse Jr. (KIA—
  September 8, 1951)
- Frank N. Sistrunk (KIA—
  September 3, 1951)
- Ken Shugart
- Lauren D. Smith (KIA—
  August 26, 1951)
- Cordice Isaac Teague (KIA—
  October 6, 1951)
- Robert Wood

VC-3 (Detachment B; F4U-5NL)
VC-11 (Detachment B; AD-4W)
VC-35 (Detachment B; AD-4NL)
Pilots:
- Felix Bertagna
- Sam Murphey
- Loren Dickerson Smith (KIA—
  August 26, 1951)
- Red Stillwell

Air Crewmen and Enlisted Personnel:
- Phillip Kendall Balch (KIA—
  August 26, 1951)

VC-61 (Detachment B; F9F-2P)
- Sutt Jaynes, OinC
- Earl Ray
- Ralph Risdal

HU-1 (Detachment; HO3S-1)

Rendova (CVE-114) (July 1951–December 1951)

VMF-212 (F4U-4; aboard September–
  December 6)
VS-892 (TBM-3S/W; aboard July–
  September, December)
HU-1 (Detachment; HO3S-1)

Antietam (CV-36) with CVG-15 (September 1951–May 1952)

VF-713 (F4U-4)
- Dorsey
- William Walter Marwood (KIA—
  January 29, 1952)
- Glenn Alton Riley (KIA—
  December 19, 1951)
- L. O. Warfield

VF-831 (F9F-2B)
- Anthony J. (Tony) Denman, CO
- John J. Barteluce
- George M. Benas
- W. J. Betz
- W. J. Callahan (Killed September 13,
  1951 off Hawaii)
- A. C. Ciraldo
- R. A. Clark
- Charlie J. Clarkson
- Richard C. (Dick) Clinite
- A. J. Denman
- George DePolo (seriously injured
  November 4, 1951)
- J. C. Dunn
- Herman W. (Bill) Jones
- Robert R. King
- R .J. Laturno
- A. Modansky
- J. E. Joe Perry Jr.
- Larry L. Quiel
- Dave Rose
- W. E. Ryan

- Billy Jo Sanders
- George Schnitzer
- R. E. Seixas

VF-837 (F9F-2B)
- George Spencer Brainard (KIA—
  November 4, 1951)

Air Crewmen
- Edward Joseph Cavanaugh Farrell
  (KIA—January 21, 1952)

VA-728 (AD-4/L/Q)
- George Walter Johnson (KIA—
  March 2, 1952)

VC-3 (Detachment D; F4U-5N)
- Guy Bordleon
- Kramer

VC-11 (Detachment D; AD-4W)
- Masek

VC-35 (Detachment D; AD-4NL)
VC-61 (Detachment D; F9F-2P)
HU-1 (Detachment HO3S-1)

**Valley Forge (CV-45) with ATG-1
(October 15, 1951–July 3, 1952)**

ATG-1 Staff
- Fritz Crabill, CAG
- James L. Holloway III
- Ryan Johnson
- Dale Shover

VF-111 (F9F-2/B)
- Frank Welch, CO (Killed—
  December 1951)
- John Ramsey, CO
- Jack Anderson
- Carl E. Dace
- Bill Fassey
- Bill Finley
- Veron Fitch
- Norman Gear
- Ron Gerdes
- Red Hix
- George Holloman
- Bob Loomer

- Jack McCoy
- Dick Omvig
- Earl Reimers
- Emil Smutzler
- Smokey Tolgard

VF-52 (F9F-2/B)
- Herbert Lester Baslee Jr., CO (KIA—
  March 17, 1952)
- James Kinsella, CO
- Bill Brook
- John Zachary Carros (KIA—
  May 2, 1952)
- Dick Dasisman
- Alan W. Duck (KIA—
  October 23, 1951)
- Paul Hayek
- R. D. Haynes
- Ray Loux
- Warren Parr
- Howard Rutledge
- Dave Shepherd
- Bob Smith
- Mike South
- Charles Glasgow Strahley (KIA—
  March 21, 1952)
- David Franklin Tatum (KIA—
  February 19, 1952)
- Ray Volpe

VF-653
Aviators:
- Cook Cleland, CO
- Ray Edinger, XO
- B. G. Balser
- M. H. Barr
- Roland G. Busch (MIA—
  May 27, 1952)
- William R. Clarke
- Thomas Davis
- G. (Guy) Dunn
- Ralph Evans
- Frank W. M. Frankovich (KIA—
  January 9, 1952)
- Gordon Galloway (KIA—
  May 30, 1952)
- Channing Gardner (KIA—
  May 29, 1952)
- Robert Geffel
- John F. Gibbons

- John Gray
- William L. Hartman Jr.
- Robert Hermann
- Richard Jensen (KIA—February 11, 1952)
- Bob Jesswine
- Roy Johnson
- Ed Kearns
- Donald E. London (Killed—December 9, 1951)
- Sam McKee
- Paul Pierson
- James T. Porterfield (Killed—December 9, 1951)
- David W. Robertson
- J. R. (Ross) Rohleder
- Joseph D. Sanko (KIA—May 13, 1952)
- Robert L. Sobey (KIA—December 22, 1951)
- Harold Sterrett (MIA—May 26, 1952)
- Henry R. Sulkowski
- G. N. (Nip) Wilson
- Hull L. Wright (KIA—March 11, 1952)

Ground Officers and Crew:
- W. J. Zielinski

VF-194 (AD)
- Robert Schreiber, CO
- Tom Pugh, XO (KIA—December 18, 1951)
- Donald S. Brubaker, XO
- Joe Akagi
- John Berry
- George Blease
- Howard Borgerding
- Stan Broughton
- Charles Brown
- Hugh Damron
- Dean Hofferth
- Elmer Hohn
- Faye Johnson
- Dick Kaufman
- Ken Matson
- Dick McCleod
- Dean Melton
- Bo Miller
- Joe Molnar
- Oren Peterson

- Ken Schechter
- Lou Stoakes
- Howard Thayer
- John Charles Workman (KIA—April 20, 1952)

VC-3 (Detachment H; F4U-5N/NL)
- Bob Taylor, O-I-C
- Carter
- John Patrick McKenna (KIA—February 8, 1952)

VC-11 (Detachment H(7); AD-4W/2Q)
- Dave Harvey

VC-35 (Detachment H(10); AD-4NL)
Aviators:
- Mel Schluter, OinC
- Vance Askew
- Harry E. Ettinger
- Knobby Walsh

Air Crewmen and Enlisted Personnel:
- Dave Besso
- Ted Bryce
- Julian Gilleland
- Jess McElroy

VC-61 (Detachment H; F9F-2P/F2H-2P)
- Arvil Bachelor
- Alan N. Hoff (KIA—March 11, 1952)
- Jack Rollins
- Marv Warner

HU-1 (Detachment 20; HO3S-1)

Philippine Sea (CV-47) with CVG-11 (December 1951–August 1952)

VF-112 (F9F-2)
- James V. Rowney, CO

VF-113 (F4U-4)
- Morris Allen Anderson (KIA—January 28, 1952)
- Gerald Rodney Brown (KIA—June 2, 1952)
- Grover Cleveland Chick Jr. (KIA—July 4, 1952)

VF-114 (F4U-4)
VA-115 (AD-4)
- C. H. Carr, CO
- M. K. Lake
- Jerry D. Wolfe (KIA—
  February 7, 1952)

VC-3 (Unit C; F4U-5N&NL)
- Boyd Dale Knox (KIA—
  February 19, 1952)

VC-11 (Unit C; AD-4W)
VC-35 (Unit C; AD-4NL/Q/-2Q)
VC-61 (Unit C; F2H-2P/F9F-2P)
HU-1 (Unit; HO3S-1)
Aviators:
- W. K. Martin, OIC
- H. E. Talkington

Detachment Crew:
- Doug Froling
- J. C. Loughran
- G. W. Mundell
- F. G. Schafer
- C. L. Sharp
- R. A. Zahm

Badoeng Strait (CVE-116) (September 1951–March 1952)

VMF-212 (F4U-4)
VS-892 (TBM-3S/W; aboard October–
  December)
HU-1 (Detachment 18; HO3S-1)

Bairoko (CVE-115) (December 1951–June 1952)

VS-25 (AF-2S/W; aboard to January,
  returned in May)
HU-1 (Detachment; HO3S-1)

Bataan (CVL-29) (January 1952–August 1952)

VMA-312 (F4U-4/B; aboard April–July)
VS-25 (AF-2S/W)
HU-1 (Detachment; HO3S-1)

Boxer (CV-21) with CVG-2 (February 1952–September 1952)

CVG-2
- A. L. Downing, CAG

VF-64 (F4U-4)
- John Edward Kordeleski (KIA—
  May 16, 1952)

VF-63 (F4U-4)
VF-24 (F9F-2)
- Jack Walter Griffith (KIA—
  July 4, 1952)

VA-65 (AD-4)
- Walter Philip Neel (KIA—
  April 18, 1952)
- Richard Carl Rowe (KIA—
  June 17, 1952)

VC-3 (Detachment A; F4U-5N)
VC-11 (Detachment A; AD-4W)
VC-35 (Detachment A; AD-3N/4N/2Q)
Air Crewmen:
- Billy Gene Soden (KIA—
  August 6, 1952)

VC-61 (Detachment A; F9F-2P)
HU-1 (Detachment: HO3S-1)
GMU-90 (AD-2Q/F6F-5K)

Princeton (CV-37) with CVG-19 (March 1952–November 3, 1952)

VF-191 (F9F-2)
- Ralph Cross (KIA—June 14, 1952)
- Forrest Dean Swisher (KIA—July 27,
  1952)

VF-192 (F4U-4)
- Conrad Leroy Neville (KIA—
  October 7, 1952)
- Howard Wilson Westervelt Jr. (KIA—
  September 12, 1952)

VF-193 (F4U-4)
- William Ellis Pulliam II (KIA—
  August 2, 1952)

- John Russell Shaughnessy (KIA—
October 7, 1952)
- Owen Foch Williams (KIA—
September 17, 1952)

VA-195 (AD-4)
- Lynn Francis Du Temple (KIA—
July 11, 1952)
- Charles Rutherford Holman (KIA—
August 1, 1952)
- Richard Loran Jackson (KIA—
June 12, 1952)
- Durward Jerome Tennyson (KIA—
June 6, 1952)

VC-3 (Detachment E; F4U-5N)
- Robert Jay Humphrey (KIA—
June 12, 1952)

VC-11 (Detachment E; AD-4W)
VC-35 (Detachment E; AD-4NL)
Pilots:
- Richard Eugene Garver (KIA—
June 8, 1952)

Air Crewmen:
- Adler Earl Ruddell (KIA—
June 8, 1952)

VC-61 (Detachment E; F9F-2P)
HU-1 (Detachment; HO3S-1)

**Bon Homme Richard (CVA-31) with
CVG-7 (May 1952–January 1953)**

VF-71 (F9F-2)
VF-72 (F9F-2)
VF-74 (F4U-4)
- Donald Edwin Adams (KIA—
August 14, 1952)
- Ronald Dow Eaton (KIA—
June 25, 1952)

VA-75 (AD-4)
- Halbert Knapp Evans, CO (KIA—
December 5, 1952)

VC-4 (Detachment 41; F4U-5N)
VC-33 (Detachment 41; AD-4NL)
- Edward Patrick Cummings (KIA—
July 11, 1952)
- Marck Loos Tooker Jr. (KIA—
July 11, 1952)

VC-12 (Detachment 41; AD-4W)
VC-61 (Detachment N; F2H-2P/F9F-2P)
HU-1 (Detachment; HO3S-1)

**Sicily (CVE-118) (May 1952–
December 1952)**

VMA-312 (F4U-4B; aboard September–
mid-October)
VS-931 (AF-2S/W; aboard May–August
and mid-October–early December)
HU-1 (Detachment; HO3S-1)

**Essex (CVA-9) with ATG-2
(June 1952–February 1953)**

VF-23 (F9F-2)
- Leo Thomas Freitas (KIA—
November 21, 1952)
- Daniel Lorenz Musetti (KIA—
November 22, 1952)

VF-821 (F9F-2)
- Dayl E. Crow

VF-871 (F4U-4)
- Alfred Edward Nauman Jr. (KIA—
October 18, 1952)

VA-55 (AD-4)
- John William Healy (KIA—November
23, 1952)
- Gordon Harwood Chandler (deck
crewman; KIA—November 1, 1952)

VC-3 (Detachment I; F4U-5N)
VC-11 (Detachment I; AD-4W)
VC-35 (Detachment; AD-4N)
VC-61 (Detachment; F2H-2P)
HU-1 (Detachment; HO3S-1)

Badoeng Strait (CVE-116) (July 1952–February 1953)

VMA-312 (F4U-4/B; aboard October–February)
- Richard W. (Bunny) Benton
- James L. Cooper
- Bryce Howerton
- Timothy Ireland
- Alexander Watson

VS-931 (AF-2S/W; aboard August–October)
HU-1 (Detachment; HO3S-1)

Kearsarge (CVA-33) with CVG-101* (August 1952–March 1953)

VF-11 (F2H-2)
- Denny Powell Phillips, CO (KIA—January 23, 1953)
- John Brown Heddons (KIA—June 7, 1952)
- James Franklyn Lee (KIA—December 30, 1952)

VF-721** (F9F-2)
- Robert Cushman Hopping, XO (KIA—November 21, 1952)
- Charles Olan Glisson Jr. (KIA—November 1, 1952)

VF-884** (F4U-4)
- Frederick William Bowen, CO (KIA—November 8, 1952)
- Eugene Fred Johnson (KIA—October 4, 1952)
- Richard Glenn Rider (KIA—November 1, 1952)
- John William Shook Jr. (KIA—September 30, 1952)
- Harold Thomas Walker (KIA—April 7, 1951)

VA-702** (AD-4/L)
- Bruce Thomas Simonds (KIA—October 16, 1952)
- Donald Hugo Hagge (KIA—February 8, 1953)

VC-3 (Detachment F; F4U-5N)
VC-11 (Detachment F; AD-4W)
VC-35 (Detachment F; AD-4N)
Pilots:
- Francis Coleman Anderson (KIA—January 28, 1953)

Air Crewmen:
- John Robert Schmid (KIA—January 28, 1953)

VC-61 (Detachment F; F2H-2P)
HU-1 (Detachment 15; HO3-1)

---

*CVG-101 re-designated CVG-14 on February 4, 1953.
**VF-721, VF-884 and VA-702 became VF-141, VF-144 and VA-145.

Oriskany (CVA-34) with CVG-102* (September 1952–May 1953)

- G. P. Chase, CAG

VF-781 (F9F-5)**
- S. R. Holm, CO
- Samuel Parsons, XO
- Gerry Barnett
- Ed Bethel
- Harry Ross Blake
- John Bybee
- Donald (Jeff) Davis
- Claire Elwood
- Lou Ives
- Jerry McCabe
- McConell
- John Middleton
- Jim O'Connell
- Charlie Ray
- Charles (Charlie) Roberts
- David Rowlands
- Randolph Taylor Scoggan (KIA—April 20, 1953)
- Jack Stiles
- E. Royce Williams
- Robert W. (Bob) MacPhail, IO

VF-783 (F9F-5)**
- W. R. Wyrick, CO

VF-874 (F4U-4)**
- M. D. Carmody, CO

VA-923 Detachment G (AD-3)**
- John Carl Micheel, CO (KIA—
  February 1, 1953)
- George Aloysius Gaudette Jr. (KIA—
  November 15, 1952)
- James Alexander Hudson (KIA—
  December 22, 1952)
- A. L. Riker (MIA—November 4, 1952)

VC-3 Detachment G (F4U-5N)
- G. W. Staeheli, OinC

VC-11 Detachment G (AD-3W)
- H. F. Gernert, OinC

VC-35 Detachment G (AD-4N)
- W. P. Kiser, OinC

VC-61 Detachment G (F2H-2P)
- J. F. Grosser, OinC

HU-1 Detachment (HO3S-1)

———
*CVG-102 re-designated CVG-12 on
February 4, 1953.
**VF-781, VF-783, VF-874, and VA-923 be-
came VF-121, VF-122, VF-124, and VA-125.

**Bataan (CVL-29) (October 1952–
May 1953)**

VMA-312 (F4U-4/B; aboard February–
  May)
VS-871 (TBM-3S/W)
VS-21 (AF-2S/W)
HU-1 (Detachment; HO3S-1)

**Valley Forge (CVA-45) with CVG-5
(November 1952–June 1953)**

VF-51 (F9F-5)
- Kendall Courtney Gedney (KIA—
  March 9, 1953)

VF-92 (F4U-4)
- William Bernard Woerman (KIA—
  April 7, 1953)

VF-53 (F9F-5)
- Howard Maurice Davenport Jr.
  (KIA—March 4, 1953)

VF-54 (AD-4)
VC-3 (Detachment B; F4U-5N)
VC-11 (Detachment B; AD-4W)
VC-35 (Detachment B; AD-4N)
VC-61 (Detachment B; F9F-5P)
HU-1 (Detachment 6; HO3S-1)

**Philippine Sea (CVA-47) with CVG-9
(December 1952–August 1953)**

VF-91 (F9F-2)
- Donald Raymond Quinn (KIA—
  March 27, 1953)

VF-93 (F9F-2)
- Hubert T. Evans (KIA—February 16,
  1953)

VF-94 (F4U-4)
VA-95 (AD-4/NA/NL)
VC-3 (Detachment M; F4U-5N)
VC-11 (Detachment M; AD-4W)
VC-35 (Detachment M; AD-4N)
VC-61 (Detachment M; F9F-5P)
HU-1 (Detachment; HO3S-1)

**Bairoko (CVE-115) (January 1953–
August 1953)**

VMA-312 (F4U-4/B; aboard May–June)
VS-21 (AF-2S/W; aboard February–May)
VS-23 (TBM-3S/W; ashore at Agana,
  Guam, February–April)
HU-1 (Detachment; HO3S-1)

**Princeton (CVA-37) with CVG-15
(January 1953–September 1953)**

CVG-15 Staff
- Parks, CO (KIA)

- Charles Moye Jones (KIA—
  July 20, 1953)

VF-152 (F4U-4)
- William Malcolm Quinley (KIA—
  May 5, 1953)
- Leland Ralph Richey (KIA—
  May 6, 1953)
- William Charles Blackford Jr. (KIA—
  July 26, 1953)

VF-153 (F9F-5)
- Jerry F. Miller, CO
- Jim McNeil, XO
- George M. Benas
- Robert F. Chaney
- Charlie J. Clarkson
- Richard Cedric Clinite (KIA—
  May 13, 1953)
- Jack H. Crawford
- T. P. (Paul) Goodwin
- Joseph Spence Hall (KIA—
  March 17, 1953)
- Thomas (Tom) Hardy
- William C. (Bill) Hitt
- H.W. (Bill) Jones
- R. R. King
- Robert C. (Bob) Kunz
- Irvin A. (Bud) Marler
- W. J. McNeil Jr.
- G. E. Miller
- Francis Edward Painter (KIA—
  May 6, 1953)
- J. E. Perry Jr.
- Lawrence Laverne Quiel (KIA—
  April 25, 1953)
- Belmont M. Reid
- Frank W. Schindler
- George C. Schnitzer
- Theodore A. (Ted) Wagner
- William A. (Bill) Wilds Jr.

VF-154 (F9F-5)
- Anderson Mitchell Clemmons Jr.
  (KIA—April 23, 1953)
- Russell Jackson Lear (KIA—
  April 28, 1953)

VA-155 (AD-4)
- Jacob Louis Pawer Jr. (KIA—
  July 12, 1953)

VC-3 (Detachment D; F4U-5N)
VC-11 (Detachment D; AD-4W)
VC-35 (Detachment D; AD-4N)
VC-61 (Detachment D; F9F-5P)
HU-1 (Detachment; HO3S-1)

Boxer (CVA-21) with ATG-1 (March 1953–November 1953)

VF-111* (F9F-5)
VF-52 (F9F-2)
- James Kinsella, CO
- James L. Holloway III, XO (later CO)
- Van Beisbrock
- Bill Brook
- Grant Dean
- Paul Hayak
- Bob Hayes
- Dick Haynes
- Art Labelle
- Howard Thayer
- Bill Thompson

Air Crewmen
- Patrick R. Callahan

VF-151 (F9F-2)
- Jack William Ingram Jr. (KIA—
  July 25, 1953)
- Thomas Franklin Ledford (KIA—
  July 26, 1953)

VF-44* (F4U-4)
VF-194 (AD-4NA/Q)
- Art Melhuse, CO
- Walter Blattman, XO
- Edward V. (Buddy) Jordan,
  Ops Officer
- Joe L. Akagi
- Jim Anderson
- Joe Arkins
- Howard Bentzinger
- Robert Bristol
- Stan Broughton

- Sam Catterlin
- Steve (Ogre) Delancy
- John (Jack) Dunckel
- Dewitt F. (Dewey) Ferrell Jr.
- Don Lacava
- Pieree Lavallee
- Joe Molnar
- Bill O'Heren
- Oren (Pete) Peterson
- Phillips
- E. E. (Skip) Purvis
- Ralph Ripple
- Tom Smith
- Bud Spear
- Jim (Chicken) Schmidt
- Bob Wiegand
- Bill Wild
- Gary Witters
- Howard Wolfe
- Bob Dunlap, Maintenance Officer
- Bob Edington, AIO
- (Willie) Reyn, LSO

VC-3 (Detachment H; F4U-5N)
- Wilfred Wheeler III (KIA)

VC-11 (Detachment H; AD-4W)
VC-35 (Detachment H)
Pilots:
- Ralph Arthur Smith (KIA—
  July 14, 1953)

Air Crewmen:
- Thomas Edward Guyn (KIA—
  July 14, 1953)
- Jack Spencer Kennedy (KIA—
  July 14, 1953)
- Martin Joseph Wright (KIA—
  July 5, 1953)

VC-61 (F2H-2P)
- Daniel Richard Paul (KIA—
  July 23, 1953)

HU-1 (Detachment; HO3S-1)
- John Monday

_____

*VF-111 crossdecked (transferred) from
Boxer to *Lake Champlain* on June 30, 1953,

and returned to the U.S. in October 1953.
VF-44 crossdecked from *Lake Champlain* to
Boxer on June 30, 1953.

Lake Champlain (CVA-39) with CVG-4 (April 1953–December 1953)

VF-22 (F2H-2)
- Stan Montunnas, XO
- Edwin Nash Broyles Jr. (KIA—
  July 26, 1953)
- Henry Knox Wallace (KIA—
  July 23, 1953)

VF-62 (F2H-2)
VF-44 (F4U-4)
VF-111 (F9F-5)
- Dick Kaufman

VA-45 (AD-4B)
Pilots:
- Donald Edward Brewer (KIA—
  June 19, 1953)

Air Crewmen and Squadron Personnel:
- Robert H. Burnside

VC-4 (Detachment 44; F2H-2B/F3D-2)
- B. R. Allen
- Robert Sterling Bick (KIA—
  July 2, 1953)
- J. W. Brown
- G. G. O'Rourke
- Linton Calton Smith Jr. (KIA—
  July 2, 1953)
- G. L. Wegener

VC-12 (Detachment 44; AD-4W)
Pilots:
- D. Q. Joralmon, OinC
- R. W. Fenn
- W. C. Haskell
- M. S. Huff
- D. L. Williams
- H. L. Wilson, Radar Officer

Air Crewmen:
- S. E. Allen
- R. K. Belmore
- A. W. Hebert

- R. R. Ott
- Jack Sauter
- D. E. Woods
- G. F. Walls

VC-33 (Detachment 44; AD-4N)
VC-62 (Detachment 44; F2H-2P)
HU-2 (Detachment, HO3S-1)

Point Cruz (CVE-119) (April 1953–December 1953)

VMA-332 (F4U-4B)

VS-38 (TBM-3S/W; put ashore at
  Agana, Guam, at the end of April)
VS-23 (TBM-3S/W; aboard late April
  from Japan)
HS-2 (HRS-2)
HU-1 (Detachment; HO3S-1)

Patrol Squadron:
VP-6
VP-28
VP-46
VP-47

APPENDIX 2: ROLL CALL

It was small wonder that carrier pilots (despite the many challenges they faced aloft) stood in awe of the dexterity, skill, draconian work hours and death-defying choreography of flight deck crews.

Pilots who otherwise had little interest in the lives and fortunes of men in the "Black Shoe Navy" held deep personal affection and enduring memories for the ships and sailors who pulled them (or a buddy) alive from the clutches of a cold sea.

With winter coming on, [the work of sailors on ships off the coast of Korea] was cold, unglamorous, monotonous and often frustrating work, marked by dangers remarkably akin (in type if not in scale) to what the troops ashore encountered.

The largely unsung heroes of this book—and of the U.S. Navy's war off Korea's shores—are the sailors who manned the decks, space and equipment of the myriad of ships in the Korean War naval task forces.

What follows is a listing (organized by ship type and ship) of crewmembers who served wartime deployments. Appendix 2: Roll Call has been compiled based primarily on direct contacts with Korean War veterans as well as family members of veterans both living and deceased. (Included also are names identified from published casualty lists.)

Roll Call includes the names of only a small fraction of sailors who served at this time. Still, as a complement to Appendix 1: Ready Room, it is by no means an insignificant list.

Roll Call attempts to expand the circle of recognition beyond the relative handful of people and events that could be included in this book. The constraints of researching, writing and producing this book inevitably curtailed efforts to incorporate more names in Roll Call. For those whose loved ones' names are not included here, my hope is that by naming these courageous veterans we honor them all.

Roll Call Key

- ★—Korean War service battle star
- (★)—unknown number of battle stars for Korean War service
- CO—commanding officer
- KIA—killed in action (includes deaths not directly attributable to combat action)

Aircraft Carriers (Ship's crews)
Antietam (CV-36) ★★

- Charles L. Martin
- Eugene Alexander Pfeifer (KIA—11/4/51)
- Thomas Richard Russell (KIA—11/4/51)

Bon Homme Richard (CV-31) ★★★★★

- Fred Vincent Bryan (KIA—10/16/52)
- Joe Huaracha
- Raymond James Buntin (KIA—11/21/51)
- Everett Ray Willhoite (KIA—10/2/51)

Boxer (CV-21) ★★★★★★★★

- Patrick Barton
- Marvin Harold Coon (USMC) (KIA—10/15/50)
- James R. Fauber
- Arthur Masaru Kozuki (USMC) (KIA—8/6/52)
- Robert N. Kuehl
- Edward Glenn Loveless (KIA—5/13/53)
- Robert Wright MacLaren
- Tommy Charles Mann
- Terrell Ray Roulston (USMC) (KIA—8/6/52)
- James Edward Shropshire (KIA—8/6/52)
- Julian E. (Jess) Szurley
- Richard Smith Taylor (KIA—8/6/52)
- James Veryle Wark (KIA—8/6/52)
- Richard J. Yanko

Essex (CV-9) ★★★★ Navy Unit Commendation

- Wade Hilton Barfield (KIA—9/16/51)
- Roger Clark Hammond (KIA—9/16/51)
- Charles Lamar Harrell (KIA—9/16/51)
- Earl Kenneth Neifer (KIA—9/16/51)

- William James Stewart (KIA—9/16/51)

Kearsarge (CVA-33) (★)

- Walter Edmundson Bailey (KIA—10/11/52)
- Elmer Clark Coon Jr. (KIA—10/11/52)
- Harley Eugene Haigh (KIA—10/11/52)
- Fernando Magri (KIA—10/11/52)
- Kay Sherill Platt (KIA—1/22/53)

Lake Champlain (CVA-39) (★)

- Robert H. Burnside (VA-45)
- Eugene Carroll
- Douglas L. Fifer
- Louis Hirbour
- Raymond W. Hope
- Robert V. McKnight
- Anthony Peralta
- John J. Walsh

Leyte (CV-32) ★★

- Thomas Leo McGraw Jr. (KIA—3/6/53)
- Thomas Michael Yeager (KIA—3/6/53)

Philippine Sea (CV-47) ★★★★★★★★

- Russell Arthur Baker (KIA—9/1/50)
- Frank Bassett Carroll (KIA—11/13/50)
- Roger Alan Frost (KIA—3/27/53)
- Robert Logan Undersinger (KIA—2/26/53)

Princeton (CV-37) ★★★★★★★

- Harry David Nutt (KIA—6/6/51)
- John W. Purdy
- Tubby Brian Watson (KIA—7/1/53)

Valley Forge (CV-45) ★★★★★★★★
(Attack) Aircraft Carriers (CVA)
Oriskany (CVA-34) ★★
(Light) Aircraft Carriers (CVL)
Bataan (CVL-29) ★★★★★★★
(Escort) Aircraft Carriers (CVE)
Badoeng Strait (CVE-116) ★★★★★★

Navy Unit Commendation

- Don Galloway

Bairoko (CVE-115) ★★★
Point Cruz (CVE-119) (★)
Rendova (CVE-114) ★★
Sicily (CVE-118) ★★★★★

Amphibious and Auxiliary Ships
Amphibious Cargo Ship (AKA)
Oglethorpe (AKA-100) ★★
Union (AKA-106) ★★
Titania (AKA-13) ★★★★★★★

Amphibious Command Ship (AGC)
Mount McKinley (AGC-7)
★★★★★★★★
Amphibious Transport (APA)
Cavalier (APA-37) ★★★★
Henrico (APA-45) ★★★★★★★★★
Destroyer Tender (AD)
Piedmont (AD-17) ★★★★
Fleet Oiler (AO)
Cimarron (AO-22) ★★★★★★★
Navasota (AO-106) ★★★★★★★★
Passumpsic (AO-107) ★★★★★★★★★
- Baxter M. Hayes Jr.
Fleet Tug (ATF)
Arikara (ATF-98) ★★★★★
Cree (ATF-84) ★★★
Lipan (ATF-85) ★★★★
Mataco (ATF-86) ★★★★
High Speed Transport (APD)
Diachenko (APD-123) ★★★★★★
Horace A. Bass (APD-124) ★★★★★
    Navy Unit Commendation
Minesweeper (AM) and Coastal
Minesweeper (AMS)
Chatterer (AMS-40) (★)
Defense (AM-317) ★★
- Marty Strauss
Gull (AMS-16) ★★★★★★★★★ Navy
    Unit Commendation
Incredible (AM-249) ★★★★
Kite (AMS-22) ★★★★★★★★★★
Magpie (AMS-25) ★ (Sunk 10/1/50)
- Warren R. Person (KIA—10/1/50)
- Donald V. Wanee (KIA—10/1/50)
- Robert E. Wainwright (KIA—10/1/50)
- Robert W. Langwell (KIA—10/1/50))
- Robert A. Beck (KIA—10/1/50)
- Richard D. Scott (KIA—10/1/50)
- Seth D. Durkee (KIA—10/1/50)
- George G. Cloud (KIA—10/1/50)
- Lloyd E. Hughes (KIA—10/1/50)
- Roy A. Davis (KIA—10/1/50)
- Cleveland G. Rogers (KIA—10/1/50)

- Richard A. Coleman (KIA—10/1/50)
- Vincente Q. Ferjaran (KIA—10/1/50)
- Charles R. Bash (KIA—10/1/50)
- Theodore A. Cook (KIA—10/1/50)
- Stanley L. Calhoun (KIA—10/1/50)
- James C. Dowell (KIA—10/1/50)
- Harry E. Ferrell (KIA—10/1/50)
- Charles T. Horton (KIA—10/1/50)
- Eugene P. Krouskoupf (KIA—10/1/50)
Mainstay (AM-261) ★★★★
Merganser (AMS-26) ★★★★★★★★★
Mockingbird (AMS-2) ★★★★★★★★★★
Osprey (AMS-28) ★★★★★★★★★
Partridge (AMS-31) (★) (Sunk 2/2/51)
Pelican (AMS-32) (★)
Pirate (AM-275) (★) (Sunk 10/12/50)
Pledge (AM-277) (★) (Sunk 10/12/50)
    Presidential Unit Citation
Redhead (AMS-34) ★★★★★★★★★★
    Presidential Unit Citation
Swallow (AMS-36) (★)
Landing Ship Dock (LSD)
Catamount (LSD-17) ★★★★★★★
Fort Marion (LSD-22) ★★★★★
Landing Ship Tank (LST)
Crook County (LST-611) ★★★
Greer County (LST-799)
    ★★★★★★★★
King County (LST-857) ★★★★★★★
Lafayette County (LST-859) ★★★★★★
La Moure County (LST-883)
    ★★★★★★★
Lincoln County (LST-898)
    ★★★★★
LST-973 ★★★★ Navy Unit Commen-
    dation
Mahoning County (LST-914)
    ★★★★★★
Marion County (LST-975) ★★★★★★
Rescue and Salvage Ship (ARS)
Conserver (ARS-39) ★★★★★★★★★
Submarine Rescue Ship (ASR)
Florikan (SS-ASR-9) (★)
Greenlet (ASR-10) (★)
Seaplane Tender (AVP)
Suisun (AVP-53) ★★
Store Ship (AF)
Karin (AF-33) ★★
Battleship (BB)
Iowa (BB-61) ★★

Missouri (BB-63) ★ ★ ★ ★ ★
- Robert Dorman Dern (USMC, KIA—12/21/52)
- Rex Donald Ellison (USMC, KIA—12/21/52)
- Robert Leland Mayhew (KIA—12/21/52)

New Jersey (BB-62) ★ ★ ★ ★
- Robert Herman Oesterwind (KIA—5/21/51)

Cruiser
Heavy Cruiser (CA)
Helena (CA-75) ★ ★ ★ ★
Rochester (CA-124) ★ ★ ★ ★ ★ ★
HU-1 (Detachment 13; HO3S-1)
Detachment Aviators
- Donal Hollis, OinC
- Duane W. Thorin
Detachment Crew
- Ernie Crawford
Ship's Crew
- Rulon V. Bird
- Earl Lanning

St. Paul (CA-73) ★ ★ ★ ★ ★ ★ ★ ★
- Charles Lyndell Albritton (KIA—4/21/52)
- William Moran Barker (KIA—3/12/51)
- Alonzo Gene Blanton (KIA—4/21/52)
- Ray Allen Briggs (KIA—3/11/51)
- John Philip Caprio (KIA—3/12/51)
- Dennis Leroy Chatellier (KIA—3/12/51)
- Bobby Joe Cole (KIA—4/21/52)
- John Andrew Collett (KIA—4/20/52)
- George Costa (KIA—4/21/52)
- Guy Joseph De Angelis (KIA—3/11/51)
- Roy Lee Estes (KIA—3/11/51)
- Lloyd Morgan Faver (KIA—3/11/51)
- Donald Charles Ghezzi (KIA—4/21/52)
- Morgan Knowles Groover Jr. (KIA—3/11/51)
- Bennie Wilson Hamilton (KIA—4/21/52)
- Elven Newman Haney (KIA—4/21/52)

- James Robert Hudgens (KIA—4/21/52)
- Fred Curtis Hughes (KIA—4/21/52)
- Ronald Jackson Hunt (KIA—4/21/52)
- Curtis Lee Johnson (KIA—4/21/52)
- Paul Howard June (KIA—4/21/52)
- Ray Dale Kerr (KIA—4/21/52)
- James Hubert King (KIA—4/21/52)
- Milton John Kosar (KIA—4/21/52)
- Robert Hawkins Mann Jr (KIA—4/21/52)
- Lamar Howard McDaniel (KIA—4/21/52)
- James Douglas Overstreet (KIA—4/21/52)
- Commie Eugene Price (KIA—4/21/52)
- Ralph Waldo Reed (KIA—4/21/52)
- Richard William Schunke Jr. (KIA—4/21/52)
- Albert Eugene Smith (KIA—4/21/52)
- James Francis Statia (KIA—3/11/51)
- Donald Edward Tapia (KIA—4/21/52)
- Lester Paul Thurman (KIA—4/21/52)
- Arthur Hinton Wall (KIA—4/21/52)
- Adon Harry Welch (KIA—3/12/51)
- Virgile Leon Wood (KIA—4/21/52)
- Pat Augusta Worsham (KIA—4/21/52)
- Billie Dean Wright (KIA—4/21/52)
- Gerald George Zimmerman (KIA—4/21/52)

Toledo (CA-23) ★ ★ ★ ★ ★
Light Cruiser (CL)
Juneau (CL-119) ★ ★ ★ ★ ★
Manchester (CL-83) ★ ★ ★ ★ ★ ★ ★ ★ ★
Worcester (CL-144) ★ ★

Destroyer (DD) and Escort Destroyer (DDE)
Barton (DD-722) ★ ★
- Russell John Graf (KIA—9/16/52)
- Dale Phoenix Gray (KIA—8/10/52)
- Harold Joseph Savoie (KIA—9/16/52)
- John Martin Sherry (KIA—9/16/52)
- Walter Edwin Thierfelder Jr. (KIA—9/16/52)
- John Laurice Walton (KIA—9/16/52)

Beatty (DD-756) ★ ★
- James L. Barry Jr.
- Hunter Betz

- Harley A. Cloud
- George A. Ellwood
- Clarence D. Haugen
- Harry L. Sidor
- Ronald K. Wharton Sr.
- Wed Wilson

Blue (DD-744) ★ ★ ★ ★ ★ ★
- F. Donald (Hambone) Collins
- Duane F. Johnson
- Sam Zuccaro

Borie (DD-704) ★ ★ ★ ★

Boyd (DD-544) ★ ★ ★ ★ ★
- Robert Broadway
- Ray L. Clark
- Albert Neudauer
- Holland Powell
- William R. Smith

Brinkley Bass (DD-887) (★)
- Morris Ladner Jr.
- John Dwayne Bryan (KIA—8/20/51)

Bristol (DD-857) ★ ★
- Robert E. Bogart
- George A. Ellwood
- Carl Graham
- James C. Taylor Jr.

Brush (DD-745) ★ ★ ★ ★
- Donald F. Quigley, CO
- John David Beagles (KIA—9/26/50)
- Bennie Joe Berryman (KIA—9/27/50)
- James Robert Colleran (KIA—9/26/50)
- Frank Allen Davis (KIA—9/26/50)
- Willie Henry Fisher Jr. (KIA—10/2/50)
- Bobby Eugene Freeman (KIA—9/26/50)
- Meyer Louis Getz (KIA—9/26/50)
- Jim McClenahan
- David Morrell Grubb (KIA—9/26/50)
- Dale Lloyd Hoover (KIA—9/26/50)
- Gordon Eugene Johnson (KIA—9/26/50)
- Henry Dean Little (KIA—9/26/50)
- Russell Maxwell
- William Duffy Morris (KIA—9/27/50)
- John H. Peyton Jr.
- Charles La Verne Piester
- Lloyd G. Sellers
- Oliver Clyde Sexson (KIA—9/27/50)

- Warren Maxwell Shepherd (KIA—9/26/50)
- Eugene Leroy Timmons (KIA—9/26/50)

Buck (DD-761) ★ ★ ★ ★ ★ ★
- Milo Andersen
- George J. Anderson Sr.
- Maynard C. Smith
- Nicol Douglas Vandever

Carpenter (DDE-825) ★ ★ ★ ★ ★
- James R. Attleson
- Angelo Barnabae Jr.
- Stewart A. Cross Jr.
- Edwin E. Falor
- Jimmie Kennedy
- James H. Lazalier
- Phil (Shep) Shepard
- Louis Smith Jr.
- Victor B. Smith
- Robert B. Stevens
- Bert Van Houten

Chauncey (DD-667) ★ ★

Collett (DD-730) ★ ★ ★ ★ ★ ★ Navy
Unit Commendation
- Wilmer (Shorty) Abshire
- Murvin Darnell

Cotten (DD-669) ★
- Norman R. Isherwood
- Charles W. Lehr Jr.
- James M. Pundsack

Daly (DD-519) ★
- Hal Boyer
- Frank R. Carlson
- Forrest M. (Bud) Daniels
- David D. Gilboe
- Robert Henry Carter Kalechman

De Haven (DD-727) ★ ★ ★ ★ ★ ★
Navy Unit Commendation
- Clarence R. Conkle
- John L. Miller
- Roland (Nick) Nixon
- Bill White

Douglas H. Fox (DD-779) ★
- Joseph J. Cicardi
- Dennis E. Crooke
- Albert G. Jaeger
- Edward J. McElroy Sr.
- Anthony Pionegro
- Leonard V. Rizzolo

- Anthony F. Rykiel
- Tom (Windy) Sherman
- Dean E. Wheeler
- Alfred Wing

English (DD-696) ★ ★ ★ ★
- Dick (Red) Davis
- James F. Knight
- Baxter Patton
- Frederick F. Schreppel Sr.
- Eugene Staciokas

Ernest G. Small (DD-838) ★ ★ ★ ★
- Frank Clark Grubb (KIA—10/27/51)
- Thomas Ray Hamilton (KIA—10/27/51)
- Edward N. Kravetz (KIA—10/27/51)
- Elija Keith Manning (KIA—10/27/51)
- Robert Patrick Martin
- Rex B. Middleton (KIA—10/27/51)
- Joseph Francis Munier Jr. (KIA—10/27/51)
- Melvin Dale Obee (KIA—10/27/51)
- Ramiro (Raymond) Prieto
- Ronald John Porter (KIA—10/27/51)
- Quentin C. Saylor
- Allen Francis Schlueter (KIA—10/27/51)

Eversole (DD-789) ★ ★ ★ ★ ★ ★ ★
- Joseph H. Bays
- Robert Leland Cole
- John P. Donnelly
- Ben F. Wood Jr.

Fiske (DD-842) ★ ★
- Howard MacDonald
- Hurshall G. Marshall

Fletcher (DDE-445) ★ ★ ★ ★ ★
- David Bruce Gatliff
- George G. Henderson
- Abelardo (Abe) Marquez
- Robert Edward Sanchez
- Frank C. Vasquez

Floyd B. Parks (DD-884) (★)
- Benny James England
- William B. Hudson
- John L. (Woody) Woodrum

Forrest Royal (DD-872) ★ ★ ★ ★
- William (Bill) Connor
- Richard Downing
- Joseph A. Kearney
- Richard A. Kowalski

- Thomas J. Lucchesi
- Frank Herbert McCandless
- Constantino (Cozzy) Procopis
- Thomas B. Simmons
- Warren D. Stevens

Frank Knox (DDR-742) ★ ★ ★ ★ ★
- W. G. Atkins Jr.
- Robert T. Baird
- Raymond N. Diemert
- George W. Glaze
- Frank Haupert
- Orville S. (Buzz) Krieg
- Lonnie McCain
- Lyle D. Somerville

Gatling (DD-671) ★
- Robert Andrew Bachich
- Hyman K. Cohen
- Walter W. McKay

Gurke (DD-783) ★ ★ ★ ★ ★ ★ ★
- Robert L. Bumgarner
- Donald A. Bennallack, M.D.
- Herman Roy Bozeman
- Crague H. Emerson
- Kerwin Carl Roe

Halsey Powell (DD-686) ★ ★
- Cornell (Corky) Anton Jr.
- Dennis M. Babb Jr.
- Warren (Red) Belden
- Stuart I. Hoffman
- Eugene (Skee) Lisle

Hank (DD-702) ★ ★ ★ ★
- A. D. Bergstrom
- John Joseph Krajeski
- Charles LaFaTa
- Norlan M. Wells

Hanson (DD-832) ★ ★ ★ ★ ★ ★ ★
- Merrick W. Creagh III
- Jimmy Lee Davisworth (KIA)
- Carl E. Hunnell
- Francis A. Jeffries
- Dennis W. Moser
- John R. Pigg
- Denton E. Spurlin
- Kenneth Watson

Harry E. Hubbard (DD-748)
★ ★ ★ ★ ★ ★
- Don Lorimer
- Roderick M. Maybee
- Louis W. Radosevich

Hawkins (DD-873) ★★
Henderson (DD-785) ★★★★★★★★
Navy Unit Commendation
- Urban C. Goodwin
- Robert Hasty
- Roddis Jones
- Chas (CJ) McGrillen
- Joseph S. Nanista
- Robert Radach
- Theodosia F. Spilinek
- Louis J. St. John
- Orin L. Thomas
- Bill Whitlow

Herbert J. Thomas (DD-833)
★★★★★★
- Jack Cross
- Gordon M. Gold
- Alan L. Myers
- Gene S. Wilbur

Higbee (DD-806) ★★★★★★★
- Robin Adair
- Harold L. Allen
- Stanley E. Ault
- James R. Campbell
- Herbert McRoy
- Charles P. Moore
- Kenneth Norris
- Alton J. Philibeck

Hollister (DD-788) (★)
- Richard Andis
- Vince Cirillo
- James Custer
- Marion (Neil) Davis
- Richard Mosca
- Darrell Dean Payne
- William Don Payne
- Harold Gene White

Hyman (DD-732) (★)
- Donald Norman Barnett (KIA—11/29/51)
- Gerald Calderone
- Vince Cirillo
- John Rufus Cleveland (KIA—11/29/51)
- Richard L. Condon
- Ralph Regis Giles (KIA—11/29/51)
- Robert John Neilson
- William Pitz
- David A. Thompson

Ingraham (DD-694) ★
Irwin (DD-794) ★
James C. Owens (DD-776) ★★
- Loren F. Artus
- Stanley Howard Emond (KIA—5/7/52)
- William Joseph Murphy III (KIA—5/7/52)
- John (Bud) Murray
- Thomas Eugene Ramsey (KIA—5/7/52)

James E. Kyes (DD-787) ★★★★★★
- Chester Bennett
- Robert C. Dickson
- Harley H. Ellis
- Joseph R. Miller, M.D.

Jenkins (DDE-447) ★
- Charles H. Carroll, XO
- Fred L. Babbitt
- Bernard A. James
- Daniel L. Shea
- Robert Neil Schumacher
- Marvin C. Siebke
- Ronald J. Taylor
- Theodore Zborowski

John A. Bole (DD-755) ★★★★★★★
- Charles Eugene Sellers
- Tracy Winslow

Joseph P. Kennedy Jr. (DD-850) ★★
- Franklin P. Jackson
- Robert V. Terry
- Benjamin E. Wagner

Kidd (DD-661) ★★★★
- William Lovey Mozingo

Kimberly (DD-521) ★
Laffey (DD-724) ★★
Leonard F. Mason (DD-852) ★★★
Lowry (DD-770) ★★
Lyman K. Swenson (DD-729)
★★★★★★ Navy Unit Commendation
- Ben Blackburn
- Richard E. Day
- Herbert W. Docken Jr.
- LeeRoy Eugene Meadows
- David H. Swenson (KIA—9/13/50)

Maddox (DD-731) ★★★★★★
- Frank Nick Cataldo (KIA—4/7/53)
- William Lovey Mozingo

Mansfield (DD-728) ★★★ Navy Unit
Commendation
- Richard A. Bowman

McKean (DD-784) ★★★
- Max D. Phillips
- Richard P. Shaw
- Robert M. Tokarczyk

McNair (DD-679) ★★
- James Custer

Moale (DD-693) ★
- Joseph M. Cowern

Nicholas (DDE-449) ★★★★★
- Lewis W. Easter
- Joe Huaracha
- Joseph W. Hiykel Sr.
- William Clarence Klaus (KIA—5/20/53)
- Robert R. Ridihalgh

O'Brien (DD-725) ★★★★★

Ozbourn (DD-846) (★)
- William Jones
- Jessie Junior Kestner Jr. (KIA—12/24/50)
- Robert C. Whitten

Picking (DD-685) ★

Porterfield (DD-682) ★★★★
- Dan Willis Brown
- Wallace F. Caldwell
- Benjamin N. Gurule
- Robert Huffman

Preston (DD-795) ★

Purdy (DD-234)

Radford (DD-446) ★★★★
- Michael (Mike) Cullen
- Leonard E. (Gene) Gibson
- Joe Huaracha

Renshaw (DDE-499) ★★★★★
- Larry N. Charness
- David Grove
- Jerry Allen Hert
- Charles C. Johnson
- Harold (Hal) Monroe
- Thomas W. Shirley

Rowan (DD-782) ★★★★
- Ronald William Adrian
- Loren R. Melton
- Duane C. Peterson

Samuel N. Moore (DD-747) ★★★

- Leo Dwaine Andrews (KIA—3/7/53)
- James E. Bagley
- Norman Baker
- Richard Benton
- George Brining
- Melvin Floyd Bydalek (KIA—11/6/51)
- Joe A. Duran
- Henry Christian Jensen Jr.
- Wayne Allen Krueger (KIA—11/17/51)
- Cecil A. Oliver Jr.
- Donald W. Rank

Shelton (DD-790) ★★★★★★★★
- Charles E. Barclay
- Barney Alford Cull Jr.
- James E. (Pete) Peterson
- Derwood B. Posey

Stormes (DD-780) ★★★

Sproston (DD-577)

Taussig (DD-746) ★★★★★★★★
- Waylon Muton Bell
- Walt Burkett Sr.
- Teddy L. George
- Roy D. Hendricks
- John James Housos
- Bobby G. Jackson
- Daniel R. Pieronek
- Jimmy F. Roberts Sr.
- Chester Z. Wodarski

Trathen (DD-530) ★
- David A. Thompson

Twining (DD-540) ★★★★★
- Herman L. Greene
- William G. Kueny
- Gordon Emerson Pelton

Walke (DD-723) ★★★★
- Jack Atnip Sr.
- Herman Kuettle
- Robert Neil Schumacher
- Douglas Perret Star

Wallace L. Lind (DD-703) ★★★★
- James F. Clark
- Richard DeLong
- Charles Geoffery Prahl
- Carl W. Toreson

Wedderburn (DD-684) ★★★★
- Thomas B. Gray

William R. Rush (DD-714) (★)
- Thomas Topham

Yarnall (DD-541) ★★

Zellars (DD-777) ★ ★ ★
Destroyer Escort (DE)
McCoy Reynolds (DE 440) ★
- Robert R. Ridihalgh

Destroyer Minesweeper (DMS)
Carmick (DMS-33) ★ ★ ★ ★
- George Burge
- Edwin Raphael
- Marty Strauss
Doyle (DMS-34) ★ ★ ★ ★ ★ ★
- Charles H. Morrison Jr.
Endicott (DMS-35) (★)
- Rene Leonard Redelsperger
Thompson (DMS-38) ★ ★ ★ ★ ★ ★
- Ronald Virgil Essex

- Chester Lazzarino
- William J. Luttig
- Thearo Snider
- Milton M. Trujillo

Frigate (PF)
Bayonne (PF-21) ★ ★ ★ ★ ★ ★
- Robert L. Bumgarner

Submarine (SS)
Cabezon (SS-334) (★)
Catfish (SS-339) (★)
Remora (SS-487) (★)
Pickerel (SS-524) (★)
Segundo (SS-398) (★)
Tilefish (SS-307) ★

INDEX